Morning PRAISE

Morning PRAISE

J. R. (Bob) and Marie Claytor Spangler

REVIEW AND HERALD® PUBLISHING ASSOCIATION
HAGERSTOWN, MD 21740

The author assumes full responsibility for the accuracy of all facts and quotations as cited in this book.

Bible texts credited to ASV are from the American Standard Version.

Bible texts credited to Jerusalem are from *The Jerusalem Bible,* copyright © 1966 by Darton, Longman & Todd, Ltd., and Doubleday & Company, Inc. Used by permission of the publisher.

Scripture quotations marked NASB are from the *New American Standard Bible,* © The Lockman Foundation 1960, 1962, 1963, 1968, 1971, 1972, 1973, 1975, 1977.

Texts credited to NEB are from *The New English Bible.* © The Delegates of the Oxford University Press and the Syndics of the Cambridge University Press 1961, 1970. Reprinted by permission.

Texts credited to NIV are from the *Holy Bible, New International Version.* Copyright © 1973, 1978, 1984, International Bible Society. Used by permission of Zondervan Bible Publishers.

Texts credited to NKJV are from The New King James Version. Copyright © 1979, 1980, 1982, Thomas Nelson, Inc., Publishers.

Texts credited to Phillips are from J. B. Phillips: *The New Testament in Modern English,* Revised Edition. © J. B. Phillips 1958, 1960, 1972. Used by permission of Macmillan Publishing Co.

Texts credited to RV are from the Revised Version.

This book was
Edited by Richard W. Coffen and Eugene Lincoln
Designed by Bill Kirstein
Cover photos by Mary Kaye Jenks
Typeset: 10/11 Century Light Condensed

PRINTED IN U.S.A.

97 96 95 94 93 92   10 9 8 7 6 5 4 3 2 1

R & H Cataloging Service
Spangler, J. Robert
    Morning praise, by J. R. (Bob) and Marie Claytor
Spangler.

    1. Devotional literature. 2. Devotional calendars—
Seventh-day Adventist authors. I. Spangler, Marie (Claytor) jt.
author. II. Title.

                    242.2

ISBN 0-8280-0675-X

To order additional copies of this book,
call your local Adventist Book Center at **1-800-765-6955.**

Thoughts on Dedication and Appreciation

Lao-tze, one of China's sages, stated, "One actor cannot make a play." So with the writing of a book. Into the making of this book is poured the help of many, even some we have never met and do not know! People around the world have touched our lives during our travels. A smile from a passerby, a mother playing with her baby, a gracious hostess on the plane, an author's passage in an inspiring book or magazine article, a preacher or layperson sharing a heartwarming sermon or talk—from all these and more we have gleaned thoughts and ideas.

We are indebted to the 7 million Seventh-day Adventists, most of whom we have never met and who will never read this book. Nonetheless, God's remnant people have inspired us with courage, and many have provided us with illustrations to keep walking the straight and narrow path.

We thank Miriam Gair, Barbara Middag, Lynetta Murdoch, and Pat Orange, who dedicated some of their life's energy when they typed the original manuscript.

We have valued the numerous suggestions made by Gerald Wheeler and his wife, Penny, our contact person with the Review and Herald. Richard Coffen and Eugene Lincoln, the final editors of this book along with their associates, had part in the production of this volume. We owe a debt of thanks to the entire Review and Herald staff from editors to engineers, from personnel in the shipping department to the president. This group of faithful workers, who produce Adventist literature for our church and the world, may be unsung heroes, but they will not be forgotten in the kingdom.

Our immediate family—Christian parents, sisters, uncles, aunts, nieces, nephews, cousins, and in-laws—all have made their contribution in the shaping of our lives and have impacted our writing.

Finally we pay tribute to two persons whom we love and respect the most—our two precious daughters, Patricia Anne and Linda Marie. Next to the Lord Himself these young women have made the greatest impact on our lives.

So we dedicate this book to literally thousands—no, millions—of people with whom we plan to get better acquainted in eternity. If what we have written gives you greater insights into the Christian life, remember that we are merely dwarfs who have stood on a giant's shoulder who has enabled us to see a little farther than the both of us could alone.

Meet the Spanglers

Marie and Bob Spangler are well-known—and loved—by thousands around the world because of their widespread and personable Christian influence. Despite their academic achievements and the heavy challenge of involvement in church business, Bob and Marie have always been people-oriented. Their greatest desire in life is to be ready to meet Jesus when He comes and help others to do the same.

Marie, born in Newport News, Virginia, and Bob, in Dayton, Ohio, met as students at Washington Missionary College (now Columbia Union College) and were married two days after their college graduation. They labored together as a pastor-evangelistic team in the Ohio, Florida, Gulf States, and Texas conferences. Eight years of mission service were spent in the Far Eastern Division, where Bob served as the Division Ministerial Secretary and Marie taught at the Far Eastern Academy and did secretarial work.

After returning from the Far East in 1962, Bob served in the General Conference Ministerial Association as associate secretary, secretary, and editor of *Ministry* magazine (his tenure as *Ministry* editor—27 years—set a record for longevity of service in that capacity). He has also been a much appreciated camp meeting and week of prayer speaker.

Because of Bob's interest in building friendships with pastors of other denominations, he initiated the ambitious and highly successful *P*roject for *R*eaching *E*very *A*ctive *C*lergy person at *H*ome, more familiarly known as PREACH. As a result, 200,000 non-Adventist clergy received a complimentary subscription to *Ministry* for a number of years. Bob's vision also prompted him to coordinate the writing, production, and distribution of the book *Seventh-day Adventists Believe . . . ,* which explains Adventist fundamentals in-depth and in a Christ-centered context. Nearly 500,000 copies of this book have been distributed. He developed what was known as "Project 27," which included the sending of 200,000 volumes of *Seventh-day Adventists Believe . . .* to non-Adventist clergy as a gift. The second and third phases of Project 27 will place this book as a reference work in every library in the world as well as the editorial offices of the leading magazines, books, and newspapers.

Marie has also served God in various capacities. She holds an M.A. in early childhood development. In addition to her roles as mother of two daughters, Patricia and Linda, and pastor's wife, she has taught school, done secretarial work, and coordinated the General Conference Shepherdess International organization, which she founded and organized. This special support system sponsored by the General Conference Ministerial Association ministers especially to pastors' wives, providing materials, encouragement, and counsel. She has a two-fold passion—advocacy for ministers' wives and child training.

Marie has also been active in recent discussions about the role of women in the church, having served on the Women's Ministries Advisory—the original committee set up by the General Conference — and has also sat on the Commission on the Role of Women.

If and when they have time, which is rare, Bob enjoys a bit of tennis and changing oil in their automobile, which seems to be the limit of his mechanical abilities. Marie loves music, making memory books, sewing, and entertaining.

Their recent retirement has not slowed down the Spanglers. They have been very much involved in the ongoing work of the church in the former Soviet Union. Bob is currently serving as evangelism consultant for the newly formed Euro-Asia Division. Under his direction this new division has experienced the greatest yearly growth of any division in the history of our church. He has often stated that this experience has been the most exhilarating time of his entire ministry!

Before their retirement, Bob and Marie conceived the idea of writing a daily devotional that would encourage active participation of the readers. *Morning Praise* is the fruit of their endeavors.

How to Get the Most Out of This Book

We want to help you experience a more personal walk with the Lord as you use this book. We have found that the element of praise makes this walk with Jesus real and tangible. Thus we have designed this book with a twofold purpose in mind. In the first place, the daily content focuses on what we call the praise factor, which enriches our spiritual life. Second, we have provided space at the end of many of the readings for you to record your own praise testimony to the Lord.

In our own experience we have learned that the more we praise God for who He is and what He has done and is doing for us, the more wonderful it is to love and serve Him. We have also discovered that a spirit of praise and thankfulness to our Creator, Redeemer, and Sustainer does not come naturally, nor is it a onetime achievement. The spirit of praise to our Lord is an attitude that results only from constant practice, practice that must never cease. Thus, for us to develop an attitude of praise, we must do it always in the framework of continuing praise. Praise makes Jesus real! Praise to Him enormously increases the joy of daily fellowship with Him.

So when you reach the end of a reading that has a place for you to respond, feel free to record a sentence or two of praise to the Lord for a specific blessing, perhaps one that you received only yesterday. If you have a spouse or children, let them express their praise for the blessings they have experienced. You may want to purchase several copies of this book so that each person has the privilege of recording a praise thought. Or you may prefer to select a family member to record the praises. The act of writing down why you are thankful to Jesus makes the blessing more tangible. True Christianity is a real and personal experience with God.

We promise you that if you faithfully jot down a word of praise and the reason for it, you will find your life greatly enriched. You will understand more fully the joy of salvation. Furthermore, at the end of the year you will have a precious diary for the year 1993.

Bob and Marie

Paper Ebenezers

Then Samuel took a stone, and set it between Mizpeh and Shen, and called the name of it Ebenezer, saying, Hitherto hath the Lord helped us. 1 Sam. 7:12.

In 1862 General Ulysses S. Grant won the first major federal victory of the Civil War. The site where he gained it now forms part of Fort Donelson National Military Park in Tennessee. The 600-acre park has a six-mile-long driving tour that is dotted with markers of historical interest. The monuments remind us of victories and even defeats during the Civil War.

In Old Testament times God's people often set up stones to memorialize His leadership and blessing. At times they wrote inscriptions on the plastered surfaces of the pillars. The stones were, in effect, a national diary. When the Israelite children would ask what the monuments meant, it gave the parents a wonderful opportunity to explain how God had led His people to victory. Samuel named the one he set up, between Mizpah and Shen, Ebenezer, which means "stone [*eben*] of the help [*ezer*]."

Imagine what would happen if every Christian erected a stone column to commemorate some divine blessing. Monuments would crowd the planet's surface. So instead of using stones, why don't we make paper memorials?

Ellen White wrote about those who want to work for the Master by sharing their faith. They may not have a great amount of knowledge or ability, she admitted, but "they will be blessed in their humble efforts to impart light to others. Let such ones keep a diary, and when the Lord gives them an interesting experience, let them write it down, as Samuel did when the armies of Israel won a victory over the Philistines. He set up a monument of thankfulness, saying, 'Hitherto hath the Lord helped us.' Brethren [and sisters], where are the monuments by which you keep in view the love and goodness of God?

"Strive to keep fresh in your minds the help that the Lord has given you in your efforts to help others" *(The Seventh-day Adventist Bible Commentary,* Ellen G. White Comments, vol. 2, p. 1012).

To help keep these blessings fresh in our hearts, she specifically recommended that we record God's leading in our lives in a diary—a paper Ebenezer, if you please! As you go through this book, take just a moment to record a few words of praise and thanks for God's leading in your life. Some days you may not feel like writing anything, but other days you will. You will find that the more you record, the more you will want to write and the more you will find to write.

The Baby Named Ichabod

And she named the child Ichabod, saying, The glory is departed from Israel: because the ark of God was taken, and because of her father in law and her husband. And she said, The glory is departed from Israel: for the ark of God is taken. 1 Sam. 4:21, 22.

The background of Israel's great victory over the Philistines at Mizpah, near the place where God's people erected the Ebenezer, the "Stone of the Help" monument mentioned in yesterday's reading, involved a baby named Ichabod.

Prior to Samuel's victory at Mizpah, Eli had judged Israel for 40 years. During the last days of his leadership, the army of Israel resisted the Philistines, who were invading the hill country of Palestine from their bases along the coast. Unfortunately, Israel went against them without God's direction, and God's people were defeated, losing approximately 4,000 men. Their defeat puzzled Israel's leaders. But instead of seeking the Lord's guidance as they faced their next skirmish with the Philistines, they decided to use the ark of the covenant as a talisman.

They shared the idea, common at the time, that a nation's god or goddess went into battle along with his or her people. Because they had lost the previous battle, God's people assumed that their God was not doing His part. By taking the ark with them, they would force Him to fight for them. God's people regarded the ark as little more than a good luck charm. The Philistines, although fearful of the ark, fought valiantly anyway and defeated the Israelite forces. They even captured the sacred object.

Eli's two wicked sons, Hophni and Phinehas, perished in the battle. The news of the ark's loss shocked the overweight and elderly Eli, causing him to fall backward from his seat by the gate of the tabernacle and break his neck.

At the very same time, Eli's God-fearing daughter-in-law, the wife of impious Phinehas, went into labor after hearing the terrible news and died giving birth to her baby. Just before her death she whispered, "The glory is departed from Israel: for the ark of God is taken." The most amazing part of this tragic story is that the Lord still loved His people, and under Samuel's leadership He brought them victory.

Even though we make mistakes and fail the Lord, if we submit ourselves again to Him, we may have the assurance of His acceptance. None of us can escape the shadows of life's deep trials, but with God's help we can find victory in every experience. Can you think of a more wonderful reason for praising Him?

I praise God for _____

Remember and Record
Your Blessings!

And he appointed certain of the Levites to minister before the ark of the Lord, and to record, and to thank and praise the Lord God of Israel. 1 Chron. 16:4.

What would you do and how would you feel if the most precious article you ever owned was stolen, only to be returned many years later? The thing that God's people most valued was the ornate ark that served as the depository for the stone tablets containing the Ten Commandments. Constructed of acacia wood and covered with gold leaf both inside and out, it had a top that symbolized God's throne. It was the focal object of the sanctuary furnishings and services. During the days of Eli the Philistines had captured it, producing the most terrible calamity that could have happened to Israel. The ark represented God's presence and power among His people. The news of its loss had led to Eli's death and had plunged God's people into depression and horror.

Now, years later, King David brought the ark to his new capital city, Jerusalem. Israel's leaders made the event a tremendous time of rejoicing. The entire nation celebrated more than we do on New Year's Day, July 4, Thanksgiving, and Christmas combined.

David was beside himself with ecstasy. A mighty musical ensemble of trumpets and other instruments played, while a choir sang praises to the Lord. In fact, "David danced whirling around before Yahweh with all his might" (2 Sam. 6:14, Jerusalem). A vital part of all worship is joy, and David knew how to be joyful before the Lord.

After the arrival of the ark, more burnt offerings were offered, and David "distributed to everyone . . . a loaf of bread and a portion of meat and a raisin cake" (1 Chron. 16:3, NASB). Then he did what our text for today states. Please read it again and note carefully the words "to record, and to thank and praise the Lord." The Hebrew word for "record" means to mark, to remember, to recount, to make to be remembered.

Why not write down an event in your life in which God has signally blessed you? The more you record, the more you will remember. And the more you remember, the more you will praise God. And the more you praise God, the more exhilarating your Christian experience will be!

Expression Deepens Impressions

O give thanks to the Lord, call upon His name. . . . Sing to Him, sing praises to Him; speak of all His wonders. Glory in His holy name; let the heart of those who seek the Lord be glad. 1 Chron. 16:8-10, NASB.

Yesterday we studied David's transfer of the ark to Jerusalem. For this joyous occasion he used his extraordinary musical abilities to compose a praise hymn for a special Levitical choir led by Asaph. Our text today contains just a portion of this marvelous poem of praise.

As we attend various churches around the world, we notice that many of our members do not sing during the worship service. Sometimes as we look into their faces, we see what appears to be joyless, unhappy faces. Some are furrowed with fear and even anger. We cannot read hearts and judge, and we certainly have no knowledge of the condition of their vocal cords. However, we believe that our Lord does expect us to at least try to sing praises to Him, even if what comes out of our mouths is only a "joyful noise."

One of our minister friends does just that. He cannot sing a single note on key, but he praises the Lord with sounds that one can accurately describe only as noise! In fact, to stand by him in a worship service can be disconcerting. However, we smile and keep on singing, even if his noise gets us off key. We can praise God with him, for at least he is trying!

If timidity inhibits your singing, at least heed the words of our text: "Speak of all His wonders. Glory in His holy name." The more we talk about the glories of His creative power in nature and the more we speak about His unmatched love seen in Calvary, the deeper the impression of His character and goodness will be made on our own hearts.

Right now, pause a moment to think about what God means to you. Then write down your thoughts. _____

_____

Praise Is a Daily Experience

Sing to the Lord, all the earth; proclaim good tidings of His salvation from day to day. Tell of His glory among the nations, His wonderful deeds among all the peoples. For great is the Lord, and greatly to be praised. 1 Chron. 16:23-25, NASB.

The Lord never created a person with a heart big enough to supply the circulatory system with sufficient blood by beating only once a month. Nor did He make our stomachs large enough so that we could eat just one meal every six months without starving to death. And He never designed our lungs with such capacity that we could survive on only one breath a year. All our bodily functions operate on a frequent and regular basis. The average heart beats approximately 70 times a minute. A normal stomach operates best on two or three meals a day. And the typical set of lungs needs to breathe every few seconds.

As in the world of nature, so in the spiritual realm. We cannot fully enjoy a healthy religious experience if we participate in spiritual activities only spasmodically. Many Christians have assumed that attending church once a week is all that is necessary for a strong relationship with our Lord. Such thinking blinds them to the fact that a relationship with Christ needs to be cultivated more zealously than even that between husband and wife. After all, isn't it Satan's main objective to destroy any kind of tie between humans and their Maker? The devil knows that if we have no connection with God, then we have no salvation.

One of the most important ways to build spiritual strength is found in praising and proclaiming God's goodness. Praise to the Lord does not come naturally. It develops by practice.

The words "Tell of His glory among the nations" is another way of saying that all who follow the Lord will witness to those about them. As we examine our witnessing experiences, we should consider what and how we witness. We may witness about the day we observe or our health habits. But the witnessing that proclaims the good tidings of His salvation, telling of His glory and His wonderful deeds among us, is what really attracts people. Happy, joyful, praising people have a magnetic influence on those about them. Then when people want to know why we're so happy and joyful, we can go into more detail about our beliefs and physical habits.

Why not write down now some of the things you can praise the Lord for?

_____

_____

How Do You Value Yourself?

For through the grace given to me I say to every man among you not to think more highly of himself than he ought to think; but to think so as to have sound judgment, as God has allotted to each a measure of faith. . . . We have gifts that differ according to the grace given to us. Rom. 12:3, 6, NASB.

A speaker once lectured to a group of senior citizens on the subject of liking yourself. When he finished, an elderly man approached him and said, "I discovered something this evening that has always troubled me. All my life I have been critical of others and wondered why. After what you said tonight I realize that I have never really been pleased with myself. In fact, I cannot tell you one thing I like about myself."

The elderly are not alone in suffering from such a problem. People of every age struggle with it. Someone has observed that "our attitude toward ourselves influences the quality of our relationships with God and others."

We can depreciate ourselves in many ways. Have you ever heard anyone say "I'm *only a* layperson"; "I'm *just a* secretary"; "I'm *just a* student in school"? The words "only a" and "just a" reveal that we feel we are not what we want to be or that we are measuring ourselves by what others are or do. To do that puts a low value on the gifts God has given each of us to work with. What would happen if we didn't have all types of people to carry all the various responsibilities in the church? Or young people who bring new ideas, creativity, and enthusiasm? And older ones to share experience and insight?

How can we properly value ourselves? God expects us to estimate ourselves according to the way He does. "Christ paid an infinite price for us, and according to the price paid He desires us to value ourselves" (*The Ministry of Healing*, p. 498). In fact, "the Lord is disappointed when His people place a low estimate upon themselves. He desires His chosen heritage to value themselves according to the price He has placed upon them" (*The Desire of Ages*, p. 668).

Can you praise God for the priceless value He has put on your life? And can you praise Him regardless of how small or seemingly insignificant your talents may be? Remember, how you regard yourself greatly determines your attitude toward God.

Why not praise Him in your own words for how great He is and thank Him for the gifts He has given you?

_____

_____

January 7

Acceptance in the Lord

For while we were still helpless, at the right time Christ died for the ungodly. Rom. 5:6, NASB.

Nothing is more helpless than a newborn baby. A tiny infant contributes nothing to a family in terms of financial or physical support. From a human standpoint the greatest example of unconditional love is that of a mother who night and day cares for a helpless, nonprofitable nursling.

An infant would never think of "doing" in order to gain acceptance and love. Such a concept enters our minds only when we are old enough to think and act for ourselves. Unfortunately, we live in a society that tells us that we are really loved only if we are successful. Love thus becomes conditional. Rarely do we think that we can be accepted or loved without doing something to deserve it.

The same notion spills over into the spiritual realm. We feel that we must *do* something for love. Doing things in order to win love and approval either from God or society is like eating a potato chip or salted peanut. Who can stop with eating just one? "No matter how many 'badges of love' you collect, they are never enough, because they are empty of real nourishment and cannot seem to feed the hunger gnawing deep inside. So you keep doing more, working a little harder, hoping this time it will take the awful emptiness away" (Sue Monk Kidd, *God's Joyful Surprise*, p. 24).

Our text makes it clear that God loves unconditionally. Can you imagine anything more wonderful than to know that you are in God's loving embrace regardless of what you have done? He loves you for who you are, not for what you do. God doesn't wait for you to become perfect. Rather, He loves you now, fully and completely.

How do we know this? "The value of all the world sinks into insignificance in comparison to the value of one human soul" (*Counsels to Writers and Editors*, p. 126). How could God not help loving anyone so infinitely priceless?

God treasures us for two reasons: He created us in His own image, and He gave His Son to die for us. We can understand our worth only as we go to Calvary. Only in the mystery of the atonement made by Christ can we place a true estimate on ourselves. Each of us must be very valuable to God for Him to create us and then to redeem us from Satan's clutches. God gave His Son so that we might live now more abundantly and with Him forever when He returns.

Grasping the reality of God's unconditional love converts the heart and causes us to respond in obedience to His will.

We cannot overestimate the importance of a correct sense of self-worth. It alone can lead to positive attitudes, productivity, and ultimate success. A lack of this sense has caused countless adults—as well as young people and even children—to feel miserable about themselves, to be unable to get along with others, to take wrong courses in life, and to make wrong decisions.

Please write out a sentence of praise to God for His unconditional love.

_____

_____

God's Love Exceeds Human Love

For while we were still helpless, at the right time Christ died for the ungodly. For one will hardly die for a righteous man; though perhaps for the good man someone would dare even to die. Rom. 5:6, 7, NASB.

One of our pioneer aviators, while piloting a mail plane from New York to Cleveland, crashed in the mountains of Pennsylvania and was killed. On his body the search party found a letter addressed "to my beloved brother pilots and pals." The words "To be opened only after my death" were written on the envelope. What he wrote is worth thinking about. "I go to my death, but with a cheerful heart. I hope what small sacrifice I have made may be of use to the cause. When we fly we are fools, they say, . . . but everyone in this aviation service is doing the world far more good than the public can appreciate. We risk our necks, we give our lives, we perfect a service for the benefit of the world at large, . . . but stick to it. See you all again."

Here was a person who made the supreme sacrifice for an earthly cause. Millions have also given all, including life, for God's cause. Yet to give your life for another person at a precise moment of time is a bit different. Paul's statement seems to say that while some might die for a good person, hardly anyone alive would die for a righteous person. Paul may be comparing two types of individuals. One is a self-righteous, pharisaical person, whereas the other is a plain, good, lovable person. If you had to die for either one, you would probably choose the good person whom you could at least identify with and respect.

Regardless of the text's exact meaning, it is hard to imagine anyone sacrificing his or her life for another person, good or righteous, especially if the individual is neither a friend nor a relative. And certainly no one would die for an enemy. Paul wanted his readers to focus on the utterly incredible love of Christ, who, while we were still helpless and ungodly, died for us. And who are the "us"? All human beings. We are all aliens and sinners—disloyal and lost.

As you ponder the story of the aviator who crashed, wouldn't it be a good idea to carry an envelope in your heart that reads, "I die, but not for long, and I do so with a cheerful heart for the One who loved me, converted me, and rescued me from eternal death. Yes, some may call me a fool for serving Christ. Whatever small sacrifice I may have made for Him, it was worth doing for the greatest cause on earth. Even though the world may not appreciate what our Lord has done for all on Calvary, yet I praise Him for His reconciling love."

Is this the way you feel about Jesus? If so, please write it out now!

A Few Seeds of Happiness

Vindicate the weak and fatherless; do justice to the afflicted and destitute. Rescue the weak and needy. Ps. 82:3, 4, NASB. Happy is he who is gracious to the poor. Prov. 14:21, NASB.

Dr. Thomas Dooley, a Navy doctor, earned fame supervising refugee camps in North Vietnam for the thousands who fled in 1954 from the Communists. In 1959 Dooley was diagnosed as having cancer, but he returned to help maintain his medical work in Laos. In 1961 he died at the young age of 34.

In his final book, *The Night They Burned the Mountain*, he wrote: "Are you willing to admit that probably the only good reason for your existence is not what you are going to get out of life but what you are going to put into it? To close your book of complaints against the management of the universe and to look around for a place where you can sow a few seeds of happiness?" (in Lincoln Steed, *The Last Mountain*, p. 114).

The misery in our world today is beyond comprehension. Natural events as well as man-made catastrophes have killed hundreds and thousands and crushed the hope in millions more. Most of us in countries such as America and Australia are blessed with material blessings. Yet even in affluent societies many live in poverty and fear. We may feel helpless to aid the millions, but surely we can seek out one person or family in need. The suffering are the special objects of God's care.

But He does not meet their needs through a shower of daily manna or by ravens bringing food. Rather, God works "by a miracle upon human hearts, expelling selfishness and unsealing the fountains of Christlike love" (*The Ministry of Healing*, p. 202).

As Christians we must first take care of the members of our own church. One of the major reasons for a church organization is to help the needy in our midst. "While we have the chance, we must do good to all, and especially to our brothers in the faith" (Gal. 6:10, Jerusalem).

The result? "Happy is he who is gracious to the poor." Whom have you helped lately? Write it down, or at least record your intentions!

We Are Rich Because He Became Poor

For you know the grace of our Lord Jesus Christ, that though He was rich, yet for your sake He became poor, that you through His poverty might become rich. 2 Cor. 8:9, NASB.

A Nazi guard in a concentration camp taunted a Jew whom he had forced to clean out the toilets. "Where is your God now?" the guard asked.

The Jew quietly replied, "He is right here with me, in the muck."

Our travels have carried us to certain poverty-stricken areas where even the poor in America seem rich by comparison. We have lived for short times under conditions such that we found ourselves hoping the Lord would never call us to labor permanently in these places.

On the other hand, we have also visited regions of extraordinary wealth. We have walked through extravagant palaces and presidential mansions. For example, we have seen the unparalleled luxury of the Hermitage and Catherine's palaces in St. Petersburg. Everywhere we marveled at gold leaf ceilings, polished white grand pianos, brilliant crystal chandeliers, magnificent paintings, mirrors framed with gold leaf, and ballrooms in which the world's notables have danced to music played by talented orchestras.

Constantly we find ourselves contrasting the regions of poverty and luxury with what Jesus abandoned in heaven to come to our planet. Had He lived in earth's most extravagant palace, it still would have been miserable compared to His home in heaven. We cannot comprehend what our Lord left to live among the poor on earth. Instead, we can only stand in awe that He chose to leave the beauties of the universe and the companionship of unfallen beings in order to redeem us. During His ministry He had no place to call home. His lifestyle was that of a poor person. But He did it for you and for me! Once we grasp His humility, we can never doubt His love for the human race.

Scripture tells us that not only did Jesus accept poverty, but He also "did not come to be served, but to serve, and to give His life a ransom for many" (Matt. 20:28, NASB).

All Christians know that our Lord is right here with us in the muck! Do you love Him? If so write a short note of your appreciation for His becoming poor in order that you might become rich in Him.

_____

_____

The Brain Change

Fixing our eyes on Jesus, the author and perfecter of faith, who for the joy set before endured Him the cross, despising the shame, and has sat down at the right hand of the throne of God. Heb. 12:2, NASB.

Scientists inform us that children's brains are plastic in the sense that whatever they see and do changes the brain functionally and even structurally. What goes into a child's brain is crucial, since by age 7 the human brain attains 90 percent of its adult weight. It is no wonder that one particular religious organization boldly has stated, "Give us a child until he is 7 years old, and you can have him the rest of his life." They realize that the first few years of a child's life make indelible impressions on the brain, impressions that last a lifetime.

Educational psychologist Jane Healy in her book *Endangered Minds: Why Our Children Don't Think* (Simon and Schuster) claims that we are unwittingly rearing a generation of "different brains." She believes that electronic media, fast-paced lifestyles, unstable family patterns, environmental hazards, and faulty teaching methods seem to be changing not only the way children think but also their actual brain structure. Perhaps the greatest single factor in changing children's thinking patterns, as well as that of adults, is television viewing.

If seeing and doing can alter a brain, then the concept of a new-birth experience is possible as well. The difference is who or what we fix our attention on. Both satanic and Godly influences vie for our time and attention. How is it possible for us to be changed? Simply, we must view Jesus daily through reading and meditation. We must pray for the Holy Spirit to increase our desire for more of Jesus and less of the world. This means we take decisive steps to study prayerfully His ways and will for us.

We speak of the miracle of the new birth, and it is indeed one. Since we are born in an alienated state from Jesus, it is truly a miracle even to want to look to Him. Furthermore, it is a miracle that human beings living in a world that encourages evil in a thousand subtle—and not so subtle—ways can, despite that fact, still choose to look to Christ.

Our decision to focus on Jesus is a specific act on our own part. But once we fasten our attention on Him, the Holy Spirit begins a lifelong process of changing our brain functionally and structurally. The unconverted, world-loving person will not understand it. Dedicated Christians are a mystery to society. The world accuses them of thinking and acting differently. In fact it regards some as being mentally unbalanced.

But we thank our Lord for miraculously placing in our minds a willingness to look to Him. Everything connected with conversion is truly a miraculous gift of the Spirit. Are you thankful for the Spirit's attempts to influence you to look to Jesus? _____

Looking in the Right Direction

And he had a dream, and behold, a ladder was set on the earth with its top reaching to heaven; and behold, the angels of God were ascending and descending on it. And behold, the Lord stood above it and said, "I am the Lord." Gen. 28:12, 13, NASB.

Do you have a fear of falling when you climb up or down a high ladder? One secret that helps some people overcome the fear of high places is to look in the proper direction.

Some years ago we visited the tiny island of Guam, where friends took us to explore a deep cave. After walking a narrow path through the jungle, we discovered that the only way to get into the cave was to climb down an extremely long ladder. One slip of the foot could spell death. It made us dizzy as we stared down to the bottom. In fact, we were strongly tempted to abandon the idea of exploring the cave. The ladder appeared to be at least 100 feet long, and maybe it was.

However, encouraged by our friends, we carefully started down rung by rung. To glance down produced a sensation of fear and falling. But if we kept looking up at the sky through the opening above us while clinging for dear life to the ladder and slowly placing one foot on the next rung, we remained calm. On the return trip, as we stared up from the depths of the cave to the entrance high above us, fear nearly paralyzed us. It appeared that even the Washington Monument was shorter than that seemingly endless ladder! But again, as we ascended the ladder, we concentrated on looking up and not down.

When Jacob was fleeing from Esau to his uncle Laban's home, he dreamed about the longest ladder in the universe. Its bottom rested on earth, while the top reached heaven. Multitudes of angels traveled up and down it. Note carefully that, according to the *New American Standard Bible*, "the Lord stood *above"* this ladder.

The only safe way to climb this ladder connecting heaven and earth is by looking up to the Lord. If you glance down or in any other direction, you are in trouble! Practice constantly focusing on Jesus. Satan does everything within His power to get us to glance at the world, enemies, friends, even at the church and its leaders. To look at anything else but up to Him results in eventual discouragement. To be attracted to anyone else except Jesus can lead to loss of eternal life.

Praise the King for the privilege of looking to Him. Praise Him for being worth focusing on!

The Ladder of Life

And He said to [Nathanael], "Truly, truly, I say to you, you shall see the heavens opened, and the angels of God ascending and descending on the Son of Man." John 1:51, NASB.

Whether Philip had a horse or not, Scripture does not say. But the disciple's Greek name, Philip, means "fond of horses." He came from the same fishing village as Andrew and Peter—Bethsaida, located on the north shore of the Sea of Galilee. Undoubtedly, as boys they played together, and now they were young men who made their living fishing in partnership.

Christ denounced Bethsaida for its unbelief. Yet out of it came three of His leading disciples: Simon Peter, Andrew, and Philip.

Philip was a decisive person, a quality he showed by skillfully bringing Nathanael to Christ. Philip did not pressure Nathanael, nor did he argue with him. Skeptical Nathanael, when learning that Jesus had come from Nazareth, exclaimed, "Can any good thing come out of that town?"

Philip's response was masterful. "Come and see for yourself. I am only telling you what I have found and experienced in Him." A personal testimony is the greatest possible witness in favor of Christ. It applies to every area of life. How often all of us have bought a particular brand because some friend or advertisement gave a personal testimony about how wonderful the product was!

The central theme and object of Christianity is the person Jesus. Come and see! Taste for yourself! Talk with Him! Listen to His voice through the Word! There is nothing or no one like Him. Why? He is the ladder upon which angels of God ascend and descend, bringing hope and help to our needy souls. Without the ladder there would be no communication between heaven and earth. Without it earth would be disconnected from God. Our world would be doomed to extinction.

The ladder is a Person. There is no other way to heaven except through and by Jesus. No wonder Philip was eager for Nathanael to see for himself this divine-human ladder.

Thank God for Christ our ladder. Spend a few moments describing your own feelings about Jesus the ladder. Also, jot down a name or two of those you would like to see find Him.

_____

_____

The One and Only Way

Jesus said to him, "I am the way, and the truth, and the life; no one comes to the Father, but through Me." John 14:6, NASB.

We have heard these words repeated many times. The question is Do we really believe that the gate to heaven is not a church, not a system of beliefs, but a Person? It does not mean that organization and doctrine are useless. Rather, it means that the church and its teachings are meaningful only as they lead us to the person Jesus.

Our text excludes any other way to heaven. Numerous passages of Scripture teach this same fundamental fact. The parable of the good shepherd frankly tells us that Jesus is the door into the sheepfold. If anyone tries to get into that fold other than going through Him, that person is a thief and a robber (John 10:1). What stronger language could our Lord use? Why did He make such an exclusive statement?

If you want a good-tasting loaf of bread, you must carefully and precisely follow a bread recipe. To drive from New York to California in the most direct manner, using the finest highways, you must follow a carefully marked map. So with Christianity. Jesus is the recipe for eternal life. He is the way, the road to heaven.

Jesus was speaking to Thomas, who should have known the route to the Father's house, but clearly he was uncertain or he would not have asked, "How do we know the way?" (John 14:5, NASB). Christ's answer rules out any alternative. From Adam and Eve until this moment, Jesus has been the *only* way. He was the way for Abel, Abraham, Moses, Isaiah, and Malachi. Jesus was the path to salvation for Huss, Luther, Wycliffe, and hundreds of other Reformers. And He was the road to eternal life for William Miller, James and Ellen White, Joseph Bates, S.M.I. Henry, Anna Knight, and Kate Lindsay. Read Hebrews 11 for a long list of biblical heroes who knew that Jesus, the Messiah, was the only channel to salvation.

He is our way. We don't want any other path but Him! We praise His name for showing the way—and being the way—for Bob and Marie Spangler. Is He the way for you now? Why not write down how precious Jesus, the Way, is to you today?

_____

_____

The Richness of a Penny

And He sat down opposite the treasury, and began observing how the multitude were putting money into the treasury; and many rich people were putting in large sums. And a poor widow came and put in two small copper coins, which amount to a cent. And calling His disciples to Him, He said to them, "Truly I say to you, this poor widow put in more than all the contributors to the treasury." Mark 12:41-43, NASB.

In 1990 an international identity management firm polled the effectiveness of brand names. Not surprisingly, the brand name Coca-Cola topped the list as the best known product. McDonald's fast-food chain took second place. We have no statistical proof, but we suspect that the name Jesus Christ probably would be much farther down the list. Furthermore, the majority of the world's inhabitants know virtually nothing about the details of God's plan to redeem the human race. Even multitudes of professed Christians have little or no understanding of how God saves a person.

Wanting to share Jesus with others, some Christians carry bumper stickers with the words "Honk if you love Jesus." Others hang crosses from their neck and even ears. But isn't making Jesus known to others a lot more effective when we know Him ourselves? A converted Christian filled with the Holy Spirit is infectious. He or she makes an unexplainable impact on others. Consider the widow who quietly slipped a penny into the offering box. She "put in all she owned, all she had to live on" (Mark 12:44, NASB). Even beyond that, she also gave her magnanimous gift to the treasury of a religious organization filled with corrupt leaders. In fact, the high priest led his committee to vote an unwarranted and illegal death decree against the Son of God. Surely the widow knew what they were like. It was common knowledge. But she had a true relationship with God. Thus, she was giving to God, not just to an organization. Her gift is a powerful lesson for us today.

Such simple human beings, converted to Jesus, will spread the good news of salvation to every nation, tongue, and people. Then the brand name "Jesus" will rate number one.

Is it your desire to let those whom you meet sense the difference the indwelling of Jesus through His Spirit makes in your life? Can you recall any incident when the Holy Spirit used you to touch someone else's life? If so, jot it down.

_____

_____

God Lives!

Of this Gospel I, by his appointment, am herald, apostle, and teacher.
. . . I know who it is in whom I have trusted, and am confident of his
power to keep safe what he has put into my charge, until the great Day.
2 Tim. 1:11, 12, NEB.

"It's a strange feeling to realize that the thing you've got is the thing that is going to kill you, that there is nothing between you and death but more of the same. You start to feel dead. . . . For the first time I seriously began to wonder if there is existence after death. . . . What if there really is a God? Won't that be extraordinary!"

Agnes Collard—kept alive only through chemotherapy and injections and transfusions—recorded her thoughts. At 67 she was dying in the last stage of a four-year siege of leukemia.

Her words appeared in the December 1990 issue of *Life* magazine. The front cover had only one caption—"Who Is God?" Twenty-three individuals shared their inmost thoughts about their personal, private faith in God. Agnes was one of them. She continued, "I don't know what or who He is, but I am almost sure He is there."

Paul's words in our passage today have no hint of doubt. He is not almost sure but unconditionally positive that he knows "who it is in whom" he trusts.

The tribal chieftain Job, a man of impeccable piety and integrity who was known as "the greatest of all the men of the east" (Job 1:3, NASB), said with absolute confidence, "I know that my Redeemer lives" (Job 19:25, NASB).

Both men gave a ringing testimony of confidence in God's existence while living in dire circumstances. Job's faith was at its highest when it appeared that both God and man had deserted him. Everyone, including his servants, ignored him and treated him as a foreigner. Disease had devastated his body, and his bones stuck "out like teeth" (Job 19:20, Jerusalem). His halitosis was unbearable even to his wife (verse 17). Yet in spite of total rejection, he triumphantly declared, "I know my Redeemer lives."

Paul wrote his testimony while he was in a filthy Roman prison. His days were numbered, like many a person with a terminal illness, but his mind clearly trusted in the Lord's existence and power.

Do you trust God? If you do, write down why you believe in Him. I believe in God because _____

_____

Bury Me Standing!

And blessed be His glorious name forever; and may the whole earth be filled with His glory. Amen, and Amen. The prayers of David the son of Jesse are ended. Ps. 72:19, 20, NASB.

In most countries the people known as gypsies are despised and must labor at hard tasks to survive. They have a saying that declares "When I die you should bury me standing, because I have been on my knees all my life." The same words could well apply to the praying Christian. Some people such as John Wesley have worn the rug thin with their knees as they wrestled in prayer with the Lord.

The word "pray" and its derivatives occur several hundred times in Scripture. Prayer is the heartbeat of a solid Christian experience. Imagine, talking with God! We covet the opportunity to meet a prominent civil or religious leader. All of us would consider it an honor if some well-known person would either call us, even in the middle of the night, or invite us to phone him or her at any hour. Yet the King of the universe, the all-powerful Creator, the everlasting God, has done just that. How dare we not take advantage of the opportunity to converse with Him?

If for no other reason, praising the Lord in prayer is good because it energizes us physically as well as spiritually. No wonder the apostle Paul, that great prayer warrior, put rejoicing and praying together when he admonished us to "rejoice always; pray without ceasing; in everything give thanks; for this is God's will for you in Christ Jesus" (1 Thess. 5:16-18, NASB).

The book of Psalms, so filled with praise, might be just as well named the Book of Prayers. The dominant theme of this praise-prayer book is humanity's great need and God's loving provision to meet it. When we truly pray to our Father, we are free to speak frankly about our whole range of experience. Although we may present to Him our sorrows, disappointments, and need of forgiveness, let our prayers also contain praise and thanksgiving. We gain more courage and strength from praising God in prayer than in begging Him. Our text today tells how David concluded his part of the Psalms with the best possible ending—praise.

Why not jot down a praise prayer? It will make your day go better.

How Much Is Jesus Worth?

You should not go out; for if we indeed flee, they will not care about us, even if half of us die; they will not care about us. But you are worth ten thousand of us. 2 Sam. 18:3, NASB.

Absalom was scheming to take the kingdom from his father, King David. His aggression forced David, along with his loyal followers, to flee from Jerusalem and across the Jordan River. The day finally came for a showdown. David divided his forces into three groups. Then he offered to lead his small army against the overwhelming odds of Absalom's forces. The king's officers flatly rejected his offer. His devoted troops made it clear that their beloved leader should stay behind. Why? Because David was worth 10,000 of them. They considered his life to be extremely valuable.

What *is* a person worth? According to some surveys, the minerals and trace elements that make up the human body were worth 98 cents in 1970. Inflation has increased their value 643 percent since then. Someone else has calculated the cost of the working chemicals in the body. For example, one gram of the follicle stimulating hormone would sell for more than $4 million, and prolactin has an estimated value of about $17 million a gram. By this standard one person would be worth approximately $6 million.

From God's standpoint the glorious news is that you can't put a monetary value on a person. Each human being is priceless. None are worth less and none are worth more in Heaven's sight. Each of us cost the very life of Jesus Christ Himself. We may not consider ourselves equal to the life of Jesus, but that is the way He looks at us! Lecturers hold seminars on the subject of self-worth, but do they teach the real value of a person? Real self-worth? True self-worth can be judged only in the light that streams from Calvary.

Jesus did not pay a bargain price to redeem us. Rather He paid the ultimate! Have you ever praised Him for the high value He places on you as a person? Do you thank Him for paying such an enormous price for you? If you really appreciate what He has done for you, why not take a moment to record your feelings on this subject?

The Key of Knowledge

For in Christ Jesus neither circumcision nor uncircumcision means anything, but faith working through love. Gal. 5:6, NASB.

The battle between salvation by faith and salvation by works is a never-ending one. It began when sin entered the world and will continue until the coming of Christ. One of the main issues in this struggle centers on a person's understanding of faith.

Faith operates on several levels of motivation. Every human being exhibits enormous faith of a certain type on a daily basis. We can call this historical faith. For example, we sit in chairs by faith. None of us would ever recline in one if we thought it would collapse. Every meal is an act of faith. No person in his or her right mind would eat food, either at home or in restaurants, he or she believed was contaminated with a deadly poison. Furthermore, we board airplanes by faith. We have flown hundreds of times in many parts of the world, but never once have we checked the licenses of the pilots. And we could multiply such examples of faith endlessly.

Historical faith rests on a track record, a past history. For instance, we know from experience that chairs usually hold up and that food is usually not poisonous and that pilots generally fly airplanes safely.

Another common type of faith has its motivation in fear. When driving we stop at red signal lights. Why? Is it because we love the police? No, we really are fearful that if we don't stop we may be arrested or get injured or killed in a collision.

Neither type of faith has any merit when it comes to salvation. God accepts only that faith which is prompted by love. When we speak of righteousness or salvation by faith, we mean a faith that works through love. To know God requires that we love Him. "Faith working by love is the key of knowledge, and everyone that loveth 'knoweth God' " (*The Desire of Ages*, p. 139).

We constantly praise our Lord for the quality of faith that operates on a love basis. Why don't you thank Him for this kind of faith now?

_____

_____

It Is Character That Counts

Then Moses said, "I pray Thee, show me Thy glory." Ex. 33:18, NASB. Then the Lord passed by in front of him and proclaimed, "The Lord, the Lord God, compassionate and gracious, slow to anger, and abounding in lovingkindness and truth." Ex. 34:6, NASB.

The word "glory" must be important, because it appears about 400 times in Scripture. Often we use it or one of its derivatives in our daily conversation. "What a glorious sunset!" "It was a glorious event!" "When Rome was in her glory . . ." It appears frequently in religious services—in sermons and song. The dictionary's definition of "glory" includes the concept of great honor and admiration won by doing something important or valuable. The word has the connotation of fame, renown, splendor, and prosperity.

But how does Scripture use it, especially as it relates to God's glory? To begin with, the biblical word "glory" in Hebrew and Greek includes all the points just mentioned that are in the English word. However, the Lord gave it a special meaning in response to Moses' request for God to show him His glory. Note carefully the descriptive terms the Lord proclaimed as He passed by Moses. The words "compassionate," "gracious," "slow to anger," etc., give new meaning to "glory." God regards the qualities and virtues of His character as His glory!

Too often we overlook these dimensions of character. We hear the voice of a Pavarotti and exclaim "What a glorious voice!" and give no thought about the singer's character.

God's very special glory is His character. Heaven judges a person's true value by character, not by talents, wealth, or position.

In stressing His own character, God shows us how to be people of glory. Are we compassionate, or are we harsh and critical? Are we gracious, or are we stern and mean? Are we slow to anger, or do we fly off the handle at the least provocation? It is the greatest possible honor to allow the Holy Spirit to create God's qualities in us. We have daily opportunities to be "glorious" people as we develop the same character traits that our Lord has.

Thank God for your qualities that are like His, but also ask Him for those that you need to strengthen. Why not jot them down in the form of a short prayer? Lord, help me to develop qualities of _____

_____

The Current of Life

For this is My blood of the covenant, which is poured out for many for forgiveness of sins. Matt. 26:28, NASB.

The sight of human blood often produces a reaction of shock. Why? It represents life, especially if it's our own blood! When talking about salvation, we often hear the expression "Christ shed His blood in order to save us." The word "blood" appears more than 400 times in the Bible. Often the word occurs in the context of the plan of salvation and especially the sanctuary system in the Old Testament. Blood is an absolute necessity to life.

The average human body has more than five quarts of the life-sustaining fluid. The blood travels in a tubing system made up of arteries, veins, and capillaries. The heart pumps the blood at a rapid rate, causing it to make a complete circuit every two or three minutes. Its flow is so important that if any part of the body gets shut off from the blood flow for just an hour, that part may die. The brain will die within minutes from lack of blood.

One of the important roles of blood is to provide nourishment for the body tissues. In the digestive process the blood miraculously absorbs nutrients from the stomach and intestines, which it then carries to every living cell of the entire body. From hair, toenails, and eyelash production to kneecaps the blood is the waitress dispensing food to hungry cells. It is the reason God told His people in Deuteronomy 12:23, "The blood is the life."

Now apply this concept to the blood of Jesus being shed for us. While His spilled blood symbolizes His death, it represents life for us sinners. When our Lord died on the cross, His poured-out blood, like a transfusion, resulted in death to Himself but life for those who accept Him as Saviour. In fact, all life on earth depends on His shed blood. "To the death of Christ we owe even this earthly life. The bread we eat is the purchase of His broken body. The water we drink is bought by His spilled blood. Never one, saint or sinner, eats his daily food, but he is nourished by the body and the blood of Christ" (*The Desire of Ages*, p. 660).

As we study the plan of salvation, we can see how carefully the Godhead engineered its every detail. Not only do we stand amazed at the way Christ saved us to live this life, but we also are thankful for His willingness to lose His life that we may live eternally. Surely it is not difficult to express our thanksgiving for His blood being shed for us.

The Current of Cleansing

But if we walk in the light as He Himself is in the light, we have fellowship with one another, and the blood of Jesus His Son cleanses us from all sin. 1 John 1:7, NASB.

Yesterday we discussed Christ's blood, which represents His life poured out for us that we may have eternal life. Blood, to a large degree, controls everything a person does. One important aspect of blood is its cleansing activity. Much of our body consists of water—perhaps 60 to 75 percent or more. Dr. Fritz Kahn, in his two-volume set titled *Man in Structure and Function*, claims that if we squeezed a human being like a lemon, we would get no less than 11 gallons of water. The blood itself is a water-based liquid. The remarkable cleansing action of blood occurs as water, or plasma, oozes through the walls of the minutest vessels, the capillaries, and flows around the cells. This clear "body water" constantly bathes every living cell.

Today's text refers to the cleansing action of Christ's blood on the sinner. This symbolic statement, although a sign of a spiritual action, uses as its comparison a tangible process found in the human circulatory system. The Holy Spirit, moving on the hearts of the men who wrote the Scriptures, marvelously brought to their minds illustrations and concepts tied to concrete events, processes, and actions—sometimes they spoke more insightfully than they themselves realized. Thus inspiration uses the literal action of real blood cleansing real bodies to illustrate the spiritual concept and lesson of Christ's blood cleansing us from all sin.

This fact gives us an added dimension to our spiritual experience. Blood really bathes and cleanses every cell of our being. Symbolically, the blood of Christ cleanses us from the rot and filth of sin.

However, one important condition comes attached to this spiritual cleansing. Cleansing comes to those who walk in the light. What is light? Again we find a word connected with a literal element used figuratively to signify the joy and happiness of obedience to God's will. Light is the opposite of darkness, which Scripture uses to symbolize ignorance, evil, and misery. Praise the Lord for the light! Praise Him for the opportunity of walking in it! Praise Him for the fellowship we have with others who also walk with us in the light! And multiply praises to our Lord for the cleansing action of His blood on our lives as we fellowship with one another and walk in the light together!

God is so good. His Word has such wonderful depths of meaning. What a thrill it is to meditate upon it and to praise Him for His goodness! Jot down your own feelings about today's text. I thank Jesus because _____

_____

January 23

The Current of Nourishment

Truly, truly, I say to you, unless you eat the flesh of the Son of Man and drink His blood, you have no life in yourselves. He who eats My flesh and drinks My blood has eternal life, and I will raise him up on the last day. John 6:53, 54, NASB.

The sixth chapter of John records some of the most profound truths that Jesus ever uttered. It "contains the most precious and important lessons. . . . The whole chapter is very instructive, but is only faintly understood" (*Fundamentals of Christian Education*, p. 456). His enemies could not fathom what they thought was a cannibalistic idea—eating Christ's flesh and drinking His blood. In fact, the concept "led to a fierce dispute among the Jews" (verse 52, NEB). They were as slow to comprehend spiritual things as was Nicodemus, who had a hard time understanding how a person could be born again when he was old.

Both Christ's body and blood bring nourishment and life for us. Just as the blood coursing through our network of blood vessels carries with it food for our tissues, so the blood of Jesus carries rich spiritual nourishment when we understand what the atonement really means. Is this a mystical, unrealistic concept? Not at all.

What, then, does it mean to eat His flesh and drink His blood? First, by faith we accept Him as our personal Saviour. Such acceptance involves believing that His shed blood cleanses us from sin through His forgiveness. Then we are spiritually nourished daily by eating His flesh and drinking His blood through beholding His magnificent love. We meditate on His character. By dwelling on His life and works we drink in His goodness. Through the Word and its promises we partake of His divine nature. Thus we practice the same principle of growing and maintaining life spiritually as we do physically. Food and drink are to the body what the life and character of Jesus are to the soul.

We maintain both physical and spiritual health by eating and drinking. While this is easy to grasp and do in the physical world, it is difficult to really believe and practice in the spiritual realm. All of us recognize that a faulty physical diet produces physical problems, but do we believe that a faulty spiritual diet leads to spiritual sickness? To feed regularly upon Jesus is just as mandatory to maintain spiritual life as to eat regularly our meals in order to sustain physical life.

One interesting sidelight is that eating between meals is not the best physically. But in the spiritual world we urge you to eat as much as you can between meals all through the day! Eat and drink Jesus! Wouldn't you like to praise Him for this privilege?

_____

_____

The Cleansing Wave

For if the blood of goats and bulls and the ashes of a heifer sprinkling those who have been defiled, sanctify for the cleansing of the flesh, how much more will the blood of Christ, who through the eternal Spirit offered Himself without blemish to God, cleanse your conscience from dead works to serve the living God? Heb. 9:13, 14, NASB.

Our blood, as it circulates through the body, consists of a marvelous variety of elements that perform a number of functions. Primarily they are to feed and to cleanse the body. Spiritually we symbolically drink Christ's blood for both nourishment and cleansing. The cleansing symbolism is central to the baptismal service. How often we sing the hymn "The Cleansing Wave" at baptisms. Since childhood its tune and words have sounded in our minds at every baptismal ceremony.

> O now I see the crimson wave,
> The fountain deep and wide;
> Jesus, my Lord, mighty to save,
> Points to His wounded side.
>
> I see the new creation rise,
> I hear the speaking blood;

It speaks—polluted nature dies,
Sinks 'neath the cleansing flood.

The refrain powerfully reminds us of the cleansing action of Christ's blood. Meditate carefully on these words:

The cleansing stream I see, I see,
I plunge, and O, it cleanseth me!
O praise the Lord! it cleanseth me,
It cleanseth me, yes, cleanseth me.

We can understand the horribleness of sin only in the light of what it cost Heaven to cleanse us of it. When you are tempted to sin stop, look upward, and send a message through to God's throne room. Request the Holy Spirit to impress your heart again with the high cost of forgiveness and cleansing from sin. Additional help can be yours if you jot down the words of this hymn on a card. Carry it with you. Read it often. It will point you to our Lord's wounded side. Meditating on the Crucifixion awakens our conscience and creates a desire to serve the living God. Thank Him for His marvelous cleansing blood. Thank Him for the thoughts of Calvary that awaken sacred emotions, motivating us to obedience.

January 25

Power in the Blood

And they overcame him because of the blood of the Lamb and because of the word of their testimony, and they did not love their life even to death. Rev. 12:11, NASB.

Who among us has not struggled to overcome temptation? At times our sense of failure nearly snuffs out all hope. Even when we cannot think of what we might have done wrong, Jesus' perfection can easily make us feel that if salvation depends on our being like Him, we are lost. It is like chasing the pot of gold at the end of the rainbow. We can be eternally thankful that our performance is not the key to salvation. If it were, salvation would be impossible!

Aside from Jesus, the only people ever good enough to have eternal life were Adam and Eve before they sinned. Since the moment sin entered human history, not one human being except Christ has deserved eternal life.

Yet the Bible repeatedly admonishes us to overcome evil, to reject the world, to walk the narrow way. The question is How do we overcome? There is no single formula for victory. Like a spiderweb, the Lord weaves about His willing servants numerous strands and threads to hold them in His life-giving control. This does not imply that He uses force, but rather that we need to accept the strands of strength He gives us to aid us in performing as Christians should. Our text refers to one major strand—the blood of the

Lamb. Our physical blood contains different varieties of cells that fight for our lives. Platelets, for instance, rush to any injury of a blood vessel and plug the hole. So with the blood of Christ. His blood, in a spiritual sense, closes the holes of weakness and fights for our very lives. By faith when we accept Him, we become motivated through the Spirit to obey right and reject wrong. If we concentrate on the meaning of Christ's shed blood, it makes a powerful impact on our minds. To remind ourselves that God the Son poured out His lifeblood for us helps us turn against evil. It glorifies right and encourages us to reject wrong.

As we meditate on the old hymn "Power in the Blood," it will do something incredible for our lives. Note some of its words.

> Would you o'er evil a victory win? . . .
> Would you be free from your passion and pride? . . .
> Would you live daily His praises to sing?

Then the repeated response to these questions is

> There is pow'r, pow'r, wonder-working pow'r
> In the precious blood of the Lamb.

We are grateful, we are overwhelmed, we are thankful to Him who shed His wonder-working blood for us. Express your feelings in just a few words.

The Price of Heaven Is Jesus

This is My body, which is for you; do this in remembrance of Me. . . . This cup is the new covenant in My blood; do this, as often as you drink it, in remembrance of Me. 1 Cor. 11:24, 25, NASB.

The Old Testament taught the plan of salvation in a most realistic way through the sanctuary system. It was a specific building with special furniture. The offering of sacrifices, and the other services performed there, were tangible events. You could see the blood, smell the incense, touch the lamb, and hear the bells tinkling on the hem of the high priest's robe. Everything in the sanctuary service had as its goal to make an impact on all the senses of the repentant sinner.

Since New Testament times we have the simple baptismal and Communion services to remind us of salvation through Christ. Through the bread and wine of the Communion service, we members of the church understand and experience the reality and depth of our unity in Christ. When we eat the unleavened bread and drink the unfermented wine, our imagination carries us not to the shadows of the cross, but to its saving light.

The service brings a very special blessing to our lives. Everything in it reminds us that the price of heaven is Jesus. We cannot buy Him with our tainted works. Rather, we acquire heaven with our acceptance, by faith alone, of Jesus. He is our priceless admission to heaven! He means everything to us and must be the center of our love and affection. As you participate in the Communion service, imagine the One adored by angels who shares Himself with us fallen beings in a very tangible way. To miss the service means to lose a precious blessing.

Since Jesus is the link between God and us, we receive great blessing when we participate in such a spiritual experience that so dramatically touches our senses. As the eaten bread and swallowed wine are assimilated into our bodies and become a part of our physical being, so Christ through the Holy Spirit wants to—and will—stamp Himself on every aspect of our being.

But this service reaches beyond the Lord's table in the church. It touches the dining table in our homes. When you sit down to eat, every mouthful of food should reflect Jesus' sacrifice. Every drink speaks of His love. Jesus is the bread and water of life for us.

Do you desire the self-sacrificing love of Jesus to take possession of your entire being? Do you want the love of Heaven to flow out from you? If so, express that longing in your own words.

_____

_____

January 27

The Anatomy of Sin

When the time of mourning was over, David sent and brought her to his house and she became his wife; then she bore him a son. But the thing that David had done was evil in the sight of the Lord. 2 Sam. 11:27, NASB.

The story of David and Bathsheba has captivated multitudes, including the scriptwriters of Hollywood. It contains intrigue, deceit, adultery, murder, and heartbreak. What lessons can we learn from it that will help us in our personal fight against temptation? We will number our points for your convenience.

1. Yielding to temptations, even seemingly small ones, can (and does in many cases) prepare us to succumb to even bigger ones. How many bank robbers have started their career by stealing a few stamps at the office? Hardened drug addicts begin with a pill before they graduate to a needle.

David seems to have had a weakness for women. When he became king over all Israel, "David took more concubines and wives from Jerusalem"

(2 Sam. 5:13, NASB). Thus 20 years later David had conditioned himself to yield to lust when he saw Uriah's gorgeous wife, Bathsheba, ritually washing herself on the housetop. A major defense against major temptation is to overcome by God's grace the small ones before they get any bigger!

2. Rationalization is a dangerous pitfall. Conventional wisdom during David's lifetime permitted rulers to get away with crimes not tolerated among the general populace. When faced with temptation, ask the Holy Spirit to help you forget about what others may do. Let your motto ever be "Others may; I cannot!"

3. "Pride goeth before destruction, and an haughty spirit before a fall" (Prov. 16:18). Pride involves the deadly habit of looking and trusting to self rather than to Jesus. Dare we leave home for work before spending time with the Word and seeking God on our knees in prayer? Is there any inoculation against temptation if we confidently march through life without taking daily doses of the Word? Confidence in God and distrust in self have as their foundation time spent with our Lord.

4. When things are going smoothly, be especially aware of Satan's traps. David was now king of a powerful nation. Under such flourishing conditions of power and prosperity, he felt no concern to be on guard. He felt little need of God's protection.

Have you ever been in a similar situation? Have you been delivered from a severe temptation and want to praise God for it? Or are you plagued with a temptation and feel your need of God's special help? If so, express it in writing.

The Oneness of a Person

Hear, O Israel! The Lord our God is one Lord; and you shall love the Lord your God with all your heart, and with all your soul, and with all your mind, and with all your strength. Mark 12:29, 30, NASB.

When we study the Hebrew and Greek words that are translated "soul," "heart," and "mind" in our English Bibles, it is surprising to see their all-inclusiveness. When we use the word "mind" we generally limit its meaning to a function of the brain. "Heart" usually refers to that marvelous organ that can repair itself while pumping endless gallons of blood through a network of veins and arteries. But the Hebrew words translated "heart," "mind," and "soul" in our English Bibles can apply to various functions of the individual. They can refer to breath, vitality, appetite, lust, greed, self, heart, emotions, intellect, concepts, and imaginations.

Our point is that the Bible clearly teaches that a person is so integrated physically and mentally that we cannot separate the effects of the mind on the body any more than we can separate the brain from the skull and still have a viable human being. The reverse is also true. The way we treat the body in terms of eating, drinking, exercise, etc., has an effect on the mind.

In the introductory part of Christ's answer to the scribe as to which commandment was most important, Jesus used an Old Testament text that the Hebrews knew well. Although it begins with the oneness of the Godhead, it can also imply the oneness of a human being, who is created in God's image.

When Jesus dwells in our heart, in a special sense He dwells in the whole of us. To surrender our mind to Him means to give Him everything—which includes our eyes, ears, feet, stomach, lungs, muscles, brain, and liver!

Praise Him for this privilege of being one in Him! _____

The Powerless Law

For what the Law could not do, weak as it was through the flesh, God did: sending His own Son in the likeness of sinful flesh and as an offering for sin, He condemned sin in the flesh, in order that the requirement of the Law might be fulfilled in us, who do not walk according to the flesh, but according to the Spirit. Rom. 8:3, 4, NASB.

Traffic laws cannot force drivers to apply their brakes when approaching red lights. People must choose to do that themselves. Our Creator gave Adam and Eve a law that commanded, "Don't eat the fruit of the tree of the knowledge of good and evil," but it had no power to prevent them from eating the forbidden fruit. Neither divine nor human laws can by themselves enable those who live under them to obey. In this respect, the law of God is weak!

Paul gives further insight. He claims the law was weak through the flesh. Our sinful nature has destroyed the law's power. Unredeemed sinners find it impossible to keep the law in all respects. Only those who have experienced the new birth can agree to and even delight in obeying God's law. Even then they encounter times when the flesh—the "lower nature"—slips and rebels against it.

Although the law is weak, the Lawgiver is strong. God in "sending His own Son in the likeness of sinful flesh and as an offering for sin . . . condemned sin in the flesh." Our Lord sacrificed His life because of sin. His death condemned sin. Even His life as a human being passed judgment on it. His life and death on earth is our passport to freedom from both the penalty and power of sin.

The law is not only weak in keeping us from sinning but even more powerless in forgiving us for transgressing its demands. The law of gravity can never forgive and restore to life the person who violated it by jumping off the top of the Washington Monument. But in a spiritual sense, Christ has performed the impossible. Through His life and death He has reversed the effects of a transgressed law for all those whose faith centers on Him and on Him alone. First and foremost Jesus forgives us as lawbreakers. He declares us innocent of any wrongdoing. That is justification. In addition, Jesus obtained victory over sin "in the flesh," or in His humanity. Why? "In order that the requirement of the Law might be fulfilled in us." His victory is ours by faith. Through His Spirit we walk the pathway of sanctification.

Take a moment to express thanks to our Lord for His great salvation.

January 30

Kingly Character or Kingly Form?

He has no stately form or majesty that we should look upon Him, nor appearance that we should be attracted to Him. Isa. 53:2, NASB.

Isaiah 53 predicted in detail the type of person our Lord and Saviour, Jesus, would be and the type of ministry He would embrace. The chapter opens with a question that brings into focus the radical and unbelievable way our Lord would look, live, and act when He came to our planet as the Son of man. The question demands, "Who has believed our message?" (verse 1, NASB).

From a human standpoint Jesus didn't look the part of a heavenly king, and He certainly didn't live like one while on earth. Who would have ever believed that the carpenter from Galilee was the King of kings in human form? Conceived out of wedlock? A king? Born in a barn? A king? Grew up in Nazareth? A king? Reared in a carpenter's home? A king? No formal education? A king? No place to lay His head? A king? Any way you look at it, Jesus did not fit the expected description. His only singular characteristic was His character.

Contrast Jesus with the first king of Israel, Saul. Saul was "a choice and handsome man, and there was not a more handsome person than he among the sons of Israel; from his shoulders and up he was taller than any of the people" (1 Sam. 9:2, NASB).

Compare the Bible's description of him with our text today. Nothing about the way Christ looked would of itself have attracted followers. Our Saviour's appearance and lifestyle were quite the opposite of the world's standard for a king, prince, or president. Humanity still judges by external appearance, whereas God still examines the inside. Outwardly Jesus had "no stately form or majesty," but inwardly He was the king of peace, the king of purity, the king of honesty, the king of love! He was the king of perfection in every aspect of goodness.

Applying these principles to our own lives, we should rejoice over the truth that we do not have to be rich, pompous, or physically attractive to be part of King Jesus' family.

In your own words, write out a short statement praising God for the character of Jesus Christ and His willingness to impart His attributes to you.

_____

_____

January 31

Hiding by the Baggage—
The New Saul

"Then the Spirit of the Lord will come upon you mightily, and you shall prophesy with them and be changed into another man." . . . Then it happened when he turned his back to leave Samuel, God changed his heart. 1 Sam. 10:6-9, NASB.

Our text records a remarkable incident in the life of Saul that took place immediately after the prophet Samuel anointed him as ruler over God's people. Israel had clamored for a king, and the Lord responded by telling Samuel to anoint Saul as king.

Was Saul a converted man before his anointing? Or does Saul's experience prove that when God calls someone a conversion takes place? In what way did Saul have a changed heart after the Holy Spirit caused him to prophesy?

The record simply tells us that Saul joined a group of prophets, and "the Spirit of God came upon him mightily, so that he prophesied among them" (verse 10, NASB). Saul became a changed man, and the people knew it. They asked, "What has happened to the son of Kish?" (verse 11, NASB). At this time God's people did not know that Saul had been anointed king.

One of the results of Saul's being a changed person appeared in his reticence and even timidity at being chosen for the highest office in the land. When Samuel summoned the people together at Mizpah to present to them their new king, no one could find Saul. They prayed to God, asking Him to reveal Saul's whereabouts. The Lord told them, "Behold, he is hiding himself by the baggage" (verse 22, NASB).

When the people located him, they exclaimed, "Long live the king!" (verse 24, NASB). Interestingly, Saul did not have unanimous support. Some whose hearts God touched supported him, while "certain worthless men said, 'How can this one deliver us?' and they despised him and did not bring him any present" (verse 27, NASB). Yet Saul truly was a changed man, for the record states that even though rejected by some, "he kept silent" (verse 27, NASB).

What is your testimony about being asked to serve in some position, especially in the church? Did you feel qualified, or did you feel that only with God's help could you perform the task requested of you? Why not praise God for the abilities He has given you to serve others?

February 1

From Saint to Suicide

And Samuel came no more to see Saul until the day of his death: nevertheless Samuel mourned for Saul. 1 Sam. 15:35.

Tragically, what you just read has been, is now, and will be repeated multiplied millions of times until that day when salvation history ends forever.

Jesus' parable of the sower, seed, and soil finds its fulfillment in every heart. Spiritual seed falls into four types of heart soil. The sower—Jesus—and the seed—the Word of God—never change. But the type of soil depends upon our own choices. King Saul's heart had become like the thorny ground where God's word, through Samuel, flourished for a time, but the thorns of disobedience, jealousy, and self-will finally choked it out, and Saul cut himself off from the Lord (see Matt. 13:1-23).

Tall and handsome, Saul was a converted man at one time, and he began his ministry honoring God. In fact, he received the prophetic gift. His bravery against the invading Philistines was outstanding. God was with him. But pride, impetuousness, disobedience, suspicion, and revengefulness began to crowd out the Holy Spirit.

At one time he wrongfully assumed the office of priest and offered sacrifices because Samuel was late to a special service. Saul feared that if he did not act quickly, his discouraged Israelite army would literally vanish. It showed that he lacked trust in God, and because of it Samuel had to tell him that his reign would not endure. Following this he spared Agag, king of the Amalekites, contrary to God's specific command. This disobedient act cost him his kingdom. His cruelty to David, his slaying of Ahimelech and 85 priests at Nob, and his contact with the medium at Endor further evidence the withering of God's good seed in his thorny-ground heart. Saul's choices finally led him to death by his own hand.

One could diagram Saul's life by a line that starts at a high point and gradually slopes downward to a suicide's grave. Not a pretty story, it is heart-wrenchingly sad. How often we have witnessed a similar course in the lives of some of our friends and even among some of our beloved relatives! But the joyful news is that if anyone reading these words is headed in the wrong direction, it is not too late to turn around.

Praise God for another opportunity to repent and be changed by His Spirit. Why not write a few words explaining how you feel about God and His leading in your life?

_____

_____

The Blessing of
Telling the Truth

Lying lips are abomination to the Lord: but they that deal truly are his delight. Prov. 12:22.

Dr. Ben Carson, renowned neurosurgeon, tells of retaking a final exam along with his classmates in a psychology class at Yale University. The students had been notified that the test papers they had already turned in had been "inadvertently burned." So they assembled in a designated classroom to repeat the exam. As soon as the professor passed out the test to the 150 students, she left the room.

Before Ben read the first question, he heard someone whispering loudly, "Are they kidding?" Not far away he heard a young woman say, "Forget it! Let's go back and study this. We can say we didn't read the notice, then when they repeat it again, we'll be ready." So she and her friend quietly left the room. Immediately three others followed. More and more disappeared until half the class had vanished, and strangely none of them turned in his or her test paper before leaving.

Ben could not believe the questions himself. "They were incredibly difficult, if not impossible." While each did contain a thread of what they should have known from the course, they were hopelessly involved. He prayed for help in figuring out answers to these knotty questions. Within a half hour all the students had left, leaving him alone. "Like the others," he said, "I was tempted to walk out. But I had read the notice, and I couldn't lie and say I hadn't."

Suddenly someone flung the door open, and Ben's gaze met that of his professor. She and a photographer from the Yale *Daily News* walked over to him, paused, and snapped his picture. When Ben asked what was going on, his professor replied, "A hoax. We wanted to see who was the most honest student in the class." Smiling, she added, "And that's you." Then she rewarded him with a $10 bill, which he desperately needed at that time.

Many resort to lying as a convenience or a cover-up. Someone has said that truth has only one face, but lying has many. Even a glance, a tone of the voice, or a body movement can create a false impression. "Everything that

Christians do should be as transparent as the sunlight" (*Thoughts From the Mount of Blessing*, p. 68).

How much happier Jacob would have been if he had trusted in God to work out the details of his life instead of taking it upon himself to deceive his father, Isaac, so he could receive the birthright. Let us pray along with David of old, "Deliver my soul, O Lord, from lying lips, and from a deceitful tongue" (Ps. 120:2).

Thank God now for His power in helping you be a transparent Christian.

Happiness Is a Choice

Whoso trusteth in the Lord, happy is he. Prov. 16:20.

Psychiatrists Minirth and Meier in their book *Happiness Is a Choice* tell of Abraham Lincoln, who said, "Most people are about as happy as they choose to be." They declare that Lincoln should have known, since he went through much anguish in his life, such as the death of his fiancée, lost elections, the Civil War, and other major disappointments. "At one point in his life he was so depressed he considered suicide. But Lincoln chose to overcome his depression. He chose to be happy."

If you are going through hardships and difficult circumstances, remember Abraham Lincoln. Even more important, never lose sight of Jesus, the true wellspring of all joy. He finds no delight in human misery but wants us to be happy. Even in nature, no matter how bad the storm or how heavy the rain, the sun always shines again.

Epicurus said, "No man is happy unless he believes he is." Many, dissatisfied with what they have, feel restless and discontented, so they continually chase happiness. Some never accept themselves, and others continually punish themselves because of guilt feelings. If you find yourself in one of these categories, believe that Jesus has pardoned your sins and then trust in Him. The transforming influence of the Holy Spirit can bring happiness. Faith in God inevitably brings happiness, peace, and joy.

Satan tricked Eve into becoming dissatisfied. He led her to believe that she needed something more than God had given her to be really happy. She abandoned her trust in God. He does the same today with anyone who will listen to him. Many seek happiness in materialism, pleasures, or power, but they still find themselves feeling unfulfilled. They have everything our world can offer, but they do not have that inner peace and joy that alone bring true happiness.

To share our means and ourselves with others is a wonderful source of happiness. Luke 12 points out that the foolish rich man worked only for his own selfish interests. In the end he could not use all that he had, and was lost. A word of cheer, an act of kindness, or a look of sympathy not only lightens

41

the burdens of those around us, but it is a spiritual shot in the arm to those who give it. Write down ways you can choose to be happy, and thank God for your power of choice.

_____

_____

Conceal or Reveal?

He who conceals his transgressions will not prosper, but he who confesses and forsakes them will find compassion. Prov. 28:13, NASB. And there is no creature hidden from His sight, but all things are open and laid bare to the eyes of Him with whom we have to do. Heb. 4:13, NASB.

Six-year-old Bob had dressed up in a new white shirt for Sabbath school and church. While he waited for his parents to leave, he decided to go into the backyard and take a pole with cloth wrapped around the end, dip it into some kerosene, and set fire to it. His father had been using it during the week to burn the caterpillar nests infesting the branches of the family's fruit trees.

As Bob enjoyed himself, he noticed a sizable spark fall onto his new shirt. When it hit, he tried to brush it away but with it went a small part of the fabric. He quickly put out the fire, went into the house, and held his hand over the hole in the front of his shirt. Somehow he managed to conceal it during the entire morning. On the way home from church, both parents noticed his odd posture, but rather than confess, he simply switched hands and proclaimed that nothing was wrong—all was well. Finally his suspicious father reached over, took Bob's hand off his chest, and saw what Bob had done to his shirt. Actually it was a relief to get his spanking over with and no longer have to keep hiding his misdeed. He has never forgotten the incident!

What Bob did is what earth's majority have done since Adam and Eve tried to hide from God. Successfully concealing sin may be possible for a time, but someday it will be found out. The mental suffering from hidden evil has caused emotional breakdowns, physical disease, and even suicide. Fortunately, Jesus has the remedy for sin. He paid for all sin in full on the cross. If we confess, He will forgive. "Blessed is he whose transgression is forgiven, whose sin is covered" (Ps. 32:1). But our text clearly outlines something else. The forsaking of sin must follow confession. The purpose of confession, embarrassing or difficult as it may be, is to turn us against sin. When we make correct confessions to the proper individuals, it deeply impresses the mind and serves as a bulwark against repeating that sin.

We thank the Lord for His forgiveness. His compassion brings great serenity and warmth into our hearts. Wouldn't you like to write out your thanks to Him for forgiving and covering your sins?

The Pre-Advent Inspection

But the Lord abides forever; He has established His throne for judgment, and He will judge the world in righteousness; He will execute judgment for the peoples with equity. Ps. 9:7, 8, NASB.

For 35 years our main mode of transportation has been by air. Our travels have carried us to all parts of the world. Often we have sat in the air terminal, observing through its huge windows the preparation activities being done on the plane before we board. It has given us peace of mind to watch one of the pilots slowly walking around the aircraft as he inspected its landing gear, wings, nose cone, engine housing, and other external parts. He was checking for any visible defects that might prove dangerous—or even fatal—to our flight. In the cockpit the crew monitors internal mechanical parts by scanning the scores of gauges on the instrument panels. All this activity has only one purpose—to make certain the aircraft is safe to fly.

So it is with the greatest takeoff in our earth's history. God will transport the redeemed to the New Jerusalem. Prior to that event, our heavenly pilot Jesus is inspecting, not the vehicle that carries us home, but rather the occupants who will inhabit a sinless heaven and who will be privileged to associate with perfect, unfallen beings. We have generally referred to this pre-Advent inspection as the investigative judgment. Call it what you will, we must take it seriously. It is not a trifling matter. The ultimate purpose of His inspection-judgment is to determine whether we will enjoy membership in the community of sinless believers.

We should be thankful for our Lord's carefulness. Aren't all of us tired of evil? Isn't every true Christian eager to live in a place where we can be sure that sin will not be allowed and will never recur? Think of the peace of mind we will have in such a place! What would be your attitude toward God if He carelessly allowed any unconverted person a place in heaven? Imagine how you would feel if Hitler or Stalin entered heaven without being unchanged in personality or character? What if God were a universalist in the sense that He would save everyone regardless of lifestyle, character, and attitude?

Instead of rejecting or ridiculing God's inspection process, let us praise His name for His careful evaluation of every person. If we gain peace of mind from pilots inspecting planes, how much more should we appreciate God's carefulness as to whom He'll take to heaven. The good news is that anyone who surrenders to Jesus Christ is fit for heaven. We can be assured that "He will execute judgment for the peoples with equity."

What is your attitude toward our God, the righteous judge?

_____

_____

What Was Finished?

And I heard a loud voice in heaven, saying, "Now the salvation, and the power, and the kingdom of our God and the authority of His Christ have come, for the accuser of our brethren has been thrown down, who accuses them before our God day and night." Rev. 12:10, NASB.

The abridged edition of James Hudson Taylor's biography, written by Dr. and Mrs. Howard Taylor, should be required reading for all Christians. It has changed and redirected the lives of many through the years. Taylor's faithfulness and answered prayers in founding the China Inland Mission will warm any reader's heart. His conversion when he was 17 years old especially interested us.

His 13-year-old sister, Amelia, was his closest friend. He could speak more freely to her than to adults. Even at her young age she determined to pray for his conversion three times daily. She wrote in her diary that she would never cease praying for her brother until he came to God.

While his mother was away from home, Taylor had a holiday and went to his father's library to find something to read. There he found a gospel tract that looked interesting, and in an utterly unconcerned state, he began to read. He had no idea that his mother, 75 miles away, rose from the dinner table that same afternoon, suddenly impressed to plead for the conversion of her son.

As Taylor read the tract, one phrase struck him: "The finished work of Christ." As he thought about it, the words of Christ, "It is finished," flashed into his mind.

"What was finished?" he asked. Later he wrote: "I at once replied, 'a full and perfect atonement and satisfaction for sin. The debt was paid for our sins, and not for ours only, but also for the sins of the whole world.' Then came the further thought: *If the whole work was finished and the whole debt paid, what is there left for me to do?"*

He related how the Holy Spirit then convicted him that there was nothing in the world he could do except to fall on his knees and accept His Saviour and His salvation and praise Him forevermore. When his mother returned home two weeks later, he met her at the door to tell her the good news. She quietly replied, "I know, my boy." Then she described how she knew her prayers were answered. Her response greatly strengthened his belief in the power of prayer.

Our text today reminds us that Christ defeated our accuser, Satan, at the cross. Victory is ours through Him. Tell Him that you claim that victory.

Resting in Jesus

If we believe not, yet he abideth faithful. 2 Tim. 2:18. For he hath said, "I will never leave thee, nor forsake thee." Heb. 13:5.

Although James Hudson Taylor, founder of the China Inland Mission, was a converted person, he (like all Christians) passed through spiritual crises. Our two passages of Scripture today became the key to his victory during those times. At the age of 37 he poured out his heart in a letter to his sister, Amelia. The challenge of reaching the millions of China who had never heard the name of Jesus was not uppermost in his mind. Instead, he wrote: "My mind has been greatly exercised for six or eight months past, feeling the need personally, and for our mission, of more holiness, life, power in our souls. But personal need stood first and was the greatest. I felt the ingratitude, the danger, the sin of not living nearer to God. I prayed, agonized, fasted, strove, made resolutions, read the Word more diligently, sought more time for retirement and meditation—but all was without effect. Every day, almost every hour, the consciousness of sin oppressed me. I knew that if I could only abide in Christ all would be well, but I *could not.* . . . Instead of growing stronger, I seemed to be getting weaker and to have less power against sin; and no wonder, for faith and even hope were getting very low. I hated myself; I hated my sin; and yet I gained no strength against it. . . .

"Sometimes there were seasons not only of peace but of joy in the Lord. But they were transitory, and at best there was a sad lack of power. Oh, how good the Lord was in bringing this conflict to an end!"

A letter from a close friend who had experienced similar problems brought Taylor's struggle to a climax. After describing his own spiritual battles, the friend said, "But how to get faith strengthened? Not by striving after faith, but by resting on the Faithful One." As Taylor read on he at last understood. " 'If we believe *not,* he abideth faithful,' " the friend continued. "I looked to Jesus and saw (and when I saw, oh, how joy flowed!) that He had said, 'I will never leave you.' Ah, there *is rest!* I thought. *I have striven in vain to rest in Him. I'll strive no more. For has He not promised to abide with me—never to leave me, never to fail me?* and . . . He never will!"

Has Jesus enabled you, like Hudson Taylor, to cease striving and to rest in Him? If He has, then praise Him. But if you have not yet allowed Him to give you spiritual rest and trust, then ask Him now to bring you that peace.

Seven Times or 490 Times?

Then Peter came and said to Him, "Lord, how often shall my brother sin against me and I forgive him? Up to seven times?" Jesus said to him, "I do not say to you, up to seven times, but up to seventy times seven." Matt. 18:21, 22, NASB.

When Peter qualified the person he would forgive as "my brother," we may conclude that Jewish Peter would consider it unthinkable to pardon anyone outside his people—or the church, as we would put it today. A second indication that he had strict limits on whom he would forgive appears in the answer he gives to his own question: "Up to seven times?"

Many individuals who go to their ministers for counsel already have in mind what they want to hear. In the case of Peter, he offered Christ an answer of seven forgivenesses, more than twice the number the rabbinical code required. Peter felt that he was being most magnanimous with his suggestion of seven times, which, after all, was the perfect number.

If we could have seen the look on Peter's face when the Lord replied 70 times seven, or 490 times, it would have been one of utter shock. Our Lord's answer was 70 times more than Peter's puny suggestion.

Why did our Lord use the phrase "seventy times seven," or 490 opportunities, to forgive? The only other reference to the figure in Scripture appears in Daniel 9:24. There we also find 70 units of seven, which we have interpreted as 70 weeks of prophetic years that God decreed or marked out for His people. Was Jesus saying in effect that for 490 years He had been repeatedly forgiving His people their transgressions? For 490 years our Lord had waited for them to make an end of sin and reconciliation for iniquity. But alas, they had failed to respond.

The point was that if Jesus could be so patient and long-suffering with His people, couldn't Peter find it in his heart to do better than come up with the figure of seven times for forgiveness?

Finally, and most important of all, forgiveness cannot be given a numerical value. To limit forgiveness is to destroy its very principle. Forgiveness is not merely an act; it is an attitude! To fulfill our Saviour's law of 70 times seven we do not need to ask how often, but rather keep in mind that our Lord has forgiven us repeatedly. Can we then possibly hold back forgiveness from a brother or sister, friend or enemy, or saint or sinner?

Shall we not praise God for His forgiving attitude toward us? Where would we be or where would we go if we had no assurance of His forgiveness? What is your response to His great heart of love?

A Forgiven Slave

And the lord of that slave felt compassion and released him and forgave him the debt. Matt. 18:27, NASB.

After Jesus answered Peter's question in yesterday's reading, He related one of His most important parables. It begins with a story of a king who wants to settle accounts with his servants. Obviously the servants, or slaves, stand for each one of us, and the king symbolizes Jesus. It is the first parable that uses the term *king* for the Lord.

The king summons one slave who owes him 10,000 talents, an enormous sum that, some scholars believe, was more than the entire revenue that Rome received from Palestine for a whole year. It wittingly expresses the immensity of every sinner's transgression in thought and deed against God and His law. The Ten Commandments stand over and against the 10,000 talents, the equivalent of a multi-million-dollar debt, utterly impossible for anyone to pay.

The parable reveals that this indebted slave had absolutely nothing to pay toward his debt. So it is with sinners. If we could pile up every ounce of wealth in the world—gold, silver, jewels, stocks, homes, autos, and every other asset—into a Mount Everest of riches, it could never compensate for the smallest sin we have committed. All the combined assets of the world can never equal the blood of Christ, who died for us.

The penitent slave, hearing that he was to be sold along with his family, prostrated himself at the king's feet and begged for mercy. Perhaps the saddest words in the entire parable appear in his plea, "Have patience with me, and I will repay you everything" (verse 26, NASB). He had no sense of the enormity of his unpayable debt. So with many today. How many of us recognize what it cost heaven to pay for our individual sins?

This slave couldn't possibly feel much of a burden for his debt, since he boasted that he would repay everything if only given enough time. However, in spite of the slave's ignorant promise, the king felt compassion and did two things. First, he released him from the threat of imprisonment, which should have brought joy to his heart and changed his attitude toward everyone in the world. Second, not only did the king free him, but amazingly he canceled the debt.

Our Lord has done the same thing for every one of us. He has justified us by canceling our debt of sin, and He sanctifies us by releasing us from sin's grip. How great our Lord is! When we see amazing grace personified there on the cross, we cannot hold back from thanking Him for releasing us from the prison house of sin and for canceling the enormous debt that we owe Him.

Are you thankful for His salvation? If you are, please say so.

When Forgiveness Failed

But that slave went out and found one of his fellow-slaves who owed him a hundred denarii; and he seized him and began to choke him, saying, "Pay back what you owe." Matt. 18:28, NASB.

In the past two readings, we have been studying the parable of the unmerciful servant found in Matthew 18:21-35. From a human standpoint, we wish Jesus would have ended the parable with the passage selected yesterday. But deeper lessons still await us. Keep in mind that the king has forgiven his slave a multi-million-dollar debt and has canceled his decision to sell him and his family into the worst form of slavery. In other words, the servant was a free person.

Rather than being eternally grateful to his Lord, the forgiven servant seeks out a fellow slave who owes him about $10. And instead of just reminding his fellow slave of the debt owed, he seized him and began to choke him, saying, "Pay back what you owe." (Remember, this parable must never be used as an excuse to avoid paying just monetary debt. Jesus is talking here about great spiritual themes.)

At this point we can clearly see the great difference between the character of the king and that of his ungrateful servant. At times a similar realization pierces our own hearts as we consider our own attitude toward those whom we think may have offended us. What is anyone's offense against us compared to what we have done against our Lord? If He forgives us, can't we forgive others whether they ask for forgiveness or not? Even if we are unjustly martyred by some enemy, what is our life compared to that of God the Son, whom we have nailed to the cross?

The only way we can receive God's pardon is to give it to anyone else who needs it. This parable offers new meaning to that part of the Lord's Prayer which states, "And forgive us our debts, as we forgive our debtors" (Matt. 6:12). Notice that the verse immediately following the Lord's Prayer says, "For if ye forgive men their trespasses, your heavenly Father will also forgive you" (verse 14).

When we truly understand the nature of our debt and that our Lord has forgiven it through His death on Calvary, we cannot—and dare not—be indifferent either toward God or the entire human family. The concept of God's forgiveness is really what produces a change in our own hearts. We owe everything, even our very lives, to the Lord. "Grace in the Saviour effected our redemption, our regeneration, and our exaltation to heirship with Christ. Let this grace be revealed to others" (*Christ's Object Lessons*, p. 250).

Express both your love to our Lord for His mighty forgiveness and your intention to let His love shine through you to others.

48

Treat Others the Way God Has Treated You

Then summoning him, his lord said to him, "You wicked slave, I forgave you all that debt because you entreated me. Should you not also have had mercy on your fellow-slave, even as I had mercy on you?" Matt. 18:32, 33, NASB.

The parable of the unmerciful servant climaxes with the king's frustrated anger. The slave he had forgiven and set free refused to have mercy toward another slave, who owed him only a paltry sum. Not only did he seize and choke his fellow slave, he actually threw him into debtor's prison until he could pay the money back. Our inhumanity to each other never ceases to amaze! It really is unbelievable at times. But aren't we all guilty to a greater or lesser degree?

As the result of the unmerciful slave's behavior, the rest of the king's servants, upset by what he had done, told the ruler what had happened. Note carefully that the king now calls him a "wicked slave," an expression he had not used at the beginning of the parable. Why? Could it be that the worst wickedness possible is to claim to be a Christian—to claim to have accepted the king's forgiveness—yet continue to treat others in a critical, unmerciful way? A professed Christian who lacks an accepting, merciful spirit toward others only reveals that he or she has not received and understood and experienced God's forgiveness in his or her own life. When we are exacting and unforgiving, we show that the free gift of forgiveness, or justification, has not touched and transformed our own hearts.

Forgiveness over anything should make us appreciative and joyful. Many of us have had the unfortunate and embarrassing experience of being pulled over by the highway patrol for speeding. But if the police officer informs us that we are forgiven if we will only remember to drive more carefully, our feelings explode into ecstasy. We want to hug the officer! The sky becomes more blue, and the fleecy clouds dance with joy! The birds sing like they never have before! The grass is greener! We were guilty but forgiven. Now we are free from the penalty.

But what is forgiveness for a speeding violation compared to a pardon from an eternal death sentence? The whole world waits in death row, but King Jesus has written out a pardon with His own blood. To accept and experience this pardon should dramatically effect our attitude toward others. "If God so loved us, we ought also to love one another" (1 John 4:11). We have received freely, so let us give freely.

Our Lord's forgiveness springs from His unconditional love, and the way we treat others shows whether or not we have made His love our own. Thank Him now for His unfathomable love.

When One Body
Can Save Another

For God so loved the world, that he gave his only begotten Son, that whosoever believeth in him should not perish, but have everlasting life. John 3:16.

The lead article in the June 17, 1991, *Time* magazine had the title we use for our reading today. It dealt with heroic examples of parents and siblings who risk their lives in donating body parts to save a stricken brother, sister, son, daughter, mother, or father. Some question the morality of such actions, but the 3-year-old daughter of Teresa Schertz is alive today because of her mother's sacrifice. A healthy person may donate up to 75 percent of a liver and survive. It is claimed that the organ can regenerate itself.

One case that ended in failure was the sacrifice of Cindy and Roger Plum, parents of a 9-year-old daughter whose lungs failed. The father donated part of his lung. Then the girl's other lung failed, and this time the mother donated part of hers. Tragically, the child suffered a heart attack and died. Both Cindy and Roger have 18-inch scars that run from their chests to their backs, and both are suffering ill effects from their efforts to save the life of their daughter. But they have no doubts about their sacrifice. "If I hadn't given Alyssa a chance at life," Cindy said, "I don't know if I could live with myself."

As you read such stories, you probably find yourself asking, "Would I do it even for someone I love dearly?" Organ transplants reflect the example of Jesus in His victory on the cross. From a human viewpoint, the most dramatic way that we can give of ourselves to help others is to share our body and blood. Jesus chose not merely to donate part of His body to save us but all of it—His very life—to give us new spiritual heart transplants. He did not just risk His life; He made a total sacrifice of it for us.

Furthermore, He donated it for those who were sinners—ungodly enemies! How can we ever thank Him enough for His amazing gift? Each of us must decide how we will respond to our Lord's gracious sacrifice of His own life. Let nothing hinder you from jotting down a sentence or two of gratitude to our divine Donor!

A Marriage
Designed by God

Then they called Rebekah and said to her, "Will you go with this man?" And she said, "I will go." Gen. 24:58, NASB.

The beautiful love story of Rebekah and Isaac is one of the most moving and romantic scenes found in the Bible. Forty-year-old Isaac had lost his mother, Sarah, three years previously, and Abraham at 140 years of age was growing feeble. Feeling the urgency of finding a wife for Isaac, Abraham asked Eliezer, his most trusted and godly servant, to choose one for his son. Abraham knew that God had forbidden intermarriage between His people and the Canaanites around them because it would lead to apostasy. So his thoughts turned toward his relatives 500 miles away in the land of Mesopotamia. After carefully instructing his servant and reminding him of the solemn significance of his mission, Abraham concluded, "He shall send his angel before thee" (verse 7).

Eliezer, aware of his tremendous responsibility and with his 10-camel train loaded with gifts, arrived at the well outside the town of Nahor. He was tired, dusty, and thirsty. There he tested God dramatically by praying that the girl who offered water to him and his camels would be the one to marry Isaac. Before he had finished his prayer, however, Rebekah, the granddaughter of Nahor, Abraham's brother, appeared. Not only did she give Eliezer a drink of water, but she voluntarily watered all 10 of his camels. It stunned Eliezer how the Lord had answered every detail of his prayer so quickly.

Eliezer met Rebekah's family and told them of his mission. Bethuel and Laban, her father and brother, realizing God's leading, said Rebekah could return to Canaan with him if she chose to do so. She showed courage, maturity, and an unselfish spirit, for without hesitation she willingly responded, "I will go." She believed that from what had already happened, God had selected her to be Isaac's wife.

Meditate a bit on your own marriage and record how God has led you to your spouse.

_____

_____

Was It Love at First Sight?

And Isaac went out to meditate in the field toward evening; and he lifted up his eyes and looked, and behold, camels were coming. And

Rebekah lifted up her eyes, and when she saw Isaac she dismounted from the camel. Gen. 24:63, 64, NASB.

We left off yesterday with Rebekah preparing to travel to Beersheba to marry Isaac. Try to imagine her feelings as she jolted up and down on camelback over some 500 miles of dusty trails. The trip took many days, which gave her plenty of time to think about marrying a man she had never seen or talked to. But as she recounted the miraculous events leading to her departure, she knew without a doubt that he was the one for her.

First, there had been Abraham's staunch obedience to God that had led him to send Eliezer to a place where God was worshiped. Second, she thought about Eliezer's prayer that the first girl to offer him and his camels water would be the one God intended. Third, her family sensed God's leading. And fourth, she herself felt convicted to go.

On the evening of their arrival, Isaac, as usual, went out into the fields to meditate. Anticipating their soon return, in all probability, Isaac prayed for the safety of Eliezer and his caravan. No doubt his prayer also included a request for God's blessing upon his new home about to be established. As he looked up he saw the camels approaching. When Rebekah spotted him she jumped off her mount and, as the custom was, covered her face. Although they were strangers to each other, both felt God's leading in their lives and knew that soon they would become husband and wife.

When the camel caravan halted and Isaac and Rebekah met, she saw what a mild-mannered and meditative person he was, and she fell in love with him. Likewise the beautiful Rebekah with her kind, energetic, modest, meek, and gracious personality won his heart. Was it love at first sight? It seems that way. But everyone involved in this love story knew also that God was involved in the union in a very direct manner. The two soon found themselves bound together by bonds of mutual affection. It was an age of almost universal polygamy, yet we find no record of Isaac having another wife or concubine. Truly, theirs was a marriage designed in heaven.

Those of you who are married, record the blessings you have received by involving God in the choice of your spouse. And those of you who are planning marriage, list some things you can do as you cooperate with God in leading you to the right person.

_____

_____

February 15

In the Beginning

In the beginning God created the heaven and the earth. Gen. 1:1.

How better could God's Word possibly start? God knew how to capture our attention as He introduced the history of the human race. The Lord understood that intelligent earth beings would have a passion to discover their roots, as the genealogical tables in both the Old and New Testaments seem to demonstrate. The book of beginnings informs us of our origin. One of the reasons that scientists said they wanted to put men on the moon was that they hoped to see if they could find clues to how life began. The Bible gives the answer clearly and forthrightly.

Our text denies atheism. God was in the beginning and even before that. Something can never evolve from nothing. Today's passage also rejects the concept of pantheism. God is both *before* all things and strictly *apart* from all creation. He is not embodied personally in every tree and flower. Although He made them, He is not a part of them. Finally, our text gives us hope and security. Why? Because it declares that there is a loving Supreme Being who created an exceedingly beautiful world. A world with choirs of bees and armies of trees. A world in which God's finger touches the soil every moment, causing constant miracles of new growth to take place. A world in which all nature flames with myriads of colors to give us unending enjoyment.

In the beginning God saved the best until last when He created man in His own image, but tragedy struck when our first parents broke faith with their Creator. And death became a tyrant. We still suffer from its rule. But don't despair. God made a way out. A way that amazed Satan and all the unfallen universe. A way that especially astounds all those of fallen humanity who have found the Lord as a Saviour. It went into operation immediately after sin's entrance when God spoke the first salvation promise in Scripture: "And I will put enmity between you and the woman, and between your seed and her seed."

The "you" and "your seed" represent Satan whereas "the woman" and "her seed" point to Christ. But the thrilling part comes next. "He shall bruise you on the head, and you shall bruise Him on the heel" (Gen. 3:15, NASB). Note carefully that God now refers to the woman's seed as "He"—none other than Jesus Christ. Furthermore, the word "bruise" means to strike, break, or crush. A person's head being broken or crushed results in a mortal wound, whereas a heel wound, though terribly painful, is not fatal. Thus Christ crushed Satan at the cross with a mortal wound while He went through the painful agony of a heel wound as He died for us. But our Lord was resurrected, and Satan will eventually breathe his last as he perishes in the postmillennial fires that will cleanse the earth.

Another beginning will soon take place when Jesus comes—one that will never end! All those who have had a new start in a conversion experience will take part in the eternal new beginning of all things.

Praise Him for our opportunity to participate both in the new beginning now and the one when He returns!

Freedom in Jesus,
the Truth

You shall know the truth, and the truth shall make you free. . . . If therefore the Son shall make you free, you shall be free indeed. John 8:32-36, NASB.

In June 1503 Christopher Columbus and his crew shipwrecked on the island of Jamaica. At first local Indians supplied them with food but then stopped. When food supplies ran low, Columbus used his knowledge of lunar eclipses to trick them. The explorer told the Native Americans that God was displeased with them for withholding food from the Europeans and would turn the moon into blood. It terrified the Indians when, just as Columbus had predicted, a lunar eclipse transformed the moon into a dark-red color on February 29, 1904.

The indigenous peoples, not knowing what was happening, pleaded with Columbus to intercede with God in their behalf. Columbus said he would do his best. Just before the eclipse ended, he announced to them that God would give them a second chance on condition they would resume supplying him and his crew with food. Sure enough, the moon returned to normal, and the Indians began bringing new supplies of meat and grain.

Knowledge is power! Humanity often uses it to dominate and destroy those who have less of it. The nation with the greatest technological knowledge in manufacturing arms can win wars such as the Gulf conflict. Knowledge can also gain the upper hand in economic struggles.

In the spiritual realm knowledge is also power. However, true spiritual knowledge does not control or dominate any nation or person. Rather it enlightens, strengthens, and frees a person from superstition and ignorance.

The person enlightened about conditional immortality, for example, escapes the fear of the terrible concept of eternal hellfire. Those who do not know Scripture's teaching on it have succumbed to mental illness, and others have regarded God as a horrible tyrant. A knowledge of truth brings power and freedom.

Jesus said that those who know the truth will be free people. He is Himself the Truth, but in love He has provided us with a beautiful system of beliefs that center on Him and give us personal power and freedom in Him.

Praise Him for His Word of truth. Thank Him for the liberating knowledge that saves us from pitfalls, superstitions, and—above all—eternal death itself.

Did Jesus Have a Price?

I will not speak much more with you, for the ruler of the world is coming, and he has nothing in Me. John 14:30, NASB.

We have all heard the saying that "Every man has his price." Unfortunately, the adage is all too true. Adam and Eve had theirs. Satan's subtle reasoning that they could have their fruit and eat it too bought them off. The result has been one grand catastrophe for our entire planet.

Abraham had his price. When his faith wavered, he took his wife's advice in an attempt to fulfill God's promise of making him into a great nation.

David had his price. The sight of an innocent but beautiful woman bathing on her roof led him to destroy her husband and bring shame upon his family and nation. He murdered her husband to cover up her pregnancy.

Fear of death at the hands of Jezebel bought off Elijah. His lack of faith in God led him to run for his life.

The list is endless. In fact, every human being on earth has had his or her price, for all of us have sinned and come short of God's glory. Any sin we commit demonstrates the old adage. The price for some is alcohol, drugs, tobacco, overeating, immorality, lying, and stealing. For others it is pride, a critical spirit, jealousy, anger, and deceit.

The only person who has ever walked in our world who didn't have a price was Jesus, the God-man. Satan did everything possible to trip Him up during His 33-year life span. He dogged every step that Jesus took. For a person who had never done anything wrong in His life, He was the most cruelly treated individual who has ever lived. Yet Satan's artful, well-designed temptations in the wilderness could not buy Him off.

On the cross, Jesus withstood the greatest temptation possible. "If you are the Messiah, if you are God's Son, if you are the Saviour, come down and save yourself!" He did have the power to save Himself and to destroy His enemies. Yet even this greatest temptation in history could never cause Jesus to sell out. Nothing, absolutely nothing—power, wealth, honor, or position—could ever cause Christ to deviate from the path of integrity!

Our Lord has set a tremendous example. Even though we have made many mistakes, through the power of His Holy Spirit we can resist being bought off by sin. It can be done, praise the Lord, by trusting in Him. Think for a moment of the victories God has given you in the past. The more you concentrate on your own victories over sin through Christ's power, the more He will give you. And the more you praise His name for what He has done for you, the more He will accomplish in you. Today praise Him in writing for the victories you have had.

Mephibosheth

And the king said, "Is there not yet anyone of the house of Saul to whom I may show the kindness of God?" And Ziba said to the king, "There is still a son of Jonathan who is crippled in both feet." . . . And Mephibosheth, the son of Jonathan the son of Saul, came to David and fell on his face and prostrated himself. . . . And David said to him, "Do not fear, for I will surely show kindness to you for the sake of your father Jonathan." 2 Sam. 9:3-7, NASB.

One of the most generous acts King David ever performed was for Mephibosheth, the son of David's closest friend, Jonathan. Our story took place some years after David had become king. Perhaps one evening as David found it difficult to sleep he began reminiscing about his past life. He thought of his victory over the giant, Goliath. Immediately after David had killed Goliath, King Saul summoned him. Present at that meeting was Jonathan. When David finished speaking to Saul, "the soul of Jonathan was knit to the soul of David, and Jonathan loved him as himself" (1 Sam. 18:1, NASB). Thus began a strong relationship between two men of God. Their friendship led to a covenant in which each promised to protect the other and his descendants.

Now years later David remembered his promise. His servants discovered for him that one crippled son of Jonathan, Mephibosheth, still lived. The son knew nothing of the covenant and feared for his life as he appeared before King David. Imagine how he must have felt when David gave him back part of his grandfather's and father's estate. But even more than that, he invited him to become part of the royal family so he could regularly eat at his table.

It so overwhelmed Mephibosheth that he prostrated himself before David and said, "What is your servant, that you should regard a dead dog like me?" (2 Sam. 9:8, NASB). David reminds us of Jesus, who has bent low over the crippled human race and invites us all to become part of His royal family and to dine daily at His table on the good things found in the Word.

Someday we will sit down and eat with Him on a personal basis. Why not praise King Jesus for His invitation and the hope that we have of being with Him in the future?

No Myth About Jesus!

Jesus said to her, "Woman, why are you weeping? Whom are you seeking?" Supposing Him to be the gardener, she said to Him, "Sir, if you have carried Him away, tell me where you have laid Him, and I will take Him away." Jesus said to her, "Mary!" She turned and said to Him in Hebrew, "Rabboni!" (which means, Teacher). John 20:15, 16, NASB.

Several years ago, in England, more than a billion envelopes during a six-week period carried the postmark "Jesus is alive!" The owner of a religious bookshop paid nearly $90,000 for it to be stamped on the mail. However, such a religious postmark angered a number of people. The National Secular Society, claiming that 26 percent of Britons are atheistic or agnostic, retaliated by paying a fee to have the mail marked with the words "Jesus is a myth."

How do we know that Jesus is *not* really a myth? Ask Mary Magdalene if He was. She knew that He was real for several reasons. Jesus had cast seven devils out of her. No mythical person could rescue a person in such deep sin. She had personally experienced His power of deliverance. On Resurrection Sunday Mary was the first at the tomb.

Mary had followed Peter and John to the empty tomb and remained behind while the two disciples returned to Jerusalem. Heartbroken, she examined the empty tomb again. This time she saw two angels dressed in white sitting at the head and feet of the platform where the body of Jesus had been laid. When they asked her why she was weeping, she replied that someone had taken her Lord away and hidden His body. At this point she turned around and saw Jesus but thought Him to be the gardener. After asking Him where they had moved her Lord's body, Jesus spoke her name in His familiar voice.

With joy and excitement she recognized it. Rushing back to the disciples, she cried out, "I have seen the Lord!" Jesus was no myth to her.

Someday soon we will be able to sit down in the New Jerusalem and personally hear Mary describe her feelings when she learned that Jesus was alive.

Our Lord is alive today and forevermore. Trials and tribulations may tempt us to wonder if He is real. But faith enables us to believe that He is alive and that He is coming back soon. Jesus is no myth. Praise the Lord for the empty tomb.

Thank the Lord for Mary's testimony. From a personal standpoint, why do you believe that Jesus is real and alive?

It Will Not Stand

Devise a plan but it will be thwarted; state a proposal, but it will not stand, for God is with us. Isa. 8:10, NASB.

During the reign of Ahaz, an apostate king of Judah, the prophet Isaiah penned the stern rebuke against him found in our passage today. Not only was Ahaz an idol worshiper himself, but also he sacrificed his own son by fire to placate one of the pagan gods of the surrounding nations. Yet despite Ahaz's vile character, God sent Isaiah with a message assuring him of His help in his struggle with the northern kingdom of Israel and with the Syrians. The Lord pleaded with him not to seek aid from other nations against his enemies. But Ahaz turned his back on the appeal and sought outside assistance rather than depend upon God. The result was inevitable. "The wrath of the Lord was upon Judah and Jerusalem, and he . . . delivered them to trouble, to astonishment, and to hissing" (2 Chron. 29:8).

The important lesson we each need to learn is that whatever evil that persons either inside or outside the church plan against us, it "will not stand." Why? "For God is with us." If we maintain our allegiance to Him—seeking His counsel, walking after Him—we have the assurance that He is with us. If we keep this in mind, we will have nothing to fear from Satan's attacks, for they "will not stand." If we fear the Lord by obeying His will, nothing can come between us and Heaven.

At times it may appear that evil events are overwhelming us, and naturally we feel that life itself is hopeless. Yet even death cannot erase the fact that God is with us.

In Isaiah's appeal to Judah, he said, "Sanctify the Lord of hosts himself; and let him be your fear, and let him be your dread. And he shall be for a sanctuary" (Isa. 8:13, 14). In other words, Judah, instead of fearing and dreading their enemies, should look to the Lord, who would be their sanctuary, their haven of security. The awe of our Lord should be greater than our fear of those who attack us. Look to Him. Seek His will. He is more powerful than all our enemies, including Satan himself.

We have a wonderful refuge in God, who is always for us and with us. The Bible writers used striking images to portray Him—images that meant much in their desert land often torn by wars, raids, and military skirmishes. To them He was a rock of strength—a fortress—to which one could flee when attacked. He is the shadow from the burning desert sun. And in a tiny country surrounded by stronger and hostile nations, He would be their defense who would never fail no matter how strong the invading army.

How much do you appreciate a refuge and a fortress against the enemy? Put into your own words your thankfulness for our protecting Lord.

Why Didn't They Understand?

And He took the twelve aside and said to them, "Behold, we are going up to Jerusalem, and all things which are written through the prophets about the Son of Man will be accomplished." . . . And they understood none of these things. Luke 18:31-34, NASB.

Jesus constantly supported the authority of Scripture. He fully realized its importance to our lives. Unless we study the Word carefully and believe it fully, the Bible will be meaningless to us. We may smile at the person who superstitiously wears a good luck charm. Or we may agree with Voltaire, the famous defender of victims of religious intolerance, who said, "Superstition is to religion what astrology is to astronomy—the mad daughter of a wise mother." Yet how many people purchase large family Bibles to house genealogical statistics but seldom study its contents? All too often such Bibles do nothing more than decorate tables or shelves and attract dust.

It is difficult to believe that Christ's closest followers, His disciples, were ignorant of what would happen at Calvary. Scripture had pointed to His death hundreds of years before our Lord came the first time. Yet none of the disciples understood the prophecies that applied to the Messiah's death. To forewarn them Jesus outlined the closing events of His life on earth. "For He will be delivered to the Gentiles, and will be mocked and mistreated and spit upon," He told them, "and after they have scourged Him, they will kill Him; and the third day He will rise again" (Luke 18:32, 33, NASB).

Such clear, definitive language could not be misunderstood—or could it? Their experience has an important lesson for God's people today. Although the prophets had recorded detailed events centuries before, still the disciples did not comprehend them. If this was true of His closest followers—men who personally walked and talked with Him—what about those of us who live 2,000 years after Calvary? How serious are we in setting aside time daily to study the Word? Are we permitting unimportant things to capture our attention? Is our culture pressing us into its mold? When we do study the Bible, are we making sure that we study it as the authoritative Word of God? Some people take newspaper reports as absolute truth but find difficulty in accepting the Bible.

We are thankful to our Saviour for the glorious light of Scripture that focuses on Him. It makes Him a real Person, a real Saviour, and a real coming King. How much do you appreciate the unchangeable Word of God?

Life After Death Depends
on the Second Coming

For the Lord Himself will descend from heaven with a shout, with the voice of the archangel, and with the trumpet of God; and the dead in Christ shall rise first. Then we who are alive and remain shall be caught up together with them in the clouds to meet the Lord in the air, and thus we shall always be with the Lord. 1 Thess. 4:16, 17, NASB.

Any discussion of our Lord's return must include Paul's definitive description that he wrote to the church at Thessalonica. Both Thessalonian Epistles reveal the character of the apostle's ministry as it relates to the second coming of Jesus.

The first six words of today's text, "For the Lord *Himself* will descend," are marvelous in concept. Suppose you have a dinner appointment with the president of the United States. Your engraved invitation tells you that a limousine sent from the White House will pick you up at your home at 6:00 p.m. Wouldn't you be prepared long before it arrives? Let's say that in order not to appear excited because of this special occasion, you sit in your living room as you wait for the knock at your door. When it happens, you casually walk to the door to greet the chauffeur. But when you open it, imagine your shock and surprise to meet, not a uniformed chauffeur, but the president himself!

Jesus is not sending a celestial chauffeur. "The Lord Himself will descend from heaven." Hard to comprehend, isn't it? He is the King, the Creator, the Sustainer of the entire universe. So why expect *Him* to leave His palatial command center in heaven and personally come to this earth to rescue His people? We would feel honored if only the angels, led by Gabriel, came back to get us. None of us would think of complaining or feel slighted. But for Jesus to arrive personally—the thought should overwhelm us. We imagine that great emotion swept over Paul as he wrote these words.

Human language simply cannot describe either this point or the entire scene of His return. Thunderous events will happen in quick succession. The same angels who sang over Bethlehem's hills to announce the first coming of Jesus lead the mighty celestial caravan as it races down over the royal highway of the skies toward our heaving, shattered planet. Oh, what a magnificent scene—Jesus is here at last!

No heart can remain untouched while reading Paul's words. No heart can refuse to praise Him for His soon coming. Thank Him now!

Resurrection Day

"He has fixed a day in which He will judge the world in righteousness through a Man whom He has appointed, having furnished proof to all men by raising Him from the dead." Now when they heard of the resurrection of the dead, some began to sneer, but others said, "We shall hear you again concerning this." Acts 17:31, 32, NASB.

Paul's audience, mainly philosophers, sat on stones or on the ground while he stood as he delivered a great sermon on the true God, Creation, and judgment. The place was Mars Hill in Athens. Above him rose the beautiful Parthenon. Below him lay Athens, filled with images and idols, probably more than 3,000 public ones. It was said that it was easier to find a god than a man in Athens! Imagine Paul the Jew preaching in the hometown of Pericles, Demosthenes, Socrates, Euripides, Plato, Aristotle, and Sophocles. Their names were attached to schools and buildings everywhere. The city was a center for art and education. Yet Paul was not interested in culture—he was looking for souls! His listeners were riveted to his speech. They had never heard anything like it before. But when Paul got to the concept of the resurrection of Jesus, his hearers tuned him out. To them the idea of a resurrection seemed beyond belief.

Before the Greek philosophers brought him to Mars Hill, Paul had been reasoning with anyone in the marketplace who would listen. Because he was preaching Jesus and resurrection, some asked, "What would this idle babbler [the word means seed-picker] wish to say?" (verse 18, NASB). Others said, "He seems to be a proclaimer of strange deities" (verse 18, NASB).

We should note that the apostle was in danger of losing his life for introducing a new religion. Socrates, Athens' greatest citizen, had been forced to drink poisonous hemlock for doing what Paul was now charged with. But under the conviction of the Holy Spirit, Paul knew that he had the greatest and only true philosophy on earth. Jesus Christ—His crucifixion and His resurrection—was at the very heart of the new religion he was preaching.

The resurrection concept was diametrically opposed to Greek and Roman thinking. It undermined the fatalistic concept of "Eat and drink, for tomorrow we die." It also ran counter to the Platonic belief that the soul is eternal and survives the body after death. Not only does resurrection imply judgment, but for believers the resurrection is the only hope we have in this life. That is why the second coming of Jesus means so much to us. We know that all life after death depends on the Second Advent.

We cling to our Lord and His promise to return. What hope would we have without it? Here's an opportunity for you to express your appreciation for His soon coming.

Take Me in Thine Arms

Looking for the blessed hope and the appearing of the glory of our great God and Savior, Christ Jesus; who gave Himself for us, that He might redeem us from every lawless deed and purify for Himself a people for His own possession, zealous for good deeds. Titus 2:13, 14, NASB.

"Take me in Thine arms" were the last words our father, Chester R. Spangler, spoke prior to his death in September 1990. We write "our father" since Marie's father died two weeks before our marriage, in 1943. Dad Spangler became as dear to Marie as her own. He was 99 years old and only three and a half months from reaching 100. Although almost blind, he taught a Sabbath school class until six months before his death.

Bob preached at his funeral, and some wondered how he could do it. He couldn't have done so had Dad not been a Christian and a great believer in the Advent movement. His life centered on Jesus and His second coming. When he was a teenager he worked as a male stenographer in the General Conference office. On several occasions he traveled with the General Conference president A. G. Daniells, writing up newspaper reports of his sermons. Dad served as a literature evangelist in the California Conference when S. N. Haskell was president. Dad's life span covered the days of the church pioneers to the present.

We have kept all the letters he sent to us throughout the years. You cannot find a single one that does not contain a large paragraph or two on the coming of Jesus. The theme of Christ's return was uppermost in his mind throughout his entire life.

Bob's sermon, as you can guess, was on the blessed hope. Some years earlier he had also preached the funeral sermon of his college teacher, mentor, and officiator at our wedding, Roy Allan Anderson, former editor of *Ministry* magazine and head of the General Conference Ministerial Association for years. Both Dad's and Anderson's funeral sermons focused on celebrating "the appearing of the glory of our great God and Savior, Christ Jesus." The service for Pastor Anderson ended with an instrumental rendition of Handel's "Hallelujah Chorus."

We cannot deny that death is our worst enemy, but—praise God—Christ's victory will swallow it up. Our Lord has won the right to open every grave of His precious children who have gone to sleep and now rest cradled in the arms of the earth. How true it is that no one on his or her deathbed ever repented of being a follower of Jesus!

How can we ever complain or groan with such a bright future before us? Life has its rough spots, but never so overwhelming that we cannot find fresh grace to press forward until that day when we will be translated or will say with Dad Spangler, "Take me in Thine arms."

Honor Him who is coming soon with a few words of praise.

_____

_____

The Jigsaw Puzzle

But if the Spirit of Him who raised Jesus from the dead dwells in you, He who raised Christ Jesus from the dead will also give life to your mortal bodies through His Spirit who indwells you. Rom. 8:11, NASB.

Paul referred frequently to Christ's resurrection as a guarantee of the resurrection of God's people if their death occurs before the Second Coming. As we have already mentioned, death is our last and worst enemy, but soon Jesus' coming and the resurrection will defeat it. Jesus is alive, and we too shall live again if death's cold fingers seize us before He returns.

Until that day when God will banish death forever, our lives should be so controlled by the Lord that whether awake or asleep, our witness continues for Him. Did you know that the Lord never really lays His faithful servants aside? Whether sick or well, living or dead, God still uses us.

How often we speak about friends of ours who have gone to their long rest but who have made a deep impression on our lives. Even in death their witness still shapes not only our lives but those of others whom they knew and helped. Using the illustration of a jigsaw puzzle, we compare each of our loved ones or friends to a piece in the puzzle. Also every event in life makes still more pieces of the puzzle. The death of a loved one is still another fragment of the picture that makes up our life sketch. By itself the death piece is ugly, but when we put it with the rest of the pieces, we can see it in perspective, and a meaningful design begins to emerge.

To the Christian, death is not the end of life's picture. It is not the last brush stroke on life's canvas. As Paul said, the same Spirit who resurrected Jesus will also bring life to the mortal bodies of every friend and relative who has died in Him. Even though our Lord permits us to drink the cup of bitterness, He also holds to our lips a cup of blessing. Isaiah declared: "But your dead will live; their bodies will rise. You who dwell in the dust, wake up and shout for joy. Your dew is like the dew of the morning; the earth will give birth to her dead" (Isa. 26:19, NIV). Another biblical writer, David, said it tenderly: "Precious in the sight of the Lord is the death of his saints" (Ps. 116:15). Death is not precious, but God's saints are!

As we carefully put together the pieces in our life's picture, we see displayed a wonderful hope which assures us that "even in death the righteous have a refuge" (Prov. 14:32, NIV). We magnify our Lord, who permits us to dwell in His secret place and rest in the shelter of His everlasting arms even in death. How does this comfort you?

_____

_____

The Man With Resurrection Power

For since by a man came death, by a man also came the resurrection of the dead. For as in Adam all die, so also in Christ all shall be made alive. But each in his own order: Christ the first fruits, after that those who are Christ's at His coming. 1 Cor. 15:21-23, NASB.

Our text for today emphasizes three major points. (1) Adam and Eve's sin doomed all of us to die, but another Man, Jesus Christ, has the power and authority to resurrect the dead. (2) Christ is the firstfruits of the resurrection—He, the Lifegiver, in His humanity experienced death, but the grave could not hold Him. The fact of His escape from the grave is a pledge that we too shall be delivered from the tomb. (3) Again we see that life after death totally depends on the second coming of Jesus.

Velma Messick, of Apple Valley, California, claims to have had an out-of-body experience when she nearly died some years ago. She painted a picture of what she claims to have seen on "the other side." It portrays a dark valley surrounded by craggy rocks. Peeking over them is what appears to be a brilliant sunrise in yellow, pink, and purple. A white beam courses through the valley, hugging the ground and lighting a path toward an even brighter light.

Is what Velma saw for real? Dr. Jack Provonsha, who for many years taught at Loma Linda University, claims that anesthetics reduce the circulation in a patient's body and build up carbon dioxide in the brain cells. "This creates an illusion—almost a hallucination—of being outside the body," he claims.

No one, unless a prophet or prophetess, sees "the other side" before Jesus returns. Furthermore, "the other side" is beyond our imagination. John the revelator couldn't describe it. The apostle Paul had the experience of being in vision and was "caught up into Paradise," but he testified that what he saw and heard were beyond words and something "which a man is not permitted to speak" (2 Cor. 12:4, NASB). The reason Paul could not tell all that he had seen in vision was that "among his hearers were some who would have misapplied his words" (*The Acts of the Apostles*, p. 469).

If we really observed what life after death is like and tried to describe it, most people wouldn't believe us and probably would ridicule us. So until then we live by faith, knowing that we are guaranteed at the Second Advent life, home, and fellowship with Jesus our Lord, all of which will last forever. Express your homage to Him, resurrection's firstfruits, in words.

Signs of the Return of Christ

And there will be signs in sun and moon and stars, and upon the earth dismay among nations, in perplexity at the roaring of the sea and the waves, men fainting from fear and the expectation of the things which are coming upon the world; for the powers of the heavens will be shaken. And then they will see the Son of Man coming in a cloud with power and great glory. Luke 21:25-27, NASB.

Jesus revealed to us what would happen before He returns. Note in our passage such words as "dismay," "perplexity," "fainting," "fear," and "shaken." Not words of peace and tranquility, they powerfully describe alarming events. Leaders, attempting to maintain some sense of stability, find themselves swept away by a riptide of evil flooding across the earth. People's hearts fill with fear, not only because of physical calamities, but also because of the disastrous effects of sin.

Strong pressure for secular and religious unity accompanies the enormous rise of nationalism and other movements. Phrases such as "global consciousness," "tolerance," "peace and tranquility," and "pluralism" mingle with the political, economic, and physical upheaval that we see all around us. In our thinking, the stage is set for a sudden end, as described by Paul in 1 Thessalonians 5:3: "While they are saying, 'Peace and safety!' then destruction will come upon them suddenly like birth pangs upon a woman with child; and they shall not escape" (NASB).

The New Age movement, with its alliance with pantheism, has destroyed in the minds of many the individual personalities of God the Father, God the Son, and God the Holy Spirit. This reduction of the heavenly Trio to a mere force or universal energy destroys the very heart of a belief in a personal return of Jesus and His personal involvement in the creation of a new heaven and new earth, where we shall have the exhilarating experience of enjoying life in a deeply personal way. How can we await the Advent if Jesus is only a vague force in the world around us, and why get excited about heaven if it is little more than an abstraction?

But we praise our coming King for the reality of His return and the reality of heaven and the reality of personal association with the real Jesus. How do you feel about the reality of the Second Advent?

What Is a
Seventh-day Adventist?

He who testifies to these things says, "Yes, I am coming quickly."
Amen. Come, Lord Jesus. Rev. 22:20, NASB.

These words are among the final thoughts of the New Testament. They should be the motto of every true Seventh-day Adventist. An Adventist is a person who: (1) believes Jesus is coming soon, (2) lives as though Jesus is coming soon, (3) is prepared to live with Jesus when He does come, and (4) prays daily that Jesus will come quickly.

What is our purpose for going into all the world to preach the everlasting gospel? Why do we establish thousands of educational institutions on every continent? Why do we build and operate hundreds of hospitals and clinics worldwide? Why do we have scores of publishing houses and printing plants scattered everywhere? What is the reason for our global network of radio stations?

The ultimate reason is to prepare the way so that we can be united with Jesus when He comes. He told His followers that someday they would be where He is. It is a promise that we cling to tenaciously.

We were attending a camp meeting some years ago, and as we walked onto the campground, a rather outspoken individual demanded, "Have you got anything to say?" We may smile now at such a direct question, but it caused us to think seriously about the sermon content for that camp meeting.

The truth is that we don't have anything to say, but God, through His Word, has plenty to say, especially about the second coming of His Son, Jesus. Our text today reveals what is uppermost in the mind of Jesus: "Yes, I am coming quickly." If we could have a press conference with Jesus and ask Him all sorts of questions, how do you think He would answer?

"Jesus, what do You think about the population explosion? It took nearly 1,700 years to double the population from the time You lived on earth. It reached 2 billion by 1930 and then 4 billion only 45 years later. Our cities are bulging, and millions are starving and dying from malnutrition-related diseases every year. How can we solve this problem?"

Jesus replies, "There is no viable answer except that I am coming quickly."

Until then, thank our dear Saviour for the fact that He is returning quickly. It will truly solve everything. Pray and work and live to be ready for that moment.

The Sign of Deception

And as He was sitting on the Mount of Olives, the disciples came to Him privately, saying, "Tell us, when will these things be, and what will be the sign of Your coming, and of the end of the age?" Matt. 24:3, NASB.

Believers in all generations have seen in various events signs of Christ's coming, whether it be the First or Second Advent. It is said that Martin Luther rushed to complete the German translation of the Bible in 1530 because he feared Christ would return before he finished it. He wrote: "For it is certain from the Holy Scriptures that we have no more temporal things to expect. All is done and fulfilled: the Roman Empire is at the end; the Turk has reached his highest point; the pomp of papacy is falling away and the world is cracking on all sides almost as if it would break and fall apart entirely" (quoted in Samuele Bacchiocchi, *The Advent Hope*, p. 116).

Throughout its history our church has strongly emphasized the signs of His second advent. They remind us of both the imminence and certainty of Christ's return. Although we must ever keep in mind that the doctrine of Jesus' coming does not focus on the signs but on the Saviour Himself, He did talk about them.

In the "great signs of His coming" discourse found in Matthew 24, Jesus made one point very clear. After the disciples asked Him about the sign of His coming, Christ's immediate answer was "See to it that no one misleads you. For many will come in My name, saying, I am the Christ, and will mislead many" (verses 4, 5, NASB).

The danger of deception weighed heavily on His mind. He wanted to prevent His followers from being deceived. In verse 11 Jesus returned to His concern about deception when He said, "And many false prophets will arise, and will mislead many" (NASB). A third time Jesus warned, "If anyone says to you, 'Behold, here is the Christ,' or 'There He is,' do not believe him. For false Christs and false prophets will arise and will show great signs and wonders, so as to mislead, if possible, even the elect" (verses 23, 24, NASB). If deception constitutes a sign, and if its repetition is a measure of its importance, then deception would rank at the top of the list of signs.

Today via radio, television, and the printed page, religious deception has become an art. We do not judge motivation, but too often what is being spewed out as truth does not square with Scripture. Sometimes even our own members accept such ideas.

Pray that such deceptions will not ensnare you. If Satan can nearly deceive Christ's chosen ones, the elect, our only safe course is to make certain we are studying the Bible carefully and that our prayer life is strong and healthy. A knowledge of Scripture alone is insufficient to rescue us from deception. We need an intimate acquaintance with the Christ of Scripture.

Praise the Lord for our combined safeguard against error—Christ and His Word.

Increase of Knowledge in the World of Science

But as for you, Daniel, conceal these words and seal up the book until the end of time; many will go back and forth, and knowledge will increase. Dan. 12:4, NASB.

Many people are still alive who have witnessed the incredible advance of science and technology. Bob's father met the Wright brothers and watched them fly their hedge-hopping airplane over the fields near Dayton, Ohio, where Bob and his parents lived. The list of inventions in the past two centuries would crowd this book, while those prior to that time would probably fill only a page or two.

Up until the beginning of the nineteenth century the fastest form of travel was on a horse. Inventors toyed with steam automobiles, but few were made. Not until years later did we have working autos within the price range of most of us. In our lifetime we remember well the Model T and Model A Fords. They were extremely primitive when compared to today's sleek, smooth-running, air-conditioned, automatic transmission cars that we routinely drive 500 to 700 miles a day on coast-to-coast freeways.

It is incredible to think that throughout thousands of years of human history there were no "horseless" carriages, railroads, steamboats, electric lights, airplanes, radios, televisions, telephones, fax machines, copy machines, tape recorders, computers, submarines, atomic power, web presses, plastics, etc.

Someone has said that 90 percent of all the scientists who have ever lived are alive today. Scientific publications pile up, according to one report, at the rate of 60 million pages a year. It seems that from a scientific viewpoint the world stumbled along in the same rut year after year. Then suddenly the increase of knowledge, like an exploding can of whipped topping, covered the planet with its fantastic foam of inventions. This sign alone should cause us to realize that we are living in the time of the end. Every modern invention we use should reinforce our recognition of the soon return of Jesus.

Furthermore, God has allowed modern inventions to come into existence to aid in fulfilling the greatest sign of all: "And this gospel of the kingdom shall be preached in the whole world for a witness to all the nations, and then the end shall come" (Matt. 24:14, NASB).

"God intrusts men with talents and inventive genius, in order that His great work in our world may be accomplished. . . . He has caused that the means of rapid traveling shall have been invented, for the great day of His preparation" (*Fundamentals of Christian Education*, p. 409).

Thank the Lord for the labor-saving inventions that make life easier and help spread the gospel quickly to the world.

No Surprise to God's People

While people are saying, "Peace and safety," destruction will come on them suddenly, as labor pains on a pregnant woman, and they will not escape. But you, brothers, are not in darkness so that this day should surprise you like a thief. 1 Thess. 5:3, 4, NIV.

Alert Christians who are students of the Word recognize that the Lord in His love and mercy has given us indications to help us know when His return nears. Paul emphasizes the suddenness of Christ's coming and compares His return to a thief in the night and to a woman overtaken with labor pains. Jesus also connected labor pains with the signs of His return. After speaking of famines and earthquakes and of nations struggling with each other, He declared, "But all these things are merely the beginning of birth pangs" (Matt. 24:8, NASB). Our world is writhing in unbelievable pain of every description—surely Jesus is coming soon.

We could list the scriptural signs of our Lord's return under at least several headings. We have already discussed the lightning speed of scientific discoveries during the past two centuries, and especially the past few years. Among the inventions that have changed the thinking of secular leaders are nuclear weapons. The most ominous warnings about nuclear weapons come not from students of prophecy, but from scientists themselves. It still seems likely that some irresponsible, insane dictator will explode one or more of these awesome weapons, plunging the world into a massive holocaust. But God, we believe, will not permit a total annihilation of the whole human race, even though there will be a time of trouble such as never has been. When the human race is proclaiming "peace and safety" slogans, sudden destruction will occur.

The earthquake sign is certainly being fulfilled. One of the most destructive earthquakes in history took place in China on July 28, 1976, with hundreds of thousands of lives snuffed out in a short time.

Furthermore, we have witnessed a sizable increase of earthquakes during the twentieth century.

In fact, the rash of killer floods, cyclones, and storms caused a leading newsmagazine a few years ago to ask, "Is Mother Nature going berserk?"

Even those of us awaiting the Second Advent may find ourselves amazed at the rapidly occurring signs in the world. Yet we know that they are trumpet blasts announcing the marvelous news that Jesus is coming back to earth soon.

Magnify the Lord with a few words of praise for His soon return.

A Weed From the Devil's Garden

Isaac, who had a taste for wild game, loved Esau, but Rebekah loved Jacob. Gen. 25:28, NIV.

For 19 years Isaac and Rebekah waited and longed for the child of their dreams. Eventually God rewarded their confidence in Him, but "the children struggled together within her" (verse 22, NASB). Frightened, Rebekah sought the Lord's help again. In response, God revealed that she would give birth to two nations, two very different types of people.

So it happened. Jacob and Esau differed in temperament, inclination, occupation, and religious outlook. A daring, vigorous man, Esau lived an adventurous, freedom-loving, self-gratifying life. He was a clever hunter, roaming fearlessly over the mountains and desert. Jacob was quite the opposite, possessing a gentle, patient, and thoughtful spirit that was content to stay home and care for the sheep and garden.

Our text reveals that these parents showed partiality in dealing with their sons. The quiet, peace-loving Isaac found himself attracted more to the wild-spirited Esau, while Rebekah adored Jacob's caring and helpful manner. Isaac loved the game Esau hunted and enjoyed the exciting stories he told of his adventuresome life.

Rebekah saw in the gentle Jacob a replica of those attributes of his father that had attracted her so many years before. Unfortunately such partiality brought division into the family. When a parent singles out one child as a favorite and showers him or her with greater love and attention, jealousy, strife, and feelings of inadequacy inevitably result.

In the case of Jacob and Esau, one fled from home in fear of his life, never to see his mother again. The other lost respect for his mother and developed a murderous hate for his brother. Both parents were brokenhearted. Partiality is one of the poisonous weeds in the devil's garden.

Praise be to our Lord that "God is not one to show partiality" (Acts 10:34, NASB). Moses powerfully stated in Deuteronomy 10:17: "The Lord your God is the God of gods and the Lord of lords, the great, the mighty, and the awesome God who does not show partiality, nor take a bribe" (NASB).

Honor our impartial God with a few words of praise.

Worthy of Praise?

Finally, brethren, whatever is true, whatever is honorable, whatever is right, whatever is pure, whatever is lovely, whatever is of good repute, if there is any excellence and if anything worthy of praise, let your mind dwell on these things. Phil. 4:8, NASB.

At a critical moment during the Battle of Waterloo, the 42nd Highlanders began to waver. When General Wellington asked why they were beginning to fall back, his officers told him that the unit's bagpipers had stopped their playing. Instantly he commanded that they play their instruments at full volume. The effect, we are told, was magical. The Highlanders rallied with new determination and advanced to win the hard-contested field.

Through the ages God has used music to bring strength and encouragement to His people. Saul's demon-possessed soul calmed when David played the harp. During the Feast of Tabernacles the Levite choir, accompanied by musical instruments, led the people in singing songs of triumph and praise.

But Satan also uses music on the battlefield of our hearts to win in the great struggle between good and evil. Ellen White tells us that music is one of Satan's most successful agencies to keep the mind away from eternal things.

The communications industry is playing havoc with the morals of America. In her book *Raising PG Kids in an X-Rated Society*, Tipper Gore points out the escalating trend toward more explicit sex and graphic violence. From advertisements to entertainment, music is the most unexpected medium of this trend.

Music increasingly portrays violent images. Rock lyrics and the related music videos are often lewd and debasing. Their target audiences are preteens and teenagers, who are the heavy listeners, viewers, and buyers of rock music. Few ask what is being sung and its effect on kids — only how well it will sell. Not only does much of the music distributed by the recording industry emphasize sex and violence; it also glorifies the use of drugs and alcohol. And it is available to persons of any age through record stores and the media.

As Christians we know that "music was made to serve a holy purpose, to lift the thoughts to that which is pure, noble, and elevating, and to awaken in the soul devotion and gratitude to God" (*Patriarchs and Prophets*, p. 594).

Let us promote God's purpose in giving music to humankind by making what we listen to and play worthy of praise. Take a moment to reflect on how music affects you emotionally and spiritually. Then thank Him for that which lifts your soul heavenward.

March 6

The Thank You Syndrome

Now one of them, when he saw that he had been healed, turned back, glorifying God with a loud voice, and he fell on his face at His feet, giving thanks to Him. And he was a Samaritan. Luke 17:15, 16, NASB.

"Thank you."

"Thank you."

"Have a good day."

"Thank you."

These words, which were exchanged between customers and the store employee who helped them unload their grocery carts, flowed quickly and easily. As Marie watched and listened to the interaction while she sat waiting in the car, she asked herself, "How often do I give thanks to my heavenly Father?"

It is easy to make specific requests of God each morning, but do we remember to thank Him for all the blessings that we receive without asking? Or when we breathe a prayer of request for the Lord to help us with a knotty problem and He answers, do we think to say thank You?

A committee meets and asks God to direct in the solving of a problem. In a marked way, God answers. Does the committee thank Him? Members of a church preparing for evangelistic meetings offer fervent prayers that many will respond to the invitation and attend. The opening night arrives and with it crowds of people—so many that they don't have enough seats for everyone. Does the congregation specifically thank God for all the people He sent? Or is there just a casual nod in His direction for His blessings on the meeting?

On His way to Jerusalem Jesus passed through a village where He noticed 10 lepers huddled together in isolation. When they saw Him, they jumped up and called out for Him to have mercy on them. In response He ordered them to go and show themselves to the priest. As they went, a miracle occurred—the leprosy vanished. Imagine their excitement as they observed each other's skin now clear and clean. But one—only one—was not so concerned about himself or so preoccupied with his friends and their discovery that he forgot to hurry back to Jesus, fall at His feet, and in a loud voice praise God and thank Jesus for what He had done for him. Furthermore, he was a Samaritan—a nonmember—who alone was blessed with the "thank you syndrome."

Would you like to have the infectious habit of thanking the Lord for His blessings? Start now by specifically writing out a special note of thanks to God for some recent blessing.

Turn Your Scars Into Stars

And because of the surpassing greatness of the revelations, for this reason, to keep me from exalting myself, there was given me a thorn in the flesh, a messenger of Satan to buffet me—to keep me from exalting myself. 2 Cor. 12:7, NASB.

God works in unexpected and sometimes inexplicable ways to bring—and keep—His children close beside Him. Paul's description of his thorn in the flesh is a rather unusual testimony. Ellen White tells us that he "was ever to carry about with him in the body the marks of Christ's glory, in his eyes, which had been blinded by the heavenly light" (*The SDA Bible Commentary*, Ellen G. White Comments, vol. 6, p. 1058). Three times he pleaded for the Lord to remove his problem, but the Lord always answered no. So Paul accepted his thorn in the flesh as a way to understand the life and work of our Lord Jesus Christ.

The apostle states that his constant problem kept him from exalting himself. His unprecedented revelations from the Lord could have easily made him proud and independent of God's guidance.

Ellen White had a similar experience. Her thorn was not partial blindness, but recurring sickness. When she received her first vision with its commission from God, her main fear was self-exaltation. She records that she feared that her revelations and visions might cause her to "yield to sinful exaltation, and be lifted above the station that was right for me to occupy, bring upon myself the displeasure of God, and lose my own soul. I had known of such cases, and my heart shrank from the trying ordeal."

Her angel told her, "Your prayers are heard, and shall be answered. If this evil that you dread threatens you, the hand of God will be stretched out to save you; by affliction He will draw you to Himself, and preserve your humility" (*Life Sketches*, p. 72).

It may be difficult for us to accept such a concept, especially if it involves ourselves. But when affliction comes, perhaps it may be for our own good. Pain can be to the body what thorny trials are to our spiritual life. Look upon trials as a means God can use to help you turn your scars into stars. Thank the Lord for both the good things and not-so-good things that happen to you in life.

Can you think of something—perhaps even something painful—that has aided you in transforming your scars into stars? Write it down and thank the Lord for His help.

My Grace Is Sufficient

And He has said to me, "My grace is sufficient for you, for power is perfected in weakness." Most gladly, therefore, I will rather boast about my weaknesses, that the power of Christ may dwell in me. 2 Cor. 12:9, NASB.

Philip Yancey in the March 18, 1988, *Christianity Today* tells the story of Douglas, a model of Christian faithfulness. His wife came down with both breast and lung cancer. Following this, his family received another blow. A drunken driver crossed the center line, causing a head-on collision. His wife was badly shaken but unhurt. His 12-year-old daughter suffered a broken arm along with severe facial cuts. But Douglas received severe head injuries that led to incapacitating headaches that could strike at any time. No longer could he work full-time because of frequent disorientation and forgetfulness. The accident permanently affected his vision. One eye wandered at will, refusing to focus. He even needed assistance to walk upstairs. Douglas coped quite well with everything, but one problem remained. He could not read more than a page or two at a time.

Yancey, as he talked with Douglas, thought that if anyone had a right to be angry with God, Douglas did. When questioned about how he felt about life, Douglas replied, "To tell you the truth, Philip, I didn't feel any disappointment with God." His answer startled Yancey, who waited for Douglas to continue. "The reason is this. I learned, first through my wife's illness and then especially through the accident, not to confuse God with life. I'm no stoic. I am as upset about what happened to me as anyone could be. I feel free to curse the unfairness of life and to vent all my grief and anger. But I believe God feels the same way about that accident—grieved and angry."

Douglas concluded, "If we can have a relationship with God *apart* from the physical reality of our life circumstances, then we may be able to hang on when the physical reality breaks down. Isn't that, after all, the main point of Job?"

While we agree with Douglas' belief that God feels sad and even angry over things that happen to His children, we believe that we cannot separate God from the things that happen to us. Douglas' remark about "not confusing

God with life" is an interesting one—whatever he means by it—but we prefer to think that God permits all things to happen to us in a way that can work together for our good. Although we may not understand everything in this life, we will in the next.

Whether we agree or not with the way Douglas separated the physical and the spiritual, certainly we can base our faith on the fact that God will sustain us through anything and everything. That is what the apostle Paul did.

Praise Him now for the power of Christ dwelling in you. Jot down your feelings.

_____

_____

Who Is Honoring Whom?

I am come in my Father's name, and ye receive me not: if another shall come in his own name, him ye will receive. How can ye believe, which receive honour one of another, and seek not the honour that cometh from God only? John 5:43, 44.

We frequently give farewell parties to honor those who have served an organization. During the early years of our ministry when we moved from one pastorate to another, the churches in our districts planned a farewell for our family. We received gifts and were the object of affection as church members presented speeches. The same has been true after we conducted evangelistic meetings in the Far East and the former Soviet Union.

From time to time we have read articles in our church publications about special events given to honor people for various achievements. Our universities and colleges have bestowed honorary degrees upon individuals. The United States government and those of other countries have recognized the Loma Linda heart team for their fine work in saving many lives. They have been rightfully considered ambassadors of good will. As we have contemplated such events, the thought occurred to us that Jesus never received any official honors from humanity. The Sanhedrin naturally would not think of honoring a person they wanted to kill. Even some of those He healed joined the ranks of the mob that cried out, "Crucify Him!"

Yet who in earth's history has deserved more honor than Jesus? And who has received less than the One who has done and is doing more for the human race than all good people put together? In our passage Jesus sets forth clearly how we honor each other, yet how many of us seek "the glory that is from the one and only God" (verse 44, NASB)?

What is the secret of receiving honor and glory from God?

When Eli, Samuel's mentor, was an old man he tried to correct the ways of his worthless sons. He failed, so God sent an unnamed prophet to Eli with a most severe rebuke. Among other things God, through the prophet, asked the priest, "Why do you . . . honor your sons above Me?" Then he added, "Those who honor Me I will honor, and those who despise Me will be lightly esteemed" (1 Sam. 2:29, 30, NASB).

Obviously, when we obey our Lord we are truly honoring Him. Disobedience shows our dishonor and disloyalty to our Lord. But one very special way to honor God is to praise Him for His goodness. "He who offers a sacrifice of thanksgiving honors Me; and to him that orders his way aright I shall show the salvation of God" (Ps. 50:23, NASB).

Take a few moments of time and write down some words of thanksgiving to honor One who deserves our constant honor and loyalty. As you honor Him, He will honor you.

_____

_____

Let Honor Come From God

Jesus answered, I have not a devil; but I honour my Father, and ye do dishonour me. . . . If I honour myself, my honour is nothing: it is my Father that honoureth me; of whom ye say, that he is your God. John 8:49-54.

The world is filled with statues, monuments, and tombs erected in honor of some supposedly great person. Marie and I have visited Napoleon's tomb in France. It has been said that Napoleon, after his crushing defeat at Waterloo, stated, "All is lost save honor." One of man's greatest weaknesses is the craving of honor. One of the characters in a Shakespearean play states, "But if it be a sin to covet honor, I am the most offending soul alive." The type of honor that Napoleon sought and received, Heaven does not regard as true honor. Many seek praise even though they may realize they don't deserve it. Pride rests on the shaky pillar of honor—a pillar that can easily collapse. Samuel Johnson wrote, "No man can justly aspire to honor, but at the hazard of disgrace."

Jesus set us a tremendous example. If ever a person could rightly seek honor and really deserve it, it was our Lord. But the only honor He ever desired was that from His Father. He lived to please Him.

Only a few really honored Jesus during His life on earth. At His birth the innkeeper sent His parents to the stable, where He was born among the cattle. Yet the cattle on a thousand hills are His. As a grown man He claimed that although even the foxes and birds had homes, He didn't have a place to call His own. Even the animal He rode on into Jerusalem during the triumphal entry had been borrowed. It is true that the multitudes at His triumphal entry seemed to honor Him, but the fact is that they were praising Him not for who

He was but rather for what they hoped He would do for them. They wanted Him to deliver them from Roman oppression.

When He came to the end of the road—His retirement, if you please—the people whom He came to rescue gave Him no farewell celebration. Instead of being honored by receiving a gold watch, He shed the gold of His blood on the cross—a cross erected at the demands of church leaders! Instead of crowning Him with a diadem of honor, they pressed a crown of thorns on His head. Instead of giving Him an honorary degree, they gave Him the death decree. And instead of eulogies of praise, Jesus heard only "Crucify Him! Crucify Him!"

Please honor our Lord of love with a few words of praise. Thank Him for enduring these insults for our salvation.

The Fourth Man

Then Nebuchadnezzar the king was astonied, and rose up in haste, and spake, and said unto his counsellors, Did not we cast three men bound into the midst of the fire? They answered and said unto the king, True, O king. He answered and said, Lo, I see four men loose, walking in the midst of the fire, and they have no hurt; and the form of the fourth is like the Son of God. Dan. 3:24, 25.

Being the head of gold of the great multimetal image of Daniel 2 was not good enough for King Nebuchadnezzar. His thirst for power led him to erect a 90-foot-high image made entirely of gold. Then the king invented a national musical-chair-type game. When the Babylonian Philharmonic Orchestra played, everyone was supposed to bow down rather than sit down. Those who refused to bow received the death penalty as their reward.

If ever Shadrach, Meshach, and Abednego had any reason to start rationalizing, it was now! And if they did start discussing the rules of the king's game, we can imagine that they toyed with the idea that if they did bow, they in their hearts could reassure themselves that they were worshiping the Lord and not the golden image. Another tempting argument would have been that living witnesses are better than dead ones! Think of all the honor they could bring the Lord in the future if they just went along with the king's little whim now. Of course, they could argue with the Lord *afterward* that their hearing hadn't been too good, and when the music played they had become confused and inadvertently bowed down.

But these three young men chose to burn rather than bow. They stood straight and tall when the music played, and they remained that way when the king in rage demanded, "Is it true . . . that you do not serve my gods or worship the golden image that I have set up?" (verse 14, NASB).

Their reply to Nebuchadnezzar after he gave them a second chance to bow is classic: "O Nebuchadnezzar, we do not need to give you an answer concerning this. If it be so, our God whom we serve is able to deliver us from the furnace of blazing fire; and He will deliver us out of your hand, O king. But even if He does not, let it be known to you, O king, that we are not going to serve your gods or worship the golden image that you have set up" (verses 16-18).

Sincerely and firmly, they slammed the door quickly on temptation's fingers. It is the only safe way to deal with sin and Satan.

When the king saw four men walking around inside the blazing furnace, it was a wondrous victory for God as Nebuchadnezzar declared, "The form of the fourth is like the Son of God" (verse 25). How right he was!

The same Son of God stands by His faithful ones today. Do you believe that God has stood by you during some special time of trial? If so, tell about it below.

March 12

You Are Mine!

Do not fear, for I have redeemed you; I have called you by name; you are Mine! When you pass through the waters, I will be with you; and through the rivers, they will not overflow you. When you walk through the fire, you will not be scorched, nor will the flame burn you. Isa. 43:1, 2, NASB.

Isaiah 43 expresses God's tender love in a most beautiful way. While the book contains numerous threats and reproofs against a rebellious Israel, in this chapter God shows His love for His people despite their transgressions. The Lord was their Saviour, and "in all their affliction he was afflicted" (Isa. 63:9). We are His! Read again our verse and meditate a moment on those precious words, "You are Mine!" God is so intimately involved with each of us that He cries out, "You are Mine!"

Because Isaiah penned those words more than 100 years before the Babylonians carried Daniel and his friends off as slaves, we can be sure that Shadrach, Meshach, and Abednego probably knew and might have even memorized this passage. We can hear them repeating it as the soldiers bound and cast them into the fiery furnace because they refused to bow to Nebuchadnezzar's golden image. It was no make-believe fire. The record states that it was so hot that the poor fellows who threw them in perished in the super-heated flames that belched out the furnace door (Dan. 3:22).

The only thing that burned on the three loyal men were the ropes. As the fibers shriveled in the flames, it freed them to get up and walk around in the furnace with Jesus beside them.

The king's terrible rage immediately turned to praise. Approaching as near as he dared to the door of the furnace, he called the three men by name and ordered them to come out and appear before him. Then, surrounded by officials from his entire empire, the king saw that not even a hair of their heads was singed, nor did the smell of smoke linger on them. The lesson is that when God does a job, He does it thoroughly!

The conclusion to this episode is remarkable. Nebuchadnezzar first blessed the God of the three men who had violated his command. Then he decreed that if any person in his empire should speak against their God, they "shall be torn limb from limb and their houses reduced to a rubbish heap, inasmuch as there is no other god who is able to deliver in this way" (verse 29, NASB).

Praise God by putting in your own words what it means to you when you hear Him declare, "You are Mine!"

_____

_____

Merging of Creation and Calvary

All the inhabitants of the earth will worship it—all those whose names have not been written in the book of life which belongs to the Lamb slain from the foundation of the world. Rev. 13:8, Phillips.

"The sacrifice of Christ as an atonement for sin is the great truth around which all other truths cluster. In order to be rightly understood and appreciated, every truth in the Word of God, from Genesis to Revelation, must be studied in the light that streams from the cross" (*Gospel Workers*, p. 315).

Ellen White's statement, when applied to every teaching in Scripture, causes one to ask, "How do Creation and Calvary merge?" The answer grips the heart with an admiration for Jesus difficult to describe.

See Jesus in the Garden of Eden, bending low over a lump of clay, forming it carefully into the body of a man. With tenderness He shapes the fingers, toes, ears, and eyes. Then He breathes into the nostrils the spark of life. The heart begins beating, the lungs quiver as they gasp the first breath of air. The eyes focus on his Maker. Holding out His hand, Jesus helps lift the newly created person to his feet. Adam never learned to walk as an infant, for Jesus created him a full-grown, thinking person. As you visualize Adam and Christ meeting for the first time, you see a satisfied, loving expression in Jesus' eyes as He searches Adam's face for a response. And the adoration comes immediately. Adam is delighted to meet his Lord.

Now consider for a moment—did Jesus know when He created Adam and Eve that someday their descendants would kill Him, their Creator? Yes, He knew, but because of His love He would not change His creation plans. In deep love He made provision for the salvation of the human race even before the moment of creation.

Bob asked Marie one day whether she would bring a child into the world if she knew that the child would someday murder her. She thought for a moment, then slowly shaking her head said, "Never. That would be folly!"

Human love can never equal divine love. Jesus was slain from the very foundation of our world. The love He has for us is beyond expression. He is our Lamb of God, who foreknew His death at the hands of Adam's descendants before He brought the first man to life!

If you are ever tempted to doubt our Lord's love, remember that He made the first person in the light of the full blaze of Calvary. The shadow of the cross stretched across even Eden. Our Saviour God so loved the idea of making a new race of beings that He would not halt His plans even at the great expense of His own life.

How much do you adore and appreciate Him for such love? Write it down even if you can say no more than simply "I love You, Lord."

March 14

Our Creator Becomes Part of Creation

In the beginning was the Word, and the Word was with God, and the Word was God. . . . All things came into being through Him; and apart from Him nothing came into being that has come into being. . . . And the Word became flesh, and dwelt among us, and we beheld His glory, glory as of the only begotten from the Father, full of grace and truth. John 1:1-14, NASB.

To fully understand these verses is an absolute impossibility. John is saying that Jesus is God and that this Jesus-God made everything that has come into existence. That much we can comprehend to a degree. But what follows is mind-boggling and beyond human comprehension. This same Jesus-God, after creating our world, now through a mysterious, unexplainable act becomes part of creation itself!

If one person had the ability to invent and build a sophisticated automobile with all its parts—engine, wheels, battery, spark plugs, windshield, et cetera—then decided to transform himself into the steering wheel and become himself a part of his own creation, what would you think? That he needed to see a psychiatrist? Obviously he must be a mad man!

Our crude illustration really is ridiculous. Yet what Jesus did far surpasses it. He, the God-man, forever identified Himself with fallen human beings in order to redeem us!

In Eden Jesus created all life, and in Bethlehem He became part of His own creation. In Eden Adam stood tall in God's image. In Eden created-man was given the tree of life, while at Calvary created-man gave Christ the tree of death. In Eden Adam stood tall in God's image. But at Calvary the Second Adam, with nails and thorns piercing His flesh, died as a common criminal. Here is love that cannot be explained or comprehended, only experienced and shared. It is love that cannot be fully grasped but only accepted. In Christ Creation and salvation meet and are cemented together with His precious blood.

The doctrine of creation is extremely important when you consider it in the light of the cross. Little wonder that Satan promotes the evolutionary theory in various forms. To downplay or ignore the record of creation and the inception of sin found in the first three chapters of Genesis is to detract from Calvary itself. Christ in six 24-hour days spoke all life into existence. And ever since, our Saviour has been speaking new life into the lives of sinners, re-creating them daily into His image. By virtue of His becoming flesh and walking among humanity for 33 years, we have the marvelous hope of Eden soon to be restored.

Why not praise Him for His incarnation at Bethlehem!

A Debt We Are Glad to Owe

I am under obligation both to Greeks and to barbarians, both to the wise and to the foolish. . . . For I am not ashamed of the gospel, for it is the power of God for salvation to every one who believes, to the Jew first and also to the Greek. Rom. 1:14-16, NASB.

Our first car was a used 1940 Chevrolet that we bought partially on credit. As newlyweds we were excited to drive away in our first automobile. Our monthly obligation was only $10, yet it was a tenth of our total income at that time. We still remember the day when we made our last payment. The sense of freedom from the oppressive feeling of debt thrilled us.

But there is one debt we will always owe, yet we'll be happy for it. Like Paul, we have a tremendous obligation to our world to share the gospel with those who sit in spiritual darkness, and it is an obligation that increases in intensity as we grow older. What value does life have for Christians unless they use their time and energy in a redemptive way?

Paul describes his obligation in such an interesting way. First he refers to the Greeks. Why? Speaking the Greek language was a must for anyone who considered himself an intellectual or even civilized. Ignorance of Greek would classify one as a barbarian. But Paul includes such people as those to whom he was indebted. Then he adds both the wise and foolish to his list. To make certain he covers everyone, he states his eagerness to preach the gospel even to those in Rome (verse 15).

Why was Paul eager to preach a message that so often brought him trouble? Why be so glad to talk about a subject that got him beaten, stoned, jailed, and finally killed? His tremendous compulsion makes wonderful sense when you understand the subject matter—Jesus Christ and Him crucified.

How can we ever be ashamed of talking about Jesus? How can we ever be humiliated to share a liberating message with someone who lives in a prison of fear and despair? Can you imagine the sheer joy of meeting in the New Jerusalem a human being whom Jesus has used you to help save? To see an eternally living person in the kingdom because of your sense of obligation to share the good news will be a fantastic experience. Suppose it is someone in your own family—your child, spouse, or cousin?

Praise Him now for this grand debt that we should all gladly owe!

Righteousness From Faith to Faith

I am eager to preach the gospel to you also who are in Rome.... For in it the righteousness of God is revealed from faith to faith; as it is written, "But the righteous man shall live by faith." Rom. 1:15-17, NASB.

Yesterday we emphasized the debt that we gladly owe to others. That debt focuses on the gospel—the good news of salvation that Christ alone has provided for the entire human race.

Paul tells us that the gospel reveals the righteousness of God. The horrible conflict between Christ and Satan is actually a battle between what is right and what is wrong. Hate is wrong; love is right. Lust is wrong; purity is right. Lying is wrong; truthfulness, right. And greed is wrong; unselfishness, right. Use the dictionary and write down every good attribute in one column and next to it every evil attribute. Then put at the top of the list of good qualities the name of Jesus Christ, and place the name of Satan over the list of evil qualities. One list is the epitome of righteousness; the other, the essence of unrighteousness.

When we speak of the righteousness of God, we are referring to the qualities of His character. In simple terms, righteousness means right-doing, or that which is right. (The Old Testament reminds us that righteousness can be a relationship as well as an act. Consider, for example, Judah's strange statement in Genesis 38:26. In the New Testament a relationship with Jesus brings each one of us righteousness.) Every mind is a daily battleground upon which we wage warfare over what is the right thing to think and do. If a cashier at a supermarket checkout stand gives you an extra $10, what is the right thing to do? What would Jesus do in a situation like that?

The gospel impels the Christian to think God's thoughts, to treat others and to relate to them as God would. To do this requires faith at every step, or as Paul says, "from faith to faith." It is faith at the beginning, in the middle, and at the end of life. Never do we operate without faith in God. His righteousness is ours by faith—faith in what God does *for* us, *in* us, and *through* us. It is all of God. Every ounce of credit for our salvation goes to Him!

No wonder we love to praise Him for salvation through faith alone in Him. We gladly acknowledge our love for Him. It couldn't be otherwise. How about you?

March 17

Busyness

Thus I considered all my activities which my hands had done and the labor which I had exerted, and behold all was vanity and striving after wind and there was no profit under the sun. Eccl. 2:11, NASB.

Solomon, we believe, wrote these words. He states with clearheaded realism that constant work may achieve a certain success, but work is also vanity—unless one leads a balanced life. He does not criticize hard work, but he recognizes that a person also needs time for the better things of life—especially time for spiritual development. (See Eccl. 3:12, 13 and Eccl. 12.)

Many erroneously feel as though they need to appear busy all the time. Ethel Renwick, who spent a lifetime studying international lifestyles, wrote: "One of the great ills of American society is that they make outrageous demands upon their bodies by overwork. The work ethic, being at the very core of America, is taken to an extreme and rationalized as worthy, even noble." She particularly points her finger at Christians who "live as though God depended on them alone and had no other way of getting things done" (in Sybil Stanton, *The 25-Hour Woman*, p. 95).

A professor from Fuller Theological Seminary was invited to the North American Division Evangelism Council in Florida several years ago. He made an interesting observation about the busyness of Seventh-day Adventists. "When I came to Daytona, the first thing I did was to drive down on the beach to see the beach and ocean, for I knew this would be my last opportunity to see God's kingdom of nature, since I was attending a Seventh-day Adventist convention." Then he added, "Undoubtedly you folk teach the correct Sabbath, which is the seventh day of the week, but I wonder if you know what it means to experience and enjoy the rest that is inherent in the Sabbath!"

Have you ever visited a park and watched children on the merry-go-round? Someone keeps the large wheel spinning, making it difficult to get off. Most of the children clutch the bars for dear life as they whirl in circles until they feel sick or until someone rescues them. As children grow, they keep going back for more of this type of activity until at some point in their lives they conclude, "I don't need this anymore!" There will always be a merry-go-round in life, but you don't have to be on it. If you are discouraged, tired, and disheartened, perhaps you haven't been able to distinguish between the urgent and the important. Get off the merry-go-round and start changing your world.

George Bernard Shaw once said, "People are always blaming their circumstances for what they are. I don't believe in circumstances. The people who get on in this world are the people who get up and look for the circumstances they want, and, if they can't find them, make them" (*ibid.*, p. 59).

"Man can shape circumstances, but circumstances should not be allowed to shape the man. . . . We are to master them, but should not permit them to master us" (*The Ministry of Healing*, p. 500).

Aren't you thankful God requires only that we do our best and never to overdo! He is the One who has invited us to "come . . . apart" and "rest a while." And He is the One who complimented Mary for choosing the better things in life. Thank Him now for being such a personal, understanding God.

March 18

The Power of Influence

I make a decree that in all the dominion of my kingdom men are to fear and tremble before the God of Daniel; for He is the living God and enduring forever, and His kingdom is one which will not be destroyed, and His dominion will be forever. He delivers and rescues and performs signs and wonders in heaven and on earth, who has also delivered Daniel from the power of the lions. Dan. 6:26, 27, NASB.

Why did Darius, king of a pagan nation, speak so boldly for God? How was he so sure that the God of heaven could do what He claimed? As the chief among the Persian ruler's ministers of state, Daniel had worked closely with the king. No doubt Daniel had told him about Israel's God. Perhaps he had even seen Daniel kneeling in prayer before his window. But more than this, in all matters of government, the king saw for himself that Daniel stood for principle. Unlike any of the other statesmen, Daniel had escaped being corrupted by selfishness. The king even planned to set him over the whole realm because of what he had found in him. When forced to have Daniel thrown into the lions' den, the king was so sure of Daniel's relationship with his God that he said to him, "Your God whom you constantly serve will Himself deliver you" (verse 16, NASB).

Influence is a powerful weapon. Daniel's impact on King Darius was astounding. His faithfulness compelled the king to order his whole kingdom to serve Daniel's God. We may debate the issue of religious freedom, but we cannot overlook the influence of one God-fearing individual who served as a high officer in a world empire.

Of all the stories in the Bible, we believe that Daniel and the lions' den has had the most powerful impact on the lives of children. Daniel's experience encourages them to be true to biblical principles of integrity and uprightness. It teaches them not to be swayed by what others may think of them as they make decisions.

For Marie, this story made a deep impression on her young life while she attended church school. She grew up in a religiously divided home. Her father, although a good man, was not a member of the church, whereas her mother, a loyal member and leader in the church, centered her life on church activities. Marie's mother dearly loved the Lord and tried in every way to interest her four daughters in His ways. At the age of 14, several outside influences could have led Marie away from God. Her mother's influence, fortunately, had planted Marie's feet in the right path.

That particular year a God-fearing teacher came to teach in the one-room church school that Marie attended. The strong influence of this teacher who emulated the character of Christ in her demeanor, words, and dress reinforced Marie's early home training and helped her make her decision for Christ. At the end of that school year Marie was baptized into the body of Christ.

We all carry with us a sphere of influence. Thank the Lord that when His Holy Spirit controls our lives, we will, regardless of our position or wealth, influence others in favor of Jesus.

Jot down a personal experience in which you saw the power of a positive influence.

_____

_____

1,999 out of 2,000

Do not judge lest you be judged. For in the way you judge, you will be judged; and by your standard of measure, it will be measured to you. Matt. 7:1, 2, NASB.

The words "critic" and "criticism" do not appear in the Bible, but we do find there the term *judge*. And in a certain context it means the same as being critical. In fact, our word "critic" comes from the Greek word for "judge." It means to separate, distinguish, discriminate. There is nothing wrong in being discriminating, but prejudgment is unfair and unreasonable. Jesus could have said, "Do not criticize lest you be criticized."

Criticism is a vicious habit with some people. They criticize everyone and everything, including the weather. One of Satan's special temptations seeks to get God's people to be critical of each other.

Jascha Heifetz, known as the violinist of the century, set a standard that none, according to music experts, ever equaled or surpassed. It is said that he became convinced that out of every 2,000 people who came to hear him play, 1,999 hoped he would hit a wrong note!

Samuel Johnson, the English lexicographer, stated it well when he remarked, "Criticism is a study by which men grow important and formidable at very small expense."

It is far better to look for the good in each other. One sure way to overcome a critical spirit is to concentrate on Jesus and not others. But it takes time and determination to form new habits of positive thinking. One way we can do this is as we see others doing wrong and making mistakes, to pray for their salvation. We should think of every way possible to help and not hurt a person.

Encouraging and spreading hope to those who may be down and almost out will remedy many problems in the world. This is what Jesus did for people, and He wants to do it for us. Even more than that, our Lord, knowing the human heart, constantly spoke words of hope to those who were in the wrong. He even healed those who had brought disease upon themselves by their own wrong lifestyle.

Praise the precious name of the wonderful Lord we serve! Has He been good to you? If so, say so in writing.

What if Christ Had Failed?

And He went a little beyond them, and fell on His face and prayed, saying, "My Father, if it is possible, let this cup pass from Me; yet not as I will, but as Thou wilt." Matt. 26:39, NASB.

Can you really grasp what it meant when God the Son, doubled up in the most intense agony possible, fell onto the ground—all because of the sins of the human race for which He was about to die? It is beyond human understanding. The disciples did not understand what was going on in Jesus' mind or they never would have fallen asleep that Thursday evening. Even with the insights the Holy Spirit gives to us today, we can but faintly comprehend the sorrow our Lord was experiencing. Jesus was being numbered among the transgressors. He even said to His disciples, "My soul is deeply grieved to the point of death" (Mark 14:34, NASB).

As Jesus reviewed His life on earth, undoubtedly His human nature was tempted to think of the way that human beings had treated Him. Every step of His life had been made more difficult by the very people He came to redeem. The widespread rejection of His claim to be the Messiah made Him feel that His agony and coming death were for nought. "Terrible was the temptation to let the human race bear the consequences of its own guilt, while He stood innocent before God" (*The Desire of Ages*, p. 688).

At this point He could have gone back to heaven. He could have avoided the paralyzing hours of horrible agony. But what would have happened to us had Jesus given in to His feelings? Our world would have reverted to its chaotic condition described in Genesis 1:2. Satan would have won the victory had there been no cross.

But Jesus didn't fail! He drank the bitter cup, and He "who knew no sin" was made "to be sin on our behalf, that we might become the righteousness of God in Him" (2 Cor. 5:21, NASB). How thrilled we are, how utterly thankful, that Jesus did not turn His back on us when He was almost overwhelmingly tempted to do so. Praise His precious name for making the supreme sacrifice for us—a sacrifice that has assured us of eternal life!

Won't you praise Him for not leaving you to perish in your sins? It doesn't have to be profound—perhaps nothing more than a simple "Thank You, Lord."

March 21

Prophet, Priest, and King at Work

But Jesus turning to them said, "Daughters of Jerusalem, stop weeping for Me, but weep for yourselves and for your children. . . . Father forgive them; for they do not know what they are doing. . . . Truly I say to you, today you shall be with Me in Paradise." Luke 23:28-43, NASB.

Our passages for today come from the twenty-third chapter of Luke. The verses clearly illustrate the three phases of Christ's work on earth as prophet, priest, and king. His crucifixion remarkably demonstrated Him fulfilling all three offices. As He made His way to Calvary crowds of people followed Him. The women among them wrung their hands and wept. Jesus, instead of thinking of His own pain and weakened condition, turned toward them and proclaimed a prophecy. Armed with the prophetic gift, He looked down the hallways of time to those terrible moments when the Romans would destroy Jerusalem and slaughter thousands of Jews. A forest of crosses covered the hills around the city, and many of the children of the weeping women were crucified at that time. In deepest pity, Jesus urged them not to shed tears for Him but to save them for the time when they and their children would perish in the coming holocaust. He added that those with no children at that day would feel themselves greatly blessed.

As priest, Jesus, while being crucified, rather than being concerned for Himself, mediated for those who were pounding nails through the tender flesh of His hands and feet. Consider the love that compelled our Lord to ignore the pain and to pray for His enemies. While the thieves and others heaped curses upon their enemies, Jesus pleaded their ignorance as a basis for forgiveness.

We have no record of them, but it will not surprise us to meet some of Christ's crucifiers in the kingdom. Surely they will trace the beginning of their own salvation to that moment when He expressed His forgiveness even before they asked for it.

Finally, Jesus practiced His saving power, not only throughout His 33 years of life, but during His dying moments on the cross when the repentant thief asked to be remembered. Again we see Jesus thinking of others, not of Himself. The words "You shall be with Me in Paradise" were dependent on His return as King of kings and Lord of lords.

In these three facets of His life—Prophet, Priest, and King—Jesus illustrated His incomprehensible love. Unparalleled love that reaches out to save others. We can only stand amazed at such infinite love. How do you respond to such marvelous love?

Unclean, Unclean!

And it came about that while He was in one of the cities, behold, there was a man full of leprosy; and when he saw Jesus, he fell on his face and implored Him, saying, "Lord, if You are willing, You can make me clean." And He stretched out His hand, and touched him, saying, "I am willing; be cleansed." And immediately the leprosy left him. Luke 5:12, 13, NASB.

Some years ago Bob was visiting our hospital on the island of Penang off the west coast of Malaysia. A doctor friend asked him if he would like to see a person with a case of leprosy that he had just diagnosed. He took Bob into his office, where a frail middle-aged woman sat. The doctor held up her arm and pointed to a grayish white spot about twice the size of a silver dollar. Then he proceeded to take a needle and started pricking in various places. The woman showed no signs of pain. She could not feel a thing. Since then Bob has visited several leper colonies and has seen the horrible results of this dreaded disease.

The leper in our story had an advanced case of leprosy. He was in a pathetic condition. If his was a case of Hansen's disease, then probably his fingers, toes, nose, and even his eyelids had vanished. His voice would have been damaged or nearly gone. His joints were probably dislocated, which would have caused him to half crawl to Jesus. It seemed as if his whole body were being eaten alive by the terrible disease, for the record states that he was "full of leprosy."

Old Testament ceremonial law required that whenever people with leprosy came near people, they had to cry "Unclean! Unclean!" When this poor sufferer heard of Jesus, faith overcame fear, and with great difficulty he found his way to the Healer from Galilee.

At a distance he watched carefully how Jesus healed the sick and how the once-suffering ones shouted praises of gratitude. Finally he lunged forward and threw himself at Jesus' feet, exclaiming, "Lord, You are able to cure me if You are willing to do so." Jesus responded affirmatively and healed him.

Ellen White made a remarkable confession to a group of Avondale College students in Australia in 1894. She said, "I loathe myself. I would clothe myself in sackcloth and ashes and cry, 'Unclean, unclean.' The only cleanness that I can have is that which is in Jesus Christ" (manuscript 15, 1894). She keenly sensed her spiritual condition. But she was not alone. The entire human race is contaminated with spiritual leprosy. Whether it be physical or spiritual leprosy, the good news is that we can be made clean and whole in Him. We praise Him, we glorify Him, for His love and cleansing power.

Write down a few words of thankfulness to Jesus for what He has done for you!

The Authority of Jesus

And they were all amazed, so that they debated among themselves, saying, "What is this? A new teaching with authority! He commands even the unclean spirits, and they obey Him." Mark 1:27, NASB.

In the middle of Jesus' sermon in the Capernaum synagogue, a demon-possessed man interrupted Him and shouted, "What do we have to do with You, Jesus of Nazareth? Have You come to destroy us? I know who You are—the Holy One of God!" (verse 24, NASB). The demonic-inspired statement contains a strange mixture of truth and error. Certainly Satan's demons have nothing in common with Jesus. The question "Have You come to destroy us?" was a good one. Jesus did come to eradicate the works of Satan and to deliver people from his death grip. But He would not harm people, as the demon tried to convince the man. Christ came to liberate him. Yet this garbling of truth and error concludes with a beautiful confession of Jesus being the Holy One of God.

Reading between the lines, you can sense the wretched fellow's deep desire to escape evil's constant harassment. Satan, however, was determined not to let his victim loose.

The great controversy between Christ and Satan raged around this man in the middle of the worship service. But Jesus won . . . and Satan lost! After the demoniac's deliverance, the congregation excitedly proclaimed, "What is this? A new teaching with authority! He commands even the unclean spirits, and they obey Him."

Some wonder if the battle over souls is as real today as it was in Christ's time. Constantly we read of the tragedy that devastates the lives of those who dabble in the occult. But such stories are only the more obvious ways that Satan attacks the human race. He has countless other weapons to use against us. Many of them are so subtle that even Christians can succumb to them. The devil uses both the bizarre and the apparently respectable to entrap his victims. Yielding to evil of any form always gives him the advantage.

The same Saviour stands ready to rescue us and set us free today. His authority over Satan is no less now than it was then. Our only safety is to remain under His shadow. We praise the Lord for both setting us free and keeping us free. How about you?

The Doctrine of Discriminating Obliviousness

If then you have been raised up with Christ, keep seeking the things above, where Christ is, seated at the right hand of God. Set your mind on the things above, not on the things that are on earth. For you have died and your life is hidden with Christ in God. Col. 3:1-3, NASB.

We have taken our title from an article by Lance Morrow in the March 5, 1990, *Time* magazine. He reminds us in an interesting way of something that we already know—that we live in a time when information threatens to inundate us. Computers belch out billions of bits of data. They bury us with an avalanche of names, images, and facts. As a result, the mind must filter out this constant barrage of electronic dust. It cannot possibly store everything. We need a guard at our mind's door to let in only what is important. To maintain our sanity we need the principle of discriminating obliviousness. In other words, periodically we have to do some mental housecleaning. And to preserve a strong spiritual nature, we must not clutter our minds with nonessentials.

Satan constantly tries to distract our thoughts from God and redirect them anywhere else. He works feverishly with well-organized plans to keep us tied up even with good things—things that do not contribute toward Christian self-development or prepare us for our Lord's return. The only possible way to thwart him is to seek the things from above. To set our minds on eternal realities requires a conscious action on our part. It demands determination. Each of us is caught up in a real battle over whether we will focus our minds on the really important things.

Nobody knows this better than we do. As we examine our own lives, we can see where we have, consciously or unconsciously, gotten involved in time-consuming things that were really not that significant. Things that are not bad in themselves, but have not really contributed to our own or anyone else's salvation.

Jesus was a master of the art of discriminating obliviousness. One day a man asked Him to settle a family dispute. "Teacher, tell my brother to divide the family inheritance with me." The first thing Jesus said was, "Man, who appointed Me a judge or arbiter over you?" In other words, I have more important things to do while I am on earth. Next He warned him, "Beware, and be on your guard against every form of greed; for not even when one has an abundance does his life consist of his possessions" (Luke 12:13-15, NASB).

Isn't it time for us to praise the Lord for His example and His willingness to help us set our minds on spiritual things? Life is at its best when we concentrate on the really important. What do you think God considers most important in your life?

March 25

Fickleness

Praise the Lord! Praise the Lord, O my soul! I will praise the Lord while I live; I will sing praises to my God while I have my being. Do not trust in princes, in mortal man, in whom there is no salvation. Ps. 146:1-3, NASB.

Note the contrast in our reading today. In short, it urges us to praise the Lord but not to trust humans. Does it mean that we can't have confidence even in our friends? Not necessarily, but even then we have known of good friends who have ended up enemies. Someone broke trust, and the friendship evaporated.

Acts 14 tells how Paul and Barnabas held an evangelistic campaign in Iconium and met with tremendous success. In fact, too much success, if that is possible! Such a great multitude responded and believed the gospel that it split the city into two camps over whether or not to support the two evangelists or the local Jewish community. Finally the hatred against them turned into a murderous plot, so Paul and Barnabas fled to Lystra and other towns largely populated by superstitious pagans.

At Lystra the Lord worked a miracle through Paul and Barnabas, who healed a man lame from birth. In common with the widespread belief that the gods frequently visited the human race, the multitudes planned a celebration to honor Barnabas as Jupiter and Paul as Mercury, two leading gods in the Roman pantheon. Astounded at such adulation, the two men stopped the crowds by tearing their own clothes and crying out that they were not gods, but humans like them. They urged the crowd to serve the true Creator, the God of heaven. Even then the people still wanted to sacrifice offerings to them.

About this time, hostile Jews from Antioch arrived and turned the same enthusiastic crowd against Paul and Barnabas. Now, instead of treating Paul as a god, they stoned him! How often we have witnessed—even among Christians—enthusiasm for some leader quickly turn against him until former supporters even denounce the person they had previously championed. Oh, the fickleness of the human race!

David has given us excellent advice. Have your friends and even trust them, but above all, trust the One who alone is supremely trustworthy. Jesus will never fail you or turn against you. He is ever on your side to help you even when you make mistakes.

What does His unchanging love and support mean to you? Has it helped you endure some difficult situation?

March 26

Thanks for Freedom From Bad Habits

Always giving thanks for all things in the name of our Lord Jesus Christ to God, even the Father. Eph. 5:20, NASB.

Recently we viewed a segment of the CBS television news magazine *60 Minutes* that showed interviews its staff had conducted in a park in Zurich, Switzerland. Several hundred young people who used drugs congregate in the park each day. The city hands out free hypodermic needles to stem the spread of AIDS. The authorities had instructed the police to ignore the sale and use of drugs in this particular park. (The park has since been closed to such activities.)

Sadly, these youthful drug users were committing suicide at a rapid rate. Nearly 300 had died during the previous year. Several of those interviewed already had AIDS and were in the process of dying. One woman, a city employee assigned to work with those who had taken overdoses, stated that probably it would be best if these drug-using youth would die, because that was likely the only way they would be at peace since they had no control over themselves. She did not say this lightly, for her own son had frequented the park for five years and was himself on the verge of death. When the interviewers asked the drug users if they were happy, without exception each one said no. One commented, "How could I be happy when my life is controlled by a substance outside of myself?"

As we watched those wretched youth, some of whom were still handsome and beautiful, our hearts cried out in pain for them. If only they had known Jesus and had served Him, how different their lives would have been!

Then another thought struck both of us. We could have been victims of drugs ourselves. What if we were alcoholics or cocaine addicts? Both of us were immensely thankful for our message of temperance and for the Christian homes we had been reared in. We can't thank God enough for the freedom we have from habits that destroy life or make it miserable.

All of us should be thankful that we have escaped many dangerous habits. Freedom from them has given us a richer, more beautiful life. (Naturally, we never use such freedom as a reason to boast or exult over others.)

Why not list a few things that Scripture and our church and its lifestyle have protected you from? Thank the Lord, for example, for freedom from gambling, addiction, or cursing and swearing. Then add to that other vices such as adultery, lying, stealing, and any other evil that God has helped you stay clear of. This exercise is not designed to develop pride but thankfulness. All too often we fail to praise our Saviour for the victories He has given us or the protection He has provided. Remember, He deserves all the credit for any victories we have. Praise Him now for them.

A New Heart

Moreover, I will give you a new heart and put a new spirit within you; and I will remove the heart of stone from your flesh and give you a heart of flesh. Eze. 36:26, NASB.

For the average layperson living in 1967 the news that the South African surgeon Christiaan Barnard had made history by performing the first human-to-human heart transplant came as an amazing achievement. It was almost unbelievable. Imagine taking a beating heart from a dying individual and placing it in the body of someone else who would otherwise soon perish.

Doctor Robert G. Clouse, recipient of another person's heart, describes his experience in a graphic manner. A virus had attacked his own heart and damaged the heart muscle. His heart had enlarged to two and a half times the normal size to compensate for its weakness, but the amount of blood it pumped was only a fraction of that circulated by a normal heart. It was difficult for Clouse to lift anything heavier than two or three books. When his cardiologist suggested a heart transplant, Clouse began to study the ethics of organ transplantation.

He concluded that organ donation and transplantation is highly Christian, because death, according to Scripture, is humanity's last enemy. To choose life is certainly a Christian choice. He observed that "organ transplantation echoes the example of Jesus Christ and His victory on the cross in another sense. He saved us from sin and death, after all, by offering up His body. Celebrating the Last Supper, we remember that we live because He gave His body and His blood. The cross is the symbol of His self-giving, and when we choose to follow Him we are called to make His cross our own. There are few more dramatic ways we can give to someone else, in the spirit of that cross, than to share our body and our blood."

As wonderful as a physical transplant is, the spiritual transplant of a new heart—the heart that Jesus gives to us—is greater yet. The surgeon in spiritual heart transplantation is the Holy Spirit. He exchanges our old stony hearts of lust, greed, rebellion, and hate for soft and responsive fleshy hearts of love, kindness, and obedience. We call this transplant the new birth, and it is a prerequisite for citizenship in the new earth. There every individual will have had a heart transplant.

Praise God for new hearts! Our eternal life depends on this type of transplant. Won't you praise Him for His willingness to give you a new heart today? _____

March 28

Not of Blood, Flesh, or Will, but of God

But as many as received Him, to them He gave the right to become children of God, even to those who believe in His name, who were born not of blood, nor of the will of the flesh, nor of the will of man, but of God. John 1:12, 13, NASB.

The apostle John talked more about the new birth than did Matthew, Mark, or Dr. Luke. John had a special relationship with Jesus. Scripture reveals a dramatic contrast between his life and spirit before meeting Jesus and that afterward. He probably had as many or more character defects than Peter, and we do know that he (and his brother James) had a fiery temper. The Gospel accounts tell us that people called them Boanerges, meaning "sons of thunder." Do you remember the time when they wanted to call fire down on a Samaritan village because its inhabitants were unfriendly to Jesus and refused to give Him room and board?

Ellen White describes John as ambitious, combative, critical, impetuous, outspoken, proud, quick to resent slight and injury, revengeful, self-assertive, and violent! Bob, in one of his sermons, reads to the congregation this list of characteristics and then asks them what disciple it describes. Without fail they overwhelmingly answer "Peter!" When you look at that list, it is difficult to believe that any of us are that bad. Maybe Hitler and Stalin, but not us! Do you suppose we could be fooling ourselves?

If under the power of the Holy Spirit John could change into a person who was amiable; patient; calm; devoted to Jesus; considerate of the feelings of others; loyal; gentle; contemplative; humble; faithful in the face of imprisonment, beatings, and death; and—above all—who acquired a loving heart, surely change is possible for any one of us. That's good news!

We want to meet John in heaven. Imagine the wonderful time we will have in hearing him tell about his conversion experience! John knew that his transformation did not result from being born with a certain genealogical background. Being in the "Who's Who" books amounts to nothing when it comes to the new birth. The desires of the flesh won't give it to us. Nor will the human will. Willpower has its place, but it cannot produce the supernatural change that only the new birth can bring. The secret is in the phrase "but of God." Only the mighty Holy Spirit can give birth to a new you and me.

Write down a short prayer in which you ask God to transform you anew today.

From Red to Snow White

"Come now, and let us reason together," says the Lord, "though your sins are as scarlet, they will be as white as snow; though they are red like crimson, they will be like wool." Isa. 1:18, NASB.

When we conducted public meetings in Osaka, Japan, in 1955, we did not realize that one of those regularly attending was a prostitute. When we went to visit her one day, we were amazed to enter a beautiful section of town that contained nothing but brothel houses. We almost turned around to leave, but decided to go ahead and find the woman, which we did. She was a person who needed Christ like all the rest of us sinners. And happily she did accept the Lord.

It is so easy to slip into a pharisaical attitude and condemn those who are deeply involved in a type of sin that we may consider terrible only because we haven't been caught in it yet. All sin is vile, especially pride, and who among us is really free from this evil of all evils?

One time Jesus faced a situation that demanded Solomonic wisdom to solve. A group of neatly robed scribes and Pharisees dragged before Him a woman caught in the very act of adultery. They didn't bring her to Him so she could find salvation, but to entrap the only One who could give her salvation. Theirs was a double sin because they both tried to find fault with Jesus and used this poor woman as bait.

The Lord is in the business of saving, not destroying, people. His method of dealing with the adulteress was unique. Employing the ground as a blackboard and His finger as a piece of chalk, He traced in the dust the sins of her accusers—hate, revenge, jealousy, immorality, stealing, pride, and a host of other evils. No wonder the religious leaders slipped away quietly after seeing Him reveal their own sins.

Jesus then turned to the woman who was cowering in fear and waiting for the first stone to crash into her trembling body. But only forgiving words struck her heart! In effect Jesus said, "Though your sins are scarlet, I will make them white as snow because I forgive you. From now on please don't sin anymore."

The story is told about an outcast woman who died in a Cincinnati, Ohio, hospital. Left among her few personal effects was a handwritten poem. One of the stanzas reads:

Helpless and foul as the trampled snow,
Sinner, despair not! Christ stoopeth low
To rescue the soul that is lost in sin,
And raise it to life and enjoyment again.
Groaning—bleeding—dying for thee,
The crucified hung on the cursed tree!
His accents of pity fall soft on thine ear.
Is there mercy for me? Will He heed my weak prayer?
"O God! in the stream that for sinners did flow,
Wash me, and I shall be whiter than snow!"

It is impossible not to praise the Lord for His mercy and love. How did you feel when you first realized that He had forgiven you?

_____

_____

March 30

Spiritual Exercise Is the Most Important

Train yourself spiritually. Physical exercises are useful enough, but the usefulness of spirituality is unlimited, since it holds out the reward of life here and now and of the future life as well. 1 Tim. 4:7, 8, Jerusalem.

Many health experts rank physical exercise as one of the most important health habits to cultivate. Today in the field of sports, physical development is of supreme importance. Add to this large group the great army of joggers, walkers, and cyclists, and you have people running to and fro throughout the earth in an attempt to maintain good health through physical exercise.

The apostle Paul in his letter to Timothy was not undermining the importance of physical exercise. In his day almost everyone received plenty of exercise in such forms as walking because people had no mechanical ways of transportation other than those involving sails and animals. Jesus, Paul, and the apostles walked all through Palestine. They undoubtedly had strong hearts, legs, and muscles.

Just as today, sports activities in Paul's time could be all-consuming. The yearly calendar of holidays for sporting festivals occupied several months. The physical exercise demanded for such sports and games took the time and attention of all their participants.

For this reason Paul is admonishing young Timothy to set the example in spiritual training. While physical exercise is important, spiritual exercise is even more vital. Why? Because the development of our spiritual faculties results in unlimited blessings now and for the future. Eternal life depends on it.

If physical exercise strengthens our bodies, then what develops us spiritually? Habits of prayer, Bible study, and sharing our faith require spiritual exercising on a daily basis. Imagine what would happen to the spiritual temperature of our world if all the millions and billions of hours people spend on getting physical exercise were enthusiastically used in spiritual activities. If we expended the same amount of time on spiritual things as we do on sports, what fantastic changes would occur for the better!

Start now on a spiritual praise program. Warm up your devotional muscles by recording a time when God answered one of your prayers in an unexpected way.

The Oil of Unity

Behold, how good and how pleasant it is for brothers to dwell together in unity! It is like the precious oil upon the head, coming down upon the beard, even Aaron's beard, coming down upon the edge of his robes. Ps. 133:1, 2, NASB.

The people of the Old Testament used olive oil extensively. They considered it one of the most important elements of their diet. The widow of Zarephath told Elijah that all she had left during the terrible famine was a handful of flour and a little oil. Besides serving as cooking oil, olive oil was the main source for light at night. Moses, under the direction of the Lord, instructed Aaron to have the sons of Israel bring oil from beaten olives for the continually burning seven-branched lamp inside the tabernacle. It was also used to treat wounds and sores. The prophets employed it in the anointing services when God appointed kings.

David compares unity among God's people with the precious oil that ran down Aaron's beard during his ordination to be the high priest of the wilderness tabernacle. The ceremonial oil was not common olive oil but a sacred oil mixed with perfume.

The Lord Himself gave the formula for it to Moses. It consisted of 12.7 pounds of myrrh and cassia (an aromatic wood) and 6.4 pounds each of fragrant cinnamon and calamus or cane. These elements were all mixed in a base of nearly a gallon of olive oil (see Ex. 30:22-25).

In order for this to create a fragrant oil to symbolize the sweet aroma of Christ's righteousness, each ingredient had to lose its separate identity and blend together. It provides a beautiful illustration of the unity that Christ wants to bring to His followers. The medium through which we lose ourselves in Christ is the Holy Spirit. The price of unity comes high. It requires much knee work and a constant uplifting of the heart to God in supplication for the presence of His Spirit in our lives. The oil of the Spirit eliminates friction and self-centered independence. He effectively lubricates the lives of the members of Christ's body so that regardless of our individual abilities and talents, we work harmoniously side by side in reaching the world with the gospel. Only then are we all part of Christ's unified body.

As we praise the Lord for the oil of unity, we pray that all of us will be anointed with—more than that, bathed in—this oil so that we can be a sweet aroma to the world around us.

Wouldn't you like to thank Him for this oil of unity?

April 1

Jesus Never Role-played

For we do not have a high priest who cannot sympathize with our weaknesses, but one who has been tempted in all things as we are, yet without sin. Let us therefore draw near with confidence to the throne of grace, that we may receive mercy and may find grace to help in time of need. Heb. 4:15, 16, NASB.

In an effort to improve medical training, certain medical schools and hospitals in North America are trying an interesting technique. It seeks to counter the most universal complaint about doctors—that they lack compassion. The method is simple. The instructors assign roles, ages, and infirmities to resident physicians and medical students. For instance, a young medical student attempts to assume the role of an elderly woman who suffers from diabetes and congestive heart failure, and is recovering from a hip fracture. The student, using a walker, limps around the hospital as if he or she had all these physical problems. To make it more realistic, participants instantly age their faces with cornstarch and makeup. Yellow goggles smeared with petroleum jelly distort vision, and wax earplugs impair hearing. Splints on arms and legs make tying shoes and buttoning shirts difficult. Peas inside their shoes make walking painful. According to reports, such training has greatly increased the compassion of physicians. They begin to understand what it means to be burdened with infirmities.

Jesus, the truly great physician in the universe, knows the infirmities and weaknesses of the human race, not through a role-playing course, but by literally becoming one with us. The humanity that clothed His divinity was not make-believe. Jesus was definitely composed of real flesh and blood. His was a body greatly reduced in strength and size when compared to that of Adam.

Jesus knew what it was to experience exhaustion, hunger, cold, heat, joy, and sorrow. As a worker in His human father's carpenter shop, surely He felt the pain of splinters in His fingers and of the hammer hitting the wrong nail. Did He ever fall down and skin His knees? Why not? He became one with us. His identification with us is so complete that He could say "To the extent that you did it to one of these brothers of Mine, even the least of them, you did it to Me" (Matt. 25:40, NASB).

Jesus totally and unselfishly committed Himself to the human race. He is one with us. No wonder He is worthy of eternal praise and adoration! What you write in praise and thanksgiving to Him brings joy to His heart.

Two Golden Days

Therefore do not be anxious for tomorrow; for tomorrow will care for itself. Each day has enough trouble of its own. Matt. 6:34, NASB.

Our text today concludes the section in the Sermon on the Mount dealing with anxiety. It begins with verse 25, where Jesus admonishes us not to be anxious about life, food, or drink. He uses illustrations from nature showing how birds, lilies, and grass exhibit no fear or concern about the future, but simply go through life doing their best to get through one day at a time. Anxiety never helps—only hinders. Nor does it change any situation for the better. It only depresses us, needlessly uses up our energy, and undermines our happiness.

Mark Twain aptly said, "I am an old man and have known a great many troubles, but most of them never happened."

Robert J. Burdett speaks of two golden days about which he never worries. He makes them "two carefree days kept sacredly, free from fear and apprehension. One of these days is yesterday, with all its pains and aches, all its faults and blunders. It has passed forever beyond the reach of my recall, save for the beautiful memories, sweet and tender, that linger like the perfume of roses in the heart of the day that has gone, I have nothing to do with yesterday. It was mine; now it is God's. The other day that I do not worry about is tomorrow, with all its possibilities, adversities, its burdens, its perils, its large promise. Its sun will rise in roseate splendor, or behind a mask of clouds, but it will rise. Tomorrow—it will be mine. There is left for myself, then, but one day of the week—today. Any man can fight the battles of today. Any woman can carry the burdens of just one day. Therefore, I think, and I do, and I journey for but one day at a time. And while faithfully and dutifully I run my course and work my appointed task on this one day, . . . the Almighty takes care of yesterday and tomorrow."

Somewhere we read that yesterday is a canceled check, tomorrow is a promissory note, and today is cash that we must spend wisely. Praise the Lord for giving us today—for one day at a time.

More Precious Than Gold

I will make a man more precious than fine gold; even a man than the golden wedge of Ophir. Isa. 13:12.

Scholars are not absolutely certain where Ophir was, but the point is that people molded and trained by God are exceedingly valuable. Nothing is worth more than a human being, as the redemption price Jesus paid for us proves.

Some years ago Harry de Leyer, head riding instructor at a private girls' school on Long Island, New York, bought a sickly swayback gray horse for $80. The horse, named Snow Man, had been on its way to becoming dog food at a local slaughterhouse. But Harry redeemed him for the girls to ride as well as for a pleasure horse for his family. Soon, however, Snow Man began to amuse himself by jumping over the fences of his paddock. When De Leyer made the fences higher, Snow Man effortlessly glided over them. Harry realized that his $80 plug had real jumping talent. Soon Snow Man won countless competitions and was named Horse of the Year. He made a fortune for his new owners.

Like Snow Man, every person on earth will end up in the global slaughterhouse at the end of the millennium unless he or she accepts the redemption provided by the Lord Jesus. In our story, De Leyer bought Snow Man before he knew anything about his rare jumping abilities. In other words,

Snow Man had done nothing to earn his rescue from the dog food factory. So with us—nothing we have ever done or will do recommends us to our Master. His love for us is our only recommendation. In return, how glad Jesus is to see our lives improve because we now love and honor Him. Gladly jumping at every command He gives us, we love to bring honor to His name and blessing to those about us. We become more precious to Jesus than all the gold in the world.

It is a great privilege to understand God's love, and willingness to transform us and make us more valuable than the gold of Ophir. Praise Him for His rescue efforts. Praise Him for calling us His brothers and sisters. And praise Him for the soon-coming day when we will see Him, our Redeemer, face-to-face. _____

This Is a Ch – – ch

Not forsaking our own assembling together, as is the habit of some, but encouraging one another; and all the more, as you see the day drawing near. Heb. 10:25, NASB.

Did you ever notice that in the Creation story, recorded in the first two chapters of Genesis, you find God admiring and pronouncing everything good? Only once did the Lord say "It is *not* good" (Gen. 2:18). That was in connection with Adam's being alone. To solve the problem, God created Eve as a companion and wife. After the entrance of sin God recognized that a solitary person or isolated group of people would find it difficult to maintain their faith in God in a sin-filled environment. So He originated the idea of a church, a congregation of individuals who, sharing common beliefs, ideals, and standards, unite together to form an organization or fellowship. A church is a school to train and unite the members both for the purpose of strengthening and encouraging one another and for the purpose of bringing others into fellowship with themselves and with Christ, the principal of this spiritual school.

Former American president Theodore Roosevelt listed 10 reasons for going to church. One of them pointed out that a churchless community, where people have abandoned, scoffed at, or ignored their religious needs, is a society doomed to collapse. We have seen this fact dramatically illustrated in the former Communist nations.

Church attendance increases our feeling of responsibility for others. Many argue that one can worship the Creator in a grove of trees, by a running brook, or at home just as well as in church. Can one feel and be married by oneself? God made us social beings with a need to worship together, just as we do everything else in our lives together.

101

We look on church attendance as a marvelous privilege, especially since we have seen a number of our members denied it in areas lacking religious freedom.

One pastor put this sign on his bulletin board:

"This Is a Ch — — ch. What Is Missing?"

Praise God for the special privilege of meeting with Christ's body on a weekly basis. State in your own words why you feel church attendance is important.

_____

_____

How to Be Perfect

Therefore you are to be perfect, as your heavenly Father is perfect. Matt. 5:48, NASB.

Perfectionism is one of the most discouraging subjects that we persist in debating. What is perfectionism? It is a belief that we can and should attain moral, religious, or social perfection in this life. Some who teach it believe that any and every form of sin, whether in thought or action, will cease in the life of any person who will witness Jesus' return. To many minds it seems an impossible objective, because they sense their own weaknesses and short-comings. Such ideas have caused some to give up and declare, "What's the use? If I have to be that perfect, I will never make heaven." Another group, overwhelmed by this discouraging aspect, believes and teaches that we are not to concern ourselves with sin because it is inevitable, an attitude that can lead to a once saved, always saved position.

The debate over perfectionism is not new. Origen, a third-century theologian, attempted to solve the problem by creating a monastic movement that renounced the world. He apparently went so far as to take literally the words of Jesus in Matthew 19:12: "There are also eunuchs who made themselves eunuchs for the sake of the kingdom of heaven" (NASB). His monastic ideals became a dominant force in the Middle Ages and are still with us today in the convents and monasteries where people attempt to live isolated from the world. Although the Reformers were generally antiperfectionistic, John Wesley became a major advocate of Christian perfection. However, Wesley made a distinction between absolute perfection and Christian perfection. In his thinking, Christian perfection was freedom from sin only in the sense of "a voluntary transgression of a known law."

Two important keys help unlock the riddle of perfection. Note carefully that the Bible uses the words "perfect" or "perfection" in a relative sense. Why? To ever attain to absolute perfection would require absolute knowledge, and no person on earth possesses that. But the Scriptures do teach not only the possibility but the necessity of overcoming sin. The second key is that although our perfection is relative, still we are covered by an absolute perfection found in Christ and Him alone! This is a major part of the good news. Without His perfection, we are all lost. Our salvation and our perfection are in Jesus Christ! Does it mean we continue in sin? God forbid! Christ, crediting to our account His perfection, gives us an assurance that brings peace to the soul. It causes us to cast ourselves into the arms of Jesus in gratitude and thankfulness for His love and His perfect life.

I praise the Lord for His _____

_____

April 6

The Old Testament's Perfect People

This is the genealogy of Noah. Noah was a just man, perfect in his generations. Noah walked with God. Gen. 6:9, NKJV.

The word for perfect in this verse means complete, mature, blameless. Noah truly was a man of God, and we shall meet him in the kingdom; but he made his mistakes. When King Hezekiah bitterly complained to the Lord about the prophecy of his death, he began to proclaim his goodness and perfection. The real meaning of his "perfect heart" in Isaiah 38:3 is that he walked as a wholehearted, fully committed, loyal servant of God. But he was not perfect then and never was in an absolute sense. God set the ideal of perfection, or blamelessness, before Abraham. In Genesis 17:1, 2 the Lord told him to be perfect, or to be blameless. Perfection has been God's ideal for all His children from Eden to the end of the world. But does that mean we will ever get to the place where we will never make a mistake or fall? If it does, then we do not personally know of anyone who has reached that level of performance. This is not to say that there is no human being that perfect—just that we have never met him or her, if there is such a person.

But we do know of One who, while on earth, performed absolutely perfectly—Jesus Christ. We rejoice over the fact that Satan, with all of his temptations, could not cause Him to sin in thought, word, and deed. Our assurance of salvation depends on His perfect life and sacrifice, and our ultimate perfection in this life is in Jesus Christ. Even as fully dedicated, committed Christians, we are still maturing, still growing, still achieving, and still battling inherited and cultivated weaknesses.

Ellen White has written some challenging and comforting statements on the subject of perfection: "To be led into sin unawares—not intending to sin, but to sin through want of watchfulness and prayer, not discerning the temptation of Satan and so falling into his snare—is very different from the one who plans and deliberately enters into temptation and plans out a course of sin" (*Our High Calling,* p. 177).

She carefully delineated between premeditated sin and being trapped into sinning by carelessness in spiritual habits. Even human judges and courts recognize the difference between premeditated crimes and those that do not involve planning or malice.

Again we extol our Lord for His magnificent provision for our salvation. His perfect life on earth was an important, integral part of His plan of salvation. Satan claimed that no human being could obey the Ten Commandments, but Christ proved him a liar. Jesus perfectly kept His law, and through His Holy Spirit we too may have power to obey the law in our sphere. Why not show your appreciation to our Lord with words of adoration for His love and power?

April 7

The High Priest Who Received New Garments

Then he showed me Joshua the high priest standing before the angel of the Lord, and Satan standing at his right hand to accuse him. And the Lord said to Satan, "The Lord rebuke you, Satan! . . . Is this not a brand plucked from the fire?" Now Joshua was clothed with filthy garments and standing before the angel. Zech. 3:1-3, NASB.

Lift the veil that hides heavenly realities from our eyes and you will be amazed at the life-and-death struggle between Christ and Satan over our salvation. Zechariah in vision sees Joshua, the high priest, doing his very best to serve God, pleading for his people's salvation, but Joshua cannot see Satan standing beside him resisting his efforts. The priest has no power of his own to defend himself or his people. He knows they all make mistakes and sin, which the vision symbolizes by his filthy garments. Joshua confesses their guilt and pleads for cleansing for the entire nation. But Satan struggles with the Lord over their salvation. Let us listen to their conversation. Satan says, "These sinful people belong to me! They are citizens of my kingdom by virtue of their transgressions!"

The Angel, Christ Himself, replies, "I admit they are sinners, but they are making spiritual progress by repenting. They suffered long in Babylonian captivity. You did everything possible to keep them there and to leave their city of Jerusalem in ruins. However, this remnant returned and are doing their best to serve Me. Therefore they are citizens of My kingdom, not yours! I rebuke you now! Stand aside while I take from them their filthy garments and clothe them in My spotless robes of righteousness."

"But," Satan shouts back, "they are sinners! They are weak, faulty human beings—they are mine forever!"

"Oh, no, Satan, they are Mine, and you dare not touch them," the Lord calmly replies. "They are as a brand plucked from the fire. I forgive their sins, and I command My servants to remove the filthy garments from Joshua."

Defeated, Satan leaves, and the Lord admonishes Joshua, "If you will walk in My ways, and if you will perform My service, then you will also govern My house and also have charge of My courts" (Zech. 3:7, NASB).

We feel both solemn and grateful that Jesus stands by us to defend us against Satan's attacks. Join us in praising Him now for His protection and for giving us His robe of righteousness.

The Perfect Paul

I myself might have confidence even in the flesh. If anyone else has a mind to put confidence in the flesh, I far more. Phil. 3:4, NASB.

According to his own testimony, Paul kept the law perfectly. Note how he said it: "As to the righteousness which is in the Law, found blameless" (Phil. 3:6, NASB). And he truly was blameless, having never smoked, drank, cursed, lied, or murdered. The apostle fasted often, prayed more often, never chased women, and was a loyal church member who gave tithe and offerings regularly. Paul was perfect! Or was he?

No person in Scripture, save Jesus, understood the gospel better than Paul. He realized that he was never perfect, never could be perfect, and never would be perfect unless his life was hidden totally in Christ. Vividly he expressed it in the words "And may be found in Him, not having a righteousness of my own derived from the Law, but that which is through faith in Christ, the righteousness which comes from God on the basis of faith" (verse 9, NASB). A person can really have a righteousness by works, but it saves no one. Only Jesus and His righteousness can ever save.

As we consider Paul's experience and look at our own lives, we find quite a few things in common. Our performance probably hasn't been too bad. We may never have smoked, drunk, cursed, lied, or murdered. As health reformers we are better than some and worse than others. We may be good vegetarians and tithers; we are loyal to the church and may never have divorced. But we also know, like Paul, that if we depend on our performance for salvation, depend on being perfect for the assurance of salvation, we are hopelessly lost! In our spiritual experience we have experienced many ups and downs. We have played the entire scale of human emotions, from the high notes of joyful victories in the Lord to the thunderous bass notes of defeat. No, we probably haven't robbed a bank or done any of those "gross" sins, but sin is sin! Any sin persisted in can ruin our relationship with God. And that destroys the only source of our salvation.

Why do we mention this? Because we believe all Christians have similar struggles but never talk about them. So how do we cope with this problem? The answer is marvelous. "Jesus loves His children, even if they err. . . . When they do their best, calling upon God for His help, be assured the service will be accepted, although imperfect. Jesus is perfect. Christ's righteousness is imputed unto them, and He will say, 'Take away the filthy garments from him and clothe him with change of raiment.' Jesus makes up for our unavoidable deficiencies" (*Selected Messages*, book 3, pp. 195, 196).

If you appreciate a loving Saviour like Jesus, and we know you do, record it on the lines below.

_____

_____

April 9

When a New Song Was Sung

And they sang a new song, saying, "Worthy art Thou to take the book, and to break its seals; for Thou wast slain, and didst purchase for God with Thy blood men from every tribe and tongue and people and nation." Rev. 5:9, NASB.

When John saw in vision an important book, or scroll, sealed with seven seals, and no one appeared with the authority to unseal it, he was greatly disappointed. In fact, he began to "weep greatly, because no one was found worthy to open the book, or to look into it" (Rev. 5:4, NASB). Finally one of the elders commanded John to stop crying, because "the Lion that is from the tribe of Judah, the Root of David, has overcome so as to open the book and its seven seals" (verse 5, NASB).

As John watched, he saw the Lamb of God, Jesus, take the book. As He did so, heaven immediately rejoiced. They sang a new song ascribing praise to the only One in the universe who had the right to open the special book containing information vital to the plan of salvation. Among other things, the scroll was a prophetic outline of the history and lives of the human race. It contained detailed experiences of the cosmic struggle between Christ and Satan and revealed the destiny of every soul. Through His incarnation, death, and resurrection, Jesus, the Lamb and the Lion, won the right to open the scroll. Had He not lived and died for us, there would have been no need for a book about the future, since the world would not have had any! History would have come to an end 2,000 years ago.

The story is told of the young donkey that carried Jesus to and through Jerusalem on His triumphal entry. When the donkey returned to the stable that evening, he excitedly told the other donkeys what had happened that day. "The people cut down palm branches and waved them in my honor!" he exclaimed. "Some took off their coats and threw them on the ground for me to walk on."

"Is that really true?" the other donkeys asked.

"Oh, yes! Furthermore, some shouted, 'Hosanna!' At one point they wanted to make me king of the Jews!"

We smile at this ridiculous story, but any born-again Christian knows that salvation is all of God. We may carry the good news to others, but we must ever remember that Jesus, and He alone, is the good news. That was why John was so thrilled when he saw Jesus open the book. Only He, the perfect one, could do it. When we all get to the new earth, we will never have a praise service for ourselves. Rather, we will shout together, "Victory to our God who sits on the throne, and to the Lamb!" (Rev. 7:10, NEB). Extol Him now in a few words of praise for purchasing us from Satan's hands by His blood.

Heart Work or Handwork

The important thing is to be willing to give as much as we can—that is what God accepts, and no one is asked to give what he has not got. 2 Cor. 8:12, Phillips.

Our text today basically refers to giving offerings, but the principle of willingness to "give as much as we can" applies even more to our loyalty and commitment to Christ. God requires heart work more than handwork. What the hand gives or does may not parallel or reflect the motives of the heart. In Christ's parable of the talents, one person received two and another five. Even though one increased his talents to four and the other to 10, the master commended them equally. The parable of the laborers who, though beginning their work at the eleventh hour, received as much as those who spent the whole day in the vineyard again shows that the important point to remember is not quantity but quality or motivation. Those who came at the eleventh hour may have produced far less than those who worked longer, but they were just as loyal and committed to the master. "God regards more with how much love one worketh than the amount he doeth" (*Mind, Character, and Personality,* vol. 1, p. 207).

According to Luther, "when we deal with piety and impiety, we are dealing not with behaviour but with attitudes, that is, with the source of the behaviour" (in Arnold Wallenkampf, *What Every Christian Should Know About Being Justified,* p. 131).

The Pharisees may have had flawless performance, but they fell far short of what God expected of them in terms of attitude. The right attitude and motivation will always lead people to seek to know more of God's will. Those who do so are the perfect ones in God's eyes. They love and fully trust Him.

Will this type of Christian ever make a mistake? "When we are clothed with the righteousness of Christ, we shall have no relish for sin; for Christ will be working with us. We may make mistakes, but we will hate the sin that caused the sufferings of the Son of God" (*Selected Messages*, book 1, p. 360).

As growing, maturing Christians, we will never claim to be perfect. Our only claim to perfection is in Christ Jesus. "Christ did not possess the same sinful, corrupt, fallen disloyalty we possess, for then He could not be a perfect offering" (*ibid.*, book 3, p. 131).

Through His perfect life and death we can have the assurance of salvation. We can be free from condemnation! Free from anxiety about what God thinks about us, for we understand the real issue in salvation is what God thinks about Jesus, our substitute. And we know there is not the slightest doubt about Christ's performance of perfect obedience. Praise His name for loving and saving us!

April 11

Complete in Him

For in Him all the fulness of Deity dwells in bodily form, and in Him you have been made complete, and He is the head over all rule and authority. Col. 2:9, 10, NASB.

In October 1990 we conducted the first Week of Spiritual Emphasis at our new seminary in Zaokski, Russia. The main theme was on the much needed and much misunderstood subject of righteousness by faith. Early one morning on our way to the school's lovely chapel, we passed by the bulletin board, where a large photocopied statement tacked in the center caught our attention. The title was "Accepted in Christ." As we read it, it thrilled us and became the central theme for the sermon that evening.

Please read the statement slowly and carefully: "Perfection through our own good works we can never attain. The soul who sees Jesus by faith repudiates his own righteousness. He sees himself as incomplete, his repentance insufficient, his strongest faith but feebleness, his most costly sacrifice as meager, and he sinks in humility at the foot of the cross. But a voice speaks to him from the oracles of God's Word. In amazement he hears the message, 'Ye are complete in Him.' Now all is at rest in his soul. No longer must he strive to find some worthiness in himself, some meritorious deed by which to gain the favor of God" (Ellen G. White, in *Signs of the Times*, July 4, 1892).

It tells us that our greatest spiritual advancement, our finest religious achievement, or our highest level of self-control—whatever we have achieved even with the Lord's help—is not perfect and never good enough to satisfy the claims of God's law! Yet our current spiritual level must never discourage us from pressing forward to walk on higher ground, since we know we are perfect and complete *only* in Him!

On one of our several visits to Thailand we toured an elephant camp where they train the creatures not only for exhibition but for work in the forest. We observed powerful elephants moving huge teak logs as humans would two-by-fours. So with us: our best performance and our greatest power and strength are limited and puny when compared with Jesus' power and performance.

We applaud Him for His willingness to help us live a victorious life, and we praise Him for crediting to our account His perfect performance. It is in Him and Him alone that we are perfectly complete. Take a moment to praise Him in words for His sharing Himself with you today.

April 12

Giving Away What Is Not Ours!

Both riches and honor come from Thee, and Thou dost rule over all, and in Thy hand is power and might; and it lies in Thy hand to make great, and to strengthen everyone. Now therefore, our God, we thank Thee, and praise Thy glorious name. 1 Chron. 29:12, 13, NASB.

These beautiful words of praise and thanksgiving appear in one of David's prayers as he blessed the Lord. He was rejoicing that his son Solomon would be able to build the Temple. As you meditate on the words, you can feel David's joy overflowing. He understood well that all glory, credit, and honor for anything he and others might accomplish belonged to the Lord.

In 1 Chronicles 29:14 he confesses, "But who am I and who are my people that we should be able to offer as generously as this? For all things come from Thee, and from Thy hand we have given Thee" (NASB). Even when we bring tithes and offerings to God, we are simply presenting to Him what came from Him originally. God, like a parent, gives us an allowance, and we turn around and give a small portion back to Him. We and all we own are His and His alone! Even at best what we return to God in gifts is a pittance, since He owns all we are and have. Every blood cell is His. Every penny we have earned and saved through the strength that He gives us is His.

God help us never to be like the covetous rich man in the dramatic story Jesus told. The rich man's dissatisfaction with the volume of goods he had acquired over the years led him to want more just for the sake of being rich, with no thought of helping others or thanking God for his success. He lived for one purpose only—to serve self. The story is in Luke 12:16-21. In the nearly 70 words the rich man speaks in the story, "I" and "my" occur 11 times. No wonder Jesus called him a fool, for he failed to recognize his dependence on God or anyone else!

Repeatedly our Lord attempted to get this point across to His hearers. Our happiness, our success, our ability to find fulfillment in life, depends upon our recognition that everything that we have comes from Him.

Now is a marvelous time to start glorifying God as owner of all by writing down your appreciation of His goodness or an experience you had when God especially blessed you for your faithfulness in helping others.

The Story of a $100 Bill

O come, let us sing for joy to the Lord; let us shout joyfully to the rock of our salvation. Let us come before His presence with thanksgiving; let us shout joyfully to Him with psalms. For the Lord is a great God, and a great King above all gods. Ps. 95:1-3, NASB.

A fundamental characteristic of true Christianity is an attitude of praise and gratitude. If you haven't practiced always being on the lookout for events and happenings in your life to praise God for, what better time to begin than now? Think back over your past life and ask God's Spirit to help you remember His leading in it.

During one of our daily walks together recently, we remembered an experience that took place in 1943, our first year in the ministry. We worked in a citywide evangelistic campaign in Cleveland, Ohio, under the leadership of R. Allan Anderson, one of our most talented evangelists. After the meetings ended, we had the task of taking the evangelistic equipment in a trailer back to Washington, D.C. On our return trip we spent the night in a small West Virginia hotel. Being married less than a year and poor as the proverbial church mouse, we had borrowed $100 from Marie's mother to help us purchase furniture. (By the way, we paid it all back.) At that time, $100 for a couple on a $28-a-week salary was equal to several thousand dollars today. Marie carefully hid the $100 bill under her pillow and promptly forgot it when we left the hotel the next morning.

After we had driven 50 miles, she remembered the money. Visions of maids cleaning the room and taking the money seized our minds. To lose that $100 would have been a colossal loss for us. The first thing we did was to bow our heads and pray, "Lord, we belong to You, and so does that money. It's Your property, but please keep it safe for us!" We returned to the hotel and found it still in its hiding place.

Such experiences constantly cause us to thank God for His goodness. Life has its bitter incidents, but if we concentrate on all the good things that happen to us, they overshadow the not-so-good ones.

We had a praise meeting the rest of our journey home.

Erect a paper Ebenezer yourself by praising God in writing for some experience when He answered your prayers.

_____

_____

Except the Lord Build the House

Unless the Lord builds the house, they labor in vain who build it. Ps. 127:1, NASB.

A friend who had just separated from her husband wrote that she would give anything to relive the last several years of their marriage. She confessed that after just a few years into their marriage, when life became hectic with work, their failure to maintain family worship led to a poor Christian lifestyle. A solid, stable spiritual relationship with God is the only safe way for a couple to have a right relationship with each other.

The Rickerson diagram—a triangle with God at the apex, husband on one point of the base, and wife on the other—clearly illustrates that when both spouses move closer to God, they also get closer to each other.

"The secret of true unity in the church and in the family is not diplomacy, not management, not a *superhuman effort* to overcome difficulties—though there will be much of this to do—but union with Christ" (*The Adventist Home*, p. 179; italics supplied).

John and Millie Youngberg have found in their Marriage Commitment seminars that one of the areas of greatest perceived needs is spiritual growth and family worship. Time for God individually and the family together is a must if spiritual growth is to take place. It is not easy to get up earlier in the morning to study the Word, either alone or with your spouse, especially when you felt the urgency to see a special television program that lasted until midnight the evening before. Nor is it easy to have family worship when the children need to attend a ball game or go to choir practice.

The little book *Tyranny of the Urgent* gives us good advice when it states "Don't let the urgent take the place of the important in your life." Putting worship in first place and respecting it results in spiritual protection for all family members.

111

William Temple emphasizes the importance of worship: "To worship is to quicken the consciousness by the holiness of God, to feed the mind with the truth of God, to purge the imagination by the beauty of God, to open the heart to the love of God, to devote the will to the purpose of God. All this is gathered up in the emotion which most cleanses us from selfishness because it is the most selfless of all emotions—worship."

Thank God today for the privilege of family worship and ask Him to use it to make you a whole, selfless person.

April 15

Full of Life Worships

Ascribe to the Lord, O families of nations, ascribe to the Lord glory and strength, ascribe to the Lord the glory due His name. . . . Worship the Lord in the splendor of his holiness. . . . Give thanks to the Lord, for he is good; his love endures forever. 1 Chron. 16:28-34, NIV.

H.M.S. Richards, Sr., once said, "Family worship that my father and mother built for my brother and me meant a great deal. I learned more Bible in family worship and gained more of an interest in the Bible than I have in any other place or at any other time. We looked forward to family worship, and all took part in it even when we were very small, learning to sing and pray and read the Bible intelligently, and, to me, that is a great part of education."

Family worship should be "brief and full of life" (*Education*, p. 186), "pleasant and interesting" (*Testimonies*, vol. 5, p. 335), and "the most pleasant and enjoyable [time] of the day" (*Testimonies*, vol. 7, p. 43).

When our children were little we had a praise service on Friday evenings, thanking God for specific things. Our younger daughter, Linda, 3 or 4 years old at the time, would thank God for everything, including the dishes, by name! While it amused us, we were also grateful that she was internalizing the fact that we should appreciate God's gifts to us and praise His name for them. Often when walking in nature, we stopped in a secluded spot, remarked about the beauty of God's handiwork, and placed our arms around each other and prayed together. More and more God became the center of our lives as we practiced such habits.

Have you ever played a guessing game with your children in worship in which one member chooses and reads a passage, and the rest then try to guess where it is found? Role-playing members acting out a Bible story and then discussing it, makes the Bible come alive. One person could be Moses, another the golden calf, another Aaron. Children love such activity, and it builds their interest in the Bible. For little ones, using action songs, finger plays, and object lessons with the use of a felt board teaches them that Jesus loves them.

Someone has said, "Our nation and our world go forward or slip backward on the feet of the youth and children of today, and we are responsible for how they go." Why not set their feet toward heaven through the medium of family worship?

Record a time when family worship was special to you and the blessing you felt from it.

_____

_____

Making Family Worships Inspiring

Come, let us worship and bow down; let us kneel before the Lord our Maker. For He is our God, and we are the people of His pasture, and the sheep of His hand. Ps. 95:6, 7, NASB.

Family worship is a time to learn of God and express our love and praise to Him. It is also an opportunity to build relationships within the family. As the family members discuss personal needs and pray for one another during worship, love and understanding develop between them. Such family worship helps to establish and maintain priorities. God becomes the most important thing in their lives, and family togetherness becomes vital as well.

If family members are rarely together, the family unit can begin to deteriorate. A husband went to a Christian counselor and asked in desperation, "What can I do to keep our marriage together?" The counselor suggested that the couple start having family worship. Later the man returned and said, "It works! You know something? We have to make up and ask forgiveness of each other before we can read and pray." They are still thankful for the advice that united their marriage at the family altar.

Since our children are grown and have left the nest, for a number of years one of the first things we do when we awake in the morning is study the Sabbath school lesson together. We discuss the points brought out in the lesson, ask each other questions, make suggestions, and clarify our thoughts. When finished, we read the devotional book selection for that day. Then we read a spread (two pages across from each other) from an Ellen G. White book. Last, we kneel together, and each prays out loud. Our worships together draw our hearts closer to God and to each other.

To make worship time a unique family experience, incorporate creative activities for each age and involve every member of the family. Why not read the New Testament together, with each person who can read having a different version? Discuss and share the differences in the versions. At another time, read a verse for the family to meditate on throughout the day. Each one then shares its meaning in the evening or tells how the verse had an impact on him or her. On another occasion, read a passage together until someone discovers something new that he had not noticed before. Add the new information to your "Something New Notebook." At another worship, after reading one of Jesus' parables, invite the younger children to retell it in their own words. For another worship, read a passage from the Gospels and have family members try to identify the feelings of those in the story as well as their own reaction if they had been there.

Making a list of specific prayer requests and their answers and recording them in a "Miracle Book" increases faith in God's love and power. Implement the creative ideas of your own family members as you worship God together. Let us thank Him for this special time we can spend with our families. Tell how you feel family worship has helped to foster good relationships in your home.

_____

_____

April 17

"Gambleholics"

Why do you spend money for what is not bread, and your wages for what does not satisfy? Isa. 55:2, NASB.

In 1783 George Washington wrote of gambling, "It is the child of avarice, the brother of iniquity, and the father of mischief." We wonder what he would say today if he saw how it has permeated every facet of our society.

Researchers on gambling claim that our country has an estimated 8 million compulsive gamblers. They are literally "gambleholics." But even worse, 1 million of them are teenagers. Experts on the subject claim that the tremendous increase of addictive gambling among teenagers strikes at all economic levels and ethnic groups. One psychologist concludes that students are two and a half times as likely as adults to become problem gamblers.

Why the increase? Nearly every state in the United States permits legal betting. Many promote lotteries to raise operating funds. Perhaps we can trace much of our gambling problems today to the churches with their bingo games. They may have contributed to the creation of a whole new generation of addicted gamblers.

Some years ago a woman who won the lottery in her state started screaming while holding up her rosary. "I held this all the time," she explained. God takes no credit for those who spend money "for what is not bread."

How do we help gamblers or others with an addictive problem? Not by scathing rebukes and condemnation. We must show them something better, even as Jesus did to the woman at the well. Our text has this principle in it.

Always point out in a kindly way that while gambling may be exciting for the moment, its darker side waits to take over.

But even more important, show people that what truly satisfies is the freedom, victory, and peace that Jesus gives to those who fully surrender to Him. True liberty comes only from self-control. And true happiness results only from obedience to God's commandments.

If you do not have a problem with gambling or have escaped from it, why not praise the Lord for this tremendous benefit? If you have friends or relatives who have been trapped by gambling, write their names down and pray for them. Freedom from any vice is a great blessing.

The Solution for Evil

For out of the heart come evil thoughts, murders, adulteries, fornications, thefts, false witness, slanders. Matt. 15:19, NASB.

The striking cover of the June 10, 1991, *Time* magazine consisted of a black background with the word "Evil" in large letters printed in a darker shade of black. In smaller white letters underneath appeared the question "Does it exist—or do bad things just happen?" The essay, written by Lance Morrow, is a masterpiece of confusion based on unanswered questions. It strings together numerous ideas in an almost incoherent manner. Yet unless one really understands the biblically based concept of the cosmic struggle between Christ and Satan, it is quite impossible to come up with a consistent answer to the existence of evil. Even with an understanding of the great controversy, evil is still ultimately unexplainable.

The essay climaxes with a series of questions. One of them asks "Does the good become meaningless in a world without evil?" In other words, Is evil necessary for the human race to understand and appreciate goodness? Is black black only because we have the color white? Unfortunately such circular reasoning does not help us to understand the why of good and evil. One could argue that Jesus is good only when you compare Him to Satan.

Clearly this essay impresses the reader with the growth of evil throughout the world. Few twentieth-century thinkers any longer support the idea of evil decreasing, while good gains momentum.

Our text today reveals where individual evil begins—in the heart. Who tempted the devil? He himself. Each one of us is our own source of evil. And evil is more than an act, as Jesus makes crystal-clear. It is a state of being. Who among us has not had either all or at least some of the evil thoughts Jesus describes. Although evil is a part of the mystery of iniquity, we are not mystified as to its existence.

115

Like evil, goodness also begins in the heart. That is what the new birth is all about. This too is a mystery, but it happens by God's converting power through the Holy Spirit.

Each one of us can be thankful that through God's forgiveness we don't have to get what we deserve. And through His sanctifying power we don't have to be what we are!

The plan of salvation is the only satisfactory answer to the problem of evil. God is in the business of setting us free from both sin's penalty and its power.

Shall we not praise Him for what He has done for us? No, we are not perfect except in Christ, but we can grow in grace daily. We praise Him for this possibility and reality. What evil has He removed from your life?

_____

_____

Start With the Inside!

Woe to you scribes and Pharisees, hypocrites! For you clean the outside of the cup and of the dish, but inside they are full of robbery and self-indulgence. You blind Pharisee, first clean the inside of the cup and of the dish, so that the outside of it may become clean also. Matt. 23:25, 26, NASB.

Can you think of a worse denunciation for us to read at the beginning of a new day? But wait—the good news will come. Most of Matthew 23 exposes the evils of pharisaism. Yet we are thankful to know that our Lord delivered His strong words with tears in His voice (see *Steps to Christ*, p. 12). He was heartbroken over the scribes and Pharisees' attitude and ways. The reason the Holy Spirit guided the Bible writers to record what Jesus said to these spiritual leaders is to help us avoid their mistakes. Today, as far as we know, there is no formal Pharisee organization. But, unfortunately, the spirit of pharisaism is alive and well just the same!

What is Jesus trying to tell us? Study these verses carefully and you will find that He is using a most graphic illustration to teach the absolute necessity of a new-birth experience. Every unconverted person on earth has garbage on the inside of his spiritual cup regardless of how clean the outside looks. (Some unfortunately have garbage both on the inside and outside!) And while some converted individuals, who because of abject poverty or no opportunity to understand God's standards, may look a bit trashy on the outside, they are beautiful on the inside.

The good news is that no matter how rich or poor, educated or uneducated we may be, we all can be born again. When the rich young ruler came to Jesus, the last condition Jesus gave in response to his question of what was necessary for eternal life was unacceptable to him. This led Jesus to remark that it would be easier for a camel to go through the eye of a needle than for a rich man to get into God's kingdom. The disciples, hearing this, threw up their arms in despair and demanded, "Then who can be saved?" (Matt. 19:25, NASB). They were really asking if it was possible for a person's nature to change. Jesus' answer was wonderfully encouraging. He said, "With men this is impossible, but with God all things are possible" (verse 26, NASB).

The Lord converts people from the inside out. He knows if He can have the heart and the mind, a change will come and a reformation will occur. Zechariah's prophetic word may seem difficult from a human standpoint, but it is not impossible in God's eyes: "Behold, I am going to save My people from the land of the east and from the land of the west; and I will bring them back, . . . and they will be My people and I will be their God in truth and righteousness" (Zech. 8:7, 8, NASB).

How good God is! We can never thank Him enough for His converting power. What specific things has it done in your life?

April 20

No Balm in Gilead?

Is there no balm in Gilead? Is there no physician there? Why then has not the health of the daughter of my people been restored? Jer. 8:22, NASB.

Since childhood we have heard and sung the American Negro spiritual "Balm in Gilead." Years later we began to wonder what that balm was. Did people really manufacture some type of special medicine in an area of Palestine known as Gilead? After a little searching we found that the term *Gilead* refers to the region of the Transjordan. Moses just before his death went up to Mount Nebo across the Jordan Valley from Jericho. There the Lord showed him "Gilead as far as Dan" (see Deut. 34:1, NASB).

As for the balm, note that the desert traders to whom Judah and his brothers sold Joseph were Ishmaelites on their way down to Egypt from Gilead. They were "bearing aromatic gum and balm and myrrh" (Gen. 37:25, NASB). The balm was evidently a soothing, healing substance bought for medicinal use. When we lived in Singapore, one could purchase a popular substance known as Tiger Balm. It seemed to help arthritic pains and had made the man who produced it a millionaire.

Jeremiah used the balm of Gilead to teach a deep spiritual lesson as he mourned over the sinful condition of God's people. Although many hated the prophet for predicting the destruction of Jerusalem, yet this man of God identified himself with his people in Jeremiah 8:21: "For the brokenness of the daughter of my people I am broken; I mourn, dismay has taken hold of me" (NASB). Then he asked, "Is there no balm in Gilead? Is there no physician there?" (verse 22, NASB). If there were, why wasn't the church in a healthy condition?

The truth is "there is a balm in Gilead to make the wounded whole; there is a balm in Gilead to heal the sin-sick soul" (*The SDA Hymnal*, No. 475).

Our precious Saviour tenderly waits to heal all those who come to Him for help. He is the great balm maker, the great physician. He has never lost a case among those who have sincerely sought His aid. His balm, with its beautiful aromatic odor, permeates the life of every surrendered Christian, for this balm is Jesus Himself.

Please express thanks to Jesus for healing your wounded spirit, for being available any time, day or night, to touch you with His redemptive medicine of love. What spiritual illnesses has He cured in your life?

April 21

A Way of Escape

No temptation has overtaken you but such as is common to man; and God is faithful, who will not allow you to be tempted beyond what you are able, but with the temptation will provide the way of escape also, that you may be able to endure it. 1 Cor. 10:13, NASB.

Here is a promise that is at first glance hard to believe. After all, temptation to do something wrong afflicts everybody, and some have more problems with it simply because they have more weaknesses to deal with. Several years ago we were told the story of a church-school teacher friend of ours who had an extra portion of temper that he frequently seemed to lose. After he had exploded in anger one day, a fellow teacher attempted to help him recognize his problem. Our friend replied, "My dear brother, with the Lord's help I have overcome more temper than you have ever had to deal with in the first place!"

Ellen White tells us that "many have received as a birthright almost unconquerable tendencies to evil" (*The Adventist Home*, p. 241). But the good news is that "through the plan of redemption, God has provided means for subduing every sinful trait, and resisting every temptation, however strong" (*Selected Messages*, book 1, p. 82).

Do we really believe His promise? The core point in our text is "God is faithful." Dwell on that a moment; repeat it several times. Because you can trust Him, believe with every ounce of willpower you have that He will not allow you to face any temptation beyond what you are able to cope with. He *will* provide a way of escape because He wants to thwart the devil—especially when Satan thinks he has you in a corner. Whatever the temptation—illicit sex, lying, stealing, unkind criticism, laziness, or anything else—the Lord will make a way out for you. However, it requires belief in His faithfulness for Him to be able to rescue you. It may be impossible for you to help someone who thinks that you are powerless to do so—and that applies even to God. He forces no one to accept His aid. You have to believe and be open to His divine help.

As you think about this promise, why not write it out on a small card and carry it with you today? When Satan assaults you with some overwhelming temptation, try to get to a quiet spot where you can be all alone, and then read this text prayerfully. Ask for the Holy Spirit to flood your mind with faith in God's faithfulness to snatch you from the problem. We promise it will happen—you will be delivered!

Praise Him for His faithfulness! Write your praise to Him now by jotting down an instance in which God has provided a way of escape for you.

_____

_____

April 22

"Shipwrecked Upon God"

And call upon me in the day of trouble: I will deliver thee, and thou shalt glorify me. Ps. 50:15.

The title "Shipwrecked Upon God," found in a James Hudson Taylor biography, aptly applies to this founder of the China Inland Mission. What better compliment could any Christian have than that he or she has shipwrecked upon God? God, the rock of ages, wants us to steer our life's boat straight into Him, the stone of salvation, shattering our spiritual self-confidence and complacency.

Just a few weeks after Hudson Taylor married his wife, Maria, in China, she became very ill. He knelt beside her bed, praying with others elsewhere for God to send them a miracle. Faith was the only element he could cling to. Modern medicine was unknown in 1858, and China was far from England. His only help was to trust in God.

Taylor, later writing of his experience, spoke of his "wrestling mightily with God in prayer." He told that "the precious words were brought with power to my soul, 'Call upon me in the day of trouble: I will deliver thee, and thou shalt glorify me.' I was enabled at once to plead them in faith, and the result was deep, deep unspeakable peace and joy." The Lord answered their prayers for Maria. The Great Physician rebuked the enemy death and restored her to full and complete health.

As we read of the answered prayers in Hudson Taylor's life we begin to sense anew the privilege we have of calling upon God. Believing prayer is something we all desperately need in our lives today. We can read of the marvelous answers to prayer in the lives of others, but what about our own personal experience? If we can bring to mind even one answered prayer of our own, it will do us more good than hearing about a hundred prayers answered for someone else.

Let us take God at His word. Believe what He promises in spite of any evidence to the contrary. He may not answer our prayers exactly as we might want Him to, but He declares that He will deliver us and that we shall glorify Him because of that fact.

To cultivate an attitude of praise and thanksgiving is one of the best possible ways to truly glorify Him! Today is the first day of the rest of your life. Why not glorify Him now with a few words of praise and thanksgiving for answered prayer? In fact, jot down briefly a recent answer to one of your prayers. Ask the Lord to open your mind to what He has done in your life, and you will suddenly see His hand in your spiritual experience in ways that you never noticed before.

April 23

Suffering in the Flesh

Therefore, since Christ has suffered in the flesh, arm yourselves also with the same purpose, because he who has suffered in the flesh has ceased from sin. 1 Peter 4:1, NASB.

A dear young friend of ours has given us new insights on living a victorious life. One day while confiding in Bob, he said, "If I lose my soul, it will be over the problem of sexual temptation, and I blame it on my past record. Even though I have had a conversion experience, this does not change my brain's memory bank or wipe out the thoughts of the past."

Sharing his secret of maintaining victory over this or any other overpowering temptation, he stated, "This is one sin that causes me to get on my knees and read the promises of God in order to get the victory. Sometimes it is a terrible struggle. There's nothing compared to it in my life."

Then he pointed out that our text today reveals that Christ suffered in the flesh, not only at Calvary but throughout His entire life, in His own struggle with temptation. It was not easy for our Lord to surrender His will to His Father when temptations poured over Him. Because of our Lord's successful struggle, we should arm ourselves with the same mind as Christ. True, we will agonize at times as we part with our darling sins, but this suffering actually helps us to cease from sin. Such suffering spiritually matures us.

Peter continues his line of thought in 1 Peter 4:2: "So as to live the rest of the time in the flesh no longer for the lusts of men, but for the will of God" (NASB). This two-verse passage indicates that Christ's followers, as they overcome strong temptation, will at times experience pain and sorrow. Yet such suffering does not destroy the joy of the Christian life. Those who know the sweet taste of victory through suffering have the deepest peace and joy possible. The athlete who has struggled to win, the artist who has created beauty despite great difficulty, the person who has triumphed over impossible odds—they know what great joy really is. Pain and challenge enable us to appreciate life in ways that nothing else can.

This quotation greets us each time we open our refrigerator door: "To make it through the day, remember that *nothing* tastes as good as abstinence feels."

Our young friend also quoted Deuteronomy 4:4: "But ye that did cleave unto the Lord your God are alive every one of you this day." He excitedly told us that sometimes he prostrates himself on the floor when he repeats these texts. By clinging to them and to God, he finds victory. "It works!" he declared.

It does work, indeed; praise the Lord! Thank Him for the powerful promises that can give us the joyous victory over temptation. Record a short praise to the Lord or an experience of victory through His promises.

On the Winning Side

What then shall we say to these things? If God is for us, who is against us? He who did not spare His own Son, but delivered Him up for us all, how will He not also with Him freely give us all things? Rom. 8:31, 32, NASB.

The great French Reformer John Calvin often concluded his sermons with "If God be for us, who can be against us?" Calvin's conversion, which he described as "sudden," had one important facet that needs to be emphasized repeatedly. He gave this graphic description of the struggle in his life in a famous letter to a Cardinal Sadolet: "The law which I strove faithfully to obey took hold of my conscience, and convinced me more deeply of sin. I tried absolution, penances, intercessions, but without obtaining relief or peace of mind. As often as I looked into myself or attempted to lift my eyes to Thee, O God, I was filled with a dread which no penances could mitigate. The more narrowly I inspected myself, the deeper did the sting enter into my conscience, so that at last I could find no ease but by steeping my mind in forgetfulness" (in Philip Vollmer, *Life of John Calvin*, p. 12).

Calvin was the victim, along with millions of others, of two horrible delusions. Through the ages many people have looked to God as a tyrant. And the same people think they can win God's love and approval by their works. If God is a tyrant, you will either try to forget Him or wind up hating Him. And if you hate Him but still believe He controls the gates of heaven, you will do everything possible to appease His anger in order to win His friendship only for the purpose of gaining salvation.

Fortunately, Calvin did find the Lord as his personal Saviour through accepting salvation as a free gift. He also discovered the magnificent reality that God is not against us but for us. He is on our side! No matter what happens, remember He is still on our side! That being so, who then, including Satan himself, can possibly do anything against us? The Father spared not His own Son, but delivered Himself up for every one of us. Certainly, then, He will give us everything we need. Paul had had many struggles and reverses in his life, but he had no question about God. He knew from experience that nothing can be against us if God is for us!

You may be facing a great problem in life, but praise Him now for being on your side.

April 25

Buy From Me

I advise you to buy from Me gold refined by fire, that you may become rich, and white garments, that you may clothe yourself, and that the shame of your nakedness may not be revealed; and eyesalve to anoint your eyes, that you may see. Rev. 3:18, NASB.

When we visited Benares, India, the holy city of the Hindus—comparable in many ways to Mecca of the Muslims—we saw the banks of the sacred Ganges River crowded with worshipers who had come to wash away their sins in the muddy water. Funeral pyres flamed and smoked along its shores. The pious Hindu believes that to have his body burned along the river will open the door to salvation. One scene we shall never forget was that of an old man with a cane walking along one of the narrow, winding streets. He was absolutely naked, and blind besides. Someone told us that his blindness resulted from sacrificing his eyes to his god or gods by staring at the sun. His nakedness, wretchedness, and blindness were all in the name of religion.

So with the Laodiceans. While they are devoted to religion, yet they are "wretched and miserable and poor and blind and naked" (Rev. 3:17, NASB). The saddest part about it all is that the Laodiceans do not even realize their horrible condition. The Hindu man in Benares surely knew of his nakedness and blindness, but the Laodiceans don't. But the good news is that the Faithful and True Witness, Jesus, promises to take care of the Laodicean condition—if we will let Him.

First, He offers to sell us gold—faith motivated by love. Such gold will make us supremely wealthy, so that we will never go through life in spiritual poverty. Then He offers us white garments to hide our spiritual nakedness of self-righteousness. Self-righteousness is the greatest possible deception, one

122

that leads people to believe falsely and fatally that their deeds and life will merit God's favor and will give them passage into His kingdom. Then our heavenly merchant displays an eyesalve that when used will restore our sight. Without it we can never discern spiritual things or really understand them.

Now here is the best news yet! All these marvelous commodities are, in fact, free gifts from Him if we will only accept them. They are all ours, "who have no money," to buy "without money and without cost" (Isa. 55:1, NASB). What more can Jesus do for us? He gave us His life, and now He gives us these marvelous gifts. No one can ever blame Him for the loss of anyone!

Bring a written thank offering to our Lord now. Is it too much to ask that we express our praise to Him for such wonderful free gifts of spiritual gold, clothes, and eyesalve? Take just a minute or two to thank Him now for each one.

Positive Thinking

For as he thinketh within himself, so is he. Prov. 23:7, ASV.

A husband once asked his wife, after they had been married a number of years, how she was always able to remain so positive. Her answer amazed him. "I don't always feel happy or positive," she said, "but I choose to be that way anyway."

Ira Hayes, a popular speaker on positive thinking, once said, "Whatever you are asked and no matter how you feel, say 'Everything is *great!*'" This may be going a little too far, but we can take heed to the principle inherent in his message. Our words do have a powerful influence on both ourselves and our listeners. "The words are *more* than an indication of character; they have power to *react* on the character. Men are influenced by their own words. . . . The expression [of them] reacts on the thoughts" (*The Desire of Ages*, p. 323; italics supplied). Furthermore, "they [our words] act still more powerfully upon the characters of others" (*The SDA Bible Commentary*, Ellen G. White Comments, vol. 3, p. 1159). Our thinking powerfully determines who we are. Someone has pointed out that it would be as reasonable to argue that it does not matter which way the rudder swings as it steers a ship as to say that it makes no difference what a man thinks.

Norman Vincent Peale makes a simple yet profound statement: "There are only two ways of looking at anything—positive or negative." At a camp meeting several years ago we met a man whose child had been deprived of oxygen for too long a time during birth, permanently damaging her brain. Though it would have crushed most people, this positive-thinking father testified that the child, now in her 20s, was a great blessing to both him and his wife. One of the most important things she had taught them was what patience really means. When we heard his story, it reminded us of the old saying "I complained that I had no shoes until I met a man who had no feet."

As humans, we do tend to complain about our trials and problems as if life should be easy, but nowhere have we been promised this. M. Scott Peck begins his book *The Road Less Traveled* with the words "Life is difficult" and then points out that when once we are willing to face up to this fact, life becomes easier. Another fact we should remember is that life at times is a mystery and not always understandable. Paul tells us that "we can be full of joy here and now even in our trials and troubles. These very things will give us patient endurance; this in turn will develop a mature character" (Rom. 5:3, 4, Phillips).

A dentist who specializes in treating children entered an orphanage at the early age of 7 when his parents died. Evidently it didn't occur to him to be bitter and to feel sorry for himself. Instead, he was grateful for the love and care given him there. He determined to help other children when he grew to adulthood, largely because of appreciating the help given him when he needed it.

May God grant us the ability to think positively despite the trials that plague us from day to day. Thank God now for the positive people in your life and tell how they have helped you.

April 27

How to Diminish Disappointments

For we have brought nothing into the world, so we cannot take anything out of it either. And if we have food and covering, with these we shall be content. 1 Tim. 6:7, 8, NASB.

We have a plaque hanging in our kitchen of a silky-eared cocker spaniel dog with his nose nuzzled in the grass. His large brown pleading eyes seem to speak of loneliness and the need to have a friend. Underneath are the words "Blessed are those who expect nothing; for they shall not be disappointed."

Marie found this plaque in the basement of a home during an estate sale. Although she saw numerous items that tempted her, the plaque especially caught her attention. The little grieving dog and its caption are quite true to life. Marie happened to be going through a rather disappointing experience at that time, and when she saw the plaque it seemed to bring life into perspective.

Paul is stating a principle in our text today similar to that in our plaque. Whether it be possessions or people, don't expect too much. After all, we arrive on earth with nothing, and we will leave the same way. Have high hopes, but be content with little! Oliver Goldsmith said it well in his poem "The Deserted Village": "His best companions, innocence and health; and his best riches, ignorance of wealth."

Writing to the Philippians, Paul declared, "I have learned to be content in whatever circumstances I am. I know how to get along with humble means, and I also know how to live in prosperity; in any and every circumstance I have learned the secret of being filled and going hungry, both of having abundance and suffering need" (Phil. 4:11, 12, NASB).

The words "content" and "contentment" in Greek have the concept of being self-sufficient. It is not a self-sufficiency based on independence from God, but rather, in the Christian context, a self-sufficiency produced by a relationship with Christ. Our happiness, our contentment, does not depend on human friendships, expectations being met, amusements, alcohol, sexual activities, or anything else that life offers, but rather on a sense of serenity and peacefulness that stems from a close walk with Jesus. Paul knew how to be content even in prison.

Praise the Lord for sharing Himself in a way that brings us peace and contentment regardless of our situation. What has God made you content about in life?

_____

_____

When Terror Loses Its Power

But some days later, Felix arrived with Drusilla, his wife who was a Jewess, and sent for Paul, and heard him speak about faith in Christ Jesus. And as he was discussing righteousness, self-control and the judgment to come, Felix became frightened and said, "Go away for the present, and when I find time, I will summon you." Acts 24:24, 25, NASB.

According to the Roman historian Tacitus, Felix, the Roman procurator of Judea and Samaria, practiced every kind of cruelty and lust, "wielding the power of king with all the instincts of a slave" (see *The SDA Bible Dictionary*, p. 364). His despotic rule and murderous ways, which Paul knew very well, could have caused the apostle to be extremely cautious in his words.

Paul was a prisoner. After an initial hearing, Felix put off a decision about the apostle's fate until a later date. Not too long afterward both Felix and Drusilla summoned him for a private interview to hear "him speak about faith in Christ Jesus."

We have often wondered, Had we been in Paul's place standing before the couple, what approach would we have used in preaching on the subject of salvation? After all, it includes the concept of repentance from sin, a topic that could have caused the despotic and haughty husband and wife to create great trouble for Paul and even to take his life.

We greatly admire the apostle for his forthrightness. He never let fear of man silence him. While we are certain that he preached in a diplomatic way, we are equally sure that he did not fawn over them with praise for their position or cringe because of their power. Paul served as an ambassador of One who was far more important and powerful than Felix and Caesar combined.

He spoke to them on three important subjects. The first was righteousness by faith alone in Christ. The second dealt with the fruitage of salvation: temperance, or self-control. And the third concerned the coming judgment, when all will have their lives opened before God. Paul's sermon reawakened Felix's conscience. The Greek for the word "frightened" in our passage really means "becoming terrified." Felix and Drusilla found themselves deeply concerned over "righteousness," which they did not possess; "self-control," or temperance, which they did not live; and "judgment to come," of which they had no control. The Holy Spirit, speaking through Paul, caused both of them to think seriously about their personal salvation. In the judgment they can never say that they did not have a chance.

Praise and give thanks to the Lord for revealing to you the message of righteousness, temperance, and judgment, which all center in Jesus. We have nothing to be terrified about if we have surrendered our lives fully to the Lord Jesus. Express your thanks to Him for these great doctrines.

Thy Great Compassion

O my God, incline Thine ear and hear! Open Thine eyes and see our desolations and the city which is called by Thy name; for we are not presenting our supplications before Thee on account of any merits of our own, but on account of Thy great compassion. Dan. 9:18, NASB.

Today's verse comes from one of the most marvelous prayers found in the Old Testament, or for that matter, the entire Scriptures. This prayer, Daniel 9:4-19, contains several outstanding elements. For instance, Daniel completely identified himself as a sinner with the rest of God's people. Although he was one of God's most faithful prophets and one that the angel Gabriel described as being "greatly beloved" (verse 23), or "highly esteemed" (NASB), yet he knew himself as a sinful-natured individual always in need of God's grace. It was a wonderful testimony for the angel to describe Daniel as being "greatly beloved." Yet aren't we all "greatly beloved"? That's why Jesus gave Himself for us!

Daniel repeatedly used the words "us" and "we." He counted himself among those who had sinned. We urge you to read and meditate on this entire prayer. It is powerful and must have touched God's heart in a marked manner, for before Daniel had even finished praying, God sent Gabriel in answer to the prophet's request for an explanation of the vision in Daniel 8, which had puzzled him for many years.

In his confession in verse 8 of the prayer, Daniel said, "Open shame belongs to us, O Lord, to our kings, our princes, and our fathers, because we have sinned against Thee" (NASB). Verse 11 states "Indeed all Israel has transgressed Thy law and turned aside, not obeying Thy voice" (NASB). Even catastrophe failed to stop Israel's rebellion: "All this calamity has come on us; yet we have not sought the favor of the Lord our God by turning from our iniquity and giving attention to Thy truth" (verse 13, NASB).

Daniel continually associated himself with God's people, even though he himself had not participated in their rejection of God. His prayer contains a great lesson for us today. Despite all of the church's faults and shortcomings, we are all a part of the body of Christ, His church. The key to Daniel's rich spiritual experience is that while he admitted the failure of God's people, he still identified with them and remained loyal, because he looked to God, not to their faults. Never for a moment would he consider leaving the body of Christ either to live independently or to join some other religious organization.

Daniel was thoroughly acquainted with the concept of righteousness by faith alone in the Lord. Our text today reveals that when he prayed he presented his supplications, not because "of any merits of our own, but on account of Thy great compassion." The prophet knew that nothing good in us or done by us will ever earn His mercy and love!

Do His mercies and compassion compel you to praise Him? He surely deserves to hear you say so in writing.

Look for the Good

When there are many words, transgression is unavoidable, but he who restrains his lips is wise. The tongue of the righteous is as choice silver. Prov. 10:19, 20, NASB.

Early in life Marie became impressed with the importance of never criticizing another person. The husband of one of her family's beloved elderly friends had passed away. Marie and her parents drove over to their home to express sympathy. As Marie stood beside the casket, the wife came up and began reminiscing about her husband. Among the many good things she mentioned about him, one particularly caught Marie's attention: "During all the years we lived together, I never heard my husband say an unkind thing about anybody." Marie instantly thought to herself, *What a wonderful thing to be said about anyone's life!* And she decided it would be a good policy to follow.

But it isn't easy to keep from saying something against someone who has hurt you or someone whom you really do not appreciate. Before you even realize it, you can put him or her down in order to make yourself look good. Without thinking of the devastating results, a person casually criticizes something his or her spouse has said or done or slips into a negative attitude toward the pastor or some other church leader. One of our former General Conference presidents, Robert Pierson, told the story of a new missionary full of zeal and eager to begin his new assignment. The first evening in the new country he listened to a steady stream of criticism of those in the mission field and at the General Conference. Months later he became so discouraged as he reflected on the shortcomings of others that he asked for a permanent return to the homeland, and eventually he left denominational employment and even the church itself. Criticism can gnaw away at the very core of our being until we become hollow and destroyed, just as tiny beetles can topple a mighty tree by boring into its bark and core until it falls to the ground.

Acceptance is a basic human need, and we must learn to accept each other at face value. If we are looking for the bad in someone else, we will surely find it, but if we search for the good, we can find that, too. "If the radiance of His Spirit is reflected from you in a Christlike character, if sympathy, kindness, forbearance, and love are abiding principles in your life, you will be a blessing to all around you. You will not criticize others or manifest a harsh, denunciatory spirit toward them; you will not feel that their ideas must be made to meet your standard" (*Testimonies*, vol. 5, p. 650).

Thank God for His power given you to overcome criticism. And thank Him also for the victory you plan to have today in this part of your spiritual growth.

Prayer Changes Things

And the prayer of faith shall save the sick, and the Lord shall raise him up. James 5:15.

Little Maranda had suffered from convulsions since she was 18 months old. After tests confirmed that she had Rasmussen's encephalitis, doctors told the parents, "It is inoperable. There is nothing we can do." Someone, however, suggested that they contact Dr. John Freeman at Johns Hopkins University Hospital. After studying Maranda's records carefully, Dr. Freeman approached Dr. Ben Carson, a renowned neurosurgeon, about the possibility of his doing surgery on the child.

When Dr. Carson met the family, Maranda was 4 years old. By then she was experiencing up to 100 seizures a day, often only three minutes apart. They originated in the left side of her brain and disrupted the right side of her body to the point that it was virtually useless. After much study, consultation, extensive testing, and prayer, Dr. Ben consented to do the surgery. Counseling with the parents the night before the surgery, he told them, "And now I have a homework assignment for you. I give this to every patient and family member before surgery. Say your prayers. I think that really does help."

Dr. Carson says he always tells parents to pray, because he believes in it himself. "I like to remind them of God's loving presence."

Maranda's brain was inflamed, and bled anywhere an instrument touched it. For eight tedious hours Dr. Ben moved slowly and carefully as the small surgical instrument coaxed tissue away from the vital blood vessels. It was one of the most difficult operations he had ever performed. The operating team had to replace almost twice Maranda's normal blood volume. During the operation Dr. Ben's thoughts turned to God. He later said, "I thanked Him for wisdom, for helping to guide my hands." After removing the left hemisphere of Maranda's brain, he sewed her skull back into place. The "impossible" had been done, but would she ever walk or talk again?

As they wheeled the gurney down the hall, the mother went up to it and bent down and kissed her daughter. Maranda's eyes fluttered open for a second. Then she spoke her first words: "I love you, Mommy and Daddy." Silently Dr. Ben Carson thanked God for restoring life to this beautiful little girl. Today she walks as well.

Thank God for the privilege of prayer. Why not jot down a few short sentences of praise and thanksgiving to God for answered prayers in your life? Better still, record an answered prayer you have experienced.

Trusting in Jesus

The Lord is my rock, and my fortress, and my deliverer; the God of my rock; in him will I trust: he is my shield, and the horn of my salvation, my high tower, and my refuge, my saviour. 2 Sam. 22:2, 3.

David wrote these words after God had rescued him from Saul and his other enemies. David had lived so long among the rocks and hills as a fugitive that he had become used to hiding in inaccessible places.

As David pours out his soul in thanksgiving to God, he uses words gleaned from those familiar surroundings such as "rock," "fortress," "tower," and "refuge." His trust, faith, and confidence in God was as sure as Palestine's rocks and hills, because God was as unchangeable and unmovable as they were. He was confident that God would never fail him no matter what might happen to him. He also knew that in time of need he could flee to God for deliverance from any evil.

David cast his burdens upon the Lord. Unfortunately, too many times with us, we may think that we have given them to Jesus, but we really haven't. We try to carry them ourselves. It is extremely difficult for the human heart to relinquish doubts and fears. Perhaps we do not trust Him to be our Fortress, our Deliverer, our Saviour. "I can do it myself," we reason. "Why should I bother Him?" Thomas à Kempis reminds us, "Put thy full trust in God. Let Him be thy love and dread above all things, and He will answer for thee and will do for thee in all things as shall be most needful and most expedient for thee."

The sick man at the pool of Bethesda knew that he could do nothing of himself. But when Jesus bade him, "Rise, take up thy bed, and walk," he believed. Without questioning or doubting, he sprang to his feet and accepted what Jesus told him to do, and through faith believed and was healed. Notice the progression: "He made the effort, and God gave him the power; he willed to walk, and he did walk" (*The Ministry of Healing*, p. 84).

Being healed of sin isn't as visible. Because spiritual healing is a more gradual process, we often depend upon ourselves instead of God for His healing power in our sinful lives. James McCord states it correctly: "Sin arises out of mistrust. Man is afraid to trust the divine destiny and to accept his limits. The rebellion that follows is a decisive act of repudiation, a trusting of self over against God."

Never forget that Christ is always on our side to help us. "You were spiritually dead through your sins and failures, all the time that you followed this world's ideas of living, and obeyed the evil ruler of the spiritual realm—who is indeed fully operative today in those who disobey God. . . . God, who is rich in mercy, because of the great love he had for us, gave us life together with Christ" (Eph. 2:1-5, Phillips). Believe what Christ can do for us, trust Him, will to serve Him, and then act upon His word.

Let us be filled with praise for such a God and trust Him to give us the power today to be victorious.

Strive to Win

Know ye not that they which run in a race run all, but one receiveth the prize? So run, that ye may obtain. And every man that striveth for the mastery is temperate in all things. Now they do it to obtain a corruptible crown; but we an incorruptible. 1 Cor. 9:24, 25.

Games and sports constituted the most exciting events in the Roman year. History records, for example, that 42 horse races of various types were run on two successive days in the Circus Maximus. Hundreds of thousands of spectators poured into various hippodromes and arenas to watch foot races, boxing, and other sports, some rather gruesome in nature, such as dressing up criminals in animal skins and throwing them to hungry wild beasts.

All of us have heard the story of Androcles, the runaway slave who was captured and forced into an arena with a lion. The lion, remembering that the man had once pulled a thorn from its paw, refused to hurt him. The authorities pardoned Androcles, and he made a living the rest of his life by exhibiting his pet lion.

Paul, well acquainted with the popular culture of his day, uses foot racing as one of his illustrations. Only one person won the prize. In the Christian race of life, all can win, but there are conditions. The apostle said, "Run in such a way that you may obtain it" (1 Cor. 9:24, NKJV). And what does the Christian obtain? A mere garland of flowers that soon fade? Our prize is an imperishable garland of gladness and joy, "for . . . your reward is great in heaven" (Luke 6:23).

To run the race of life to win requires striving for mastery over ourselves. The Greek word for striving is *agonizomai,* from which, as you can readily deduce, we get our English word "agonize." Jesus used the word in a similar context: "Strive to enter by the narrow door; for many, I tell you, will seek to enter and will not be able" (Luke 13:24, NASB).

We must never think of this agonizing or striving as working our way to heaven. Rather it is the struggle to maintain self-control over our entire beings by—and here is the bottom line—unceasingly focusing our eyes on Jesus, the only source of strength that will enable us to strive at all. A runner who wants to win does not look to the right, left, or behind him. His gaze is riveted on the goal. His mind concentrates only on winning the race.

So it is with the Christian who is determined to win in life's race. His goal is Jesus only. We are like David, who wrote, "My soul pants for Thee, O God" (Ps. 42:1, NASB). Once we have this type of experience, the pain and agony of the struggle of the race fades into insignificance. Jesus becomes everything to us, and we realize that He is worth everything as we endure the agony of looking to Him by faith. Tell what Jesus means to you.

All Prophecies
Converge on Jesus

Then I said, "Behold, I come; in the scroll of the book it is written of me." Ps. 40:7, NASB.

From Genesis to Revelation we find tucked away numerous passages pointing to the glory of God revealed in Jesus. The types in the Old Testament are not always obvious, but as we study Scripture we can see the sparkling gems of prophecy focusing on Him. Between the Old and the New Testaments stands the cross, history's supreme event. From Calvary radiate streams of light back to Eden and forward through the rest of the New Testament. Jesus is the key that unlocks both Testaments.

The purpose of types and analogies is to make Jesus real to us. Everything we can learn about Him reveals more fully His love for us. That is why He inspired the 66 books of the Bible. Why do we have four Gospels, since much of the record is repetitious? God gave them to open to us different insights on His Son. Each in a different way enriches our understanding and makes our faith in Jesus stronger and more alive.

Cleopas and his friend were walking with Jesus down the road to Emmaus. They did not understand what had happened to Him until He opened the Scriptures about Himself. Daily study of what the Scriptures have to say about Jesus is indispensable to a rich Christian experience. And a truly healthy experience depends upon knowing Jesus personally.

Our Lord wants to do for us what He did for Cleopas and his friend. But He can't open our eyes spiritually until we study the pages of the Book through which Jesus emerges.

Each one of us needs to more fully appreciate having a Bible, *a written* revelation of our Lord. The people of the ancient Near East did not believe that their gods really communicated with them. While they assumed that the gods were constantly punishing them for violating divine laws, they held that the gods would never reveal what those laws were. The worshiper had to constantly repent of everything he could think of, hoping that he would then stumble on whatever his transgression was. But the Israelite thanked his God for revealing Himself to him. God revealed not only His commands, but also His person and character. That is why we find constant praise of God's law, His revelation to mankind.

Today we have different translations that bring out additional ideas and meanings in the text. But more than new Bible translations, we need a daily new understanding of Jesus and His love for us. We need the power to carefully follow Him and walk as He walked. If the people of the Bible could praise God for the limited revelation they had, how much more should we thank Him for revealing Himself to us through His life and death.

Burning Hearts!

And they said to one another, "Were not our hearts burning within us while He was speaking to us on the road, while He was explaining the Scriptures to us?" Luke 24:32, NASB.

Picture three persons walking together on a narrow, dusty mountainous road from Jerusalem to Emmaus. It was a seven-mile journey and probably took two or three hours, especially since one of them, Jesus, was giving the other two an intensive study of the Old Testament. It is clear that their hearts and minds responded to Jesus' words while He was talking. Of course their hearts burned more after He revealed Himself to them. They were both tremendously excited and shocked when the Holy Spirit opened their eyes and they *recognized Him* as the resurrected Christ, but before this they felt their hearts on fire as Jesus studied prophecy after prophecy and explained Scripture to them.

Luke recorded the incident to prove that Jesus truly was resurrected. But more than this, he wanted his readers to understand that a study of inspired Scripture is the key to faith in Christ.

As Cleopas and his friend walked with Jesus they at first did not realize who He really was. Only after He went through the prophecies with them did they begin to see that Jesus was the Saviour of the world. Faith in Jesus comes from believing the scriptural record in the light of the cross. For more than three years Jesus had tried to teach them the same points that He was now going over with them. But before the cross they had been unable to understand them. Now, as Jesus put passage after passage together, they could understand.

Delighted that someone had explained the Scriptures to them, they gained renewed hope in Jesus. The terrible events of Pilate's judgment hall and Calvary had numbed their minds into terrible disappointment. Now their hearts burned with delight. They felt amazed that they had been so stupid in not grasping the meaning of the Scriptures before then.

Starting with Moses and other prophets, Jesus piled up evidence after evidence that His death and resurrection were actually foretold. While He performed a miracle by vanishing from their sight at suppertime, the greater miracle had taken place in the two men's hearts when they heard and believed the Word.

Jesus still speaks to those who study the Word. How often our hearts have burned within us as we have seen new evidence of God's truth from the Bible. It is an exhilarating experience, and one we continue to have as flashes of truth, like lightning, pierce our hearts when we take the Scriptures and pray for the Holy Spirit to reveal Jesus to us.

Praise God for His Word and His love revealed in the Word.

The Power of the Word

It is written, "Man shall not live on bread alone, but on every word that proceeds out of the mouth of God." Matt. 4:4, NASB.

When Satan attempted to get Christ into the breadmaking business, our Lord quoted a well-known passage from Deuteronomy 8:3. The Old Testament context of the passage referred to Israel's rebellion and subsequent punishment of being forced to wander in a desert land, a "waste howling wilderness." There God attempted to teach His people through Moses and other prophets that His word is even more important than physical food. Both Moses and Jesus knew that Scripture was vital. Our every heartbeat depends on physical nourishment. But if forced to choose between the baker's bread and the bread of life, choose the latter. Jesus did!

Notice that the three statements Jesus used to answer Satan's temptations all came from the book of Deuteronomy. Today we hear and read much *about* the Bible, but what we need to hear *is* the Bible.

The Old Testament was the only Bible Jesus had, but He knew it well. He referred to at least 20 Old Testament characters and quoted from at least 19 different books. Jesus not only believed the Scriptures, but He had inspired the prophets to write them.

The idea that man shall not live by bread alone strengthened Jesus during a critical moment of His life. The world's destiny hung on His response to Satan's temptation. Had Jesus, with His stomach gnawing with hunger pangs, turned those stones into bread, Satan would have conquered. But Christ held appetite power subject to His faith in the power of God's Word—truly "man shall not live on bread alone"!

In a world overflowing with every possible temptation to live the way we want to, we can praise the Lord that we have a Saviour who won His desert victory—a victory that can be ours! Praise the Lord that we do not have to succumb to Satan's teaching, since we have access to that same powerful Word. The "It is written" answer that causes Satan to flee is ours today as much as it was Christ's in His day. Perhaps you have just had a victory over some temptation. If so, jot it down now and rejoice.

Don't Tempt God

Then the devil took Him into the holy city; and he stood Him on the pinnacle of the temple, and said to Him, "If You are the Son of God throw

Yourself down; for it is written, 'He will give His angels charge concerning you; and on their hands they will bear You up, lest You strike Your foot against a stone.' " Jesus said to him, "On the other hand, it is written, 'You shall not tempt the Lord your God.' " Matt. 4:5-7, NASB.

"Every promise in God's Word is ours. 'By every word that proceedeth out of the mouth of God' are we to live. When assailed by temptation, look not to circumstances or to the weakness of self, but to the power of the Word. All its strength is yours" (*The Desire of Ages*, p. 123).

The first two temptations Jesus met in the wilderness cast doubt on His being the Son of God. Satan urged Him to prove that He really was the Son of God by performing a miracle. The devil had used the same deceitful logic with Eve in the garden. There he had questioned God's command forbidding the human pair to eat from the tree of knowledge of good and evil. In effect Satan was saying that God knows how hungry you are and surely would not want you to suffer this way. Now demonstrate that fact.

Every temptation that Satan creates always has as its root not taking God at His word. Satan constantly seeks to create distrust of God and His revelation in Scripture. In the case of Jesus, He knew that He was God's only begotten Son and had no reason to prove it either by turning stones into bread or by throwing Himself off the Temple pinnacle, even if it was apparently a tradition that the Messiah would reveal Himself in that way. At His baptism a voice from heaven had declared Him to be God's beloved Son, and that was sufficient. He believed His Father's word.

So we today are victorious over the evil one when we believe God's Word. We sing " 'Tis so sweet to trust in Jesus, just to take Him at His word; just to rest upon His promise, just to know, 'Thus saith the Lord.' "

Join us in being thankful for the Word made flesh. Also join us in thanking our heavenly Father for the Written Word that we can turn to anytime day or night. Our Father will never fail us no matter what may come our way. It will do you good to express your faith in both the Written Word and the Word made flesh.

God or Possessions?

"All these things will I give You, if You fall down and worship me." Then Jesus said to him, "Begone, Satan! For it is written, 'You shall worship the Lord your God, and serve Him only.' " Matt. 4:9, 10, NASB.

Don't think Satan's final temptation to Christ was easy to overcome. How would you feel, after being weakened by a 40-day fast, if someone offered you the world and its wealth in exchange for simply bowing at the feet of Satan, a creature who still possessed much of his original glory? Millions bow at his feet for much less—a shot of cocaine, a binge on alcohol, another round of sexual immorality, or some other momentary gratification. Others kneel at his feet through lying, murdering, or politicking to gain position and power. But, thankfully, Jesus didn't fall down and worship Satan. Had He done so, you wouldn't be reading this page, and even if you were, it would not do any good.

In His answer Jesus brings to bear the short but powerful first commandment. It is first for a reason. All obedience to God's Word and will rests on the premise of God being supreme. You cannot love God supremely if you do not make Him number one in your life.

Jesus conclusively defeated Satan with His command to depart, because—and here is the key—Scripture reminds us that God alone has exclusive rights for worship from His created beings. Satan knew it to be true from the first moment of his existence. When Satan developed an incurable case of sin, his ego demanded that he serve self, and he seduced the human race into doing the same.

Jesus exhibits the opposite of self-serving. By putting His Father first in His life, His whole objective was to live in order to bless others. When God has first place in our lives, we live for others. The great law of life and happiness is worshiping God supremely and serving others.

Jesus won the battle with Satan. We owe our very lives to Him for His victory. And He stands ready to help us in our own struggles today. Do you want His power in your life now? Let your fainting soul rejoice in our Lord's victory, which is yours by faith. Describe your rejoicing on the following lines:

_____

_____

May 9

A Mother's Love

And the woman conceived and bore a son; and when she saw that he was beautiful, she hid him for three months. But when she could hide him no longer, she got him a wicker basket and covered it over with tar and pitch. Then she put the child into it, and set it among the reeds by the bank of the Nile. Ex. 2:2, 3, NASB.

Moses was fortunate to have Jochebed as his mother. She did everything possible to save him from Pharaoh's decree ordering the destruction of all Hebrew male infants by casting them into the sacred Nile River. Jochebed put her baby in the Nile, but in a safe, comfortable basket, or ark.

A larger ark saved a remnant of the human race under Noah's leadership. Now a miniature one cradled the future leader of God's remnant of Israel held captive in Egypt. Moses is a marvelous symbol of Christ, who came to deliver

His people from the bondage of sin. The influence of his godly mother as she risked her life to save him reveals anew the love of a mother for her children.

In our travels to the former Soviet Union we visited one of the most moving war memorials we have ever seen. Babi Yar is located in the city of Kiev in the Ukraine. The monument itself stands on the edge of a huge grass-covered ditch. It is a memorial to 100,000 people machine-gunned down by Hitler's invading armies. The Nazis then threw the bodies into a large ditch. After the war the Soviets excavated as many bodies as possible and gave them a decent burial. The grass-covered ditch and monument grimly remind us of man's inhumanity to man.

The agony carved on the faces of the metal statue reaches a climax on the face of the figure of a mother at the very top. The woman's hands are cruelly tied behind her. A large lock of hair hangs from the side of her forehead. Her body bends over a baby cradled in her lap. As you look closer, you see her struggling to lower her bared breast to feed her baby in the final moments of life.

We will never be able to erase that vivid scene from our minds. As we think of this mother cast in metal, we always connect it with our Saviour, who died to save us. He bent low over the human race in drinking the cup of death until He finally cried out, "It is finished!" His love surpasses all love, including that of a mother.

Praise His name in a few sentences for His exalted sacrifice.

A Mother Who Did Not Forget

Can a woman forget her nursing child, and have no compassion on the son of her womb? Even these may forget, but I will not forget you. Behold, I have inscribed you on the palms of My hands; Your walls are continually before Me. Isa. 49:15, 16, NASB.

Martina seemed perfectly normal until about the age of 6 months. Then, after she failed to develop as other children did, doctors told her mother, Leola Beck, that the girl had suffered a birth injury. It was June 1991 when we visited Mrs. Beck's immaculate apartment on the campus of Highland Academy in Portland, Tennessee. The mother led us into the bedroom where Martina was. Nearly 56 years old, Martina had never spoken a word or taken a step. Her gnarled fingers lay useless on her chest. Martina looked at us, and she seemed to try to talk. After prayer we had a conversation with Mrs. Beck.

It gripped our hearts as we sensed this mother's loyalty to her bedridden daughter. Mrs. Beck stated that it had never crossed her mind to place her in a home. "I wanted her near me. She is my life, and we enjoy each other in our own way."

One of Mrs. Beck's longtime friends said of her, "She is one in a million." Mrs. Beck gives all the praise and credit to her Lord for the strength and endurance He has given her to care for her Martina.

She is one mother who has not forgotten her child! Unfortunately, some mothers and fathers do abandon their children.

Often we read about a newborn baby found in a garbage can in an alley. Or a helpless child left at someone's doorstep. But there is One who will never forget us, His children! How can our Lord forget us? He endured hardship and suffering for more than three decades before paying the ultimate price. Jesus will never forget His suffering on Calvary. Gethsemane is as vivid in His mind this moment as it was 2,000 years ago. He carries with Him the healed wounds forever. Every time Jesus looks at His own hands, He remembers you and us. We are His blood-bought children.

A mother may forget her nursing child, but never let the thought enter your mind as long as you live that Jesus has forgotten you. Why not express your appreciation for His love for you?

_____

_____

May 11

Judgment by the Saints

And I saw thrones, and they sat upon them, and judgment was given to them. And I saw the souls of those who had been beheaded because of the testimony of Jesus and because of the word of God, and those who had not worshiped the beast or his image, and had not received the mark upon their forehead and upon their hand; and they came to life and reigned with Christ for a thousand years. Rev. 20:4, NASB.

The thrilling event you have just read about takes place at the beginning of the millennium. Picture the redeemed from Eden until the end of time reigning with Christ 1,000 years. Among them will be a great throng of martyrs who lost their lives simply because they followed the testimony and Word of God. Others in this scene endured persecution and ridicule for refusing to worship the beast or his image. It seems that the majority of the saved will have suffered persecution for worshiping the Lamb.

These saints now participate in a judgment role. "Do you not know that the saints will judge the world?" asks the apostle Paul. Then he adds, "Do you not know that we shall judge angels?" (1 Cor. 6:2, 3, NASB). The context for his two questions is the argument that, of all people, Christians should be able to resolve problems in the church among themselves without resorting to secular courts. If, as he says, they are competent to judge the world and even angels, then surely they can now make proper decisions for disputes among church members (see verses 1-7).

The redeemed will judge the cases of lost sinners as well as Satan and his fallen angels. In order for sin never to rise a second time, God's justice must be seen and accepted by not only the saved from earth but the loyal inhabitants of all the universe. "Therefore do not go on passing judgment before the time, but wait until the Lord comes who will both bring to light the things hidden in the darkness and disclose the motives of men's hearts" (1 Cor. 4:5, NASB).

God puts great trust in His people as we play a major part in defending His character not only by our daily lives but through the growth experience that prepares us for the immense responsibility of being "kings and priests to His God" (Rev. 1:10, NKJV). We "will be priests of God and of Christ and will reign with Him for a thousand years" (Rev. 20:6, NASB). When we realize how much the Lord trusts us, it makes us want to rise to the occasion.

We praise our Lord for another chance to make a fresh beginning this day. Even more we thank Him for blotting out our past and for giving us a special assignment of being His priests and kings. What is your response?

May 12

A Chosen Instrument

But Ananias answered, "Lord, I have heard from many about this man, how much harm he did to Thy saints at Jerusalem."... But the Lord said to him, "Go, for he is a chosen instrument of Mine, to bear My name before the Gentiles and kings and the sons of Israel; for I will show him how much he must suffer for My name's sake." Acts 9:13-16, NASB.

If we knew God had specifically selected us before our birth to fulfill a particular role, we would naturally feel excited. And that is exactly what God has done for every person on earth. The problem is that most of us go our own self-determined way. We, however, believe that the Lord has a map for our lives that is just as real as any earthly road map. Will we walk in the paths He has ordained for us?

In the final judgment God will reveal to the lost what could have happened to them had they sought God's plan instead of their own, while the saved, even though they may have taken some detours, will know that God has used them according to His goals.

In the case of Paul, part of his life was a complete departure from God's plan. His murder of Christians under the assumption that he was doing God's will was certainly a terrible detour from God's will. Afterward, though the apostle seemed to be in a continual state of repentance for his past life, he never forgot that Jesus chose him before he chose Jesus. He was a chosen vessel, but one that displayed "the surpassing greatness of the power" that came from God and not himself (2 Cor. 4:7, NASB). So it should be with us!

Paul, writing to Timothy, stated, "Therefore, if a man cleanses himself from these things, he will be a vessel for honor, sanctified, useful to the Master, prepared for every good work" (2 Tim. 2:21, NASB). As His chosen vessels, we must also be clean, undefiled ones that God can use for His purposes.

We will make little spiritual progress unless we have a deepening awareness of God's guidance in our lives. His will must manifest itself in our will. If you are tempted to be discouraged, remember Paul, of whom Christ said, "I will show him how much he must suffer for My name's sake." Following God's plan for your life is not necessarily a walk through a thornless rose garden, but it is a journey with a sure destination.

We thank the Lord for knowing us and praise Him that He has mapped out a plan for our lives before we were born. How about thanking Him for this assurance in your life?

_____

_____

May 13

Fearfully and Wonderfully Made

My frame was not hidden from Thee, when I was made in secret, and skillfully wrought in the depths of the earth. Thine eyes have seen my unformed substance; and in Thy book they were all written, the days that were ordained for me, when as yet there was not one of them. Ps. 139:15, 16, NASB.

These sublime thoughts reveal the magnificent truth that a personal, self-existing Lord brought us into existence. God—through Christ and the Holy Spirit—with love and concern, created man and woman, masterpieces of design and function. Sin has effaced the perfection of our creation to a great extent, but we can still sense the fantastic arrangement of our original state in the delicate and intricate design of our bodies. What greater motivation can there be to cause us, His children, to constantly cast ourselves at His feet in adoration and love? Furthermore, this passage should compel us to search with determination for God's will for our lives that we may accomplish all that He desires for us.

David knew very well how wonderfully God had made him. His ability to skillfully use a slingshot, play a harp, write psalms of confession and praise, accumulate wealth, and fearlessly map out and execute battle plans all testify to the truth that God had a plan for his life. God had in His mind goals for every day of David's life, even "when as yet there was not one of them."

The murder of Uriah and adultery with Bathsheba reveal that for a time David departed from God's plan for his life. Although he repented of his crimes, they still brought suffering to his family and nation. But in spite of David's detours in life, he ended up at God's intended destination. And regardless of your own deviations from the route God has mapped out for you, you can start this day and make it the best one yet. Believe, as David did, that God's eyes saw your "unformed substance" before birth. Believe that the Lord has a record of this day and the rest of your life written in His book. Take God's hand now and permit Him to lead you in the direction that He knows is best for you. You may not be able to understand why things happen the way they do, but you can trust that He really does know best. Someday He will open the book of plans for your life and make everything plain.

We love our Saviour and testify to His goodness in leading us thus far in our lives. The future is His, and we praise Him for adding honey to the dregs we taste in our cups at times. Do you want to join with us in praising Him?

Check Stubs and You

Do not lay up for yourselves treasures upon earth, where moth and rust destroy, and where thieves break in and steal. But lay up for yourselves treasures in heaven, where neither moth nor rust destroys, and where thieves do not break in or steal; for where your treasure is, there will your heart be also. Matt. 6:19-21, NASB.

One of the leading members of the millionaire's club is the sultan of Brunei, who rules over a little spot of oil-rich earth carved out of the large island of Borneo. He has often been listed as the richest man on earth, with around $50 billion in assets. A few years ago Bob visited his country, and as he saw his palace in the distance he wondered how the sultan's account stood in heaven.

At church dedications Bob likes to use a particular illustration. He asks the congregation if they have made any investment in their new home church. Most of the members usually respond with uplifted hands. Then he points out that what they put into the structure in terms of dollars and cents could actually be translated into various amounts of physical property if someone took the time to figure it out. Parts or all of various items such as the carpet, pews, plasterboard, mortar, paving, and windows could be assigned to the members in proportion to the amount of dollars they donated. Then Bob points out that the building is a part of their entire being. This means that a part of Brother and Sister X went for this much of the carpet or for a certain section of the wall. Our money not only represents us; it is *us* in a very real sense! We invested our life's energy, our heartbeats, our minds, in the money-making process.

Jesus, the righteous judge, could judge many people simply by their check stubs, bank statements, and credit-card invoices. As He looks at their financial records He can easily see what they valued in life. A certain amount of *us* went for food, clothes, home, cars, books, tithe, barbers or beauty parlors, offerings, travel, ice cream. When we go through our records at income tax time, it often amazes *us* to see where *we* went during that year. Our hard-earned money represents us! It is quite a challenge to think of our possessions in this way.

Remember the ancient story of the penurious wealthy person who got to heaven and tried to locate his mansion? An angel led him past glorious castles and mansions until finally they stopped in front of a tiny cottage. The rich man was offended when the angel informed him that this was his eternal abode.

"Why is my place so small when others have lovely, spacious homes?" he demanded.

Replied the angel, "Well, we did our very best with what treasure you sent us."

Have you ever put in words your thanks to God for the privilege you have of transferring part of your possessions from earth to heaven through faithful giving of tithe and offerings? Do it now.

May 15

No Spot or Wrinkles

Husbands, love your wives, just as Christ also loved the church and gave Himself up for her; that He might sanctify her, having cleansed her by the washing of water with the word, that He might present to Himself the church in all her glory, having no spot or wrinkle or any such thing; but that she should be holy and blameless. Eph. 5:25-27, NASB.

Endless discussions have centered around the nature of the church. Is the church visible, invisible, or both? Both the Old and New Testament Scriptures clearly indicate that there is a visible church. The word "church" in New Testament Greek means "called out," signifying a group of individuals who have certain beliefs in common that are different from those of the world and even other religious organizations. In the early New Testament times the "called out" concept applied to those who left the world and were united by a common confession of Jesus as Lord. They made a distinct category in Roman society.

Jesus started the New Testament church only after the Old Testament church had refused to acknowledge Him as the Messiah. Christ had to bypass self-righteous Jewish authorities and choose mainly uneducated, humble fishermen to lead a church that He desired to become world renowned for "having no spot or wrinkle or any such thing." To do that He poured out the Holy Spirit on them at Pentecost, empowering them to effectively preach the gospel in all the world.

The power and growth of the church were never to depend on human genius or wisdom but on the Holy Spirit. Those who would join the church were to be a new humanity united in fundamental beliefs and with Christ crucified at the heart of all doctrine. Gifts given by the Holy Spirit to individuals would help equip them "to the building up of the body of Christ; until we all attain to the unity of faith, and of the knowledge of the Son of God" (Eph. 4:12, 13, NASB).

It is a sacred privilege to become a part of Christ's body, His church. Yet all who belong to His visible body may not, because of being unconverted, belong to His invisible body. Membership in the visible church does not guarantee membership in the invisible. But we believe that membership in both is of utmost importance.

The church has its spots and wrinkles, but Christ still loves it. He gave Himself for it, and He wants to present us, His church, to Himself in all its glory.

Thank the Lord for the marvelous privilege of being a part of Christ's church, a worldwide movement that has as its objective to carry the good news of salvation to every nation and tribe on the globe. If you appreciate this privilege, please express your thankfulness in a few words of praise.

Born for a Purpose

Now the word of the Lord came to me saying, "Before I formed you in the womb I knew you, and before you were born I consecrated you; I have appointed you a prophet to the nations." Jer. 1:4, 5, NASB.

Did Jeremiah's experience apply only to him? Actually it illustrates God's design for all His children. Since this is the case, then the person who longs for security will find this text a valuable insurance policy. So powerful and wonderful was the concept of God's plan for Jeremiah's life that the prophet introduces his book with it. Whether in a mud pit or smashing pottery as a visual aid, Jeremiah's mind was constantly undergirded by the thought *I have been selected by God for a specific purpose and work.* At times his sense of calling was the only thing that kept him going.

You can't break a person who tenaciously holds to the conviction "I am here for a reason, I have a work to perform given to me by divine appointment, and by God's grace I will do my best to honor His investment in my life." Jeremiah could easily have doubted his appointment. When he stood unflinchingly in proclaiming the devastating prediction of Jerusalem's collapse, his family turned against him even to the point of wanting to kill him. In fact, the whole nation eventually rejected him. He worked under the most distressing circumstances. His spiritual anguish over God's people was unparalleled. Despite all of his appeals, it appeared unthinkable that God's people would ever repent. But he knew God had planned his life and work.

Because God forbid Jeremiah to marry and have children, from a human standpoint he went through life a lonely man. Once he complained, "O Lord, Thou hast deceived me and I was deceived; Thou hast overcome me and prevailed. I have become a laughingstock all day long; everyone mocks me" (Jer. 20:7, NASB). In fact, he became so distressed at one point that he decided not to speak anymore in God's name. But it was impossible for him to keep his mouth shut when he knew that God had a plan for his life. The Word of God, like a fire in his bones, burst into ever more powerful sermons.

All of us have been in God's mind before we were born. That includes the little mother of five children living in poverty. It means the person born with a clubfoot as well as the individual with an IQ of a genius. Whoever we are, wherever we are, the Lord has a plan for us. Hold fast to that fact. When times get rough and life seems futile, remember you cannot defeat the Lord. He is with you to make your mark for good on this earth.

Won't you praise Him for the plan He has for you now?

Two Determining Truths

You were the anointed cherub who covers, and I placed you there. You were on the holy mountain of God; You walked in the midst of the stones of fire. You were blameless in your ways from the day you were created, until unrighteousness was found in you. Eze. 28:14, 15, NASB.

The "anointed cherub who covers" is none other than Lucifer, the pinnacle of all of God's creative acts. Ezekiel refers to God's ultimate masterpiece of creation as the seal, or the summit, of "perfection, full of wisdom and perfect in beauty" (Eze. 29:12, NASB). Next to the death of God's Son on the cross, Lucifer's defiance that led to war in heaven was the greatest crisis and heartbreak God ever experienced. A valuable truth we have discovered in the Word, and one that every follower of Jesus needs to find, is that life and God's plan for our lives are not by accident. God emphatically declared to Lucifer that He, first of all, had brought him into existence and second, had appointed him the definite responsibility of being the angel who should stand by His throne. A refusal to abide by these two determining truths gradually transformed Lucifer into Satan.

All through history the deceiver, through every conceivable means, has dulled, blunted, and calloused mankind's perceptions to the point where the majority of people grope blindly through life until the grave mercifully ends their meaningless existence. They do not know where they came from and what they are here for.

God had a purpose and plan for our lives before we ever came into existence. That fact should give us the greatest possible sense of certainty and security in our lives. If God has a goal for our lives, He will never permit anything to happen to us that He has not foreknown and made allowance for in His plan. This thought will carry us through many a disappointment.

All of us have had difficulties and conflicts that have plunged us into the iron cage of despair, and all of us will sit behind those bars some more. But as our faith in Christ helps us to crawl out of these brief dungeonlike experiences, we can grasp anew our Lord's love for us.

We thank our Lord for helping us bear our burdens, for we can't carry them alone. Every day we give Him our heartfelt gratitude for His protection and power in our lives. How would you express your thanks to Him for giving meaning and purpose in your life?

_____

_____

Where Do Wars Begin?

What causes wars, and what causes fightings among you? Is it not your passions that are at war in your members? You desire and do not have; so you kill. And you covet and cannot obtain; so you fight and wage war. James 4:1, 2, RSV.

James speaks of the internal conflict that rages within the human heart as well as war in the family, community, church, or world. He also shows that wars start with greed, covetousness, criticism, and selfishness. Such internal struggles will never end until the eradication of sin and sinners. They began when the seeds of sin took root in the hearts of Adam and Eve. Psychiatrist William Menninger stated correctly, "Wars begin in the minds of men. We should quickly add that this refers to your mind and my mind. We therefore need to recognize more clearly the evidences of hate in our own relationships—selfishness and resentment and prejudices and jealousy and bigotry—with the intent of more effectively controlling and reducing them."

Whether it be a global conflagration or a bitter heart war, hate is the basic ingredient of every conflict. Hate lies at the core of crime and murder. It often leads to suicide, which usually results from hating one's self.

The remedy for war and hate must begin in the individual heart. James appeals to us to "submit therefore to God. Resist the devil and he will flee from you." He also speaks of the indwelling of the Holy Spirit that alone enables us to overcome hatred in all forms. Although the Lord is "opposed to the proud," He "gives grace to the humble." James invites us to "draw near to God and He will draw near to" us (verses 5-8, NASB).

Temperaments differ with individuals. But regardless of hereditary and cultivated wrong tendencies, God has a power that is available to all of us if we "fight the good fight of faith" (1 Tim. 6:12). What assurance do we have of receiving help from Jesus? "God longs to breathe into prostrate humanity the breath of life. And He will not permit any soul to be disappointed who is sincere in his longing for something higher and nobler than anything the world can offer. Constantly He is sending His angels to those who, while surrounded by circumstances the most discouraging, pray in faith for some power higher than themselves to take possession of them and bring deliverance and peace" (*Prophets and Kings*, pp. 377, 378).

Surrendering self to God becomes easier the more we bow in prayer, the more we study His promises, and the more often we relinquish our will to His will. The art of surrendering to Jesus finally becomes natural and habitual (though never permanent in the sense that we no longer need to keep praying, trusting, and surrendering to Him).

The experiment of life is a grand challenge. The battle never stops, nor do our victories over self ever cease as long as we practice surrendering to Him. Aren't you thrilled over the fact that our Lord stands by to help us in every step in life? Then tell Him so.

Jesus Was No Myth

Because He has fixed a day in which He will judge the world in righteousness through a Man whom He has appointed, having furnished proof to all men by raising Him from the dead. Acts 17:31, NASB.

It was not until the eighteenth century that some scholars began to raise the possibility that Jesus never lived. Even Voltaire, who believed God to be a vague, impersonal being with little concern for the human race, found himself shocked by the idea. "Higher criticism," as it was called, soon mounted an attack on the authenticity of the Scriptures and the Christian faith that has never stopped. Some scholars wrote books that attempted to prove that Jesus was a myth.

What valid secular historical sources do we have that demonstrate the existence of Jesus? The earliest non-Christian reference to Jesus appears in the works of Flavius Josephus, a Jew who became a historian of his people. In Book XVIII of his *Antiquities of the Jews*, written before the end of the first century, we find a controversial passage that states, "At that time lived Jesus, a holy man, if man he may be called, for he performed wonderful works, and taught men, and joyfully received the truth. And he was followed by many Jews and many Greeks. He was the Messiah." While later Christian scribes may have embellished it, most scholars recognize that Josephus wrote at least its core.

Another early mention of Christ and Christianity appears in a letter sent about A.D. 110 by Pliny the Younger, asking advice of the Roman emperor Trajan on how he should deal with Christians. A few other early references to Christians by Tacitus and the largely unknown Mara bar Serapion, as well as early rabbinical traditions, help establish the authenticity of Jesus Christ and His founding of the Christian faith.

The New Testament is the greatest historical source of evidence for the existence of our Lord. Naturally, all true Christians accept the reality of Jesus based on Scripture. One great Russian-born Jewish scholar, Joseph Klausner, said, "If we had ancient sources like those in the Gospels for the history of Alexander or Caesar, we should not cast any doubt upon them whatsoever" (in Will Durant, *Caesar and Christ*, p. 557).

Even though we have only a few secular historical sources testifying to Christ's existence, there are other strong evidences. Can anyone deny that the most fascinating event in Western civilization is the life, character, work, and teaching of Jesus? Even most of the world's calendars date back to Him. No man in history has ever influenced literature, art, music, doctrine, and philosophy as much as Jesus has.

If you wiped out every particle of influence Jesus has had on the human race, you would find a massive vacuum in the minds and books of the human race. But praise God He is our resurrected Lord, and is alive and well today!

The supreme evidence of His existence occurs in what happens in the believer's heart. Jesus changes our hearts, making transformations that would otherwise be impossible. Isn't your heart filled to overflowing with the satisfaction He has brought to your life? Please describe how He is real in your life.

_____

_____

The Art of Fleeing

Flee immorality. Flee from idolatry. Flee from these things. Flee from youthful lusts. 1 Cor. 6:18, NASB; 10:14; 1 Tim. 6:11, NASB; 2 Tim. 2:22, NASB.

The apostle Paul knew that the only safe course to follow in overcoming temptation is to quickly decide against it. He uses the word "flee" four times, more than any other New Testament writer. Since the word means "to run away," Paul is saying, "Don't linger around, contemplating the advantages of the enticement, but vanish; instantly shut the door in Satan's face." Doing so will prevent Satan from having easy access to us. Also the word "flee" means "to escape." When someone tries to escape from prison or from harm's way, he does not move sluggishly. Temptation will be greatly weakened, and in many cases completely thwarted, if we act swiftly and decisively. To think about the temptation, to examine it from many angles, will almost inevitably place us on a disaster course.

Youthful Joseph set us an example in how to deal with temptation. He was a slave in a country flooded with idolatry and immorality. Everything that he saw was designed to divert him from worshiping the God of simplicity, purity, and truth. His decisiveness against sin appears in his reaction to the attempted seduction by Potiphar's wife. The record states that when she caught him, he "left his garment in her hand, and fled" (Gen. 39:12). Joseph fled from immorality. Again we see the importance of making a swift decision when faced with temptation.

The principle of fleeing evil applies to all avenues of life. Television advertisements and programs are extremely seductive. So many programs, even talk shows, are laced with subtle and not-so-subtle impure materials and scenes—scenes that play an important part in undermining society's moral foundation. The safe way to handle such programs is to avoid them. The command of Paul to flee immorality involves not only immoral acts but immoral thoughts, sights, and sounds.

When escaping temptation, we cannot flee from something to nothing. We must have a destination. After admonishing young Timothy to flee from youthful lusts, Paul adds "pursue righteousness, faith, love and peace" (2 Tim. 2:22, NASB).

We should praise the Lord that we can flee from evil to good, from Satan's seductions to Christ's allurements. Thank Him who will not lead us into temptation but will always deliver us from evil. We serve One who has promised never to allow us to be tempted above what we are able to bear. Thank Him now for some temptation you have overcome by faith or that you know that He will give you the victory over.

"It's the Word of a Gentleman"

All authority has been given to Me in heaven and on earth. Go therefore and make disciples of all the nations, baptizing them in the

name of the Father and the Son and the Holy Spirit, teaching them to observe all that I commanded you; and lo, I am with you always, even to the end of the age. Matt. 28:18-20, NASB.

David Livingstone, the Scottish missionary and explorer, was converted at the age of 17 and dedicated his life to spreading the gospel in Africa. He is honored not only as a missionary but as a writer, poet, linguist, scientist, doctor, and geographer. With all his talents one could call him a modern Moses.

His astonishing drive led to one of the greatest journeys of exploration ever made by one man. But above and beyond his accomplishments is his outstanding faith in God's leading in his life.

In 1856 as he traveled through the hostile territory of the native chief, Mburuma, the African leader tried to arouse the countryside against Livingstone's expedition. One night before crossing a river Livingstone pitched his camp. His guides brought him reports that Mburuma's men were creeping toward them. As usual, he studied his Bible and wrote in his journal alone in his tent.

His journal entry states: "January 14, 1856. Evening. Felt much turmoil of spirit in view of having all my plans for the welfare of this great region and teeming population knocked on the head by savages tomorrow. But I read that Jesus came and said: 'All power is given unto me in heaven and in earth. Go ye therefore, and teach all nations . . . and lo, I am with you alway, even unto the end of the world.' It's the word of a Gentleman of the most sacred and strictest honour, so there's an end on it! I will not cross furtively by night as intended" (in Catherine Marshall, *Adventures in Prayer*, p. 84).

The next day Livingstone took charge of his company of 114 men with their oxen and led them across the river while Mburuma and his warriors watched from the edge of the jungle. It is said that one of his men pleaded with him not to be the last to cross, for fear that the Africans would shoot him in the back. He replied, "Tell him to observe that I am not afraid." Then Livingstone walked over to Mburuma and his men, thanked them, and wished them God's peace. Then he returned to his canoe. His entire group crossed safely without incident.

This kind of trust in God is what we need today in our own lives. Thank Him in advance for creating a fearless faith in your own heart.

_____

_____

Know Yourself

Pay close attention to yourself and to your teaching; persevere in these things; for as you do this you will insure salvation both for yourself and for those who hear you. 1 Tim. 4:16, NASB.

Scripture admonishes us to examine ourselves carefully not only to ascertain whether our lives harmonize with God's will but also to discover how we may better please Him. The way to do that is through study of God's Word. Too often we come to the Bible with preprogrammed beliefs and limit our study to confirming those beliefs. Some search the Word for proof that some brother or sister in the church is wrong. The only safe and profitable way to approach the Bible is to let God speak to us personally through it. It is in this way that we can "pay close attention" to ourselves. The self-knowledge revealed in the mirror of Scripture is powerful. The Chinese philosopher Lao-Tzu said, "He who knows others is clever, but he who knows himself is enlightened."

Someone has said, "It's not the parts of the Bible I don't understand that bother me—it's the parts I do." The Word, sharp as a two-edged sword, cuts into our complacency and our conformity to worldly standards. The Spirit through the Word challenges us to live in a more powerful relationship with Jesus. It is in this sense that we are to examine ourselves—to know ourselves.

The world of counseling and psychiatry has as one of its major objectives to help people understand themselves. However, we agree with Dr. William Menninger, who, before his death in 1966, as one of the national spokesmen for the vital cause of mental health, stated, "I've never felt that psychiatry, which is my specialty, can save the world all by itself. It presents no patent pill for ending war or meeting the threat of the atomic bomb—or even for getting children to stop biting their nails. Psychiatry, however, does help one understand himself better, and it helps us understand other people."

Paul speaks of knowing yourself in order to ensure salvation for yourself and those to whom you witness. Writing to the Corinthians, he added, "Test yourselves to see if you are in the faith; examine yourselves! Or do you not recognize this about yourselves, that Jesus Christ is in you—unless indeed you fail the test?" (2 Cor. 13:5, NASB). We need to understand both our strong and our weak points. Only then can we intelligently maneuver through life—guided by the Holy Spirit—in a way that will outwit Satan and please our Lord.

Examining yourself can produce nothing more exhilarating than to confirm that you have a good relationship with Jesus. The more you praise Him for this privilege, the stronger your relationship becomes. Praise God for the fruit of faith becoming more apparent in your daily life!

"If I Perish, I Perish"

Then Mordecai told them to reply to Esther, "Do not imagine that you in the king's palace can escape any more than all the Jews. For if you remain silent at this time, relief and deliverance will arise for the Jews from another place and you and your father's house will perish. And who knows whether you have not attained royalty for such a time as this?" Esther 4:13, 14, NASB.

The decree had gone forth to kill the Jews scattered throughout the Medo-Persian kingdom. Under the reigns of Cyrus and Darius, God in His mercy had provided an opportunity for the Jews to return to their homeland, but many voluntarily remained in the land of their exile. Now they faced destruction.

Queen Esther and her cousin, Mordecai, made a most difficult decision to appeal to King Ahasuerus to save their people. They realized that once the king had issued a decree, nothing could revoke it. Mordecai, after reminding Esther that her people's fate would be hers as well, concluded, "Who knows whether you have not attained royalty for such a time as this?"

Esther instructed him to summon all the Jews in Shushan to join her and her maidens in fasting and prayer. She had decided to risk her life by illegally appearing before the king. "If I perish, I perish," she said. Her courage and faith undoubtedly stemmed from her early life when Mordecai had taught her the faith of her people. Her life had its focus on God instead of self. She made the decision to sacrifice her life if necessary for the sake of her people. Esther's belief that God had a plan for her life compelled her to let Him use her in fulfilling it.

God had a plan for each of us even before we were conceived. Do you believe He has led you just where you are now in order to do a work for Him, perhaps even "for such a time as this"? You can choose to be disgruntled, critical, and fearful, *or* you can confidently and joyfully accomplish great things for God.

Esther, by following God's leading, brought salvation to her people. The king proclaimed a counter-decree that allowed the Jews to defend themselves. The record states, "No one could stand before them, for the dread of them had fallen on all the peoples" (Esther 9:2, NASB). Their marvelous victory resulted in the establishment of the festival of thanksgiving known as Purim, which Jews still celebrate today.

God may not have used us to dramatically deliver an entire nation, but any victory we have had is an occasion for a thanksgiving celebration. Mark down briefly how God has led you victoriously through some experience or how He has recently worked through you to bring relief to someone in great need.

Sweet Unreasonableness

The kingdom of heaven may be compared to a king, who gave a wedding feast for his son. Matt. 22:2, NASB.

Our parable begins with a special invitation to a royal wedding feast. But the invited guests refused to come, a terrible insult to the king. We recall seeing on television the tremendous pomp and ceremony accompanying the wedding of one of England's royal family. Can you imagine anyone rejecting a special invitation to a royal wedding? But the king in our parable, although insulted, had a great heart of love, so he issued another invitation. This time he made the invitation in greater and more specific detail. "Tell those who have been invited, 'Behold, I have prepared my dinner; my oxen and my fattened livestock are all butchered and everything is ready; come to the wedding feast'" (Matt. 22:4, NASB). Who in his right mind would even think of turning it down?

Yet the response in our parable is unbelievable. Some insulted the king again by ignoring the whole affair and going about business as usual. Far worse, the rest seized the king's servants and mistreated and even murdered them. Enough was enough! This time the king sent his armies, executed the murderers, and set the city on fire. The third invitation now went out, not to any special group, but to everyone—high and low, rich and poor, learned and ignorant. The king invited good and bad people alike. The result? Guests filled the banquet hall.

Now for the explanation. The king in our parable represents God the Father, who sent His beloved Son to earth. The feast was in His honor. The first invitation to the wedding feast took place before Calvary and went to God's people, the Jews, through John the Baptist and Jesus Himself. But "they were unwilling to come" (verse 3, NASB). Our Lord's sad commentary on them was "O Jerusalem, Jerusalem. . . . How often I wanted to gather your children together, the way a hen gathers her chicks under her wings, and you were unwilling" (Matt. 23:37, NASB).

The second invitation represents the gospel carried by the apostles and others to the lost sheep of Israel after the Resurrection. But they mistreated and killed the Christians instead of accepting God's gracious invitation to the gospel feast. The third and final invitation went to everyone—Jews and Gentiles. We are living today in its time.

As we have studied these parables of heartache, we marvel at God's love for us! From a human viewpoint His longsuffering is unreasonable—but what sweet unreasonableness! Tell how you respond to such love.

The Royal Wedding Clothes

But when the king came in to look over the dinner guests, he saw there a man not dressed in wedding clothes, and he said to him, "Friend, how did you come in here without wedding clothes?" And he was speechless. Matt. 22:11, 12, NASB.

The climax of the wedding feast parable involves a wedding garment that "opens before us a lesson of the highest consequence" (*Christ's Object Lessons*, p. 307). As the curtain rises on the third and final invitation to the wedding feast, we witness a rather motley crowd of people seated at the beautifully prepared banquet table. Their backgrounds are varied—some wealthy, some educated, but most of them are simple, down-to-earth individuals who gladly accepted the banquet invitation. Everyone is exuberantly joyful.

Suddenly a most embarrassing incident interrupts the scene. The king comes "in to look over the dinner guests." As his royal eyes sweep over the vast throng, he examines the dress of each person. Finally his eyes rest on one individual who conspicuously stands out from all the rest because he has an obviously inferior garment that is most unacceptable to the king, especially on this important occasion. This person figured that his own clothes, made by his own hands, were better than the ones the king supplied. Some commentators tell us that ancient Oriental custom for wedding banquets included the provision of wedding garments as a gift for the guests. You can imagine the king's surprise when he saw one whom he addressed as "friend" present at the banquet without the clothes the host had provided for him—clearly another insult to the king.

The king's inspection to see who is and who is not clothed in the king's garments represents the work of judgment prior to Jesus' second coming. The garment depicts Christ's righteousness, or the putting on of Christ. Paul declares that those who have been baptized into Christ have clothed themselves with Christ (see Gal. 3:27).

When we are clothed with Jesus, we wear His white raiment—His righteousness—which covers our nakedness. This robe, woven by the bloodstained hands of Christ, symbolizes both the justifying righteousness of Christ and His sanctifying holiness. Spend a moment praising Him for His gift of a wedding garment to wear to His banquet. Praise Him for not having to wear your own self-designed, trendy, but unacceptable, garments of self-righteousness to His feast.

"A Long Time"

For this reason you be ready too; for the Son of Man is coming at an hour when you do not think He will. Matt. 24:44, NASB.

Some in our church are perplexed about the prophetic timing of our Lord's return. Is He coming soon, or will there be a longer delay? Some feel that the Lord intended to return shortly after His ascension in the first century. If He did not come then, how do we know that He will now? But our study of Christ's parables and teachings suggests that He did not have in mind an immediate return after His resurrection.

In one of our Lord's illustrations He refers to a "faithful and sensible slave" (Matt. 24:45, NASB) in charge of cooking for the household. While the master was away the slave had orders to provide food at the proper time for the household. The master said the servant would receive a blessing if he was doing his duties in the kitchen when he returned.

In contrast, Jesus then refers to a servant who was evil because he was not at his post when the master got back. In fact, he was persecuting his fellow slaves, thinking in his heart, *My master is not coming for a long time* (verse 48, NASB). Could it be that our Lord was trying to teach us that there just might be "a long time" before He returns? We recognize that the main thrust of this story is for us always to be ready for His return, whether it be a distant or a short time off. But the fact is it has been "a long time" since Jesus bade His disciples farewell on Olivet's hillside nearly 2,000 years ago.

In the parable of the talents, after each person received "according to his own ability" a certain number of them, Jesus pointed out that "now after a long time the master of those slaves came and settled accounts with them" (Matt. 25:15, 19, NASB). Again Jesus mentions a "long time" before the master returns.

Peter, describing certain conditions in the last days, speaks of mockers "following after their own lusts, and saying, 'Where is the promise of His coming? For ever since the fathers fell asleep, all continues just as it was from the beginning of creation' " (2 Peter 3:3, 4, NASB). Why would Peter under inspiration write such a thing if the coming of Jesus was imminent in his day?

Delay or no delay, our Lord will return. That is certain. Christ's parables do suggest that the idea of "a long time" must have been in His thinking. But the timing of Christ's return is secondary to the question of whether we are ready to meet Him.

If you would like to thank Him for the surety of His return, write out a statement of praise.

Nothing More Important

So Christ also, having been offered once to bear the sins of many, shall appear a second time for salvation without reference to sin, to those who eagerly await Him. Heb. 9:28, NASB.

Which is more important: the birth, death, resurrection, or second coming of Jesus? That's like asking whether your heart or your brain is more vital. They are all important. No birth of Christ, no death; no death, no resurrection; and no resurrection, no Second Coming. And the lack of the Second Coming would spell doom for the entire human race. Our text points out that those who truly want Jesus to return "eagerly await Him." How eager are we to talk about His return? It should be often in our minds and on our lips.

An editor of a small-town newspaper had cherished a font of old-fashioned wooden display type. On more than one occasion his assistants had tried to get him to use the large type when some momentous newsworthy event transpired. But he always firmly vetoed the idea.

One summer the old editor went away for a short fishing trip. In his absence a tornado struck the town, tore the steeple off the church, unroofed several houses, sucked a couple of wells dry, and scattered a few barns around. It was the biggest catastrophe that had ever hit the town. So figuring "Now's our chance," his assistants got down the 144-point type from the shelf where the editor had kept it hidden, and they set it up and printed a sensational front-page headline on the tornado.

Two days later the editor came storming into the office shouting, "What do you folks mean by taking down that special type and using it for a tornado? All these years I've been saving it for the second coming of Christ!"

We smile at this story, recognizing that this editor was a bit mixed up in his theology. When the Lord comes, there won't be any time for newspapers to print bold headlines about His return. But he was right about its importance. Even more vital, however, is the fact that the time to headline His return is now! Signs of His coming are evident everywhere. We must all ask ourselves, Are we really ready to meet Him?

Praise the Lord that now is the time to get ready for His return.

The Sabbath and the Second Coming

"For just as the new heavens and the new earth which I make will endure before Me," declares the Lord, "so your offspring and your name will endure. And it shall be from new moon to new moon and from sabbath to sabbath, all mankind will come to bow down before Me," says the Lord. Isa. 66:22, 23, NASB.

Isaiah vividly describes the redeemed worshiping God on the Sabbath in the new earth. The last chapter of his book certainly refers to the climax of history when "the Lord will come in fire and His chariots like the whirlwind to render His anger with fury and His rebuke with flames of fire. For the Lord will execute judgment by fire" (Isa. 66:15, 16, NASB). Our Lord's return is not a quiet secret but a cataclysm of unprecedented proportions.

When God created our world, He intended to personally fellowship with us. Sin interrupted it, but it will resume when we see Jesus face to face. God planned the seventh-day Sabbath rest as a special time when He Himself would have intimate communion with His created beings. When we honor Him by coming before Him each Sabbath to worship, we anticipate, by faith, the time when the One we worship will be visibly present with us. Thus each Sabbath day should be a weekly reminder of our rest in Him when He returns again.

The Sabbath also memorializes His creative power. The seventh-day Sabbath, a 24-hour segment of time, comes at the end of six 24-hour units of time, and together they constitute a literal week. "For in six days the Lord made the heavens and the earth, . . . and rested on the seventh day" (Ex. 20:11, NASB). It indicates an abrupt beginning of our earth and everything, including ourselves, on it. So with the end when Jesus returns. It will happen abruptly when the heavens will split wide open and the Lord will appear. In other words, Creation was a speedy event, and so will be our world's destruction! God will establish the new-heavens and the new-earth creation in a short time.

Most important of all, Isaiah points out that our names will endure. Everything we see, do, or are is transient, but when eternity begins—and it will begin soon—it will endure forever.

Thank the Lord for His Sabbath that both points to a creation in the past and has the seeds of eternity planted in it for the future when Jesus returns. I praise Jesus for _____

Seventy or Eighty Years

As for the days of our life, they contain seventy years, or if due to strength, eighty years, yet their pride is but labor and sorrow; for soon it is gone and we fly away. Ps. 90:10, NASB.

Someone once asked Somerset Maugham, the English novelist and playwright, how he felt when he reached his ninetieth birthday. "Not bad when you consider the alternative," he replied. The older one gets, the more the thought of death flashes across one's thoughts. The theme of life after death must be a money-making subject if you go by the number of headlines on the tabloids at the supermarket checkout stands. Many refer to someone who came back to life after death. Life after death certainly is the uppermost thought on the mind, if still conscious, of a person about to die.

Many suffering constant illness and plagued with aches and pains must feel like the person who exclaimed, "I wish I had known I would live to be 80. I would have taken better care of myself." Although we are not yet 80, we can testify to its truth.

When we consider our past lives, we marvel at the excellent degree of health we possess today. We did not smoke or drink or violate any other major health principles, but in spite of that, we wish we had done better in terms of proper diet and exercise. Though we were both reared in Adventist homes, our overindulgence in eating too much of everything, including sweets and fats, was not the best, especially as we grew older.

Yet we have found that it is never too late to improve health habits, and that a number of conditions are to some extent reversible. You will always feel much better following God's plan rather than indulging your taste buds. To know that you are master of your life—to know that you are practicing the principles of healthy living—to know that you are pleasing God with your total lifestyle—that knowledge contains the seeds of unending joy and delight.

Do you remember the feeling that you had as a child when you followed your parents' instructions fully? You felt just plain good all over. The same thing happens when we seek to please God, not only in the area of healthful living but in all facets of life.

Whether you live to be 70, 80, or 100, cultivate habits that produce blessings to yourself, honor to God, and a positive witness to those around you.

We praise you, O Lord, for _____

Total Surrender

By faith Abraham, when he was called, obeyed by going out to a place which he was to receive for an inheritance; and he went out, not knowing where he was going. Heb. 11:8, NASB.

Barbara Nelson, in telling the story of her son Dwight's close brush with death, shares what it means to surrender. Dwight, water-skiing as a child, smashed into the dock and cracked his skull. He lay motionless before his parents. Soon a helicopter whisked him away. It had room for only the pilot, physician, and the unconscious patient. This was a terrible disappointment for Barbara, since she was hoping that she, as his mother, could accompany her son to the hospital. But in order for her child to get medical attention immediately, she had to totally surrender Dwight to God and place him in the care of people she did not know. God rewarded her trust, and today Dwight is a successful minister.

Likewise, in our daily Christian walk it is of utmost importance to surrender totally to God if we are to experience His healing power in our lives. Andrew Murray tells us that a life of absolute surrender is one that genuinely and sincerely obeys God day by day and has a fellowship with Him through His Word and prayer. Surrendering is the most difficult action in life. We want the last word! We want things to go our way! We demand our rights! Webster defines surrendering as giving up possession of, or power over, or yielding to another. Today we hear much about being our own person and maintaining our rights. Seminars teach us how to win and how to get ahead and even intimidate others. Wouldn't it be wonderful if we could have seminars that teach us how to surrender?

Total surrender is not a normal part of our vocabulary. In the morning we may pray, "Lord, I give myself to You today. Work out Your life in me." But how often we get up from our knees and take control instead of waiting for God to lead. For a peaceful life in Christ, there must be a complete—*total*—surrender on our part, a giving up of ourselves completely to His will. We must be willing to do what He wants and allow Him to do with us what He sees is best. Although this is not easy, remember that God does not expect us to surrender in our own strength or by sheer willpower. He is more than willing to help us. Pray for trust in Him and belief in His power to help. "For it is God who is at work in you, both to will and to work for His good pleasure" (Phil. 2:13, NASB).

Abraham lived a life of total surrender. It was not easy to leave the familiar home territory and move away from relatives and friends, not knowing where he would go. But his unquestioning obedience showed his faith and trust in God. Because Abraham knew the secret of surrendering, he blessed many with the fragrance of his life. All knew that he was connected with God. The zenith of his surrender came when God asked him to sacrifice his son of promise on Mount Moriah.

We receive God's full blessing only through *total* surrender. Thank God today for the Holy Spirit, who enables us to yield our lives to Christ in total surrender to Him.

The Potter and the Clay

Then I went down to the potter's house, and there he was, making something on the wheel. But the vessel that he was making of clay was spoiled in the hand of the potter; so he remade it into another vessel, as it pleased the potter to make. Then the word of the Lord came to me saying, "Can I not, O house of Israel, deal with you as this potter does?" ... "Behold, like the clay in the potter's hand, so are you in My hand, O house of Israel." Jer. 18:3-6, NASB.

Every time we see a person molding a piece of clay into a lovely bowl or vase on a potter's wheel, we always think of Jeremiah. He had witnessed the sight on numerous occasions, but this time God wanted to teach him a spiritual lesson. For some reason the workman marred the piece of pottery. Instead of throwing away the clay, the potter reworked it while it was still pliable. Jeremiah instantly recognized the spiritual analogy. God was the potter, while Israel was the clay. Today God is still the potter while we individually are the clay.

The first lesson we must learn is that both in Jeremiah's day and ours, this illustration does not portray what is, but rather what God desires to do. Although the clay represents people, God does not mold us against our wills. The clay is the variable, whereas the potter is the constant. Following this illustration, the Lord clearly reveals the formula for making His people into a beautiful piece of pottery. If we turn from evil, then the Lord can take us and mold us into His image. Even if we "blow it," rebel, fail, backslide, and miserably mar the work the Lord is attempting to do in our lives, He will patiently try and try again.

To be made into an honorable vessel requires pain at times. The potter uses knives, chisels, firm hands, and the whirling wheel to shape the clay. Fire is required to permanently harden the vessel and protect it from water. No step in the process of making a lovely piece of pottery can be eliminated if the potter is to obtain the best results. "For those whom the Lord loves He disciplines, and He scourges every son whom He receives" (Heb. 12:6, NASB).

In one phrase of the chorus "Spirit of the Living God," we ask the Spirit to break, melt, mold, and fill us. How often we have sung that line, but do we really stop to think that the key to becoming a vessel of beauty and honor is total surrender? God can use only surrendered clay—clay that will allow the Potter to do with us what He needs to.

Thank the divine Potter for His skillful, loving hands that are willing and eager to mold us. And thank Him for His pierced hands that try again and again to make something out of our confused, distressed, and at times rebellious lumps of clay!

Twice-born People

Jesus answered and said to him, "Truly, truly, I say to you, unless one is born again, he cannot see the kingdom of God." Nicodemus said to Him, "How can a man be born when he is old? He cannot enter a second time into his mother's womb and be born, can he?" John 3:3, 4, NASB.

John Wesley, founder of Methodism, wrote in his journal after failing in his evangelistic mission in the New World, "I went to America to convert the Indians; but, O, who shall convert me? . . . It is now two years and four months since I left my native country in order to teach the Georgian Indians the nature of Christianity; but what have I learned myself in the meantime? Why, what I the least of all suspected: that I who went to America to convert others was never myself converted to God."

We spent eight years in the Orient as missionaries conducting evangelistic meetings and seminars for pastors and other denominational employees. We worked with Buddhists and Hindus. At times we wondered what we as Christians had to offer them that would make a difference in their lives. Were we born-again people who were offering the new-birth experience to others?

Such a question should sober all Christians, especially ministers and their spouses. We may look religious, act religious, and use religious talk. And we may be employed full-time as religious workers. But the question still confronts us, Are we offering something to others that we ourselves don't possess?

The good news is that all of us can be born again! The fact that Jesus said that we cannot see God's kingdom unless we have the new birth is really supreme proof that it *can* happen to us! Surely Jesus would never require anything unless He, in His great love, made it possible Himself. Our Lord never asks for the impossible; His promises are guaranteed.

Christ carefully taught Pharisee Nicodemus, His special night school student. John 3, the 1,000th chapter of the English Bible, not only emphasizes the importance of the new birth but also reveals how a person can be born again. Nicodemus, being a seminary graduate, must have been terribly embarrassed that night long ago. He had believed that his ancestry guaranteed eternal life. Now he found out that race has nothing to do with it. The new birth is available to every person in the world.

Jesus' offer to us to be born again is beyond price. It compels us to praise Him and adore Him. Thank Him today for the new-birth experience, and if you need to be born again, thank Him for making it available to you now!

June 2

A Disturbing Bible Study

Unless one is born again, he cannot see the kingdom of God. . . . Truly, truly, I say to you, unless one is born of water and the Spirit, he cannot enter into the kingdom of God. John 3:3-5, NASB.

Nicodemus was one of the 71 or so members of the Sanhedrin, the highest judicial body in the Jewish nation. Before the Roman domination of Palestine, the Sanhedrin had had power over life and death. For Nicodemus to come to Jesus even during the hours of darkness was a remarkable thing. We wonder what would have happened had Judas been present when Jesus confronted this Pharisee, one of the top leaders of the Jewish world. In all probability Judas would have been more disturbed than Nicodemus. Judas was the treasurer for the disciples. His greedy spirit, which caused John to call him a thief (John 12:6), would have surely led him to take Jesus aside and labor with Him. You can almost hear Judas reasoning with Christ about the wealth and influence of this top church official and how Jesus should avoid saying anything that might upset him. Judas could see shekels coming into their bank account if Jesus would only stop talking about being born again. After all, the core concept of the new-birth experience as Jesus taught it meant that Nicodemus and everyone else who lacked it would be banned from heaven. While the disciple would have been interested in Nicodemus' prestige and money, Jesus felt greater concern about Nicodemus' soul.

In today's text Jesus emphasized two words: "see" and "enter." First, He declared that a nonborn-again person cannot "see" the kingdom of God. Those who have never had a new-birth experience cannot see, or understand, why a converted Christian acts the way he does. It is a mystery. We have met several non-Christians or professed Christians who asked us, after finding out our lifestyle and standards, "If you don't smoke, drink, dance, go to movies,

161

and eat meat, what do you do to enjoy life?" Only converted people can understand and believe the principles behind the kingdom of heaven.

Then Jesus pointedly told Nicodemus, Unless you are born again, you will not enter God's kingdom. The statement is unequivocal. There is a finality about it. Citizenship in God's kingdom requires the new-birth experience. To accept unchanged people into the kingdom would be a catastrophe both for the unchanged and for heaven itself.

We are thankful not only for the new-birth requirement but above all for the fact that we can be born again through His Spirit. He changes us daily. How has Jesus transformed your life through the new-birth experience?

_____

_____

June 3

Transformation, Not Improvement

That which is born of the flesh is flesh, and that which is born of the Spirit is spirit. Do not marvel that I said to you, "You must be born again." The wind blows where it wishes and you hear the sound of it, but do not know where it comes from and where it is going; so is everyone who is born of the Spirit. John 3:6-8, NASB.

Our hearts are inherently evil, though not all of us have the same degree of evil. We have discussed these points between ourselves numerous times. According to Bob, Marie is by nature a much better person, with less hereditary and cultivated traits of evil to deal with than he has. Marie reminds Bob that there is no such thing as a "natural Christian." We all need to be born again!

When Bob was pastoring in Florida in 1945, we rented one of our rooms to a mother and her 12-year-old son. They were not members of our church but were Christians. After a few days of getting acquainted we noted how obedient and submissive the son was. It so impressed us that one day we asked the mother how she had trained such a lovable, compliant son. Her answer astounded us. In effect she said that she had never needed to discipline him, and that from infancy on her son had never been a problem. "In fact," she stated, "I don't know what I would do if he ever disobeyed."

Yet regardless of how good this boy was, he still had a fallen nature and needed the Saviour. The concept, so popular today, that all we need to do is to develop the good traits that reside in us is a fatal deception. All of us have minds inherently hostile toward God. We rebel against God's law and will continue to do so if left to ourselves.

But, praise be to God, we don't have to stay that way. Change happens only through the activity of the Holy Spirit. Jesus compared the Spirit to the unseen wind. You know the wind jostles and buffets everything that can be moved, but you can't see the wind itself. When we permit the Spirit to work on our hearts, changes come, sometimes gradually, sometimes quickly. We are not talking about perfection, but something that happens and strengthens as time goes by. It is more than an improvement—it is a transformation!

For the power and influence of the Holy Spirit we praise our Lord. We thank Him for sending to us One, whom physical eye cannot see, from heaven above expressly to mold our lives into the image of Jesus. How much do you appreciate this Supernatural Power whom you can daily call upon to change your life?

How Can These Things Be?

Nicodemus answered and said to Him, "How can these things be?" Jesus answered and said to him, "Are you the teacher of Israel, and do not understand these things?" John 3:9, 10, NASB.

The natural mind cannot understand the new-birth experience. Nicodemus, although gradually finding himself drawn to Jesus as His personal Saviour, expressed doubt about the possibility of any radical change in the human life. In addition, being a conscientious religious leader, he could not believe he needed to radically alter his way of living. Christ chided him for being a teacher of theology and yet professing to know nothing about the need for spiritual transformation.

Nicodemus certainly was acquainted with the idea but probably paid little attention to it as being relevant in his day. After all, his people had given up many of the sins that the prophets had chastened them for. He knew Ezekiel 36:25-27, an Old Testament counterpart to what Jesus was trying to teach him: "Then I will sprinkle clean water on you, and you will be clean; I will cleanse you from all your filthiness and from all your idols. Moreover, I will give you a new heart and put a new spirit within you; and I will remove the heart of stone from your flesh and give you a heart of flesh. And I will put My Spirit within you and cause you to walk in My statutes, and you will be careful to observe My ordinances" (NASB). God's people had stopped worshiping idols, and they were careful about obeying God's law.

Ezekiel describes the new-birth experience in a beautiful way. He uses the two elements of water and the Spirit. Both are necessary—we must be born outwardly of the water and inwardly of the Spirit. The whole life, internally and externally, must reflect conversion. An outer change without an inner one is pure hypocrisy. And any professed transformation that does not express itself in an outward way is pure delusion. Born "of the Spirit" indicates a character change through the powerful impact of the Holy Spirit upon our minds. To be born "of the water" (baptism) is insufficient if we are not born of "the Spirit."

The new-birth experience is God's way of reconciling us to Himself. He reconciles us to Himself legally through justification. Then He reconciles us to Himself experientially through the new birth and growth in grace, the latter being a process that lasts throughout the rest of our lifetime.

Thank Him, praise Him, for this bridge from death to life. If He sat down in the chair in front of you right now, how would you thank Him for your new birth?

_____

_____

The Key to Conversion

And as Moses lifted up the serpent in the wilderness, even so must the Son of Man be lifted up; that whoever believes may in Him have eternal life. John 3:14, 15, NASB.

Every Jew was familiar with the fiery-serpent story. The episode had taken place during Israel's journey to Canaan from Egypt. The record states that because of the lack of water, the heat, and the food—which they didn't like—they began to complain against both Moses and God. It undoubtedly was a difficult trip, but rather than remembering God's blessings and deliverance from bondage in Egypt, they now bitterly found fault. They failed to recognize that each day was a miracle for them. God had shielded them from all types of danger. But discontent—like rumors—spreads rapidly.

To help them learn an important lesson, the Lord removed His protection; poisonous serpents bit many, and many of the bitten died. When the people begged Moses to intercede with God on their behalf, the Lord instructed him to make a bronze serpent and erect it on a pole. Then he urged those who had been bitten to look by faith at the serpent on the pole. If they did, they would live. Many did, but others refused to do so.

The lesson was obvious. They knew the bronze serpent had no power in itself to heal. Faith in God, and faith alone, brought life to their dying bodies. It was a tremendous lesson in righteousness by faith, which is the same as life by faith.

When Jesus reminded Nicodemus of the ancient story, the Jewish leader finally began to put it all together. He began to sense that the new-birth idea was the result of looking to Jesus by faith.

After the crucifixion of Christ, Nicodemus knew for a surety what the serpent story meant. The Father had sent "His own Son in the likeness of sinful flesh and as an offering for sin, . . . [condemning] sin in the flesh" (Rom. 8:3, NASB). Writing to the Corinthians, Paul makes it even clearer when he said, "He made Him who knew no sin to be sin on our behalf, that we might become the righteousness of God in Him" (2 Cor. 5:21, NASB). Jesus vicariously became sin for us on the cross. That fact will save us if we will only look to Him, our sin-bearer. Our sins went to the cross in the form of Jesus. The very least we can do in response to such great love is not only to look but to keep on gazing at Him every day of our lives.

Are you willing to focus on Him today? Look to Him, not to your faults and weaknesses. Look to Him, not to your enemies. Look to Him and not to an organization. Look to Him and not to the world with its sinful enticements. Look to Him and not to your bank accounts. Look to Him now and every moment.

Praise Him for being lifted up for you. Tell Him in any way you want or can that you are thankful that He heals the poison of sin in your veins.

To Save, Not to Condemn

He that believeth on him is not condemned: but he that believeth not is condemned already, because he hath not believed in the name of the only begotten Son of God. And this is the condemnation, that light is come into the world, and men love darkness rather than light, because their deeds were evil. John 3:18, 19.

Jack was an uneducated huckster who used to go from village to village, selling his goods. One time he heard an old woman singing a simple little ditty: "I'm a poor sinner and nothing at all, but Jesus Christ is my all in all." He began to sing the same words, and by God's grace they burned their way into his heart until he soon experienced the new birth. He quit swearing and drinking and began regularly attending church.

Finally he asked the minister if he could join the church. The pastor inquired on what basis the church should accept him as a member. He replied, "The only basis I have is that I'm a poor sinner and nothing at all, but Jesus is my all in all."

"Well," the minister replied, "you must tell me more than that."

"No," Jack said, "I can't, for this is my confession of faith, and that is all I know."

In time Jack went before the membership committee for more questioning. He met some rather stern-faced church officers who seemed bent on finding some fault with him. When they asked him about his Christian experience, he replied, "I'm a poor sinner and nothing at all, but Jesus Christ is my all in all."

One officer inquired if perhaps he didn't have many doubts and fears.

"No," said Jack, "I never can doubt but that I'm a poor sinner and nothing at all, for I know I am; and I cannot doubt that Jesus is my all in all, for He says He is, and how can I doubt what He says?"

The entire community of villagers used to call him Happy Jack because no one could move him from his conviction. "There is nothing in me," he said. "I deserve punishment! Of myself I am a lost person, but I trust Him who came into the world to save sinners, and He will not let me perish."

This refreshingly simple story needs to burn its way into our hearts. Jesus came not to condemn us but to save us! Condemnation vanishes when we accept Him. But if we love darkness rather than light, we pronounce judgment against ourselves.

Let gratefulness ring from your life and heart in a few words now.

June 7

People in the Book of Life

I urge Euodia and I urge Syntyche to live in harmony in the Lord. Indeed, true comrade, I ask you also to help these women who have shared my struggle in the cause of the gospel, together with Clement also, and the rest of my fellow workers, whose names are in the book of life. Phil. 4:2, 3, NASB.

Euodia and Syntyche were two energetic Christian women living in Philippi whom Paul urges to dwell together in harmony. Evidently some difference of opinion existed between them. Then he requests help for these women, who have shared his struggle in the great cause of preaching the gospel. After naming Clement and referring to the rest of his fellow workers, he tenderly speaks of their names as being in the book of life.

Our text constitutes a personal insight into the struggles of the people associated with Paul as they established the early church. They had their problems and trials, even as we do today.

Women were prominent in the formative years of the Macedonian church. It was at Philippi on a Sabbath beside the river in the countryside where Dr. Luke records that Paul and his companions sat down and began speaking to the women who had assembled there (Acts 16:13). In Thessalonica many "leading women" joined Paul and Silas (Acts 17:4, NASB), and in Berea the believers included "a number of prominent Greek women" (verse 12, NASB).

166

Our own church owes much to faithful women believers. In fact, the majority of our members around the world are women. Their faithfulness and service in our church is a major reason for its growth.

Anna Knight learned to read and write by listening to neighbor children and practicing writing by scratching on the ground with a sharp stick. She became one of the denomination's leading Black educators.

Mrs. Henry Gardener invited some women to come to her home in Battle Creek for a prayer band; in 1874 it became the first Dorcas and Benevolent Association. Under the leadership of Martha Byington Amadon, its first president, the Dorcas Society flourished. From this small beginning it evolved into Community Services centers, and finally led to the Adventist Development and Relief Agency, known as ADRA.

Kate Lindsay graduated at the head of her class with the first group of women to receive medical degrees from the University of Michigan Medical College. She founded our church's first Adventist school of nursing in 1883.

As in Paul's day, so in modern times: women, along with men, have played a prominent role in the work of our church.

It is time again to express our praise in writing to the One who has inspired so many—both men and women—to do so much.

My House

For we know that if the earthly tent which is our house is torn down, we have a building from God, a house not made with hands, eternal in the heavens. For indeed in this house we groan, longing to be clothed with our dwelling from heaven. 2 Cor. 5:1, 2, NASB.

Paul, by trade a tentmaker, compares the body to a tent. Houses and tents are quite destructible. So with our earthly bodies. But, praise God, when Jesus comes, we shall have an everlasting tent, or body, to dwell in. Our earthly bodies are temporary dwellings, but our heavenly bodies will be eternal! In this passage Paul clearly expresses his confidence in the resurrection.

The tent in which we dwell inevitably grows older and shabbier. The teeth, like stars, come out every night. Bifocals graduate to trifocals to corneal transplants. Hair becomes scarce, while the skin sags and wrinkles. But we may and should delay the aging process as long as possible through a good lifestyle. Although we cannot stop aging, our characters—the only component of these earthly tents of ours to leave our world—can be continually improved. While the outside of the tent disintegrates, we can enhance the inside.

Sunshine magazine printed a touching and beautiful description of this concept, written by 87-year-old Mother Conger. "I am the sole owner of a house I have lived in over 87 years. In the beginning it was a splendid structure, large enough, tall enough, and on a solid foundation. It was an attractive house. I was proud of its appearance. I have never paid much attention to the repairs on the outside; only to keep it fresh and healthy looking. But I have striven to make the interior clean and beautiful. No unwelcome guests, such as anger, jealousy, and unkindness, were allowed to linger long within its sacred walls, but rather such lovely ones as love, sympathy, prayer, and goodwill every day. So it has been a joy to dwell in this house of mine.

"But time is proving that all things, however beautiful, must fade, and so my house is going down. The windows are not so clear, the door is a bit squeaky, the roof is near to cracking, and the foundation is getting trembly. And I know that someday, not far off, I must move out and let this old house crumble into dust. But the tenant within is quiet, patient; living on the food of the promises of the Good Book, to guide to the house not made with hands.

"So I say to this old house of mine, as we have grown old together: 'O House, we have been long together, in pleasant and in cloudy weather. . . . Choose thine own time; say not "Good night," but in some brighter clime, bid me "Good morning." ' "

For the promise of an immortal tent to dwell in at Your return, O Lord, we want to thank You. For the privilege of perfecting through Your Spirit the character equipment to fit into that new home, we praise You.

June 9

Women of Vision

Now Saul, still breathing threats and murder against the disciples of the Lord, went to the high priest, and asked for letters from him to the synagogues at Damascus, so that if he found any belonging to the Way, both men and women, he might bring them bound to Jerusalem. Acts 9:1, 2, NASB.

The word "Way," used as a synonym for Christianity, appears a number of times in the book of Acts.

Bob, in his early public evangelism, used large billboard entrances to his tents with the title "Way of Life" emblazoned in letters across the top.

Scripture uses "way" in several phrases, such as "the way of the Lord," "the way of the righteous," and "the way of the wicked." Jesus Himself employed the term in its greatest sense when He said of Himself, "I am the way." He alone is the only way to the Father in heaven. Thus it is an honor to be people of "the Way."

Another important concept in our text is one that we may have overlooked in our reading of Paul's call by God on the Damascus road. It states clearly that he had sought permission from the high priest to arrest "both men and women." Three times the book of Acts mentions that the future apostle persecuted the women along with men. In Acts 8:3 we read of him "dragging off men and women," putting them in prison (NASB). Again, in Acts 22:4, he acknowledged that he had persecuted "this Way to the death, binding and putting both men and women into prisons" (NASB). Why did Paul so cruelly mistreat women, and why did Luke record the phrase "men and women"? We believe one major reason is that women played an important role in the establishment of the early Christian church.

When it comes to the Seventh-day Adventist Church, we find many women helped to build our infant organization. It was our privilege while in Australia to visit the grave site of Maud Sisley Boyd. We met her granddaughter, Nona Coombs, who thrilled us with stories of God's leading in her grandmother's life.

Maud Sisley was our first Adventist woman missionary to Europe. After 10 years of service at the Review and Herald Publishing Association, she asked for a six-month vacation to distribute Adventist publications in Ohio with her friend Elsie Gates. Maud supported herself during this time with the savings that she had managed to put away from her 10-cents-an-hour wages at the publishing house. Then she volunteered as a single young woman to join J. N. Andrews in Switzerland and assist him in our first publishing branch overseas. Later, after marriage, she went with her husband, C. L. Boyd, to South Africa, becoming the first woman missionary to that region. After her husband's death, she taught at Avondale College in Australia. She seemed to have one purpose in life—to carry God's message both abroad and in her homeland. God honored her vision and blessed her efforts mightily.

Jot down a word of praise for any woman you know who has built faith in your life.

_____

_____

June 10

How God Overcame the Communication Problem

"For My thoughts are not your thoughts, neither are your ways My ways," declares the Lord. "For as the heavens are higher than the earth, so are My ways higher than your ways, and My thoughts than your thoughts." Isa. 55:8, 9, NASB.

This classic statement illustrates a problem God faces in trying to get the gospel across to the sinful human mind. Some years ago Bob experienced for the first time what it meant to try to communicate with people who could not read and write and had little contact with the outside world. He had traveled by boat and foot through heavy jungles with a minister-translator guide.

Several of the villages they visited had no knowledge of the gospel. Jesus was a totally unknown entity. Bob had a small battery-operated projector with slides on various doctrinal topics. The projector itself was a fantastic revelation to these people. Among the slides were a few pictures of airplanes, skyscraper cities, and automobiles—that Bob used to illustrate the increase of knowledge. When he showed the slide of the New York City skyline, the audience began laughing and talking among themselves. Bob's translator explained that the people had never seen any village like this before, and furthermore, they did not believe it was real.

In spite of Bob's attempts to help them understand that cities and buildings of such magnitude actually exist, they would not accept the photographs as authentic. How do you communicate God's love to people in such situations?

God faces the same kind of problem. We may think we are well educated, talented, and knowledgeable, but actually we know very little compared to Him. But our God is one of love. The verse preceding our passage today is a call for wicked and unrighteous people to return to God. Why? Because He will have compassion on us and "will abundantly pardon" our sins. It is in this context that the Lord reveals the magnitude of His ways and thoughts when compared with ours. Humanity finds it hard to have compassion and to forgive, but God reveals His utter supremacy through His forgiving and compassionate love.

We stand dumbfounded before the cross, the supreme exhibition of His love. Only the Holy Spirit can get it across to our minds. God's ways are higher than ours, as the heavens are higher than the earth, but He has found a way to communicate with us. He sent His own Son to live, breathe, eat, walk, and talk as a man among men. Lift God up in praise and gratitude because, in a world of darkness, Jesus has pierced it with the light of His life and love forever.

June 11

Silent Cal
and Coals of Fire

If your enemy is hungry, give him food to eat; and if he is thirsty, give him water to drink; for you will heap burning coals on his head, and the Lord will reward you. Prov. 25:21, 22, NASB.

Calvin Coolidge, thirtieth president of the United States, has been best remembered more for what he didn't say than for what he did. He was a miser with words, hence the nickname Silent Cal. As vice president, he succeeded to the presidency when President Warren G. Harding died in August 1923.

While staying in the Willard Hotel in Washington, D.C., Silent Cal caught an intruder who had climbed through a window from a ledge. As the thief searched the president's clothes and prepared to make off with a charm, wallet, and watch, Coolidge remarked with perfect economy of words, "I wish you wouldn't take that," referring to the charm, which had the inscription "Presented to Calvin Coolidge, Speaker of the House, by the Massachusetts General Court."

"Are you President Coolidge?" the intruder asked after reading it.

"Yes, . . . if you want money, let's talk this over."

The intruder told the president that he needed money so he and a friend could pay their hotel bill and train fare back to college. Coolidge gave him $32, calling it a loan so the intruder would not be a thief. The incident remained a secret at President Coolidge's request until he and a person whom the president informed had died. Then the story came out. The record shows that the young intruder repaid the $32 loan in full.

Many a person on the road to disaster could be saved if someone would only offer help that includes trust and confidence. We all, as intruders, have been dealt with mercifully by the Saviour. All of us are hungry enemies whom Christ has fed, and penniless enemies whom He has made rich. And we all are thirsty enemies to whom Christ has supplied the water of life.

What He has done for us is what awakens in us admiration and love for Him. Do not "think lightly of the riches of His kindness and forbearance and patience, . . . [for such] kindness of God leads you to repentance" (Rom. 2:4, NASB).

Thank the Lord profusely for heaping coals of fire on your head, and pray for strength to do the same for others—including your enemies.

Walk a Mile in Their Moccasins

Do not speak against one another, brethren. He who speaks against a brother, or judges his brother, speaks against the law, and judges the law; but if you judge the law, you are not a doer of the law, but a judge of it. There is only one Lawgiver and Judge, the One who is able to save and to destroy; but who are you who judge your neighbor? James 4:11, 12, NASB.

All of us have suffered the criticisms of others, and we know how it hurts, especially if the criticism rests on falsehood. Some have honed the terrible art of criticism to an evil science by constant practice. But now and then you meet someone who never speaks against anyone. Bob during his academy days worked as a bellhop in one of our hospitals, under the leadership of an efficient desk clerk. One thing Bob never will forget about his boss is that he never heard the man say a derogatory remark about any person. If anyone came to the clerk with criticism of someone else, he would either remain silent or say something good about the individual being attacked. One day Bob asked him what caused him to be so uncritical of others. His boss replied that he had learned an old Indian prayer that said "Grant me the ability to never criticize my neighbor until I have walked a mile in his moccasins."

Too many people are involved in the science of garbology. They examine the garbage of other people's lives and take great pleasure in sharing what they find.

We all need to learn the lesson of silence like Jacob the middle-aged Pennsylvania Dutchman who one evening was riding with pretty young Clara in his buggy. He finally turned to her and said, "Clara, will ye marry me?"

She bashfully mumbled, "*Ja* [yes], Jacob." Then followed a long silence till Clara asked, "Will ye not say something more, Jacob?"

Jacob replied, "Ach, I think I say too much already!"

Many of us have said too much already and have regretted it afterward.

How would Jesus relate to all the criticism and rumors if He were present in our midst today? First, He would be saddened but would do His best to help, rather than to condemn, those suffering verbal abuse. And then He would encourage all the critics to practice the art of praising the good and ignoring the supposed faults in others.

Think of someone right now whom you may be critical of, and write down something good about him or her. Then praise the Lord for putting the desire in your heart to speak positively about the individual!

I Will Fear No Evil

Yea, though I walk through the valley of the shadow of death, I will fear no evil; for You are with me. Ps. 23:4, NKJV.

Death is ever-present, whether it be represented by a falling leaf, a wilted flower, a run-over pet, a fish floating upside down in the aquarium, or a Memorial Day weekend. On that particular holiday we decorate the old graves and dig new ones for the speeders.

Our text today contains a principle that the Lord in His love has given us. If we are going to walk through the dark valley of death with no fear, the only way to do it is to make sure that the Lord accompanies us on our journey. And to pass through the valley with Jesus without fear means that we must discard all encumbrances.

Eddie Rickenbacker once told of how he had to throw everything he could out of a crippled B-17 plane during World War II. He and his crew knew they were going to crash, and they were desperate to lighten the load. Finally he made the decision to eject even his briefcase of secret papers.

We have never forgotten stories recounted by our missionaries in South Korea, of how they escaped from the Communists during the Korean War shortly before the capture of the airport at Seoul. The authorities told the missionaries that they could have only one suitcase each to carry on the plane, but even that they took from them in order to lighten the plane for more people. One missionary vividly described how he drove his relatively new car up to the plane, climbed the steps, turned around at the top, and threw away the ignition keys.

When you face death, *things* become quite unimportant.

The really important aspects of life are few and cost little. What are they? Taking time with God through prayer and study. Sharing ourselves more with others around the dinner table in our homes. Spending more time with our immediate families and close relatives. Savoring the beauties of nature— walking through the woods near sunset and smelling a rose in the garden.

A Mrs. Busybody was pumping the local doctor about the death of the richest man in town. "You knew him well," she exclaimed. "How much wealth did he leave?"

With a tip of his hat, the old doctor replied, "All of it, madam, all of it."

Enjoy every day as if it were your last. If you knew your final day to live had come, what would you thank God for giving you to enjoy during the last precious few hours?

Limited Editions

And He made from one, every nation of mankind to live on all the face of the earth, having determined their appointed times, and the boundaries of their habitation, that they should seek God, if perhaps they might grope for Him and find Him, though He is not far from each one of us. Acts 17:26, 27, NASB.

During a visit to Interlaken, Switzerland, we noticed figurines for sale in a shop window with certificates of guarantee that each one was a limited edition. One figurine of a boy leading a donkey with a girl on it had a certificate with the words "750 edition"—meaning that only 749 other figurines just like it had been manufactured.

God has made a limited edition of every human being who has ever lived or ever will live on earth. His edition is extremely rare—only one of a kind! The entire human race has the same initial ancestor—Adam. From that one individual, along with Eve, has come everybody else on earth. Although all have two ears, two eyes, two feet, and two arms, yet each of us is absolutely unique. Our thinking processes, our cultures, our knowledge, our personalities—all are different. The count of the hairs on our heads and the number of brain cells we each possess are each unique.

Sin has made us even more individually different, because of hereditary and environmental factors. The internal struggle each of us has in following God's will is also unique, a fact that should cause us to be careful in our attitudes toward others.

Writing to three members who were critical of others in the church, Ellen White said, "We are not all organized alike, and many have not been educated aright. . . . Some have a much better organization than others. While some are continually harassed, afflicted, and in trouble because of their unhappy traits of character, having to war with internal foes and the corruption of their nature, others have not half so much to battle against" (*Testimonies*, vol. 2, p. 74).

Speaking of mothers who indulge in selfishness and peevishness, and are exacting in their demands on their children, she stated, "Many have received as a birthright almost unconquerable tendencies to evil" (*The Adventist Home*, p. 241).

In every respect of our characters we are each different from others. But the good news is that our Lord knows our differences and takes them into account as He judges us. He has a special tender care for those who possess the worst traits of character and have had the most difficulty overcoming them.

While you still have time and are alive, praise Him now for His recognition that we are each unique and different, and for the fact that He deals with us as individuals.

Divine Warfare Weapons

For though we walk in the flesh, we do not war according to the flesh, for the weapons of our warfare are not of the flesh, but divinely powerful for the destruction of fortresses. We are destroying speculations and every lofty thing raised up against the knowledge of God, and we are taking every thought captive to the obedience of Christ. 2 Cor. 10:3-5, NASB.

Paul was well acquainted with military terms and used them magnificently in our passage. We cannot miss the point that we are in a raging spiritual battle. As Christians we find ourselves caught up in a war of eternal life versus eternal death. No earthly conflict can compare with the spiritual battle we each face. Its two commanders, or generals, are Christ and Satan. All of us belong to one of the two opposing armies. Our Commander is Christ, and though His army is outnumbered as far as human followers are concerned, He has heavenly divine forces that far overwhelm Satan's hordes. In other words, as Christians we are on the winning side.

The war we each fight, better known as the great controversy between Christ and Satan, is more than a spiritual one—it touches every cell of our bodies. We have already mentioned the word "psychoneuroimmunology" several times. In simple terms, we could call it the mind/nervous system/ immune system connection. The lead article of the June 1986 *National Geographic* magazine has the title "Our Immune System: The Wars Within." The article begins with a remarkable introduction: "Every minute of every day wars rage within our bodies. The combatants are too tiny to see."

The article contains astounding photographs taken by electron microscopes of the battles between enemy viruses and various types of immune system fighters such as the helper T cells, killer T cells, and B cells. Each type of immunological cell has its own particular expertise, even as various soldiers in an army have certain assignments.

Also, Disney World has a spectacular ride through a reproduction of the human body in EPCOT Center's Wonders of Life pavilion. It is called Body Wars.

The battle against sin and evil encompasses our entire being. In fact, Satan attempts to destroy us physically and mentally in order to render us less capable of understanding the plan of salvation. He is aware that wrong thoughts if not taken captive to the obedience of Christ can depress our immune system. A weakened immune system leads to illness, which then affects our ability to make spiritual decisions.

For the weapon of knowledge on how to care for our bodies, praise God. For the weapon of the Holy Spirit to empower us to control our appetites and passions, praise God. And for the weapon of Christ and Him crucified, who is the focal point of all life, praise God. Write down your praises now to strengthen yourself spiritually, mentally, and physically.

Help Needed for Our Bones

Be gracious to me, O Lord, for I am pining away; heal me, O Lord, for my bones are dismayed. And my soul is greatly dismayed; but Thou, O Lord—how long? Ps. 6:2, 3, NASB.

Did you notice how the psalmist intertwines the mental, emotional, physical, and spiritual aspects of his being? His mind and emotions are "pining away," or withering, while his body needs healing because his "bones are dismayed," or vexed. Then David comments, of his spiritual nature, that his "soul is greatly dismayed." He must have been in intense agony mentally, physically, and spiritually when he wrote this psalm. He ends his thought by asking, "O Lord, how long?"

When we suffer from any cause, all of our being reacts. Or in other words, when you suffer for any reason, all of you feels the pain! Therefore, God in His mercy has instructed us on how to live in a way that, when coupled with true medical science, will help us avoid unnecessary suffering, especially that which we inflict on ourselves.

An interesting concept is David's reference to his bones. Scientists tell us that our bone marrow is the major producer of our 1 trillion-strong white blood cells. They constitute a highly specialized army of soldier cells that battle against the enemy viruses and germs constantly invading our bodies. Our army of helper T cells, killer T cells, macrophages, and B cells constitute an important part of our immune system. Seventh-day Adventists have as their heritage a wonderful amount of counsel that teaches us how to live properly so our immune system army can remain in full combat readiness.

Whether the biblical characters knew of the bone marrow's role in producing white blood cells, we don't know. But interestingly, they make a number of references to bones. Job comments that the "marrow of his bones is moist" (Job 21:24, NASB). Several writers speak of bones being made fat. David repeatedly declares that his bones were wasting away because of his sins. In Psalm 38:3 he states, "There is no health in my bones because of my sin" (NASB). Psalm 51, David's great penitential psalm, requests that God "let the bones which Thou hast broken rejoice" (verse 8, NASB). King Solomon, as he urges people to fear the Lord and turn from evil, claims that doing so will result in a healing experience for the body and "refreshment to your bones" (Prov. 3:8, NASB). If the Bible writers were not aware of the immune system built on the cells produced in the bone marrow, God certainly was.

Our lifestyle and thoughts can depress or strengthen our immune system. As we have seen already, one way to strengthen it is to praise the Lord regularly for His life-giving power through the Holy Spirit. I want to praise God because _____

June 17

Sadness of Heart

So the king said to me, "Why is your face sad though you are not sick? This is nothing but sadness of heart." Then I was very much afraid. Neh. 2:2, NASB.

Nehemiah was a trusted officer in the court of King Artaxerxes I. One day as the Jewish exile served the monarch, Artaxerxes could see depression written on Nehemiah's face. Perhaps the cupbearer had been weeping over the condition of Jerusalem with its broken walls and gates. Desperately longing to go back and help rebuild his beloved city and encourage his destitute people, he could not hide his anguish from the king, who recognized that something was wrong, even though Nehemiah otherwise appeared to be in good health.

Again we see the inevitable interaction between mind and body. Our thoughts affect our facial expressions, as well as our immune system. That is why it is extremely important to form habits of praise and thanksgiving to our Lord.

Hippocrates, the Greek physician known as the Father of Medicine, lived about 400 years before Christ. Until recently, graduating physicians would take the Hippocratic oath that tradition says he wrote. It is said that he would rather know what sort of person had a disease than what sort of disease the person had. In other words, health and healing depend not only on the treatment but also on the patient's personality, attitude, and psychological makeup.

Sir William Osler, the brilliant Canadian physician and medical historian, made a similar observation. He rightly claimed that the outcome of tuberculosis had more to do with what went on in a patient's mind than what occurred in his lungs.

The story is told of a debate carried on between Louis Pasteur, the famous nineteenth-century French chemist, and Claude Bernard, the French physiologist. Pasteur claimed that the greatest factor in disease was the germ that attacked the "soil," or the body. But Bernard argued that the soil, or the body that the germ attacked, was more important. Pasteur, it is claimed, admitted on his deathbed that Bernard was correct.

If our bodies, including our minds, are in tip-top shape, germs have less chance of getting us down. But more important, our thinking patterns and our attitudes are the most important factor of all in the area of health. If 80 to 90 percent of diseases originate in the mind, how careful we should be in screening our thoughts. How cautious we should be in filtering out any sight or sound that might tend to break down our immune system.

Nehemiah's sadness of heart may not have made him physically ill, but it could have cost him his life. Note what he said after the king saw him sad and spoke to him: "Then I was very much afraid." A despotic king could have a person killed if he brought displeasure in any way. As we live before the King of the universe, however, we have every reason to be glad, thankful, and happy. I praise Him constantly because _____

Do You Love Life?

Let him who means to love life and see good days refrain his tongue from evil and his lips from speaking guile. And let him turn away from evil and do good; let him seek peace and pursue it. 1 Peter 3:10, 11, NASB.

Peter is here quoting from David's Psalm 34. It would seem that David had a good grasp of the relationship between our minds and our bodies. He urges us to be careful what we think, because this shapes and influences how we perceive and enjoy the world around us. To speak evil first requires evil thinking. Evil thoughts will warp our attitude toward life and destroy our ability to enjoy it. If we want to enjoy life and bless those around us, we must have a positive outlook. We must avoid evil and concentrate on the good. Sin is by its very nature self-destructive, and because of the intimate relationship between mind and body, evil, self-destructive thoughts will affect the body and every other aspect of life.

"The condition of the mind affects the health to a far greater degree than many realize. Many [not all] of the diseases from which men suffer are the result of mental depression. Grief, anxiety, discontent, remorse, guilt, distrust, all tend to break down the life forces and to invite decay and death" (*The Ministry of Healing*, p. 241). Although Ellen White wrote this years ago, it accurately describes the findings of medical scientists today in the area of psychoneuroimmunology. The mind's negative effects on the nervous system and the immune system because of grief, anxiety, discontent, remorse, guilt, and distrust have been scientifically demonstrated. Evil thoughts destroy, while peaceful ones build up.

The July/August 1987 *Hippocrates Journal* contained an article dealing with an experiment conducted on 111 healthy Harvard University students. Each student received a comprehensive personality test that measured tolerance, confidence, and self-esteem. From blood samples taken from the students the researchers isolated a subset of white blood cells called natural killer cells. They exposed the killer cells to cancer cells and measured how many tumor cells the killer cells destroyed in a four-hour period. Then they compared the results with the personality tests and found a startlingly consistent pattern. The cells in the blood samples of those who had a healthy, positive attitude and personality managed to overcome more cancer cells than any other personality group.

Those who ranked high on the depression scale in the personality test were people inclined to withdrawal, maladjustment, and low self-esteem. Their killer cells were less active. Again, these results strongly indicate a relationship between the mind and the immune system.

How do we build a positive attitude? Seek peace in the Lord. Turn from evil. By the grace of Jesus dwell on those thoughts that are life-building.

Guard your words. Above all, form the habit of being thankful. Constantly praise the Lord for His mercy, which endures forever! Write words of thankfulness to God for any blessing you have had in the past 24 hours. I am thankful because _____

The Blessings of a Cheerful Heart

A joyful heart makes a cheerful face, but when the heart is sad, the spirit is broken. . . . All the days of the afflicted are bad, but a cheerful heart has a continual feast. Prov. 15:13-15, NASB.

In the Bible the term *heart* is interchangeable with what we would term our thoughts, feelings, will, intellect, and mind. Again, we recognize in our reading today the relationship between mind and body. Sooner or later, what is on the inside shows on the outside. And hearts, or minds, that are despondent, critical, discouraged, or under stress for whatever reason will have an adverse effect on the entire bodily system. But when a person has a relationship with Jesus, he or she will have a continual feast of good things that will make a cheerful heart. And a cheerful, happy spirit creates an atmosphere in which the immune system can flourish. When the immune system thrives, foreign invaders such as viruses or cancer cells have less chance to survive.

According to some medical researchers in the field of psychoneuroimmunology, cancer is more common in people who suffer major emotional problems and fail to cope with them. These researchers claim that the link between emotions (our attitudes and thoughts) and our state of health is so strong that certain psychological tests are better predictors of cancer than some physical examinations. That does not mean that all persons plagued with cancer or any other disease brought it upon themselves by wrong thinking. Disease involves numerous factors. The best attitude possible will not prevent problems caused by genetic malfunction, aging, accidents, or some chemical or biological hazards.

But Christ-centered Christians have a greater advantage in warding off disease and maintaining health than others do. Our hope in Jesus, our assurance of eternal life, our belief in our Lord's soon coming, our thoughts of being in heaven with the redeemed—all strengthen our life forces. The reality of these truths and many others creates a joyful spirit in the heart.

Add this to the fact that "nothing tends more to promote health of body and of soul than does a spirit of gratitude and praise" (*The Ministry of Healing*, p. 251), and you possess a powerful combination.

Jesus invites us to rest in His love and care. We are still learning to trust Him with the cares and perplexities that face us personally, but we know that a life-giving power results from turning over our problems to Him. We can stop struggling with overwhelming difficulties as we pray, "Lord, You know what is best. We commit all our perplexities into Your hands. Then, whatever happens, we believe that with You sustaining us, all will be for the best."

We praise the Lord that the more we encourage thankful thoughts and feelings, the more blessed, happy, and healthy we will be. We want to write out a few words of praise today for some specific blessing. Would you like to join us?

_____

_____

June 20

Jesus Is No Placebo

It is the Spirit who gives life; the flesh profits nothing; the words that I have spoken to you are spirit and are life. But there are some of you who do not believe. John 6:63, 64, NASB.

While faith is a powerful medium, it cannot stand alone or exist by itself. Faith is always connected with something or someone. It has an object, is centered in some definite thing or person. In medical studies, patients given a placebo—a preparation totally neutral in content but used only for its psychological effect—reported an improvement about one third of the time. Of course, the patients taking a placebo do not realize that the medicine they are taking contains nothing but some inert material. But their belief and faith in what the doctor prescribes for them—the placebo—has a good effect on their health. Sometimes the placebo is the only or main source of value in some treatments. It is claimed that bitter placebos work better than pleasant-tasting ones, and that injections are more effective than pills. The important element is the patients' belief, or faith, factor.

In a study of people who survived supposedly incurable cancers, all had a strong faith in something—doctors, medical treatment, or God. The faith component aided them in maintaining hope and escaping an attitude of helplessness. An interesting nonreligious book on this subject is titled *Love, Medicine, and Miracles,* by Bernie S. Siegel, a surgeon who has concentrated on cancer patients. He organized what one might call a club that he named Exceptional Cancer Patients (ECaP). They are people who normally would have died quickly from their terminal illness, but who developed faith and positive attitudes. They outlived patients with similar types of cancer but whose defeatist attitude and hopelessness, according to Siegel, produced swift death.

If faith in a placebo or a human physician helps to improve a person's health, what about faith in the Great Physician? Jesus is no placebo. His matchless love and power are the real thing. If we talk of His goodness and His healing power and have a dynamic faith in Him, it will surely improve our lot in life, whether we be sick or well. But it requires habitual focusing on Him through the Word. Educate yourself to take His promises and apply them to yourself. After all, He said that His words are spirit and are life.

Thank Him for your lips that can praise Him for His goodness. Thank Him for your eyes that can read His Word. Praise Him for a heart that will respond to His love. And finally, express your gratitude with ours now.

Psychoneuroimmunology and the Sermon on the Mount, Part 1

Blessed are "the poor in spirit," "those who mourn," "the gentle," "those who hunger and thirst for righteousness," "the merciful," "the pure in heart," "the peacemakers," "those who have been persecuted," "you when men revile you, and persecute you." Matt. 5:3-11, NASB.

We have collected in our passage today the kind of qualities God admires in us, the ones He wants to develop in us. In English we call them the Beatitudes, derived from the Latin word for blessedness.

During his earlier years, as Bob preached on the principles found in the Sermon on the Mount, he wondered at times if we should take them literally or consider them just nice-sounding platitudes. He preached that only truly born-again people can understand and practice these teachings. Although he still believes this, his growing knowledge of psychoneuroimmunology has given him new insights that cause both of us to accept more readily the literalness and reality of the principles that Jesus gave. When we understand clearly how God put us together, how our minds work, and how our thoughts affect our nervous system and in turn our immune system, then we stand back in grateful amazement at our Lord's insightful teachings.

To begin with, ask yourself a difficult question: "Am I really able to rejoice and be glad if I am persecuted, insulted, and lied about because I am a follower of Jesus? Is it possible to actually 'rejoice, and be glad' [Matt. 5:12, NASB] for such ill treatment?" It seems like a rather questionable reward for being like Jesus—that the more you are like Him, the more hostility you may provoke. But now we have an additional reason to rejoice and be glad. We recognize that if we respond to persecution, insults, and falsehood with fear, worry, anger, retaliation, and revenge, we only add to our own sufferings by depressing our immune system, leading to physical illness. Jesus knew this, so He urged us to rejoice. Even if martyred, we can die rejoicing in Him!

To surrender all to Jesus is not just a nice religious platitude. It demands an actual decision to place ourselves in His hands and focus our minds on Him in absolute trust when everything around us seems dark and foreboding.

We thank our Lord for the life-giving effect on both our physical and spiritual natures, that results when we sincerely practice rejoicing in His name. Thank Him now for any sorrows you have faced for His sake while you at the same time knew that He stood beside you, ready to help you victoriously cope with them.

June 22

Psychoneuroimmunology and the Sermon on the Mount, Part 2

You have heard that the ancients were told, "You shall not commit murder" and "Whoever commits murder shall be liable to the court." But I say to you that everyone who is angry with his brother shall be guilty before the court; and whoever shall say to his brother, "Raca," shall be guilty before the supreme court; and whoever shall say, "You fool," shall be guilty enough to go into the fiery hell. Matt. 5:21, 22, NASB.

Some mistakenly believe that in Old Testament times the sixth commandment condemned only the act of murder. The truth is that in Moses' day God commanded the people not to hate their fellow countrymen in their hearts. Nor were they to take vengeance and bear grudges. Rather, they were to love their neighbors as themselves. (See Leviticus 19:17, 18.) Through the years, accumulating scientific research has shown conclusively the emotional factors involved in all illness. It is not mysticism or magic but fact that our emotions have a direct effect on us physiologically as well as psychologically.

Remember that term *psychoneuroimmunology* simply means how the mind, or psyche, affects the nervous system, which in turn impacts on the immune system.

Dr. Karl Menninger in his book *Whatever Became of Sin?* titles one of his subchapters "The Sins of Anger, Violence, and Aggression." In it he lists a broad range of wrong feelings, actions, and attitudes—among them "ill humor, sharp words, denunciation or destructive criticism, glares, curses, and even blows" (p. 143). Then he points out lesser but still important forms of violence that he defines as sin. Menninger speaks of sheer rudeness, discourteousness, ill mannerliness, coarse speech, shouting, hurling epithets, and pushing people (as on the subway) as also being sin. While they may be lesser forms of anger, they still all have a negative effect on our immune system.

Ellen White speaks of the mental activity of the brain vitalizing the whole system and aiding the body in resisting disease. Talking about the preservation and recovery of health, she refers to "the depressing and even ruinous effect of anger, discontent, selfishness, or impurity" (*Education*, p. 197). Not only does anger in all its ramifications ruin social relationships but it keeps us from experiencing maximum health.

On the other side of the coin, we, through Christ, can have "the marvelous life-giving power to be found in cheerfulness, unselfishness, [and] gratitude" (*ibid.*). A sweet temper makes the body operate better. Write out a praise thought now on how His Holy Spirit helps us control our emotions.

June 23

Psychoneuroimmunology and the Sermon on the Mount, Part 3

Make friends quickly with your opponent at law while you are with him on the way, in order that your opponent may not deliver you to the judge, and the judge to the officer, and you be thrown into prison. . . . And if anyone wants to sue you, and take your shirt, let him have your coat also. Matt. 5:25, 40, NASB.

Lawsuits appear to be the order of the day in much of the Western world. Jesus' advice seems most unreasonable—or does it? In the early 1950s psychiatrist Thomas Holmes and psychologist Richard Rahe prepared a life change rating scale. When we first read about this newfangled study that claimed to show the devastating effects of stress on the body by assigning a certain number of points to each crisis a person encounters in life, we smiled and considered it another fad. But through the years this test has been refined, and it is impossible to ignore its validity.

The scale lists more than 40 events that can cause harmful stress. At the top of the list is the death of a spouse, which rates 100 points. Divorce, loss of job, moving to a new location, or even taking a vacation—any one of these has a negative impact on a person. An individual who accumulates more than 300 stress points will in all probability experience some form of illness within a relatively short time. The key to staying well depends on the attitude and coping mechanism of the individual under the stress.

As practicing Christians, we have a marvelous coping mechanism when they put on the whole armor of God. It shields us from the harmful effects of the stress darts hurled at us daily. Our Lord wants us not only to cope with stress but to choose to avoid all harmful stresses when possible.

This is the reason, we believe, that Christ advised us to agree with our enemies, in order to avoid the stressful situation of going to court. Jesus took it a step further when He said that if anyone wants to sue you (he has not yet gone to court), let him have both your coat and shirt, to spare you the terrible experience of hiring lawyers, getting depositions, and going before a judge and/or jury. As someone has said, a dog may win a fight with a skunk, but is it worth it?

The Sermon on the Mount contains fantastic counsel that when followed can be a blessing to the total person. Our Lord's wisdom makes tremendous sense when you see His advice in the context of its effect on the whole system! The basic idea behind it all is to place your trust in God.

How has the Lord helped you deal with stress?

June 24

The Lust Factor

You have heard that it was said, "You shall not commit adultery"; but I say to you, that everyone who looks on a woman to lust for her has committed adultery with her already in his heart. Matt. 5:27, 28, NASB.

Read this passage to most people today and they will respond with sneers and snickers. But Jesus makes it clear that lust, sexual or otherwise, begins in the mind and always precedes the outward act. "The eye and the heart are the two brokers of sin" (*Robertson's Word Pictures*, p. 46). Augustine claimed that "sinful lust is not nature, but a disease of nature."

The Greek word for *lust* in our passage means to set one's heart on a person or thing, a sense that also includes coveting and an intense abnormal desire. Scripture uses the same Greek word in both a good and an evil sense. In the good sense, Peter speaks of the angels who "long to look" into the gospel (1 Peter 1:12, NASB). Thus here the word for lust is translated as a longing—a deep, strong desire. But in our passage today the Lord deals with illicit sexual desires.

Christ emphasizes the danger of such lust when He states in the next verse, "If your right eye makes you stumble, tear it out, and throw it from you" (Matt. 5:29, NASB)). Jesus was not here advocating self-mutilation, but rather was making a powerful plea for us to be resolute in our determination to gain victory over sin, especially sinful thoughts that particularly debase and corrupt a person.

Impure thoughts precede impure actions. We believe impurity in thought or deed always has an accompanying guilt, which has a depressing effect on the body, especially the immune system. Impure thoughts short-circuit our connection with Christ. But pure, elevated thinking and acting brings us closer to the Lord. Those who let their minds dwell on pure themes display sunny attitudes and dispositions. As future citizens of a heaven of purity and holiness, we will shun any thought, sight, or sound that will drag us down mentally, physically, and spiritually. When Satan thrusts debasing thoughts into our minds, the Holy Spirit stands as a mighty guard to protect us by closing the door to them.

"O that the youth may realize how important it is to keep the mind guarded, pure and clean, from corrupting thoughts, and to preserve the soul from all debasing practices; for the purity or impurity of youth is reflected upon old age" (*Sons and Daughters of God*, p. 78).

When we think of the absolute purity reflected in our Saviour's life, we rejoice that we worship and serve One who has set us such a pattern of goodness. We thank Him for teaching us that purity not only elevates us spiritually but also has a positive, effervescent effect on our physical nature. Do you want Him to more fully display His spotlessness in your life?

June 25

Enemies Are to Be Loved, Not Hated

You have heard that it was said, "You shall love your neighbor, and hate your enemy." But I say to you, love your enemies, and pray for those who persecute you in order that you may be sons of your Father who is in heaven; for He causes His sun to rise on the evil and the good, and sends rain on the righteous and the unrighteous. Matt. 5:43-45, NASB.

Jesus quoted from Leviticus 19:18 when He said, "You shall love your neighbor." But the last part of that sentence, "and hate your enemy," is not a quote from the Old Testament but a concept found in Jewish teachings that Jesus rejected. The parable of the good Samaritan teaches us how we are to act as neighbors to all people. The word "neighbor" means one who lives near another. Thus neighbor is "nigh-bor," one who is nigh. As Christians, we should live nigh to all people — even our enemies. To be true children of God requires loving our enemies. Paul adds action to this concept: "But if your enemy is hungry, feed him, and if he is thirsty, give him a drink; for in so doing you will heap burning coals upon his head" (Rom. 12:20, NASB).

Jesus helped us to know how to love our enemies when He said to pray for those who persecute us. To pray for an enemy requires a special measure of the Holy Spirit in our lives.

In the year 1569 the authorities searched for a Dutchman named Dirk Willems, because of his Protestant beliefs. One day as he fled, Willems dashed across a pond covered by thin ice. He successfully made it to the other side, but his pursuer was not so fortunate. The man broke through the ice and started to drown. Willems, hearing his shouts for help, turned back and rescued him.

In spite of saving his enemy's life, Willems was not set free but was imprisoned, and after a trial he was put to death in a slowly burning fire at Asperen, Holland. Concern for the life of his enemy led to the loss of his own. The record of this man's martyrdom reveals no bitterness or hate on his part against his pursuers, and had he the opportunity of saving an enemy's life again, he undoubtedly would have done so.

To hate others regardless of what they have done results in harm to ourselves, not just spiritually but physically, as well. To love is God's gift for health and happiness. Following His way of love leads to peace, security, and joy.

We praise our Saviour for loving us when we were so unlovely and thank Him for helping us even while we were yet enemies. Even beyond that, we praise Him for enabling us, not to hate, but to love our enemies. What praise is in your heart for Him who is love personified?

One Thing Only

For this reason I say to you, do not be anxious for your life, as to what you shall eat, or what you shall drink; nor for your body, as to what you shall put on. Is not life more than food, and the body than clothing? Matt. 6:25, NASB.

Anxiety destroys the entire being, just as rust corrodes weather-beaten autos sitting out in the junkyard. But anxiety is a symptom, not a cause. It is analogous to a fever, not the infection that plunges the body into its struggle to resist the invading germs. Anxiety attacks a person's physical and psychological nature. Add guilt and resentment to anxiety and you have an unholy and self-destructive trinity. Many individuals carry with them an unbearable load of anxiety without realizing it. If not dealt with properly, it will inevitably lead to some form of emotional or physical illness.

Martha the sister of Mary was a most anxious person. The story of Christ's visit to their home in Bethany reveals that "Martha was distracted with all her preparations" (Luke 10:40, NASB). When she complained about her sister's lack of interest in helping to prepare and serve the meal, Jesus frankly replied, "Martha, Martha, you are worried and bothered about so many things" (verse 41, NASB). Then He stated a truth that people living in today's technological societies know little about: "But only a few things are necessary, really only one, for Mary has chosen the good part, which shall not be taken away from her" (verse 42, NASB).

What is that "really only one" ultimate element? One thing—how can this be true when you have a child on drugs? One thing—when you have just lost a job and have house payments to make? One thing—when your daughter is getting married and there are a thousand preparations to attend to for the wedding and reception? One thing—when a close relative comes down with a terminal illness? Is Jesus unreasonable? Is He exaggerating?

No. The one thing He is talking about is the ultimate concern—salvation, eternal life. It overshadows all else. When we make salvation top priority in life, anxiety will fade, and faith and confidence in Jesus will not only survive but flourish. We develop a calm, trusting spirit between Jesus and ourselves. Faith displaces fear. Does this mean that we are no longer concerned about all the things we have just mentioned (and more, too)? Never! But the one thing—the relationship with Christ—is of prime importance.

As an example of this "one thing" experience, Jesus referred to the birds of the air, who do not sow, reap, or hoard food for future use. Yet if our heavenly Father watches over them, how much more will He take care of us. Jesus also referred to our anxiety over clothes and asked us to observe the gorgeous dress of the lilies. (In the ancient world, clothing was like what an automobile is to us today—an expensive but vital necessity. People did not have closets bulging with things they needed to get rid of. Most people owned only one or two garments at a time.) If we are anxious at all, we should make sure it is over a saving relationship with our Lord.

We are thankful to Jesus for inviting us to lay down the cares of this life at His feet. Can you put into words your own thankfulness that you can trust Him?

First Things First

Do not be anxious then, saying, "What shall we eat?" or "What shall we drink?" or "With what shall we clothe ourselves?" For all these things the Gentiles eagerly seek; for your heavenly Father knows that you need all these things. Matt. 6:31, 32, NASB.

Yesterday we studied about God's medicine for anxiety. Our verses today touch on the three major concerns of even today's society—food, drink, and clothes. Christ did not teach here that they are not important or that it makes no difference as to what you eat, drink, and wear. Rather, we are not to be overconcerned about them. It is an excessive preoccupation with them that causes stress in our lives and produces unhealthful anxiety. But more than that, Jesus knew that our worry about such necessities can easily divert our thoughts from the even more important spiritual things of life. In life's battle for peace of mind we quickly discover that we can spend most of our waking hours fretting over pleasing our appetites and making ourselves look good on the outside.

The advice Jesus gives us starts with the inside. He knows that if we care for the mind, then everything else falls into place. First He asks us to consider the birds and how they get along in life. They joyfully depend on God for their needs. Then He interjects the idea that if our anxiety cannot add an inch to our stature, then what is the purpose of such emotional turmoil? Be satisfied with your present possessions, including the body God has given you, He says, and be at peace with yourself and others. Jesus knew by experience what He was talking about, for He practiced what He preached.

The next illustration deals directly with clothing. He compares Solomon's man-made royal robes with the God-made clothing of the field flowers of Palestine. Several times we have visited the botanical gardens in Washington, D.C., around Eastertime. The magnificent display and arrangement of lilies always reminds us of Jesus' illustration. As we view these perfectly formed, brilliantly white lilies, we seem to be dressed in rags when compared with their fine clothing.

The next example He employs to help us overcome anxiety deals with the plants; they can shrivel so quickly in Palestine's dry season that they can be used for fuel the next day. If the Lord has written His love on blades of grass, which are quickly cut and destroyed, then what about people for whom His Son died in order to save? Why should we fear or worry? Jesus pinpoints our problem with the words "O men of little faith" (Matt. 6:30, NASB). The greater the faith in Him, the less the anxiety.

His concluding remedy for anxiety is to seek first, not temporal blessings, but rather His kingdom and His righteousness. All other necessary things will then be ours.

We invite you to write out a sentence or two of thanksgiving for His simple cure for anxiety.

_____

_____

The Two Foundations

Therefore everyone who hears these words of Mine, and acts upon them, may be compared to a wise man, who built his house upon the rock. And the rain descended, and the floods came, and the winds blew,

and burst against that house; and yet it did not fall, for it had been founded upon the rock. Matt. 7:24, 25, NASB.

A few years ago a hotel in Singapore suddenly collapsed. Where a once fine-looking building had stood, now one saw only a heap of rubble. No earthquake or severe storm had toppled it. The only cause for this tragedy that cost several people their lives was found in the shabby construction of the foundation.

When we lived in Florida during our early ministry, we experienced the fury of several hurricanes. After boarding up our windows and barricading the doors before the wind reached its full intensity, we would sleep under a table for added protection. As the storm reached its height the house would shake with each gust, but its foundation was solid.

In the physical, mental, and spiritual realm, wise people build on rock, never on the sand. The foundation Rock, Jesus Christ, is the only place upon which to safely anchor a life. How often we have sung the chorus of the hymn "My Hope Is Built on Nothing Less," which says "On Christ, the solid Rock, I stand; all other ground is sinking sand, all other ground is sinking sand" (*The SDA Hymnal*, No. 522).

Our only Hope, Christ, is a foundation that nothing can ever shake. If we solidly build our lives on Him, the rains of stress—reverses, sickness, accidents, hardship, privation, injustice, and loss of loved ones—may jolt our lives, but we will not collapse.

And if the winds blow—winds of rejection, of opposition, slander, insult, temptation, and ill-treatment—our bodies, minds, and spirits may reel and tremble, but we will not crumple in despair or defeat, because our feet are planted firmly on the Rock of Ages.

David, though hounded and hunted during his early life, wrote of our Lord's sustaining power: "He brought me up out of the pit of destruction, out of the miry clay; and He set my feet upon a rock making my footsteps firm. And He put a new song in my mouth, a song of praise to our God; many will see and fear, and will trust in the Lord" (Psalm 40:2, 3, NASB).

You can have absolute confidence in our Rock of salvation. Stand on Him all day long and all life long. Bless His precious name, for He will guard our ways and lead us safely through life, even though the winds and rain will plague us as long as time shall last.

Haven't you found this to be true? Write out a short experience in your own life that illustrates this, and praise Him for His goodness.

_____

_____

Live for Heaven Now

Whatever your hand finds to do, do it with all your might, for in the grave, where you are going, there is neither working nor planning nor knowledge nor wisdom. Eccl. 9:10, NIV.

On December 7, 1877, Ellen White made some startling comments in a letter to her 19-year-old nephew, F. E. Belden. She was apparently urging her young nephew to do his very best in life now so that he would not suffer remorse in the present life and would also enjoy the life to come to the fullest:

"Every time one of the glorious faculties with which God has enriched man is abused or misused, that faculty loses forever a portion of its vigor and will never be as it was before the abuse it suffered. . . . Though God may forgive the sinner, yet eternity will not make up that voluntary loss sustained in this life. . . . However high we might attain in the future life, we might soar higher and still higher, if we had made the most of our God-given privileges and golden opportunities to improve our faculties here in this probationary existence" (*This Day With God*, p. 350).

The question is Could we enjoy heaven more had we done better while on earth? Of course, we don't believe Ellen White or anyone else would even consider the idea of saved persons suffering or being upset or restless in heaven because they failed to reach their full potential here. When we all get to heaven, the thief on the cross, the eleventh-hour laborer, and the deathbed convert all will enjoy heaven immensely. Rather, the point is that the longer and the more consistently a person serves the Lord, the greater will be his or her capacity for loving and knowing Him.

The younger a person learns this concept, the less remorse and guilt he or she will experience. The less a person falls into sin, the less scarring of the soul. Pound a nail into a board, and then pull it out. The nail is gone, but the scar remains.

We praise the Lord for His forgiveness, and His encouragement to use every ability and talent we possess to honor and glorify His name. Also, we should praise His name every time we have won a victory, through His power, over evil temptation. Then we will never be plagued with remorse for sins we could have committed. The life of victory and self-control yields rewards now and for eternity. It always pays to serve Jesus. Thank God for that fact.

Making Disciples
in the Home

And He said to them, "Follow Me, and I will make you fishers of men." Matt. 4:19, NASB.

One morning at daybreak Jesus was walking on the shore of the Sea of Galilee, hoping to spend a quiet hour by the water. Suddenly He noticed two men in their boat, fishing. As they drifted closer, He discovered they were His friends, Peter and Andrew. They had been fishing all night and had caught nothing. Jesus told them to row out a ways and cast their net again. This time it was so full of fish that it began to break, and they signaled to their partners, James and John, who were fishing close by, to come and help them. Both boats were soon so full that they began to sink under the weight. Shortly Jesus suddenly declared, "If you follow Me, you'll fish for men!" The men had already accepted Jesus, but His invitation now commissioned them to become His full-time disciples.

What does being a disciple involve? A disciple is a pupil, a learner, a follower; one who believes in certain teachings, follows a certain lifestyle, and develops a capacity for intimate relationships.

Jesus gives the same invitation to be His follower, or disciple, to everyone. What more effective place could there be to develop such discipleship than in the home? The home teaches and models certain truths, values, and lifestyle. As we endeavor to be and to make disciples, we have the privilege of leading our children by precept and example to Jesus.

A college student once talked with Bob during a Week of Prayer. She stated that when Bob spoke of a loving Father in heaven, it had only a negative effect on her heart. Then she described the terrible treatment she had received daily from the hands of her alcoholic father, who abused her physically and verbally. Only God, through His Spirit, could ever heal the wounds this lovely student had received as a child.

The family structure is where we learn relational skills for better or for worse. Our acts and words make indelible marks on each other in the family unit. If close, tender ties exist among the family members, then discipling for Christ becomes easier. Family members who experience warm relationships, unconditional love, affirmation, and encouragement, along with times of loving discipline and forgiveness and healing, are more likely to view God as a kind, loving, forgiving Father, and they will want a close relationship with Him, to become His disciples.

Children brought up in such homes will develop friendships within the community that could lead to fruitful witnessing. Becoming disciples of Jesus within the family is like a pebble dropped into the water, making never-ending ripples.

Thank Jesus today for the privilege of making disciples for Him. Write down relationships with your family that have been vital to you, and tell how they have helped make you disciples.

July 1

The Peril of Possessions

Then He said to them, "Watch out! Be on your guard against all kinds of greed; a man's life does not consist in the abundance of his possessions." Luke 12:15, NIV.

Charles Swindoll, in his book *Living on the Ragged Edge*, tells the story of Yussif the Terrible Turk—a 350-pound wrestling champion in Europe a little more than two generations ago. He agreed to wrestle the United States champion, Strangler Lewis, a small fellow in comparison with Yussif. Lewis had earned the name Strangler because his method of winning fights was to get his arm around his opponent's neck and cut off his supply of oxygen. The problem was that Yussif didn't have much of a neck; his body went from his head to his massive shoulders, with practically nothing between. Yussif won the match, demanded his $5,000 reward in gold and wrapped the championship belt around his huge waist. Stuffing the gold into his belt, he then boarded the S.S. *Bourgoyne* and set sail for Europe.

When the ship was halfway across the Atlantic, a storm struck and the *Bourgoyne* began to sink. Yussif, with his precious gold still weighing down his body, jumped over the side. But the added burden was too much for the Turk, and before other survivors could haul him into a lifeboat, he sank out of sight, never to be seen again.

Successful people usually don't wear their gold. They stash it away in banks or invest it in the stock market. But either way, greed is the bottom line for many of earth's masses. If it wasn't true, do you think Jesus would have given the strongly worded warning in our text? Jesus cautions against all kinds of greed—greed for position, for power, for acclaim.

Any individual who contemplates Jesus, the most ungreedy person to ever walk on earth, cannot help being touched by His simple, plain, loving, unselfish life. Living what He taught, Jesus demonstrated more clearly than anyone else that a happy life does not depend upon an abundance of possessions.

If it is your desire for Jesus to take your life more fully into His hands and unburden you from the tyranny of things, write out your praise appeal now.

Shields of Gold or Shields of Brass?

So Shishak king of Egypt came up against Jerusalem, and took away the treasures of the house of the Lord, and the treasures of the king's house; he took all: he carried away also the shields of gold which Solomon had made. Instead of which king Rehoboam made shields of brass. 2 Chron. 12:9, 10.

Rehoboam, the son of Solomon, by a rash decision and subsequent discourse, divided God's people into two separate nations—Israel in the north and Judah in the south. Attempting to rectify his mistake, for three years Rehoboam encouraged Judah to follow the ways of the Lord, but his vacillating character led the southern kingdom into idolatry. Ultimately, he and all Judah forsook God. Shishak, king of Egypt, knowing that the division had weakened God's people, attacked Jerusalem and carried away the decorative gold shields that Solomon had made. Because his treasury was too poor to replace the gold shields, Rehoboam substituted brass or bronze shields.

The shields dramatically symbolized the downward trend of Judah's power and position. Just as brass was inferior to the gold and silver in the image Nebuchadnezzar later dreamed about (Dan. 2), so Rehoboam's brass shields were far inferior to the gold ones that Shishak had taken as booty.

After the days of power and glory that marked the reigns of David and Solomon, a decided change came as both Israel and Judah declined through the years. Finally, Israel, the northern kingdom, met its tragic end in 722 B.C., all because of its unwillingness to walk in the ways of the Lord. Judah, with its checkered history, followed the same pattern to its downfall during the Jewish-Roman wars of the first and second centuries A.D.

Just as God's ancient people replaced their lost shields with inferior ones, so those who ignore God's will or rebel against Heaven exchange their gold shields for brass ones. Many trade their gold shields of integrity for the brass ones of dishonesty. Others substitute the gold of sexual purity for the brass of immorality. Still others replace their gold shields of faithfulness to God's church with the brass of rebellion and criticism. The list could go on.

Ask the Lord to help you treasure the gold shields of faith and love and keep you from ever exchanging them for anything else. Our God longs to keep Satan from stealing the gold shields of honor, morality, kindness, love, and faithfulness. Thank and praise Him for your shields of gold.

The World's Greatest Sinner

Here is a trustworthy saying that deserves full acceptance: Christ Jesus came into the world to save sinners—of whom I am the worst. 1 Tim. 1:15, NIV.

Paul claimed the dubious honor of being the worst of sinners. Note carefully that he does not say he *was* the worst, but that he *is* the worst. In Ephesians 3:8 he claimed to be the very least of all saints. One of the greatest evidences of being born again is that the sense of sinfulness and unworthiness is never lost and perhaps becomes more acute. To all who pursue righteousness, their only safeguard is to remember the pit from which Christ has rescued them (see Isa. 51:1).

John Knox, sixteenth-century Reformer and founder of the Presbyterian Church, would probably debate with Paul over who is the worst sinner. Knox was a man of tremendous conviction and courage, but he possessed character traits that he had to struggle against all his life. One of the most moving confessions we have ever read was one he made during the last year of his life.

"Lord Jesus, receive my spirit, and put an end at Thy good pleasure to this my miserable life: for justice and truth are not to be found among the sons of men. Be merciful unto me, Lord. Now after many battles, I find nothing in me but vanity and corruption. For in quietness I am negligent, in trouble impatient, tending to desperation.

"Pride and ambition assault me on the one part, covetousness and malice trouble me on the other: briefly, O Lord, the affections of the flesh do almost suppress the operation of Thy Spirit. . . . In none of the aforesaid do I delight, but I am troubled and that sore against the desire of my inward man which sobs for my corruption, and would repose in Thy mercy alone to which I claim, and that in the promise that Thou has made to all penitent sinners of whose number I profess myself to be one" (in Mark I. Bubeck, *The Adversary*, p. 33).

In your Christian struggle, do not get discouraged over your evil traits, but rather look to Jesus. He is your perfection. He is your justifier. He is your sanctifier. And He is the One who has saved you. Praise His wonderful name for all this and more, too!

Jesus Sets Us Free

Therefore if any man is in Christ, he is a new creature; the old things passed away; behold, new things have come. 2 Cor. 5:17, NASB.

All of us have problems that keep our minds in turmoil. Perhaps we have relatives, friends, or neighbors who upset us. In our prayers we may frequently ask God to work a miracle by transforming those who trouble us. Then something wonderful happens. As we pray we begin to feel different, not because *they* have changed, but because *we* have. We begin to see others through the eyes of Jesus. Love and compassion for them fill our hearts. Perhaps they may even change too, but if they don't, we find ourselves able to cope with the situation because God has helped us alter our own attitude.

When Jesus dwells in our hearts, He reveals to us our true and often erratic feelings and attitudes. Jesus gives us a glimpse into the real person we are and then sets us free. Free not only from wrong attitudes, but from any sin that enslaves us. While on earth Jesus said: " 'If you abide in My word, then you are truly disciples of Mine; and you shall know the truth, and the truth shall make you free.' . . . 'If therefore the Son shall make you free, you shall be free indeed' " (John 8:31-36, NASB).

As He liberates us from our critical and jealous attitudes and other sins, He molds us into the image of God. "We all, with unveiled face beholding as in a mirror the glory of the Lord, are being transformed into the same image from glory to glory" (2 Cor. 3:18, NASB).

Prayer especially changes us. We behold the glory of Jesus while communing with Him, and His glory in our hearts transforms us into His likeness. Although our progress may seem slow, the Spirit of God lets us know that transformation is indeed taking place in our lives.

We do not set out to change ourselves by making a plan for ourselves and then asking God to help us fulfill it. Rather, as we commune with Him we get to know Him and trust Him, and this leads us to ask Him to take control of our thoughts, motives, and actions. When we ask Him to fill our hearts and lives with His glory, change naturally follows.

Has prayer become obsolete in your life? If so, start praying today for renewed hope and determination to visit daily with Him. It will transform you into the likeness of Christ. Thank Him today for His marvelous transforming power in your life.

Newborn Babes

Like newborn babes, long for the pure milk of the word, that by it you may grow in respect to salvation. 1 Peter 2:2, NASB.

Here the word "newborn" refers to new Christians who have little knowledge or personal experience in walking the Christian pathway. As an infant craves its mother's milk, so a newborn Christian has a similar desire for the "pure milk" of the Word. Longtime Christians should have the same longing as well.

If salvation is our goal in life, how do we make room for God in an already jam-packed day? Taking time for the study of God's Word involves both organization and self-discipline, especially for busy parents of growing children. In today's fast-paced world, every conceivable problem pummels us. Such things as flat tires, leaking water pipes, broken-down washing machines, or baby Sue's measles stretch us to the limit. Modern inventions have made life easier, but with them come new sets of problems that make it difficult to squeeze in time for Bible study.

Interestingly enough, we never miss time spent with God, because it recharges our batteries for maximum efficiency the rest of the day. What we have to do we will get done wisely and lovingly. "In the midst of this maddening rush, God is speaking. He bids us come apart and commune with Him. . . . Many, even in their seasons of devotion, fail of receiving the blessing of real communion with God. They are in too great haste. . . . They have no time to remain with the divine Teacher. With their burdens they return to their work. . . . They must give themselves time to think, to pray, to wait upon God for a renewal of physical, mental, and spiritual power. They need the uplifting influence of His Spirit. Receiving this, they will be quickened by fresh life. The wearied frame and tired brain will be refreshed, the burdened heart will be lightened" (*Education*, pp. 260, 261).

A friend in Australia told Marie in a letter: "I rise each morning at 4:00 a.m., so that gives me two hours to devour the written Word, one hour with God, and then another reading and studying. Praise God I am an early riser, for I work full-time and that is my only spare time." Each of us has to make his or her own plan, but this is how one person organized her time and work so that she could schedule time alone with God.

Because God is invisible and His voice inaudible to our physical senses, our relationship with Him is easy to neglect. We won't hear Him complain, nor will we see the hurt on His face when we skip time with Him. Patiently He waits and continues knocking at our heart's door until we open it through communion with Him.

If you are one who is caught up in the bustle and hustle of life and have forgotten to take time to commune with the Lord, determine anew today to reorganize your life so that you can spend time with your best Friend. You will never regret it. Thank Him today for His Word, which is like a lamp to feet walking on a dark path (Ps. 119:105).

How to Treasure God's Word

Be diligent to present yourself approved to God as a workman who does not need to be ashamed, handling accurately the word of truth. 2 Tim. 2:15, NASB.

In our text today Paul tells Timothy that the only way he can rightly represent the Lord to God's people is to carefully and systematically study Scripture. As a tentmaker Paul believed in producing a product that he would not be ashamed of. He carried the same attitude into his preaching from the Word. We too need to be careful to interpret Scripture carefully and not distort it. Every aspect of truth should receive its proper emphasis so that nothing will obscure the principles that help us overcome sin and live a victorious life.

As His followers and students, we have Jesus' assurance: "I have called you friends, for all things that I have heard from My Father I have made known to you" (John 15:15, NASB).

Studying God's Word is an exciting experience. Choose a quiet place where you can be alone with God. Pull an imaginary curtain around you to shut the world out. As you read God's Love Letter, keep in mind that He is speaking to you individually and personally. Establish a pattern for reading your Bible.

We suggest that you select a book and stay with it until you have finished it. Underline those passages that specifically speak to your heart, and note any blessings you have received, as well as questions that come to you.

Another approach is to choose a topic and thoroughly study its meaning through the aid of the writings of Ellen White, a Bible concordance, *The Seventh-day Adventist Bible Commentary*, and other helps. Study one verse at a time, meditate on it, figure out how it fits into its context, and then think how you can apply it to your own life and your particular circumstances. Ask the Holy Spirit to impress you. As you do, new ideas will open before you. You will feel God's presence as never before and sense a close relationship with Him. A new determination to do right will flood your soul. You can then say as David did: "With all my heart I have sought Thee; do not let me wander from Thy commandments. Thy word I have treasured in my heart, that I may not sin against Thee" (Ps. 119:10, 11, NASB).

When we really get to know Jesus through Bible study and prayer, the words we speak will be His and the things we do will be from His prompting. We will live out our lives in Him moment by moment. Then we can say with the psalmist: "I have set the Lord continually before me; because He is at my right hand, I will not be shaken" (Ps. 16:8, NASB).

197

If . . .

Thy testimonies are wonderful; therefore my soul observes them. The unfolding of Thy words gives light; it gives understanding to the simple. Ps. 119:129, 130, NASB.

If the words that Christ spoke are spirit and are life (John 6:63);

if the Scriptures "cannot be broken" (John 10:35, NASB);

if the Scriptures testify of One who alone can give eternal life (John 5:39);

if we are commanded to rightly handle the Word of Truth (2 Tim. 2:15);

if the proper study of the Word keeps us from sinning against God (Ps. 119:11);

if the rise of the Advent movement is traceable to the study of the Scriptures (*The Great Controversy*, pp. 410, 411);

if we are to demonstrate to others that we "consider it more important to obtain a knowledge of God's Word than to secure the gains or pleasures of the world" (*Child Guidance,* p. 571);

if "through the study of the Scriptures we obtain a correct knowledge of how to live so as to enjoy the greatest amount of unalloyed happiness" (*Testimonies*, vol. 3, p. 374);

if when the Bible is studied with the aid of the Holy Spirit, the result is a well-balanced mind and a harmonious development of the "physical, mental, and moral powers" (*Fundamentals of Christian Education*, pp. 433, 434);

if the Bible creates "a better moral atmosphere . . . and a new power to resist temptation" (*ibid.*, p. 434);

if the Bible is "more effective than any other book in guiding wisely in the affairs of this life" (*Counsels to Parents and Teachers,* p. 448);

if "the Bible will teach us what nothing else can teach" (*Messages to Young People,* p. 257);

if through the Word of God we live and fellowship with heaven and finally will find ourselves at home in heaven's companionship (*Education,* p. 127);

then rejoice and praise the Lord for the privilege of having God's precious Word and the freedom to study it!

Thank the Lord in a few words for what the Scriptures mean to you. Be specific, if possible.

We Still Believe

Until we all attain to the unity of the faith, and of the knowledge of the Son of God, to a mature man, to the measure of the stature which belongs to the fulness of Christ. As a result, we are no longer to be children, tossed here and there by waves, and carried about by every wind of doctrine, by the trickery of men, by craftiness in deceitful scheming. Eph. 4:13, 14, NASB.

In 1975 General Conference president Robert H. Pierson wrote a book entitled *We Still Believe*. It encouraged many of us to have confidence in our basic doctrines. Doctrine, which is simply a belief, is extremely important. How we understand the person of Christ is a doctrine, a belief. The meaning of His atonement is another. The purpose of doctrine is simply to give us an expanded knowledge of God's character and His plan of salvation.

If you ever walk by the seaside and watch the restless waves roll in, you will get a sense of what it means to be "tossed here and there by waves, and carried about by every wind of doctrine, by the trickery of men, by craftiness in deceitful scheming." True doctrine gives stability to the believer.

We praise God for the clarity and simplicity of the Bible doctrines that our church has put together in its list of 27 fundamental beliefs. If studied properly, our beliefs give a solid foundation to stand on. They provide security and a positive reason and hope for our existence.

In his book Pastor Pierson tells the well-known story of the Roman orator Cicero, whose speeches caused his hearers to say, "How well you speak." In contrast, when Demosthenes, the great Greek leader, finished his orations, the people cried out, "Let us march!" Drawing a lesson, Pierson said: "I do not want anyone to come to me and say, 'How well you wrote'; but I pray that God by His Holy Spirit will light a spark that will kindle a fire in the hearts of our workers all around the world and that it will compel every member to cry out, 'Let us march!' " (p. 193). He wanted our doctrines to capture and motivate our people, and lead them to the source of all doctrine—Jesus Christ.

Are you thankful for the system of beliefs that God has led this church to rediscover from His marvelous Word? If so, list some belief that is of particular importance in your life and praise God for it.

_____

_____

Sounds of Joy

Then David spoke to the chiefs of the Levites to appoint their relatives the singers, with instruments of music, harps, lyres, loud-sounding cymbals, to raise sounds of joy. 1 Chron. 15:16, NASB.

Included in David's plan to take the ark from the Philistines and bring it to Jerusalem was a special musical tribute of joy to God. Music touched both the private and public lives of the Hebrews in the Old Testament. In their social gatherings and their processions—whether religious, triumphal, bridal, or funeral—music played an integral part. In David's and Solomon's court, choirs of men and women were organized.

How we wish we could have compact disk or tape recordings of the music from both Old and New Testament times! The Psalms were undoubtedly sung to chants or short simple melodies accompanied by appropriate instruments. Alternate singing from side to side was frequent.

In the New Testament we read an interesting experience of Jesus coming into the home of a synagogue official whose daughter had died. The record states: "When Jesus came into the official's house, and saw the flute-players, and the crowd in noisy disorder, He began to say, 'Depart; for the girl is not dead, but is asleep'" (Matt. 9:23, 24, NASB). One wonders what part the music played in causing the crowd to be disorderly and noisy.

However, music, when rightly used, is a powerful form of praise. It is an effective way to help young people memorize words as they repeat them in song.

Music "has power to subdue rude and uncultivated natures; power to quicken thought and to awaken sympathy, to promote harmony of action, and to banish the gloom and foreboding that destroy courage and weaken effort. . . .

"When Christ was a child . . . He was tempted to sin, but He did not yield to temptation. As He grew older He was tempted, but the songs His mother had taught Him to sing came into His mind, and He would lift His voice in praise. And before His companions were aware of it, they would be singing with Him. God wants us to use every facility which Heaven has provided for resisting the enemy" (*Evangelism*, pp. 496-498).

Unfortunately, Satan realizes the power of music and is skilled in exciting and charming human minds with music that does not elevate our thinking.

After listening to the final notes of the latest rock hit song, a teenage girl said, "Did you ever hear anything so wonderful?"

Her father replied, "Only once, when a truck loaded with empty milk cans bumped another truck filled with live ducks!"

We recognize that personal taste plays a large role in what kind of music people appreciate. Nonetheless, too often even some Christian music with discordant sounds does not elevate our souls.

Praise God for music that builds us spiritually. Thank Him for the marvelous hymns we have in our hymnal. Tell what good music means to your soul, and try to be specific.

Prophets and Prosperity

Yet the Lord warned Israel and Judah, through all His prophets and every seer, saying, "Turn from your evil ways and keep My command- ments, My statutes according to all the law which I commanded your fathers, and which I sent to you through My servants the prophets." 2 Kings 17:13, NASB.

What would happen if we abruptly removed the writings of Ellen White and their influence from the Seventh-day Adventist Church? It would have a devastating effect on most of us.

We were but a disorganized handful of Advent believers when God gave Ellen White her first prophetic vision in December of 1844. That she was a mere 17 years old and had only a few years of formal education and yet claimed to have direct revelations from the Lord didn't help the image of our movement during its infancy.

When you add to it the stigma of poverty, the fanatical behavior of a few individuals, and unpopular doctrines such as the seventh-day Sabbath, you can understand why the chances of Adventism surviving were not too encouraging.

F. D. Nichol, in his work *Ellen G. White and Her Critics*, stated the case eloquently. "Onlookers in the late 1840s, and for some time beyond, dismissed this little Sabbathkeeping Adventist group as a ragtag end of a raveled-out movement that would soon be nothing more than a curious paragraph in the history books" (p. 22).

Without the Spirit of Prophecy in our church, we would probably number a few hundred at best today, if even that. Unity, despite endless discussions on some points, would have disappeared. The Spirit of Prophecy has amplified and strengthened our concepts of last-day events. Our world missions would never have existed without the powerful instruction and urging of God through Ellen White.

How is it that this rather small group of Adventists eventually entered nearly 200 countries and grew to a world membership in the millions? Our early, poverty-stricken leaders reacted in dismay at the thought of their little church trying to reach every nation, kindred, tongue, and people. But can you imagine Seventh-day Adventism today without its mission pageant at General Conference sessions? Without Dr. Harry Miller, Fernando Stahl, or John

Nevins Andrews? Without medical launches on the Amazon? Without airstrips in the jungles? Without dental clinics, hospitals, or educational institutions? We owe an incalculable debt to our Lord for the gift of prophecy.

Take time to thank God for how it has helped the Adventist Church spread wide and far, bringing this message to the attention of leaders and governments around the world. Write a few words of praise and thankfulness to God for His prophetic leadership.

_____

_____

July 11

Born of God

For whatever is born of God overcomes the world; and this is the victory that has overcome the world—our faith. And who is the one who overcomes the world, but he who believes that Jesus is the Son of God? 1 John 5:4, 5, NASB.

Being born of God was a special theme of the apostle John. The only New Testament writer to include the story of Nicodemus, he made it clear that those who receive Christ have power to become God's children. He further elaborates that the new-birth experience is not one of being born of blood or of human will, but of God (see John 1:12, 13).

John emphasizes that a supernatural experience must happen in the heart and life of any person truly born of God. It does not mean that he or she must have some earthshaking experience, but rather a definite change in attitude toward God and fellow human beings.

In our text today, John combines a new-birth experience with victory over the world. We could say that if the new birth is a result of justification, then sanctification leads to victory over evil. Then John states that the person who does overcome the world "believes that Jesus is the Son of God." It is all a Christ-centered, Christ-oriented experience.

Every bookstore today contains an amazing number of titles dealing with how to change or how to overcome this or that. Both our daughters have taken considerable course work in psychology, and they have shared with us some of the textbooks they have used. Only those written by Christians introduce the concept of a person's need of God, especially to effect lasting change. Others promote such things as shock therapy, brain surgery, chemotherapy, supportive psychotherapy, assertion training, and even yoga.

We do not deny the usefulness of certain behavior modification techniques in aiding people to face life's stresses. The human race can stand all the improvement it can get by any legitimate means, and we must not underplay the role of the will in effecting change. After all, we are made in the image of God. But the new-birth experience constitutes more than outward transformation. It gets to the real heart of the problem.

To alter the deepest motives of a person's life, only an understanding of the atonement and a sense of Christ's pardoning love can effect any permanent change. "The light shining from the cross reveals the love of God. His love is drawing us to Himself. If we do not resist this drawing, we shall be led to the foot of the cross in repentance for the sins that have crucified the Saviour. Then the Spirit of God through faith produces a new life in the soul. The thoughts and desires are brought into obedience to the will of Christ. The heart, the mind, are created anew in the image of Him who works in us to subdue all things to Himself. Then the law of God is written in the mind and heart, and we can say with Christ, 'I delight to do thy will, O my God' " (*The Desire of Ages*, p. 176).

It is our desire to share how much Jesus means to us. He is a precious jewel that sparkles and shines in the brilliant sunlight of the cross. As we look to Him we will be attracted to Him and forget our obsession with ourselves. It is God's love, and His love alone, that leads to this new-birth experience. We praise Him for His magnificent love, and urge you to jot down a few words of praise and thanksgiving for what He has done for you.

Love,
the Greatest Medicine

Walk in a manner worthy of the calling with which you have been called, with all humility and gentleness, with patience, showing forbearance to one another in love. Eph. 4:1, 2, NASB.

One evening Winston Churchill attended a banquet. After the guests had finished eating, someone asked them who they would like to be if they had to be someone else. When Churchill's turn came, he walked over and stood behind the chair of his wife, Clementine, took her by the hand, and said, "If I could not be who I am, I would like to be Lady Churchill's second husband." His was certainly a unique way to express affection, respect, and appreciation for his spouse.

Love, like life, is a gift from our wonderful Creator. He created every human with the innate capacity to give and receive love, and He planted within our hearts the need to love and be loved.

Someone has said, "To be manifestly loved, to be openly admired, are human needs as basic as breathing." Why is it, then, that we so often fail to express our love to others when we feel such a great need of it ourselves? A plaque hanging beside our kitchen window reminds us to "give the world a little love today." "If you love somebody, show it" announces another plaque close by. It depicts a little boy with an expression of exhilaration as four little puppies express their love for him by climbing all over him and licking his neck and cheeks.

Love is not just an emotion—it is action. "Love can no more exist without revealing itself in outward acts than fire can be kept alive without fuel" (*Testimonies*, vol. 1, p. 695). Like a plant, love must be fed and handled with care if it is to grow. What are some of the ways we can nurture love? What about being flexible, not always insisting on having our own way, giving more than receiving, showing genuine concern for others through a willingness to take time to listen? We can put ourselves second instead of first, accept the feelings of another instead of belittling them, and admit when we are wrong.

"Let there be no more bitter resentment or anger, no more shouting or slander, and let there be no bad feeling of any kind among you. Be kind to each other, be compassionate. Be as ready to forgive others as God for Christ's sake has forgiven you" (Eph. 4:31, 32, Phillips).

Dr. Karl Menninger, the famous psychiatrist, once said, "Love is the medicine for the healing of the world." What a different world we would live in if love were the motivating force between people and nations!

Thank God for the love He has planted in your heart and for His power to forgive and forget. Describe your last experience of forgiveness and tell how you felt about it.

_____

_____

July 13

Marriage, a Divine Institution

And the Lord God said, it is not good that man should be alone; I will make him a helper comparable to him. Gen. 2:18, NKJV.

As the Creation story unfolds in Genesis, we read that God caused a deep sleep to fall on Adam so that He could take one of Adam's ribs to create Eve. Then He proudly presented her to the man. Adam's response, "This is now bone of my bones and flesh of my flesh" (Gen. 2:23, NKJV), implies the close relationship that God intended them to have forever. Jesus confirmed the divine intention when He said, "And the two will become one flesh. So they are no longer two, but one" (Mark 10:8, NIV).

In the marriage union the "one-flesh" concept fuses a man and a woman in their relationship to each other without the loss of individual personality. It signifies a unity, a complete partnership in which each complements and enhances the other. It was not God's plan for one spouse to be superior to or rule over the other.

"Eve was created from a rib taken from the side of Adam, signifying that she was not to control him as the head, nor to be trampled under his feet as an inferior, but to stand by his side as an equal, to be loved and protected by him. . . . She was his second self, showing the close union and the affectionate attachment that should exist in this relation" (*Patriarchs and Prophets*, p. 46).

In marriage God does not bestow upon one person all the family talents, gifts, and decision-making ability, but He has stipulated certain responsibilities that each person should have. The husband, as head of the family corporation, does not have a superior position above the rest of the family, but rather has a special office of service to help the family relationships grow and thrive. He is to show initiative in guiding the family in the ways of God by lovingly leading them as a shepherd tenderly cares for his flock.

"The father is to stand at the head of his family, not as an overgrown, undisciplined boy, but as a man with manly character and with his passions controlled" (*The Adventist Home*, p. 213). As Karl Barth said: "It is not 'dominium' but 'ministerium.'" The husband loves his wife as Christ loved the church and gave Himself for it (Eph. 5:25) — a self-sacrificing love. He loves his wife as his own body (verse 28) and is willing to offer life itself for her well-being.

What wife would not be glad to recognize, acknowledge, and support the headship of such a husband? It does not mean she loses her personhood, dignity, or self-respect. While the husband is head of the marriage, she is equally as important as its heart. "Next to God, the mother's power for good is the strongest known on earth" (*ibid.*, p. 240).

If you are married, thank God for this divine institution of marriage and for the part you play in it.

The Visited Planet

Therefore, He had to be made like His brethren in all things, that He might become a merciful and faithful high priest in things pertaining to God, to make propitiation for the sins of the people. For since He Himself was tempted in that which He has suffered, He is able to come to the aid of those who are tempted. Heb. 2:17, 18, NASB.

J. B. Phillips in his book *New Testament Christianity* describes an imaginary conversation between a senior angel and a very young one whom he was showing around the universe. The little angel was getting a bit tired and bored of viewing whirling galaxies and blazing suns. Finally the experienced angel showed him the galaxy containing our tiny planetary system. As the two drew near our sun, the senior angel pointed to a small, rather insignificant sphere turning slowly on its axis.

"I want you to watch that one particularly," the older angel said.

"Well, it looks very small and rather dirty to me," the new angel commented. "What's special about that one?"

"That," replied his senior solemnly, "is the visited planet."

"Visited? You don't mean visited by—?"

"Indeed I do. That ball, which I have no doubt looks to you small and insignificant and not perhaps overclean, has been visited by our young Prince of Glory."

As the conversation unfolds, the senior angel reveals the amazing story of how Jesus became one of us. It so shocked the new angel that he asked, "Do you mean to tell me that He stooped so low as to become one of those creeping, crawling creatures on that floating ball?"

"I do, and I don't think He would like you to call them 'creeping, crawling creatures' in that tone of voice. For, strange as it may seem to us, He loves them. He went down to lift them up to become like Him."

The little angel considered it quite incomprehensible. The story continues with the senior angel taking the little angel back in time. He shows him how "the Light visited our planet, lived among us in our stupidity and darkness. When he came to the part of how the people He came to save killed Him rather than accept Him as their Saviour, the little angel responded, 'The fools, the crazy fools! They don't deserve—'

"Neither you nor I nor any other angel knows why they were so foolish and so wicked," the senior angel commented.

This imaginary experience reminds us that the angels are utterly astounded over God's love and our feeble response. Do we really understand that we are in the middle of the drama of the ages?

Honor Jesus in a few words for His coming to our planet to redeem you.

July 15

R_X for Spiritual Growth

The Jews therefore were marveling, saying, "How has this man become learned, having never been educated?" Jesus therefore answered them, and said, "My teaching is not Mine, but His who sent Me." John 7:15, 16, NASB.

Their question obviously did not mean that Christ was illiterate, but rather that He had no formal theological training. Even as a 12-year-old Child He astounded the best minds in Jerusalem with His questions and answers. The deep truths He skillfully brought to the surface by His innocent questions intrigued the Jewish scholars. "All who heard Him were amazed at His understanding and His answers" (Luke 2:47, NASB).

Christ did not enter our world with a head filled with divine knowledge and wisdom. Instead, because He had assumed the garb of humanity, His spiritual, mental, physical, and social powers expanded as He conformed to and obeyed those principles that govern all human development.

When tempted by Satan in the wilderness, Jesus responded, "It is written, That man shall not live by bread alone, but by every word of God" (Luke 4:4). As Jesus learned the Scriptures from childhood, He understood that the Bible is our only safeguard against error and illusion. Note Christ's reply to the wily Sadducees who tried to trip Him on a sticky theological question: "You are mistaken, and surely this is the reason: you do not know either the scriptures or the power of God" (Mark 12:24, NEB).

The Holy Spirit does not guide people apart from the Scriptures—if they are available. Numerous religious books and magazines flood both secular and denominational presses around the world. We do not condemn the reading of such publications, but we appeal for you to spend more of your energy and time in studying the Word of God itself.

The authoritative, infallible revelation of God must be our source of power, our standard of right and wrong. Our minds, fickle as they are, cannot know the right way unless controlled by biblical principles. How thankful we are for His Word! What does it really mean to you?

This Man Receives Sinners

What man among you, if he has a hundred sheep and has lost one of them, does not leave the ninety-nine in the open pasture, and go after the one which is lost, until he finds it? Luke 15:4, NASB.

The story behind this story is the vying of tax gatherers and sinners to be part of Jesus' audience. As a result, the Pharisees, Sadducees, and scribes began to grumble, saying, "This man receives sinners and eats with them" (Luke 15:2, NASB). No wonder the sinners and outcasts gladly heard what He had to say! Jesus did not despise them as the religious leaders did. While His own pure life was a constant rebuke to evil, at the same time His message of salvation offered them hope and awakened a desire in their hearts to serve Him.

The three parables in this chapter have the same intent. Jesus skillfully designed the stories to show the Pharisees how unlike God the Father they were in their attitude toward sinners. The parables illustrate the tremendous joy of a shepherd locating his lost sheep, a housewife finding her precious piece of money, and a father being reunited with his lost son. The first two parables illustrate how God's love constantly seeks out the object of His love; whereas the prodigal son parable reveals a proper response to that love.

No parable can adequately illustrate God's love, of course, but sinners cannot help but get a clearer view of our Saviour's love if they study the three parables of Luke 15.

The story about the lost sheep must have struck a sore spot in the Sadducees' hearts. The Old Testament writers often described the priests as shepherds of Israel. As they glanced at one another, the question undoubtedly flashed into their minds as to how lax they were in really searching out the lost souls among them.

Undoubtedly, fear and longing to be home with the other sheep filled the mind of the lost sheep, if sheep can be said to have minds. This poor, bleating animal presents a pathetic picture. Sheep are helpless creatures and need constant loving care. It is pitiful to see any animal lost, but the real loss is on the part of the shepherd. A lost sheep simply cannot understand the heart of the shepherd. This is doubly true of the Divine Shepherd, who searches for lost sinners. Our Shepherd, Jesus, suffers the greatest loss, not the sinner for whom He is searching. Can you imagine how our Lord feels when His efforts to find a sinner fail? The agony is totally beyond our comprehension.

We believe that if every sinner on earth realized the heartbreak our Saviour-Shepherd experiences over His lost sheep, he or she would desperately want to come back to the fold and truly follow Him forever!

Please praise your heavenly Shepherd for finding you! If you need to be found, then praise Him for His efforts to return you to the sheepfold. Let Him know that you want to come back home now.

God's Feelings Toward Us

As a shepherd seeketh out his flock in the day that he is among his sheep that are scattered; so will I seek out my sheep, and will deliver them out of all places where they have been scattered in the cloudy and dark day. Eze. 34:12.

In Christ's parable of the lost sheep, the shepherd goes to find the smallest possible number of lost sheep—one. Jesus does not save mobs, crowds, or multitudes. He delivers people one at a time. Jesus loves one. He saves one. Our Saviour would have died for just one! According to Ellen White, He risked the safety of the unfallen universe to rescue our world, and He would have done it even for one individual. Although it is beyond our comprehension, it is nonetheless true.

The heart of Jesus cries out for His lost sheep. In the Old Testament He agonized through His prophet Hosea: "How can I give you up, O Ephraim? How can I surrender you, O Israel? . . . My heart is turned over within Me, all My compassions are kindled" (Hosea 11:8, NASB). Could anyone imagine a more powerful description of how God feels toward us, His lost sheep? Too often we think of how we feel, but the element that touches our hearts redemptively is how He feels. Jesus seeks our salvation not merely for our sakes, but because He is a God of love. He seeks us because He misses us terribly. This is why there is such incomprehensible joy in heaven even over one sinner who repents (Luke 15:7).

Our Lord's feelings of self-sacrificing love for us should give both sinners and saints alike food for thought. When Bob attended the theological seminary, one of his assignments involved researching the subject of the objective atonement. It meant studying the plan of salvation from God's viewpoint, not ours. In other words, how did *God* feel when He gave His only begotten Son to save the human race? If we carefully tried to see salvation through God's eyes, it would open up to us a whole new perspective on His incomparable love. We cannot begin to grasp God's love fully when we concentrate exclusively on how we react to Christ's death on the cross.

The parable of the lost sheep emphasizes the objective atonement—God's viewpoint of the plan of salvation. It is the shepherd who makes certain the 99 are accounted for, and it is he who seeks the solitary lost sheep. Our Lord came from the green pastures of heaven to our desert world where billions of sheep have been and are lost. He left the safety of the heavenly fold and did not turn back as the thorns lacerated His head and the nails tore into His flesh. He left a trail of blood across the earth as He searched for His lost sheep.

"And when he has found it, he lays it on his shoulders, rejoicing" (verse 5, NASB). Could He more tenderly demonstrate His love than by laying us on His own shoulders and carrying us back home? He does not whip us or drive us—never! He "who bore our sin in His body" loves us even to the point of death (1 Peter 2:24, NASB).

How much do you really appreciate our Divine Shepherd? Imagine yourself as a sheep. How would you show your love and gratitude to Him?

_____

_____

What Causes Joy in Heaven?

And when he comes home, he calls together his friends and his neighbors, saying to them, "Rejoice with me, for I have found my sheep which was lost!" I tell you that in the same way, there will be more joy

in heaven over one sinner who repents, than over ninety-nine righteous
persons who need no repentance. Luke 15:6, 7, NASB.

The lost sheep parable ends in great joy. Jesus takes delight in championing the cause of the lost, and He uses beautiful illustrations to defend His actions. It is important to remember that the Lord Himself searches for His lost sheep. The sheep don't seek Him. Many believe that sinners must repent before God bestows His love on them. Unfortunately this is righteousness by works in its worst form. Repentance becomes a work that earns God's love. Because the Pharisees reasoned this way, they angrily protested, "This man receiveth sinners." Note the contempt in their words "This man."

"In the parable of the lost sheep, Christ teaches that salvation does not come through our seeking after God but through God's seeking after us" (*Christ's Object Lessons*, p. 189). Scripture states: "There is none who understands, there is none who seeks for God. All have turned aside" (Rom. 3:11, 12, NASB). A person cannot truly repent unless he or she first experiences God's love. Repentance itself is a wonderful gift that comes only from God Himself.

The parable ends with the shepherd returning home and holding a grand party. True rejoicing cannot exist apart from fellowship. Imagine yourself a mother bringing home from the hospital your child after he has just recovered from serious surgery. How would the rest of the family react? Everyone, brothers and sisters included, would naturally celebrate his return with great joy.

The idea of more joy over one sinner who repents than over the 99 who need no repentance rebukes the self-righteous. All of us are sinners, and we all need to repent. But only those who understand and experience God's greatness really sense that fact. Jesus can save only those have a deep sense of their lost condition. He cannot help those who feel no need for help.

We have no idea of the amount of joyous celebration that goes on in heaven when one sinner turns around and repents. All heaven reverberates in a praise service, and it will celebrate just as joyously for each one of us.

Why not praise the Lord right now for finding you?

July   19

The Woman Who Lost
One Coin

Or what woman, if she has ten silver coins and loses one coin, does not light a lamp and sweep the house and search carefully until she finds it? Luke 15:8, NASB.

When we visited the traditional site of Mount Sinai in the Egyptian desert some years ago, we met several Bedouin groups. We were able to take close-up photographs of several women who had headdresses decorated with numerous coins hanging down over their foreheads. Our guide told us that the coins in these headdresses were part of their dowry and represented an important part of their wealth and possessions. When we saw the coins we immediately thought of Jesus' parable.

Palestinian homes, in Christ's day especially, were not known for their large, bright, airy rooms or for their cleanliness. They had only one or two tiny windows at best, and an oil lamp would burn in them even during the daytime so that its inhabitants could see. The floor was packed down dirt. The parable says that the woman had to light a lamp to search for her lost possession. A bronze or even silver coin could easily vanish into the dust of the dirt floor.

A dowry coin was important not only for its intrinsic worth, which the woman could replace, but also for its priceless and irreplaceable sentimental value. It was an heirloom passed on from one generation to the next. The fact that the coin was lost did not diminish its value. So also with the lost sinner. Though lost, he or she is still of inestimable value to Jesus. He did not give His life for worthless beings. We cost the life and death of Jesus! How much more valuable could we be?

There are some interesting comparisons and contrasts between the lost sheep and the lost coin. The lost sheep knew its condition, but the coin had no sense of its state. Nevertheless, it was still lost. Many in the world today have never read a Bible, never heard a sermon, and have no idea of God's love and His plan to redeem them. They have little or no concept of sin and what it has done to them. Yet they are lost. Can one think of a greater reason for supporting our church's Global Mission program?

The sheep was lost far from home; whereas the coin is lost right at home. To Christ's audience, home was Jerusalem and the Jewish people. Doubtless they understood Christ's allusion. Perhaps the lost sheep could represent the Gentile out of the fold; whereas the lost coin symbolized the Jews who were supposedly in the fold. Here in the coin parable we find God's special people, most of whom were in a lost condition. Could it apply to us today? How many of us as parents have lost coins—children—right in our own homes? The greatest and most important mission field in the world consists of our own homes.

Praise the Lord that He is sweeping the house—and that He has given us the opportunity of sweeping with Him—and finding the lost coin or coins in our own homes. Write down the names of one or two people for whom you want to thank God for allowing you to be a redemptive witness.

_____

_____

Rejoicing Angels

And when she has found it [the lost coin], she calls together her friends and neighbors, saying, "Rejoice with me, for I have found the coin which I had lost!" In the same way, I tell you, there is joy in the presence of the angels of God over one sinner who repents. Luke 15:9, 10, NASB.

The parable of the lost coin reveals that the woman had 10 silver coins to begin with, so she still had nine left when she had lost the one. The lost sheep parable had only one missing out of a hundred. Whatever the proportion, Heaven is always concerned over the lost. (*Heaven*, a term that usually includes the Godhead and the angels, was also a common substitute that the Jews used for the name of God Himself.)

The coin lost at home should concern all Christians. Home should be the place that demonstrates the ultimate in care for the spiritual welfare of each family member. But if a child or spouse is still unconverted, do not despair. Remember that God found both the lost sheep and the lost coin. No one is beyond God's reach. Some cases may appear hopeless, but God keeps His lamp lit and continues searching for the "lost coin"—and so should you.

A family member is even more important to God than that piece of dowry money was to the Israelite woman. This does not mean that God can save all the lost—especially if they refuse to accept His salvation—but it does mean that we should never give up praying and searching for them.

John Newton, the Anglican clergyman and hymn writer, was the son of a merchant sea captain. His unsettled youth led him to a rather desolate life. He tried to escape from the royal navy after having been forced to join. Arrested in West Africa, after a time he virtually became the slave of a White slave trader's African wife. In 1747, while he was on board a ship going to England, a violent storm nearly sank the vessel. The voyage was Newton's moment of truth and conversion.

Years later a minister by the name of William Jay visited him. Newton shared with Jay a letter he had just received from a person both of them knew. The minister told Newton that the man had for years regularly attended his church, "but he was a most awful character, and almost in all evil."

"But," Newton observed, "he writes now like a penitent."

Jay responded by saying that if their mutual acquaintance had changed, he would never despair of the conversion of anyone again! Newton's reply contains the thought that every truly converted sinner will never forget. He said that he also never despaired of anyone's conversion, since he himself had been saved by the Lord.

Newton's hymn "Amazing Grace" reveals that he knew from experience what those words meant. "Amazing grace! how sweet the sound, That saved a wretch like me! I once was lost, but now am found, Was blind but now I see."

Cannot we all praise our Lord for finding us? We can hear the angels rejoicing that we, as lost sheep and coins, are now safe! Even more than that, God Himself rejoices. How do you respond to that wonderful fact?

Why Leave Home?

And He said, "A certain man had two sons; and the younger of them said to his father, 'Father, give me the share of the estate that falls to me.' And he divided his wealth between them." Luke 15:11, 12, NASB.

Jesus' story about the prodigal is known as the pearl and crown of all biblical parables. The details that Jesus shared with His hearers make it the most elaborate parable that He ever taught. It never grows old with telling.

Probably the two sons represent the Jews and Gentiles, yet the lessons taught by the parable apply to every person. The preceding two parables of the lost sheep and the lost coin say nothing about the sinner's departure from God or the terrible misery of living apart from God. The stories of the lost sheep and the lost coin emphasize God's wonderful attitude toward lost sinners; in these stories, He goes in search of them. The parable of the prodigal son underscores the principle that the way of the transgressor is hard.

The son demands his share of his father's estate now, not after the death of his parents. He considers his home a prison simply because his father's rules bind his wild spirit. His desire for total, complete independence outweighs his better judgment. Sadly, he is a son only in name, not in heart. Honoring his father and mother never enters his thoughts. So he proceeds to plan his whole life for pleasure and not for responsibility.

The parable reveals that the ungrateful son went to a far, or distant, country. Anyone who willingly breaks his relationship with the Lord is spiritually in a distant land. There the boy squandered his share of his father's estate. Perhaps he had heard his father read at worship time, "A man who loves wisdom makes his father glad, but he who keeps company with harlots wastes his wealth" (Prov. 29:3, NASB). But somehow it failed to make an impression on him.

Note that although the son was wasting his health and wealth, he still was having fun. Sin really does give a certain type of pleasure. "Stolen waters are sweet, and bread eaten in secret is pleasant" (Prov. 9:17, NASB). Eventually the young man ran out of money just when a severe famine hit the country. Food prices skyrocketed until they were out of reach—and so were his so-called friends. He finally found a job caring for swine. It was humiliating for a Jew to care for pigs, of course. The parable also states that no one would give him anything to eat, so he took some of the pigs' food.

Tomorrow we will continue this story, but today praise the Lord for the knowledge and faith you have in our Father above. If you have never left His home or you did and have returned, write out your thanks to Him for His constant love.

Repentance in a Pigpen

But when he came to his senses, he said, "How many of my father's hired men have more than enough bread, but I am dying here with hunger! I will get up and go to my father, and will say to him, 'Father, I have sinned against heaven, and in your sight; I am no longer worthy to be called your son; make me as one of your hired men.'" Luke 15:17-19, NASB.

When people lose everything and are virtually starving to death, even the most stubborn heart finds itself subdued. But even then the mind can still hold out in rebellion. Ephraim and Samaria, despite having run out of hope, still traveled the road of rebellion. They continued to refuse to submit to God. They asserted "in pride and in arrogance of heart: 'The bricks have fallen down, but we will rebuild with smooth stones; the sycamores have been cut down, but we will replace them with cedars'" (Isa. 9:9, 10, NASB).

The prodigal son did not surrender to God until he found himself in a miserable, miry pigpen and had nothing to eat but pods from the carob tree. Why do so many sinners have to plummet to the bottom of the pit before they look up? He had wasted his time, possessions, and even his life at that point.

Sin is the most expensive commodity available, destroying us mentally, physically, and morally. It withers our finer feelings until we, like Samson, find ourselves shorn of our spiritual locks. Sin is like the detective who found the criminal he was searching for. He joined the criminal in his thievery, and after gaining his confidence convinced the thief to try on a pair of handcuffs, which he then snapped shut. The detective had his prey. Sin also captures its prey.

Thank God the prodigal son finally looked up and began to think of his father's home. Soon he had his speech of repentance rehearsed. Too ashamed to let himself be taken back as a son, he thought he would ask for a job as a hired servant. At least he would get decent food even if his father no longer considered him a son.

Then comes the grand reunion, something totally unexpected by the son, who didn't understand his father's character. Because he operated on the principle of salvation by works and not faith in his father's love, he assumed that he had to buy that love. We misinterpret God because we don't understand His heart of love. This parable—if it teaches us anything—reveals what kind of God we serve. He will not hold our sins against us if we acknowledge and reject them.

God will never refuse forgiveness to the vilest sinner. Christianity has as the very heart of its teaching God's love and forgiveness.

It is God's power of forgiveness—His justification—that pardons sinners and changes lives. Shall we not praise Him in writing for His forgiving power?

Kisses of Forgetfulness and Forgiveness

And he got up and came to his father. But while he was still a long way off, his father saw him, and felt compassion for him, and ran and embraced him, and kissed him. . . . The father said to his slaves, "Quickly bring out the best robe and put it on him, and put a ring on his hand and sandals on his feet; and bring the fattened calf, kill it, and let us eat and be merry." Luke 15:20-23, NASB.

This passage brings out touching details of the father's love. But before we get to that, notice that the wayward son comes home just as he is. He wears filthy rags and has wornout shoes on his feet. His long, matted hair reeks with the pigpen aroma that also floats about his unwashed body. Everything about him screams of a person truly in desperate need. He dramatically reflects all sinners who come to Christ. Even though we may look ever so nice on the outside, the inside is filthy—a fact no one likes to hear.

One time Bob was preaching in an evangelistic campaign about the subject of the sinner's need of Christ. One young woman, who had faithfully attended every night, stopped attending after this sermon. When we visited her to find the reason for her absence, she made it clear that she could not accept the idea of having a sinful nature. She strongly believed in the inherent goodness of all people. Nothing we could show her from Scripture would change her mind. Sadly, she missed the whole point of salvation. If we have no sense of our sinfulness, then we have no awareness of our spiritual need. And if we cannot sense our need, we have no desire for a Saviour.

As the son trudged home, the father spotted him "a long way off." Jesus also saw each one of us a very long way off. He recognized our condition from the courts of heaven and quickly climbed down the ladder of humiliation. Embracing the human race, He has showered us with kisses of spiritual and temporal blessings. As someone has said, He kisses the past with blessed forgetfulness. Then Jesus exchanges our filthy robes of self-righteousness with

His gorgeous garments of perfect righteousness. Finally He smothers us with an incomparable love. Jesus receives us just as the father in His parable welcomed home his wayward son.

The way the father received his son overwhelmed the prodigal. He didn't even have the chance to finish his memorized speech requesting employment as a hired servant. The father quickly interrupted him with commands to the household servants to prepare a welcoming party for his son who was dead but now was alive.

How can anyone who knows what our Lord is like not love Him? Won't you gladly write down what you think of our Father and Saviour?

_____

_____

The Resurrection of a Son

For this son of mine was dead, and has come to life again; he was lost, and has been found. And they began to be merry. Luke 15:24, NASB.

Which is the greater miracle—the resurrection of a physically dead person or of someone spiritually dead? The return of the prodigal son to his father's embrace and home is nothing short of a miracle. Only God can enable anyone to repent and be converted. We believe the prodigal son's conversion is as great an exhibition of God's power as the resurrection of Lazarus or of the widow of Nain's son.

Paul describes the spiritual resurrection in connection with baptism: "If we have become united with Him in the likeness of His death, certainly, we shall be also in the likeness of His resurrection" (Rom. 6:5, NASB). The apostle clarifies this point further in Philippians 3:10, 11: "That I may know Him, and the power of His resurrection and the fellowship of His sufferings, being conformed to His death; in order that I may attain to the resurrection from the dead" (NASB). The context makes it clear that Paul is talking primarily about his own spiritual resurrection prior to his physical resurrection at our Lord's return.

The Jews were undoubtedly shocked when Jesus told them, "I say to you, an hour is coming and now is, when the dead shall hear the voice of the Son of God; and those who hear shall live. For just as the Father has life in Himself, even so He gave to the Son also to have life in Himself" (John 5:25, 26, NASB). Commentators both liberal and conservative agree that Jesus had in mind a spiritual resurrection, as His words "an hour is coming and *now is*" demonstrate. The "now is" not only meant the physical resurrection of several people Jesus raised during His life on earth, but also all of those "who hear

216

shall live" now. Then He refers to the physical resurrection in the next verses (see verses 28, 29), where He uses the word "tombs" (NASB) or "graves" (KJV).

"This same resurrection power is that which gives life to the soul 'dead in trespasses and sins' (Eph. 2:1). That spirit of life in Christ Jesus, 'the power of his resurrection,' sets men 'free from the law of sin and death' (Phil. 3:10; Rom. 8:2)" (*The Desire of Ages*, pp. 209, 210).

Jesus, in developing the parable of the prodigal son, expressed this resurrection power when He said, "This son of mine was dead, and has come to life again." The same power He used in creating the world, He also employs in re-creating people. We experience eternal life right now in a God-given spiritual resurrection.

Aren't you glad for this power that daily provides us a resurrection from our evil ways to walk in the path of obedience? Thank Him now for His resurrection power, which He offers you today.

The Prodigal's Brother

Now his older son was in the field, and when he came and approached the house, he heard music and dancing. And he summoned one of the servants and began inquiring what these things might be. And he said to him, "Your brother has come, and your father has killed the fattened calf, because he has received him back safe and sound." Luke 15:25-27, NASB.

Jesus could have ended His parable when the father embraced his son who had come back home. But at the beginning of the parable Jesus had referred to two sons, thus indicating that the parable had yet another lesson to teach. The two sons form an interesting contrast. One leaves to live riotously, while the other stays home and faithfully works by the sweat of his brow "in the field." It is not too difficult to sympathize with the older brother if you look through his eyes, but view the situation from the father's perspective and you see things differently.

If the older brother had mourned deeply over his kid brother's departure and had been as eager for him to return as the father was, he would have immediately shared in the welcome-home party. But instead of rejoicing, he became angry and refused to join in even though his father begged him to. The older brother responded to his father's pleas by reciting his long years of service, adding that he had never neglected his father's commands. This perfect, loyal, hardworking obedient son reminded his father that he had never received a party in his honor. "But when this son of yours came, who has devoured your wealth with harlots, you killed the fattened calf for him" (Luke 15:30, NASB). Note the nasty insinuation in the words "son of yours." Angrily, he refused to refer to him as "my brother."

How does this part of the parable apply to the church today? Some years ago an extremely poor family attended one of our series of evangelistic meetings. Their ragged clothes, toothless smiles, and the shack they called home indicated their great need of help. Yet the mother and father with their four children came to every meeting. They responded to the first call for baptism. When their names went to the church board for recommendation for baptism, imagine Bob's shock when several board members complained about the family's poverty and appearance. Some of these local church leaders, like the prodigal's brother, were angry at the thought of this family joining the church because they might become a burden. Besides, they were so unsophisticated!

God accepts us just as we are, but He doesn't leave us in that condition. This family changed dramatically. Within a short time they had cleaned up and dressed up, and eventually the father became an enthusiastic church leader. The children went to our church schools and became strong lay leaders in various congregations.

We praise the Lord for how God treats His prodigal children. Really, we are all prodigal sons and daughters who have fallen into our Father's rejoicing arms. Wouldn't you like to say thank You to your heavenly Father for His welcome home?

July 26

"All That Is Mine Is Yours"

And he said to him, "My child, you have always been with me, and all that is mine is yours. But we had to be merry and rejoice, for this brother of yours was dead and has begun to live, and was lost and has been found." Luke 15:31, 32, NASB.

We call the story Jesus told about the father and his two sons "The Parable of the Prodigal Son." It would be more accurate to call it "The Parable of a Father's Love." From beginning to end it teaches God's magnificent love for the human race. Many a person has walked downhill to the valley of the pigpen, yet has returned to the open arms of our Saviour-Father. It is the Father who welcomes all sinners home. The Father who gives us a feast of joy and happiness rooted in His forgiveness. And it is the Father who removes our filthy rags of self-righteousness and sin and clothes us with His unspotted garments of righteousness.

Although Christ's parable shows the contrast between the Jews, God's people, and the Gentiles, whom the Jews had no love for, the basic lesson taught is that of righteousness by faith. The prodigal son who squandered his father's money lived in a way that could have never warranted any joyous reception home. But while he may have deserved to be cut off from the family, he wasn't. God's unconditional love welcomed him back. The father treats him royally because salvation is not earned—it is a gift.

The older brother was the truly wayward one. He felt that because of his faithfulness and long years of work he deserved his father's love and respect, that his right actions and obedience had qualified him for a feast. Even though the father assured him that "all that is mine is yours," he could not understand his supposed unfair treatment. Proud of his impeccable record of service to his father, he operated on the principle of salvation by works. In view of this, he felt that he deserved all that belonged to the father! He had earned it with his own hard labor. His self-righteousness stands revealed in his jealous attitude toward his brother.

The welcome-home feast with the new robes is a gift to all sinners, including ourselves. When we as sinners internalize the glorious truth that salvation from beginning to end is ours strictly as a love gift from God, it will change our attitude toward other sinners. None of us by any stretch of the imagination deserves to be saved, regardless of how much good we have done or how much money we have given to the church.

Thank the Lord for the free gift of salvation. We glorify and bless the name of Jesus, who, by His love, has melted our icy hearts. He alone deserves our thanks. Perhaps begin, My loving Father, I want to thank You for _____

_____ .

The Blessing of Adam's Ale

Who has woe? Who has sorrow? Who has contentions? Who has complaining? Who has wounds without cause? Who has redness of eyes? Those who linger long over wine. . . . Do not look on the wine when it is red, when it sparkles in the cup, when it goes down smoothly; at the last it bites like a serpent, and stings like a viper. Prov. 23:29-32, NASB.

Nearly 30 million Americans have seen at least one parent in the horrible grip of alcoholism. Imagine the enormous damage done, not only to the drinker, but to nondrinking friends and relatives. The January 18, 1988, *Newsweek* magazine painted a grim picture of the effects of alcohol on the family. The report included heartrending interviews with children. One child said, "I grew up in a little Vietnam." Decades after the drinking parents die, the children continue to suffer with a sense of failure for "not having saved Mommy or Daddy from drink." The article concluded that "children of alcoholics are people who've been robbed of their childhood."

One researcher listed symptoms that most children from alcoholic households experience to one degree or another. Such symptoms can pose lifelong problems: difficulty with intimate relationships, a constant seeking of approval and affirmation, attempts to guess what normal behavior is, and a tendency to lie when it would be just as easy to tell the truth. The children either become super-responsible or super-irresponsible and judge themselves without mercy.

If you have been reared in a home in which alcoholism plagued one or more family members, you know what we're talking about. Thank God daily that you are not gripped with such a horrible vice. The United States is waging war on drugs but permits the drug of alcohol to be sold virtually everywhere, including supermarkets. Our nation requires warning labels on cigarette packages, but nothing, as far as we know, appears on cans and bottles containing alcoholic beverages.

We are thankful for the church's definition of temperance: moderation in everything that is not harmful and total abstinence from all harmful substances. The greatest insurance policy against becoming an alcoholic is to never take the first drink. God has given us many marvelous fruit juices. Best of all, we have what some call Adam's ale—pure fresh water to enjoy to the fullest.

We have the privilege of praying for those being injured by alcohol. Do not condemn but uphold them before God's throne as individuals who desperately need help. And praise the Lord for your own freedom from all drug-related problems.

July 28

The Blessing of Minding Your Own Business

Peter therefore seeing him said to Jesus, "Lord, and what about this man?" Jesus said to him, "If I want him to remain until I come, what is that to you? You follow Me!" John 21:21, 22, NASB.

Timothy Eaton, a Canadian entrepreneur, built a chain of department stores across Canada. The story is told of this wealthy tycoon meeting an Irishman who was a new employee in one of his stores. When Eaton asked him how long he had been working in his company, the Irishman replied, "None of your business."

Eaton then inquired, "What are you doing here?"

Forthrightly the Irishman said, "Minding my own business, and I recommend that you mind your own. You are blocking the passageway."

Did Eaton fire him? Never! "The man was quite right," Eaton later explained. "I wish I could find 500 such who would mind their own business and make everybody else mind theirs!"

"Everyone in town is talking about the Smiths' quarrel," a wife remarked. "Some are taking his part, and some are taking hers."

"And," interjected her husband, "I suppose a few eccentric individuals are minding their own business."

Lovable Peter must have had an inordinate amount of inquisitiveness. His curious nature seems to have bordered on snoopiness. Jesus had just revealed to him that after living a life of service he would suffer a martyr's death. Our Lord described his death by stating, "When you grow old, you will stretch out your hands, and someone else will gird you, and bring you where you do not wish to go" (verse 18, NASB).

Afterward Peter saw John and asked his Master, "What about this man?" Jesus, giving him a kind but sharp rebuke, virtually said, "Peter, mind your own business and follow Me!"

Many are in danger of losing their own souls because they look to others and not to Jesus. Our duty and privilege is to mind our own business, which is another way of saying "Look to Jesus constantly."

"It is our work to look to Christ and follow Him. We shall see mistakes in the lives of others and defects in their character. Humanity is encompassed with infirmity. But in Christ we shall find perfection. Beholding Him, we shall become transformed" (*The Desire of Ages*, p. 816).

It is an honor and privilege to mind our own business by looking to Jesus. Praise Him for that.

The Blind Beggar, Bartimaeus

And casting aside his cloak, he jumped up, and came to Jesus. And answering him, Jesus said, "What do you want Me to do for you?" And the blind man said to Him, "Rabboni, I want to regain my sight!" Mark 10:50, 51, NASB.

If you were blind and knew that some eye specialist held the secret to restoring your sight, you would undoubtedly focus all your energy on getting help. You would even spend your life's savings on securing your sight again.

Let us suppose that you meet your appointment with the specialist. How would you feel if the doctor, after giving you a thorough examination, began to lecture you on the reason you went blind, emphasizing the mistakes you had made in caring for your eyes and telling you what you should have done to avoid blindness? At this point you would probably tell the specialist that you were not concerned with what you did or didn't do to lose your sight, but rather with getting back your sight!

Aesop was a Greek author said to have lived about six centuries before Christ. Legend reports that he was born a slave and was also ugly and deformed but highly intelligent. Many stories are credited to him. One concerns a lad who went swimming in a deep river and soon found himself on the verge of drowning. He cried out for help. Fortunately, a traveler, walking on the path beside the river, heard and saw the drowning boy's distress. Unfortunately, he decided to teach the venturesome lad a lesson. "Your first mistake," he told the floundering boy, "was coming to swim alone. In this deep river, you should have had someone with you to help in case of an emergency. Your second mistake was going out too far over your head. And your third mistake . . ."

"Save me now," screamed the boy. "Give me a lecture later!"

Jesus never lectured the blind man who came for healing—or anyone else in need of help. Even the woman caught in adultery and forcibly dragged into His presence did not hear reproof or reprimand, only the words of forgiveness and the gentle advice not to sin anymore. Jesus told her that He did not condemn her, which was essentially His way of forgiving her.

Today the Lord waits to heal us and not lecture us. Thank Him for His marvelous loving nature.

Kidnapped and Ransomed

For even the Son of Man did not come to be served, but to serve, and to give His life a ransom for many. Mark 10:45, NASB.

Barbara, the daughter of a wealthy businessman, was kidnapped and held for $500,000 ransom. Her abductors took her at gunpoint from a motel room to a distant and lonely spot where they had prepared a grave and a special casket for her, complete with food, water, and a battery-operated fan and lights. In spite of her pleas, they buried her alive. The fan brought fresh air into her casket prison through a pipe that extended to the surface of the ground.

Can you imagine her feelings as she heard the dirt being shoveled on top of the casket and then that deathly silence? One 24-hour period passed, and no sounds of rescue. Undoubtedly, she wondered if her father would pay the ransom. A second 24-hour period passed, and a third. We marvel at her ability to maintain her sanity under such horrible circumstances. Finally, after more than 80 hours of living death, she heard shovels scraping frantically at the dirt. Someone opened the lid, and the light dazed Barbara. Her rescuers lifted the physically and emotionally exhausted woman out of the casket, and she fell into the arms of her father, who had paid the ransom.

Consider for a moment that our entire planet is in a very real sense a giant coffin. Satan, our kidnapper, took our first parents from their Eden home. They, with every descendant down through the centuries, have been held for ransom. As the centuries have gone by, multiplied billions of additional individuals have been kidnapped. Many of them, fortunately, died believing in the One who would ransom them from the grave. That One came and paid a priceless ransom. He gave His life that we might be set free from the clutches of the great kidnapper Satan. Not only will we be delivered from death in the resurrection, but we can be rescued from the grip of sin now.

Paul understood what it meant to be kidnapped when he stated, "It is an agonising situation, and who can set me free from the prison of this mortal body?" But God ransomed him. "I thank God there is a way out through Jesus Christ our Lord" (Rom. 7:24, 25, Phillips).

If you appreciate the ransom that Jesus paid to give you the assurance of eternal life and to aid you in gaining victory over the enemy now, express it in your own words.

_____

_____

Recipe for Peace and Unity

Do nothing from selfishness or empty conceit, but with humility of mind let each of you regard one another as more important than himself. Phil. 2:3, NASB.

If every church member practiced the principle in this passage, there would exist an astounding spirit of love and unity among us. When you have a meeting with the president of a corporation, a conference, a union, the General Conference, or a state governor, most people immediately have a sense of respect, if not for the person, at least for the position or office the individual has. Now transfer that respect and esteem to everyone you know or meet. Paul admonishes: "Consider others better than yourselves" (NIV), regardless of their clothes, skin color, education, or past history. But sometimes we are unable to respect others because we don't like ourselves.

Writing to a Brother M, Ellen White attempted to help him overcome some difficult personality problems. He was struggling to overcome "powerful evil habits." Although he had "gained victories," he still had many more to reach. The man had failed to cultivate "courtesy and true Christian politeness." In her letter to him she used our text today to suggest a cure for these and other problems. After pointing out his combative spirit and his too-independent thinking, which had injured his own soul as well as others, she said, "It is as natural as your breath for you to consider the views and opinions of others inferior to yours. . . . You have possessed a reckless spirit, have felt that no one cared specially for you, that almost everybody was your enemy, and that it was of no consequence what became of you." Having gone on to reveal other problems, she concluded, "You possess many good traits of character; you have a liberal heart. God wants you to be right, just right."

Brother M's response is worth reading. "Sister White: The testimony I received yesterday I look upon as a well-merited rebuke for which I feel truly thankful to you. I earnestly hope to be an overcomer. I am fully sensible of the magnitude of the work I have to do, yet I trust that by God's assisting grace I shall be able to conquer" (*Testimonies*, vol. 2, pp. 162-165).

Irrespective of our individual problems and defects, God devoutly loves us and desires one thing only—our redemption. Praise His name for His compassion and forbearance as He molds us into His image. Perhaps you would like to write out some character defect that you need help with.

Deception and God's Love

And He said, "Take heed that you be not misled; for many will come in My name, saying, 'I am He,' and, 'The time is at hand'; do not go after them." Luke 21:8, NASB.

One of the greatest evidences that God is love is that He warns us to let nothing deceive us so that we lose eternal life. In Matthew 24, Mark 13, and Luke 21, we find Christ's outline of the important events that will transpire prior to the end of time. As He presented it to His disciples, He skillfully intermingled prophecies of two events: the destruction of Jerusalem and the terrors of earth's final hours—the former prefiguring the latter.

In answer to the disciples' question as to when these things would take place, each of the three accounts begins with the unequivocal warning: "Take heed that no man deceive you." Our loving Christ did not want us to be deceived. His concern for us is evident not only from the introduction but also from the repeated emphasis it receives throughout the rest of His discourse.

One of the most outstanding signs in Christ's lengthy answer as to when the end would come for both Jerusalem and the world we could sum up in one word: deception. In fact, Satan's great masterpiece of deception will be his counterfeit of Christ's return. As you read the combined accounts in the Gospels of the signs of Christ's coming and His warnings against deception, you must always keep certain facts in mind. First, He will return again—that is certain! Second, the deception counterfeiting His return centers not only on the fact of His second advent but also on the *manner* of His coming. Third, charlatanism among professed Christians will flourish. Fourth, false miracles will be rampant. Fifth, the deceptions relative to the time, place, and manner of His return will be so insidious that they will put even God's elect in jeopardy.

Our Lord in His great love shares with us warnings in order to help us avoid the pitfalls of deception. Almost an entire religion-nation misunderstood the manner of His first coming. Even Christ's closest followers and companions, the 12 disciples, to a man were deceived over the establishment of His kingdom. It took the shattering of their theological concepts before they began to grasp what He had been trying to teach them.

The best way to avoid deception is to pray and study for the love of Christ to possess our hearts. Love for the One who is the truth, the way, and the life is the key to not being deceived. When the hope of His return is based on a sincere search and acceptance of the Word and becomes part of our deepest emotions, then and only then can the Holy Spirit protect us from the schemes of the evil one.

As the last great crisis bursts upon the world, those who love Christ, who eagerly await His coming, will find refuge and absolute safety in clinging to the Scriptures and the Scriptures alone. "Every man that hath this hope in him purifieth himself, even as he is pure" (1 John 3:3). Write your appreciation here for God's warnings.

_____

_____

Satisfying the Heart's Longings

As the deer pants for the water brooks, so my soul pants for Thee, O God. My soul thirsts for God, for the living God; when shall I come and appear before God? Ps. 42:1, 2, NASB.

Some years ago, more than 3,000 questionnaire responses from members of 28 churches in one of our North American Division unions revealed that once they are baptized, members indicate that their spiritual welfare depends more upon Sabbath services and fellowship than on personal devotions. The survey revealed a rather dangerous trend, since the deepest fellowship with our Lord really rests upon our own personal devotional and prayer life. Those who fail to have such a spiritual experience often criticize the church for their lack of spiritual growth.

In our early ministry, despite the pressures of denominational service, we realized that we could not blame the church for our not having our own personal devotions. If we failed to study, pray, and meditate, it was our own fault. Certainly we had a thousand details to take care of, but the truth was that we had freedom of choice, and if we allowed the pressures of work to steal from us our right to spend time with God daily, we had no one to blame except ourselves.

Perhaps one of the reasons people do not spend more time in study and prayer is that they either do not really enjoy it or don't know how to enjoy it.

Robert Murray McCheyne, a nineteenth-century minister of the Church of Scotland, wrote a letter to a young man about the relationship of Bible reading to prayer life. Among other things, he stated, "You read your Bible regularly, of course; but do try and understand it and still more, to feel it. Read more parts than one at a time. For example, if you are reading Genesis, read a psalm also. Or if you are reading Matthew, read a small bit of an Epistle also. *Turn the Bible into prayer.* Thus, if you were reading the first psalm, spread the Bible on the chair before you, kneel, and pray, 'O Lord, give me the blessedness of the man; let me not stand in the counsel of the ungodly.' This is the best way of knowing the meaning of the Bible and of learning to pray."

Try this plan, and you will find that it works beautifully. You will learn to praise God for His precious promises and the truths revealed in His Word. The Holy Spirit will stand by you to aid you in such personal devotion. Thank God now for the privilege of communing with Him through prayer and study of the Word.

August 3

Procrasteventuality
Give us this day our daily bread. Matt. 6:11.

Our title is a new hybrid term we and Mr. Webster put together recently to signify the behavior of certain people who never see any value in the now or present. For example, sure, the end of the rainbow may have a pot of gold, but because it isn't right here in front of you it isn't worth thinking about or doing anything about. We could use "procrasteventuality" to describe the attitude that regards life at this moment as always dull and unimportant. Anything worthwhile must still lie only in the future.

But Jesus taught that the present is all-important. In His astounding sermon on the mount, misunderstood by the masses and misinterpreted by the spiritual leaders of His day, He urged His hearers to take no thought for their lives, what they should eat, drink, or wear. Christ meant, Don't be anxious, don't worry, don't live in the future, but live in the here and now! Then He added, "If God so clothes the grass of the field which *today* is . . ." (Matt. 6:30, NKJV). There's the point—today, now, this moment—"today is." In conclusion He stated, "Therefore, do not be anxious about tomorrow, for tomorrow will be anxious for itself" (verse 34, RSV).

As He taught His disciples to pray Christ made a statement that most modern breadmakers with their chemical spoilage retardants don't think about: "Give us *this day* our daily bread." People in the biblical world had to make new bread every day because it spoiled so quickly.

Jesus tells us that we should not hunger for yesterday's or tomorrow's bread, but only for today's. Our bodies testify to the concept's truth. We live and function only in the present moment. Our moment-by-moment living teaches us eloquently that life is always *now*.

Although we do not want to fall prey to the problems inherent in the now generation, it is also true that sin has robbed us of the joy and pleasure of living in the present. Many people, for instance, enjoy the anticipation of a vacation more than the actual trip itself. A spirit of impatience, of nervousness, prevents us from enjoying *this moment* because our agitated minds are constantly racing forward to some future objective or time when we assume that life will be different and better.

But it is a great privilege to live for the Lord this moment—now! Thank God for every second of life and every blessing. I thank God for

_____

_____ .

Now Is the Time

And behold, there was a man called by the name of Zaccheus; and he was a chief tax-gatherer, and he was rich. . . . And when Jesus came to the place, He looked up and said to him, "Zaccheus, hurry and come down, for today I must stay at your house." And he hurried and came down, and received Him gladly. Luke 19:2-6, NASB.

Zacchaeus, a capitalist of his day, was a chief tax gatherer, or publican, and very rich. The people of Palestine universally despised Jewish tax collectors and looked upon them as unpatriotic for serving the Romans.

In our story we find Zacchaeus perched on a limb from which he peered down into the face of Jesus, who urgently told him, "Zaccheus, hurry and come down, for today I must stay at your house." Note the word "today." Now came the test for Zacchaeus. Did he hesitate and say, "Lord, I don't have my house cleaned, the beds are not made, the refrigerator is empty. I'm sorry, please come tomorrow, and I will get ready for You"? The biblical record instead shows that he hurriedly slid down the tree and received Jesus joyfully. Jesus summed up the experience when He said, "*Today* salvation has come to this house" (Luke 19:9, NASB).

Too many of us procrastinate and say, "Tomorrow I will spend time with God. Tomorrow I will do better." Why not enjoy life at its best now? Didn't

Jesus say, "I am come that they might have life, and that they might have it more abundantly" (John 10:10)? Christ is not talking about an abundant life merely in the future, but also one right now.

Our Lord loves us so much that He wants us to have the very best life every moment. He longs for us to put an end to our "procrasteventuality," as we discovered yesterday.

Converted individuals do not live in the future, but the future lives in them. A daily Christian experience is what you might call a miniature coming of Christ moment by moment. The Holy Spirit never invites us to follow Christ tomorrow, but always today.

Oliver Wendell Holmes once said, "Take your needle, my child, and work at your pattern. It will work out a rose by and by. Life is like that. One stitch at a time taken patiently, and the pattern will come out all right, like the embroidery." That one stitch at a time is today.

Praise the Lord Jesus Christ for giving you this day to make the very most of it.

Grace and Faith

For by grace you have been saved through faith; and that not of yourselves, it is the gift of God. Eph. 2:8, NASB.

Dr. Herbert E. Douglass in his book *The Faith of Jesus* states that our text today has been the "crux of innumerable controversies, involving even the torture and death of millions" (p. 48).

Note carefully the two words "grace" and "faith." What is the difference between them? What function does each have? Salvation does not result from either one alone. "Salvation is not all God's part, nor is it all man's. If it were by grace alone, then it cannot be by faith. On the other hand, if faith solely provided us salvation, we would not need grace—unless we make up new definitions for faith and grace the Bible writers were not aware of" (*ibid.*, pp. 48, 49).

Grace is what God has done, is doing, and will do for us. It is His action to both forgive us and to grant us power to live a victorious life. God initiates grace, while men and women respond.

We receive grace by faith—our response. It requires faith on our part to accept pardon and power. Neither grace nor faith can be isolated from each other in the plan of salvation. Note carefully how Paul says it in 2 Corinthians 6:1: "We also urge you not to receive the grace of God in vain" (NASB). The only way to receive the grace of God "in vain" is to refuse to permit it to operate in our lives through faith in Jesus Christ.

Reconciliation to God inevitably brings us into oneness and unity with Him and His law. Christ's merits always restore people to harmony with their Maker. But this process requires a conversion experience performed by grace and resulting in a new life from above. However, faith does not possess any merit in itself. Also, faith in a biblical sense always involves action—action that is a response to God's will, and that leads to obedience.

None of us deserves to be saved. But God in mercy and love extended grace to every one of us. Our work, which is not in itself meritorious, is to accept divine grace by faith in our Lord.

How often do you thank the Lord for His salvation? How often have you thought of His grace in your life that has enabled you to overcome some wrong habit? Why not write down what God's great salvation means to you?

_____

_____

A Watchman's Duty

Now as for you [Ezekiel], son of man, I have appointed you a watchman for the house of Israel; so you will hear a message from My mouth, and give them warning from Me. Eze. 33:7, NASB.

Ellen White never claimed to be a prophet but rather a messenger of the Lord. We have often wished we could have met her. After reading her inspirational writings, we feel that it would have been a privilege to know her personally.

Elder H.M.S. Richards, Sr., founder of the Voice of Prophecy radiobroadcast, in an interview with Bob some years ago, told of hearing Ellen White in 1909 when he was a teenager. He had forgotten her topic but did remember what she looked like and how she prayed. Richards said that she wore a long, black, silk dress with a little white around the wrists and around the neckline. A small cap covered her gray hair.

"I remember her as a sweet, old, motherlike woman. She had a big floppy Bible. Just as she began to talk, it began to rain. You can imagine the noise it made on that iron roof. She had no amplifier, but she did have a tremendous preaching voice. It was just like a silver bell. You could hear it right through all that rain on the iron roof. She talked for about 30 minutes using more than 100 texts. Although she turned to the texts in her Bible, she did not stop to look at them. Instead she knew and quoted one after another. It just came as natural as part of her speech."

Then Richards told how her son Willie came up behind her after about 30 minutes and said that she had spoken long enough. "He reminded her that they had a long trip with many meetings, but she replied, 'I don't want to stop yet. I haven't prayed yet. I want to pray first.' So she talked for about three minutes more, then knelt down on the platform and began to pray. Her first words were 'Oh, my Father.' Within two minutes a mighty power came over that whole place. I was afraid to look up for fear I'd see God standing there. As she talked to Him, she forgot all about us. Her prayer lasted only about five or six minutes at the most, but as she prayed, I heard sobs all over that audience—people weeping over their sins. She didn't even look at them—she was down on her knees with her eyes closed—but Heaven came down and touched the earth, and God honored her as His prophet."

Richards went on to relate how this experience was a turning point in his life. "I have never doubted her since. A revival broke out. Those Baptists, Methodists, Catholics, and Adventists were all weeping over their sins. You know, she was a great revivalist, but she didn't get up and harangue the crowd. Instead she prayed, and men took their stand, and some of them became preachers. She was a humble woman."

We praise God for the way He has given such practical information through her to encourage us in the pathway of life.

Wouldn't you like to thank Him for her writings?

August 7

Go Prophesy to My People

Then Amos answered and said to Amaziah, "I am not a prophet, nor am I the son of a prophet; for I am a herdsman and a grower of sycamore figs. But the Lord took me from following the flock and the Lord said to me, 'Go prophesy to My people Israel.'" Amos 7:14, 15, NASB.

Another interesting incident that Pastor H.M.S. Richards, Sr., referred to in the interview with Bob was an experience that Pastor M. L. Andreasen, one of our leading Bible scholars in his day, told him. "One day as Andreasen was studying the Bible and the Spirit of Prophecy he read in *The Desire of Ages* that when Jesus approached the city of Jericho, Zacchaeus climbed up a fig tree. When he read the words 'fig tree,' he exclaimed, 'Why, here is a contradiction,' because the Bible described it as a sycamore tree. This led him to doubt our message. Pastor Andreasen exclaimed to himself, 'It looks like I'll have to give up the second coming of Christ, the state of the dead, and the Spirit of Prophecy, because Zacchaeus climbed the wrong tree.'"

Then one day Andreasen ran across our text and noticed that Amos said he was "a grower of sycamore figs."

"'They are both right,'" he exclaimed. "'I don't have to give up the faith. It's the same kind of tree!'"

When Bob asked Pastor Richards what the Spirit of Prophecy had meant to him in his life, he replied, "I have preached all of my life under the wonderful conviction that this movement was predicted in the prophecies.

Part of those predictions is that the last church should have the Spirit of Prophecy, and I am a part of the last church, and we have the Spirit of Prophecy. It gives me great confidence. In fact, I wouldn't want to belong to a church that didn't have the Spirit of Prophecy."

He stated that he didn't understand some things about it, "but I believe in the gift enough to believe that it is just like the Bible. I believe the Bible is God's Word, yet I must confess that there are things that Paul said that I don't understand. Even Peter recognized that Paul's writings had things in them that the unlearned twist to their own destruction."

We can give the same testimony. It would probably be best if we did not espouse the all-or-nothing attitude that Pastor Andreasen and others have had. Both the Bible and the Spirit of Prophecy contain things that puzzle us, but we should not let our confidence in God and His Word falter upon these difficulties. The overwhelming evidence is that God has inspired the Scripture writers as well as Ellen White.

Again we want to praise our Lord for the overwhelming amount of material He has given us through Ellen White for our edification, guidance, and comfort. How do you feel about it?

August 8

How to Make Jesus Your Friend

And in the early morning, while it was still dark, He arose and went out and departed to a lonely place, and was praying there. Mark 1:35, NASB.

Anne Ortlund, in her book *Disciplines of the Beautiful Woman*, tells the story of her 21-year-old son, Bud, who was home from college. A minister's wife, Anne was about to fill a speaking appointment when she casually asked her son what she should say to her audience.

"Mother," Bud replied, "tell them only Jesus satisfies—not a suburban house, not color TV, not a station wagon and a sexy wife. No trip satisfies, only the Lord." And then he spread out his hands on the table and said, "That's what I want. The way the planets revolve around the sun, I want my life to revolve around Him. I want Him absolutely central."

How can our lives revolve around the Lord? Is it not by making Him the foundation of our existence? And how do we do that? Unfortunately there is no such thing as push-button religion—no shortcuts to building a relationship with the Lord. Doesn't it take time for us to get to know each other and become friends on earth? We take time to cultivate friendships by inviting each other to our homes, using every opportunity to talk together face-to-face or by telephone, and finding out the things that make each other happy. This especially applies to husbands and wives who want to build a beautiful marriage. And the same is true when it comes to our relationship with God.

Scripture tells us that if we make our first priority the kingdom of God and His righteousness, then everything else will come to us in its appropriate time (see Matt. 6:33). So we seek Christ first. Jesus is at the top of the list. All other relationships are secondary compared to that with our Lord. No person, no thing, must keep us from putting Him first. Nothing must compete with Him in our hearts. He is in a class all by Himself, and we must know Him not only intellectually but experientially as well. Christ is the one person on whom everything in our lives must converge.

Determine to fight the petty larcenies that steal away your time and energy from focusing on the Lord. Determine to drop the clutter from your life. Take steps to reorganize your life, if necessary, in order to put our Lord in first place in your daily experience.

Perhaps you wonder how to do this. *I am so busy,* you tell yourself, *and have so many plans for the future. If I totally surrender everything to Him, I'm not sure what would happen to all my dreams and goals.*

The story is told of Queen Elizabeth I, who asked a man to go abroad on business for her. He explained that he would like to but really couldn't because of the demanding nature of his own business affairs, which would suffer if he left. She said that if he would attend to *her* business, she would take care of *his*.

Our text today makes it clear that Jesus attended to His Father's business by getting up early and praying. In return, the Father guided His Son through each day. So with us. If we determine to seek God first, He will take care of all the other important things.

Thank Him today for the privilege of intimate association with Him.

Prayer, Our Great Privilege

And without faith it is impossible to please Him, for he who comes to God must believe that He is, and that He is a rewarder of those who seek Him. Heb. 11:6, NASB.

If you really believe that God exists, the next step is to accept the fact that He is a personal God, not some type of universal energy or force. Our text depicts Him as personally interested in each of us. The whole idea of knowing God involves trust and faith. We use faith and trust constantly in our secular affairs. Every time we write a check, we trust our bank to honor it. Do we trust God as much as we do our bank?

Developing faith in God requires a friendship with Him that demands intimate communication with Him through prayer. We talk much about prayer, but how many of us really pray?

Prayer is not a one-sided conversation with God. Any relationship with a friend requires interaction of talk and thought. It also involves trust in each other. Our heavenly Father allows us to open up our hearts in confidence to Him. Patiently He waits for us to come to Him so He can pour out His blessings upon us. If Jesus found comfort and joy in communion with His Father, so can we!

One marvelous element about prayer is that at any time, at any place we can commune with God. In the quietness of our homes, on the crowded streets, or while visiting with friends, He is always present to hear and help us. It is comforting to know that He is there and that He cares about what happens to us. We can have great assurance in knowing that we can share anything and everything with Him. Whether it be our fears, our hopes, or our joys, our Lord wants us to talk to Him like a friend—a best friend. Tell Him your dreams, your loneliness, your successes, and your failures. The Lord is interested in what you have to say! Tell Him about your baby cutting its first tooth or how you tripped and fell and skinned your knee. Nothing that happens to you is boring to Him.

Jesus asserts that God knows what we want to tell even before we say it. Why, then, do some feel as though they aren't getting through to God when they pray? Being unable to sense His presence is really our problem, not His. Prayer requires our entire being. To truly communicate with God we have to give Him our total attention. Sometimes when we are talking with friends, our minds wander. We talk and yet hardly realize what is being said. The same experience can happen with prayer. Our minds are on something or someone else. We speak the words but don't internalize what we are saying. Thus we feel that God is not there, when we really are the ones who aren't. Robert Burns said it well: "They never sought in vain that sought the Lord aright!"

Above all, learn to praise Him in prayer. Praise Him before you petition Him. George Bernard Shaw once said, "Common people do not pray; they only beg." Try being uncommon and praise Him now!

Do You Really Know Jesus?

I count all things to be loss in view of the surpassing value of knowing Christ Jesus my Lord, for whom I have suffered the loss of all things, and count them but rubbish in order . . . that I may know Him, and the power of His resurrection. Phil. 3:8-10, NASB.

A 97-year-old woman received regular visits from her pastor. On one occasion she told him that when she was a little girl she went to Washington, D.C., and that while visiting the White House she shook hands with President Lincoln. If someone asked you if you knew President Lincoln, you would probably respond, "Of course, he was the president of the United States during the Civil War and was known as Honest Abe." But we don't know Abraham Lincoln like she did, and she didn't know him as did his son, Tad, who could burst into his father's study at any time, jump up on his knee, and get a bear hug and kiss. The son *really* knew Abraham Lincoln.

Do I really know Jesus? That is life's ultimate question.

When Marie was in college one of her teachers, Marjorie Kemmerer, impressed her with her Christian life and influence. The woman's relationship with Christ was evident to all who met her. Marie discovered that Marjorie Kemmerer's secret of knowing Him lay in the fact that even though her first class for the day began at 7:30 a.m., she would arise at 4:30 a.m. in order to have quiet time with the Lord. Communing with Him through prayer and Bible study is not an option—it is absolutely vital. The only way Jesus knew His Father while on earth was through the same avenues open to us.

E. M. Bounds states beautifully: "In prayer God stoops to kiss man, to bless man, and to aid in everything that God can devise, or man can need."

Susannah Wesley, mother of 19 children, had no secluded place to go to meet the Lord. At her chosen time she would cover her face with her apron. Her children knew never to disturb their mother when she was praying under it.

A Japanese friend of ours accepted a call to go to Belém, Brazil, to serve as a Bible instructor for the thousands of Japanese who live in that hot, tropical climate. Since her husband had deserted her, she went alone even though she didn't know anyone in Belém. While she was on furlough, she asked us, "I'm nearly 65 years of age and about to retire, but what would you think if I went back to Belém and retired there to help my people?"

Her question surprised us, since we thought she would want to retire near her two children, who lived in the United States. But then she continued, "I know this may sound strange to you, but since I have been in Brazil I have found Jesus as my Friend, my Master, my Husband, my Companion. Since I've found Him I want to do anything that He wants me to do and to go anywhere He wants me to go." Although we had known her for years, her tone of voice and attitude revealed a new depth of love for Christ.

Thank God today for the privilege of communing with Christ in prayer and Bible study. It is the only way to *really* know Him as our Friend and Saviour.

The Asking Child

If you then, being evil, know how to give good gifts to your children, how much more shall your Father who is in heaven give what is good to those who ask Him! Matt. 7:11, NASB.

In their helplessness and innocence children do not hesitate to ask their parents for what they need. When the disciples started to rebuke those who brought their children to Jesus to be blessed, He said to leave them alone and "do not hinder them from coming to Me; for the kingdom of heaven belongs to such as these" (Matt. 19:14, NASB).

Becoming like little children in our dependence upon God is a real privilege as well as a requisite for entering His kingdom. As adults we have to surrender a certain amount of pride and self in order to accept help, whether from God or from another human being. Many resist asking for any kind of aid. Pride causes some to go miles out of the way rather than stop to get directions to their destination. Some are embarrassed to let others know they desperately need food. But asking God, who has all the resources we need, puts us into a right relationship with Him. He is our Creator, and we are His creation. We will always be dependent on Him. Our Lord is happy when we seek for and accept His aid.

When in trouble or having a need—major or minor—we should go to Him as our Father and tell Him about it in a simple, direct manner. Few hesitate to pray for such things as another person's salvation or for world peace. Yet our heavenly Father is just as interested in each of our individual needs, regardless of how large or small they may be.

One evening as Bob was replacing the burned-out headlight in our car, he could not budge any of the screws that held the headlight frame. They were rusted in tight because of the age of the car. After spraying them with WD-40 lubricant he came inside to eat, then after supper he tried again but without success. Finally he decided to bow his head and offer a simple petition to God for help. Extremely busy, he did not have time to take the car to a garage and get the screws drilled out, since we were leaving on a trip shortly. After praying, he tried again. Believe it or not, those stubborn screws all came loose. Was God interested in rusted screws? We think so! Why not? Does He not note a sparrow hit by a car? All things that concern us are important to God!

Have you ever misplaced or lost anything? We have. Many a time we have prayed and then quickly found what we were looking for. The parable Jesus told of the woman searching for the one lost silver coin shows that Jesus cares about seemingly insignificant things, not because they are intrinsically valuable but because they are important to us, His children.

Take time right now to pen a few words thanking God for prayers He has answered in your life.

Alone!

And when the sixth hour had come, darkness fell over the whole land until the ninth hour. And at the ninth hour Jesus cried out with a loud voice, "Eloi, Eloi, lama, sabachthani?" which is translated, "My God, My God, why hast Thou forsaken Me?" Mark 15:33, 34, NASB.

Max Lucado, in his book *No Wonder They Call Him the Saviour,* tells the story of Judith Bucknell, who was suicide victim number 106 in Miami, Florida, during 1980. We would know little about her had she not kept a diary that reveals the terrible loneliness this 38-year-old woman endured.

Judy was not on drugs or welfare or a social outcast. Rather, she was respectable and wore designer clothes. She lived in an apartment that overlooked the bay. But her loneliness caused her to write, "I see people together, and I am so jealous I want to throw up. What about me! What about me . . . ! Who is going to love Judy Bucknell?" The diary entry continued, "I feel so old. Unloved. Unwanted. Abandoned. Used up. I want to cry and sleep forever. I am alone and I want to share something with somebody."

Cries of loneliness fill the world. We hear the voices of the singles, the divorcées, the widows and widowers, and those in convalescent homes filled with sighs and shuffling feet. More voices in our overcrowded prisons join the moans and cries of loneliness. Loneliness exists even in families, rich and poor alike. In fact, if one listed the major problems of our cruel world, loneliness would be near the top.

God never made us to be alone (see Gen. 2:18). The author of Ecclesiastes observes that "two are better than one because they have a good return for their labor. For if either of them falls, the one will lift up his companion. But woe to the one who falls when there is not another to lift him up" (Eccl. 4:9, 10, NASB).

What's the answer? We can begin by reaching out to others and making friends. But deeper than that, we must let Jesus be our constant companion, even as Jesus, who tread the winepress of suffering alone, had His Father as a constant companion. The closest that Jesus ever came to being alone was on the cross, when He cried out the words of our text today. Yet earlier He had told His disciples, "I am not alone, because the Father is with Me" (John 16:32, NASB).

Praise God that you don't have to be alone in this world, even though you may live by yourself. Jesus is always our elder brother and constant companion.

Future of the Family

Behold, I am going to send you Elijah the prophet before the coming of the great and terrible day of the Lord. And he will restore the hearts of the fathers to their children, and the hearts of the children to their fathers, lest I come and smite the land with a curse. Mal. 4:5, 6, NASB.

In the October 10, 1991, *Adventist Review*, Dr. Penny Long Marler, sociologist and churchwoman, shared her analysis of today's family. "If church leaders are to be as responsive today as they were in the fifties, the task is not to recapture the family of the past, but to discover the family of the present."

When we think of a traditional family, we visualize a mother caring for the children while the father is the breadwinner. But such families are decreasing in number, and they did not really exist in ancient times, when whole extended families worked together. Dr. Long points out that a portrait of today's family is really a composite of many family types. She lists four common ones:

1. *The traditional family.* Even it has changed, since both parents work in most cases. During the 1950s about half of North American households consisted of married couples with children. Today we could consider only one quarter of American households as traditional families.

2. *Married couples without children.* This type of home has remained virtually stable during the past 40 years.

3. *Single-parent families.* These families are mainly headed by women, some divorced, some widowed, others who never married. Statistics show that the single-parent household has increased its share of the overall household structure portrait by 4 percent.

4. *The nonfamily households.* These consist of persons who live alone or who live together but are unrelated such as young professionals, retirees, etc. During the past 40 years the nonfamily category has increased most of all—by 15 percent.

In light of such facts, we need to interpret our text today to include the church as the family in which children, parents of all types, and single people will find solace, comfort, fellowship, and above all, a closer relationship with Jesus Christ. The church is a family whose ties transcend those of blood and marriage.

Thank God for allowing you to become a friend to some lonely person in your congregation. Let the church be the focus of your life.

The Importance of Justification

But God demonstrates His own love toward us, in that while we were yet sinners, Christ died for us. Much more then, having now been justified by His blood, we shall be saved from the wrath of God through Him. Rom. 5:8, 9, NASB.

In 1890 Ellen White wrote: "The point that has been urged upon my mind for years is the imputed righteousness of Christ. I have wondered that this matter was not made the subject of discourses in our churches throughout the land, when the matter has been kept so constantly urged upon me, and I have made it the subject of nearly every discourse and talk that I have given to the people. . . . There is not a point that needs to be dwelt upon more earnestly, repeated more frequently, or established more firmly in the minds of all than the impossibility of fallen man meriting anything by his own best good works. Salvation is through faith in Jesus Christ alone" (*Faith and Works*, pp. 18, 19).

That justification is a totally free gift to undeserving sinners is a vital point we find easy to talk about but difficult to grasp, believe, and accept. Unfortunately, we often describe and explain this magnificent truth in the same manner that a math teacher might use for an algebraic equation. But to really present it, we need to pray for the Holy Spirit to be poured out as we spiritually look to Jesus—God's lamb—who "was wounded for our transgressions . . . , bruised for our iniquities" and who healed us "with his stripes" (Isa. 53:5).

It is not a subject to argue about, but one that we must internalize. Surely all of us agree that we poor sinners can take no credit for what Christ has done for us in His act of justification. God not only has taken the initiative in justifying human beings, but—note carefully—what He does is a *free gift*. Justification is totally of grace and cannot be secured by anything that we might do. In fact, we are just as helpless to perform any meritorious works as the newborn child that was cast out into the field to die, as portrayed in Ezekiel's parable. It was only when the Lord passed by that little baby and spoke the electrifying words "Live; yea, I said unto thee . . . , Live" (Eze. 16:6) that the infant had any chance for survival.

Jesus has justified us by His blood, and as a result we shall be "saved from the wrath of God through Him."

Please praise the Lord for this marvelous fact. The more you talk and write about it, the more real it will be to you.

The Robe

But the father said to his slaves, "Quickly bring out the best robe and put it on him, and put a ring on his hand and sandals on his feet." Luke 15:22, NASB.

The robe in the story about the prodigal son could well represent the robe of Christ's righteousness. Joshua, the high priest, found himself clothed with torn and soiled robes similar to those worn by the prodigal son. And the angel, Christ, commanded, "Remove the filthy garments from him" (Zech. 3:4, NASB). The same robe appears in the Laodicean message of Revelation 3:18, which urges us to buy from the Lord "white garments" (NASB) to cover the shame of our spiritual nakedness. Even the armies in heaven are "clothed in fine linen, white and clean" (Rev. 19:14, NASB). All can wear the beautiful robe of Christ's righteousness, because the one that He wears for us is a "robe dipped in blood" (verse 13, NASB).

In the Saviour's parable of the marriage feast, the king expelled the man without the wedding garment (Matt. 22:10-13). We believe that this robe symbolizes both imputed and imparted righteousness. It means that we must continually wear it in order to be covered with His justification and sanctification. For some years we thought that justification came into action at conversion to care for past sins and then reappeared periodically to forgive those sins committed after a person had accepted Christ. But such a concept made the righteousness of Christ, as far as justification is concerned, into little more than an eraser. At the moment we accepted Him, Christ used it to remove the mistakes of the past. Then He put it away until we made another mistake.

A closer study of Scripture reveals that it compares Christ's righteousness to a robe—not an eraser! And His robe must cover us constantly. That does not mean that it merely hides our confessed sins and does not eradicate them. Rather, it is to say that our sinful natures dare not be uncovered or exposed for a single second. We are in constant need of His justifying righteousness.

In order to cover the shame of our spiritual nakedness, we must wear Christ's robe continually as a part of our daily apparel. We don't take it off even when we sleep. It cannot be held at arm's length and still be effective. Nor can we carry it around in a suitcase or hang it in a closet to pull out only when needed. Christ's robe of righteousness is a garment that we must always have on, not because of fear or for diplomatic reasons, but because it is a precious gift that one cherishes and prizes even above life itself. The infinite cost that made it available to us is what makes it so valuable and desirable.

When was the last time that you praised and thanked God for this prized gift of His robe of righteousness? Do it now.

Justification, Part 1

*So then as through one transgression there resulted condemnation
to all men, even so through one act of righteousness there resulted
justification of life to all men. Rom. 5:18, NASB.*

Misinterpreting our passage for today could plunge us into the trap of
universalism—that God will save all whether they accept Christ or not, and
regardless of their lifestyle.

Our text proclaims God's mighty love for the entire human race. When our
Lord went to the cross and shed His blood there, He provided justification for
all men. But that justification must be accepted if it is to save anyone. And
that acceptance has vital consequences.

Yesterday we pointed out that we must continually wear Christ's robe of
righteousness and never hang it in the closet. Christ provided justification for
all people through an objective act. When we accept Christ, we will also
accept His robe of righteousness as a gift held out to us by nail-scarred hands.
God's forgiveness then brings us to repentance through a deep, overwhelming
experience.

The moment the heart and mind, under the Holy Spirit's influence,
understand (1) what the robe is, (2) who provided it, and (3) how it is
appropriated, justification then becomes a prized personal possession. It is no
longer a theological idea but a dynamic force in our daily existence. Some may
wish to call this development a new-birth experience and the beginning of
sanctification. We have no quarrel with phrasing it that way, but we are
convinced that a person can no more isolate and define each stage in the
development of salvation than a young man or woman who falls in love can
precisely explain the various steps that eventually led to the marriage altar.

Arnold Wallenkampf in his book *Justified* tells of the crash of Air Florida's
Flight 90 into the Potomac River on January 13, 1982. A U.S. Park Service
police helicopter dropped a rope with a life preserver to rescue the survivors
from the icy waters. Wallenkampf points out that it was the pilot in the
helicopter who was the savior of the passengers struggling in the water, not
the rope. "But the rope was necessary to connect them with the will and the
power hovering above. So, through faith, a life-giving connection must be
established between the sinner and Jesus. Jesus saves the repentant sinner by
means of faith, just as the pilot in the helicopter saved the crash survivors by
means of the rope" (p. 45).

Are you clinging to the rope that connects you to Christ? His robe of
righteousness is yours for the asking. Ask for it in writing.

Justification, Part 2

Therefore, having been justified by faith, we have peace with God through our Lord Jesus Christ. Rom. 5:1, NASB.

Some of us have tried to diagram the process of salvation, but there can be a danger in doing that. No diagram can ever fully illustrate the point or points under consideration. Furthermore, it is possible for diagrams to teach both truth and error at the same time. For instance, a favorite diagram Bob used for years to illustrate imputed and imparted righteousness had a diagonal line drawn from the bottom left-hand corner that gradually and erratically rose to the top right-hand corner. He labeled everything below the ascending line as imparted righteousness or sanctification, and everything above it as imputed righteousness or justification.

Such an erratic, diagonal line does correctly illustrate how a Christian life advances in sanctification. But at the same time the diagram implied that as Christians grow in grace and in sanctification, they require less and less justification. In other words, it gave the false impression that the closer Christians come to Christ and the more victories they have, the less they need His justification.

But we will always require His justifying grace. No matter how far we progress on the Christian pathway, true Christians will ever sense that their poor, sinful natures will always need the covering robe of both justification and sanctification.

Justification and sanctification are absolutely inseparable in the Christian experience. We may correctly define them theologically as distinct steps, but that is for discussion purposes only. Every saved person knows, however, that you can't divide them in experience.

We need justification now just as much as we did the first day we accepted Christ. And to live eternally with Him and the rest of the redeemed, we also need His sanctification for full salvation.

Thank God for these marvelous concepts. May our lives today fully depend upon His salvation and never on our own works.

Put into words your joy for the fact that God gives everything you need for complete salvation.

_____

_____

David's Repentance

Create in me a clean heart, O God, and renew a steadfast spirit within me. Do not cast me away from Thy presence, and do not take Thy Holy Spirit from me. Restore to me the joy of Thy salvation. Ps. 51:10-12, NASB.

Ellen White tells us that David composed this great penitential psalm after his great sin with Bathsheba (*Education*, p. 165). We would like to draw out of our reading today one important point. Some misunderstand God's forgiveness and teach that once people have the assurance of salvation based upon Christ's justifying act on the cross, they are forever saved. We usually term this "once saved, always saved." Did David with his double sin of murder and adultery ever intimate that he still felt assured of God's acceptance? Quite the contrary. Listen to his words in Psalm 32:3, 4, which he also composed after his sin with Bathsheba. "When I kept silent about my sin, my body wasted away through my groaning all day long. For day and night Thy hand was heavy upon me" (NASB).

As our text today indicates, David pleaded with God not to cast him away from His presence. Neither psalm reveals any attitude of spiritual arrogance or self-assurance. David regained his sense of relationship with God some months later when the prophet Nathan led him into a full confession of his terrible crimes and pointedly told the king that he had "despised the word of the Lord by doing evil in His sight" (2 Sam. 12:9, NASB).

The record clearly indicates that David had severed his relationship with God. The king was a lost man until he confessed and repented of his sin. When the prophet's finger of accusation pointed at him, "David trembled, lest, guilty and unforgiven, he should be cut down by the swift judgment of God" (*Patriarchs and Prophets*, p. 722).

David and his kingdom suffered greatly because of his sins, but when a consciousness of his sins broke his spirit, he truly humbled himself in the eyes of God and his subjects. Although we may have been once saved, nothing automatically guarantees that we will always remain in that state. Yet if we do fall, we can come back to God and cry out to Him, as the publican called to God in Christ's parable. Through confession and repentance our relationship with God can be restored.

The marvelous thing is that though David had fallen, the Lord lifted him up. "He was now more fully in harmony with God and in sympathy with his fellow men than before he fell. . . . Whoever will in faith accept God's promises, will find pardon. The Lord will never cast away one truly repentant soul" (*ibid.*, p. 726). Is this your desire—to praise God for His love?

The Law—Standard or Method? Part 1

What shall we say then? Is the Law sin? May it never be! On the contrary, I would not have come to know sin except through the Law; for I would not have known about coveting if the Law had not said, "You shall not covet." . . . So then the Law is holy, and the commandment is holy and righteous and good. Rom. 7:7, 12, NASB.

Through the decades others have consistently accused Adventists of being legalists. Undoubtedly we deserved some of the criticism. Some Adventists still believe that we are saved either by the works of the law or by a mixture of law and grace that depends partially on each other for salvation.

We can quickly clarify the relationship between law and grace if we answer a single question: Is God's law—the Ten Commandments—a standard of right and wrong, or is it a method of salvation? If we try to employ the law as a method for salvation, then we fully agree with any who accuse us of being legalists. But if the law serves as a standard of right and wrong, then law and grace fit together beautifully—as closely as the forefinger and thumb. A correct understanding of the relationship between law and grace will show that both are as important to the spiritual life as are the heart and brain to physical life.

Many Christians believe that God had a different plan for saving His people during Old Testament times than He did during New Testament times. The truth is that from Genesis to Revelation, one finds a unity of thought declaring that only Jesus Christ and His shed blood provide justification for the sinner.

The Old Testament system of sacrifice simply pointed forward to Christ's death on the cross. Just prior to His death, Jesus declared, "For this is my blood of the covenant, which is poured out for many for the forgiveness of sins" (Matt. 26:28, RSV).

God did not institute a plan of salvation involving works *before* the cross and then switch to a program of salvation by faith *after* it. The entire sanctuary system taught the blood atonement of a coming Messiah. From the first lamb offered by Adam and Eve to the last animal slain before Christ cried out on the cross "It is finished," the theme of the sacrificial arrangement was that "without shedding of blood there is no forgiveness" (Heb. 9:22, NASB).

Praise the Lord for both His grace and His law. To ignore either one spells spiritual disaster. Thank Him now for this understanding.

The Law—Standard or Method? Part 2

Lovingkindness and truth have met together; righteousness and peace have kissed each other. Ps. 85:10, NASB.

The ark of the covenant placed in the Holy of Holies of the Old Testament sanctuary illustrated the correct relationship between law and grace. Inside the ark rested the tablets containing God's law, written by His own finger, but covering the sacred chest was the mercy seat. The two golden cherubim at each end of the mercy seat had their faces turned toward each other and looked downward, signifying their respect for the mercy seat and for the holy law. Thus, in the heart of the sanctuary, "mercy and truth are met together; righteousness and peace have kissed each other."

The Scriptures clearly indicate that salvation in the Old Testament consisted of grace through faith in a Saviour. True, many then, as now, perverted God's plan of salvation into a system of earning redemption through human effort, but they did so contrary to God's will.

Read the first chapter of Isaiah, in which God declared in no uncertain terms that He wanted no more of their "worthless offerings" (Ps. 85:13, NASB). Incense was an abomination to Him. He declared that He was weary of the blood of bulls, lambs, and goats. Why? Because Israel had perverted the Old Testament plan of salvation into a system of self-works. Therefore, the Lord appealed to them, " 'Come now, and let us reason together,' says the Lord, 'though your sins are as scarlet, they will be as white as snow; though they are red like crimson, they will be like wool' " (verse 18, NASB). All the offerings in the world, and all the works that people could ever perform could never forgive sins.

One major difference between the Old and New Testaments was God's *method* of teaching the plan of salvation. Teachers may use different ways of explaining that 2 plus 2 equals 4, but the answer always remains the same. So God used a "kindergarten" system of symbols and sacrifices to explain His plan of salvation to those who had not the privilege of seeing the reality of Calvary. Naturally, this method of teaching by types and shadows has no longer been needed since the cross.

While we are fortunate to live today in a time when God's instruction in the ways of salvation is much clearer and more direct, His plan is still the same.

Thank the Lord for the privilege of living when the plan of salvation is easier to understand than ever before.

May It Never Be!

Do we then nullify the Law through faith? May it never be! On the contrary, we establish the Law. Rom. 3:31, NASB.

The King James Version translates the exclamation "May it never be!" as "God forbid." Paul used "God forbid," or "May it never be!" more than all the other Bible writers put together. The apostle emphatically declared that faith in Christ does not destroy the law—in fact, it establishes the law.

Calvary is an eternal demonstration that God's law is as unchangeable as His character and His love. When in Gethsemane our Saviour pleaded with the Father to spare Him from drinking the cup of death, the only answer He received was the immutability of the sacred law. Death is the penalty for transgression. If salvation was to become reality, Christ must die, not for Himself, but for the transgressors of that law—each one of us.

The fact that God Himself could find no other way to satisfy its claims is supreme proof of its eternal, unchangeable nature. Would God have given His Son to redeem sinners from the law's penalty if any other way existed? If God could have altered His law or its penalty, surely as a being of love He would have done so! But because the law is a transcript of God's character, He would have to change His character—change His inmost being—in order to change His law.

We cannot behold the Sacrifice upon the cross and at the same time ridicule or downgrade the law. Jesus died to uphold it. The cross, rightly comprehended, leads us to a true understanding of the terribleness of sin, which is the transgression of that law. The cross leads us as sinners to come to its foot, lay hold of Christ's merits, and with the Spirit's power transforming us cease from breaking that law.

Look at the center cross at Calvary. Witness the agony suffered by One who knew no sin. See Him, whose skin as a baby was pricked with the straw in the manger, now enduring the stabs of sharp thorns piercing His brow. Rough spikes embedded in His human flesh pinned His hands and feet against the rough wood. Watch a soldier thrust a spear into His side. And why did Christ willingly suffer all this?

The answer is clear and simple. God knew of no other way to eradicate sin, and sin is the one thing in all the universe that God hates. His great heart of love twisted in pain at the sight of a world filled with His children enduring the unrelenting onslaught of sin's crippling destruction. Such love could never allow sin to continue unchecked. He knew that the only way to destroy it was for His Son to accept the consequences personally. Jesus willingly went to the cross in order to forgive us our sins.

Rejoice with all of heaven in God's free grace provided by Christ's sacrifice.

Least of All Saints

To me, the very least of all saints, this grace was given, to preach to the Gentiles the unfathomable riches of Christ. Eph 3:8, NASB.

In 1 Corinthians 15:9 Paul declares, "For I am the least of the apostles, who am not fit to be called an apostle, because I persecuted the church of God" (NASB). He ever recognized that he needed God's grace every single moment of his life.

We believe that it is important to understand that while we may not be aware of any particular disobedient action on our part, we still are sinners by nature. More than once we have prostrated ourselves before the Lord and confessed our sinfulness—that our motives have been less than right. Often we have pleaded for the Lord to forgive us for sins committed against another, only to realize that we were more embarrassed over what that person must have thought of us than the horribleness of our sin against our Lord Himself. With Paul we can groan, "Wretched man that I am!" (Rom. 7:24). According to Greek scholar A. T. Robertson, the term *wretched* derives from words meaning to "bear" and "callus." Our sin-scarred minds are insensitive to our true condition.

That is why we have emphasized that surrendered Christians constantly need to be under the umbrella of Christ's justification.

"The religious services, the prayers, the praise, the penitent confession of sin, ascend from true believers as incense to the heavenly sanctuary,- but passing through the corrupt channels of humanity, they are so defiled that unless purified by blood, they can never be of value with God. They ascend not in spotless purity, and unless the Intercessor, who is at God's right hand, presents and purifies all by His righteousness, it is not acceptable to God. All incense from earthly tabernacles must be moist with the cleansing drops of the blood of Christ. He holds before the Father the censer of His own merits, in which there is no taint of earthly corruption. He gathers into this censer the prayers, the praise, and the confessions of His people, and with these He puts His own spotless righteousness. Then, perfumed with the merits of Christ's propitiation, the incense comes up before God wholly and entirely acceptable. Then gracious answers are returned.

"Oh, that all may see that everything in obedience, in penitence, in praise and thanksgiving, must be placed upon the glowing fire of the righteousness of Christ. The fragrance of this righteousness ascends like a cloud around the mercy seat" (*Selected Messages*, book 1, p. 344).

Praise God for Christ's righteousness in our behalf!

Forgetting the Past

Brethren, I do not regard myself as having laid hold of it yet; but one thing I do: forgetting what lies behind and reaching forward to what lies ahead. Phil. 3:13, NASB.

Paul, who wrote our words today to the Philippian church, had a lot to forget. The apostle had watched a man being stoned to death and had held the coats of those who did it. He "made havoc of the church" that Jesus Christ had started, to the point that just the mention of Saul's name produced fear in the hearts of dedicated Christians. Yet when Christ called him on the Damascus road, Paul forgot the past. Or did he? We believe he forgot the past in terms of guilt, but never how God forgave him.

Bob has a section in his card file that he has titled "God's Leading in My Life." In it he records those events that reveal the Lord's graciousness to him. Some of the experiences may seem insignificant, but to him they prove overwhelmingly that God cares for and leads His children. When Satan seeks to discourage you, pull out your diary—or this book if you have written in it notes substantiating God's leading in your life and your praise to Him. Read what He has done for you in the past. It will do wonders for your spiritual life!

Peter had a lot to forget. Imagine his denying his Lord three times. All the biblical characters had a past that needed erasing. We love what Isaiah wrote to God's people when he said, "Fear not, for you will not be put to shame; neither feel humiliated, for you will not be disgraced; but you will forget the shame of your youth" (Isa. 54:4, NASB).

However, as we forget our past of guilt, we must never forget God and His gracious hand that has constantly preserved and enriched our lives. Such vital memories enabled Paul to carry on no matter what happened to him.

Often we have seen a tiny toddler learning to walk. Mother, with outstretched arms, slowly and quietly backs away as the little one attempts to reach her. Yet she always stays within reach. Our heavenly Parent, while forgetting the past mistakes we have made, constantly challenges us to higher and holier attainments.

Praise the Lord now for helping you forget your past mistakes and giving you courage to press toward God's goal for your life.

God's Guidance

But when He, the Spirit of truth, comes, He will guide you into all the truth; for He will not speak on His own initiative, but whatever He hears, He will speak; and He will disclose to you what is to come. John 16:13, NASB.

In her autobiography Helen Keller describes the terrible illness that closed her eyes and ears and plunged her into the "unconsciousness of a newborn babe." She relates, "Gradually I got used to the silence and darkness that surrounded me and forgot that it had ever been different, until she came—my teacher—who was to set my spirit free."

Followers of Jesus have One who has set their spirits free too. The Holy Spirit guides us into all truths, and when we know and practice truth, then we become free.

Not only did the Holy Spirit inspire the prophets to produce the Scriptures; not only was the Spirit the active agency in the creation of our world; not only is the plan of redemption executed by and through the Holy Spirit; but also the Spirit guides the true Christian in all facets of life. In our fallen state we are incapable of guiding ourselves. Frantic voices may cry out "This is the way," but they usually direct us down a dead-end street. The power of the Spirit transfers a person's affections from the present world to eternal things.

"Pray that the mighty energies of the Holy Spirit, with all their quickening, recuperative, and transforming power, may fall like an electric shock on the palsy-stricken soul, causing every nerve to thrill with new life, restoring the whole man from his dead, earthly, sensual state to spiritual soundness" (*Testimonies*, vol. 5, p. 267).

Have you thanked the Lord for the Spirit of truth's guidance in your life recently? If not, why not do so now?

Four Trees and $1,000,000

The righteous man will flourish like the palm tree, he will grow like a cedar in Lebanon. Planted in the house of the Lord, they will flourish in the courts of our God. They will still yield fruit in old age; they shall be full of sap and very green. Ps. 92:12-14, NASB.

An article by Paul Harvey in the November 1990 *Signs of the Times* under the title "The Biggest Living Thing" stated that we can reap a million dollar benefit simply by planting four trees. Researchers have calculated that all the benefits we receive from one tree during a 50-year life span if translated into monetary value would be worth $282,000. Four trees would give us more than a million dollars of usefulness.

Scientists claim that the largest living thing, past or present, is not a dinosaur, but one of the great sequoia or redwood trees of California. A single such tree weighs as much as six blue whales. The tallest tree is 70 feet higher than the Statue of Liberty.

Harvey's article points out that trees in a forest seem to have the capacity to help each other by joining their roots and sharing nutrients and water. Thus a forest is not just a collection of individual trees, but a "cooperative network of trees working together for survival." Trees can do marvelous things. A single acre of maple trees puts 20,000 gallons of clean water vapor into the air every day. And think of all the fruits and nuts we get from trees.

No wonder the psalmist refers to the righteous people as flourishing like trees. Their lives yield fruit even in old age. As long as we are connected to Jesus Christ, our lives will provide great benefits to the world. We become an honor to God and a blessing to each other.

Praise God for your opportunity to flourish for Him. Are you like a tree? What good things do you think God could accomplish through your life?

The Father Himself Loves Us!

For the Father Himself loves you, because you have loved Me, and have believed that I came forth from the Father. John 16:27, NASB.

Do we really believe that God loves us? This verse is an extension of John 14:1, which tells us that because we believe in God we should not let anything trouble us. To believe in God means to recognize that He is a God of love and that His love focuses on us. Jesus loved to talk about His Father's love, for He understood that if we knew the Father correctly, we would realize that He loves us dearly.

The Father's love for us is so great that He eagerly desires to reproduce His character in us, knowing that true fulfillment and happiness in life is in direct proportion to how much we are like Him. God created us in His image, and the great object of salvation is to restore us back to that condition. If we have His character, we will be able to respond to love as He would. The restoration process never stops. "There are hereditary and cultivated tendencies to evil that must be overcome. Appetite and passion must be brought under the control of the Holy Spirit. There is no end to the warfare this side of eternity" (*Counsels to Parents and Teachers*, p. 20).

The apostle Paul was well acquainted with the struggle in the Christian life when he stated that he was crucified with Christ and that he died daily. He constantly faced the danger of death from outside foes, but he also knew that his greatest enemy lay within his own heart. For that reason, he declared that we do not fight against flesh and blood, but against dark spiritual powers.

Every child of God wages warfare. Ellen White bared her own spiritual conflict when she wrote: "The deep struggles of my own soul against temptations, the earnest longings of my mind and heart to know God and Jesus Christ as my personal Saviour, and to have assurance, peace, and rest in their love, lead me to desire every day to be where the beams of the Sun of Righteousness can shine upon me" (*Our High Calling*, p. 146).

When a rosebud bathes in the warm sunshine, it does not take long before it bursts forth in full bloom. And as we understand God's love for us and as we rest in the sunshine of His love, the petals of our lives will fully spread open to exude beauty and fragrance about us.

It is almost beyond imagination that God, the majestic ruler of the universe, loves us and wants to restore His character in us daily. But He does! Praise Him for His magnificent, personal love for you as a person.

Life's Greatest Question

And as He was setting out on a journey, a man ran up to Him and knelt before Him, and began asking Him, "Good Teacher, what shall I do to inherit eternal life?" Mark 10:17, NASB.

"What shall I do to inherit eternal life?" How much thought have you given to this question that is above all others? We hear endless discussions about what direction the church is going, but the vital question is What direction are we going—toward heaven or hell? Constantly we read detailed explanations of the elements of salvation—justification, new birth, sanctification—but the ultimate question is Have I been born again? And we listen to numerous discussions on the nature of Christ, but the fundamental question is Am I like Jesus?

The story of the youthful, wealthy ruler was considered important enough for Matthew, Mark, and Luke to each record the incident in their Gospels. It involves the issue of values. What do we consider the most valuable thing in life to obtain? In our hierarchy of values, where does eternal life really stand? Sit quietly for just a few seconds, then answer this question: How important is eternal life to me? If you place it at the top of your priority list, then ask yourself: Am I ordering my life—my time, money, and energies—in such a way that salvation gets first priority? If not, what changes should I make now—today—to make certain that I am saved for eternity?

As we write these words, we find ourselves under great conviction as to how we should respond to these same questions. Salvation is not some trivial subject to discuss and argue about. No, it is everything that counts in life. Jesus emphasized the importance of salvation in His parables and discourses. From the woman at Jacob's well to the Sadducees in the Temple, from Nicodemus to His disciples, Jesus focused His teaching on salvation through Him alone.

Even His parables centered on eternal life. From the houses built on rock or sand to the sower and his seed, from the pearl of great price to the wedding clothes at the banquet, all stressed the same theme of salvation. Another principle in our story today that needs repeated emphasis is that our surrender to Christ and His teaching is a prerequisite for salvation. No surrender, no salvation. But submission to the will of Jesus isn't easy. Self rises up constantly to interfere with our relationship with our Lord. Someone spoke truly when he said, "Seeing ourselves as others see us wouldn't do much good because most of us wouldn't believe what we saw!"

The poor rich young ruler couldn't believe his ears when the Lord told him he lacked one thing. He thought he was perfect and ready for eternal life, and just wanted Jesus, the Good Teacher, to confirm it.

Perhaps the most important facet of our young leader's story involves the perfection of Christ. We will expand on this point tomorrow.

Now it is your turn to praise the Lord in a sentence or two for giving you eternal life.

Love in a Look

And looking at him, Jesus felt a love for him, and said to him, "One thing you lack: go and sell all you possess, and give it to the poor, and you shall have treasure in heaven; and come, follow Me." Mark 10:21, NASB.

Mark, throughout his Gospel, vividly emphasizes Jesus' expressions and gestures. According to tradition, Mark recorded those events told to him by Peter. We can easily visualize Peter intently studying the face of Jesus in our story. Despite his problems, Peter loved the Lord. He was always interested not only in what Jesus said but in interpreting his Master's facial expressions. At a later time, when Peter denied Jesus three times just prior to the Crucifixion, Dr. Luke records that "the Lord turned and looked at Peter. And

251

Peter remembered the word of the Lord" (Luke 22:61, NASB). Jesus was not angry, but terribly hurt. His expression was one of compassion and forgiveness.

After the young rich man rejected the Lord's counsel to sell his possessions and went away grieved, Jesus uttered His famous statement about it being more difficult for a rich man to enter the kingdom than for a camel to go through the eye of a needle. Peter, wanting to secure assurance of his own salvation, immediately replied, "Behold, we have left everything and followed You" (Mark 10:28, NASB).

Christ not only had a look of love for the ruler, but the record says that Jesus loved him. Have you ever felt that way as you watched someone whom you know walking in the wrong direction in life? What can you say or do to change a person's course? Perhaps nothing. But by God's grace we can have Christian love for another person. As the young man left, a solemn hush must have come over the disciples.

When the ruler heard the specific conditions for him to follow, he became very sad, for he was extremely rich (verse 22). Undoubtedly the poorly dressed disciples and Jesus had watched intently to see what this man, clothed in expensive garments, would do. He probably toyed with his sandal in the dirt as he thought for a moment. A battle raged in his mind over giving up his possessions and following Jesus or keeping them all to himself and forgetting Christ. Satisfaction with his own righteousness finally won the day. Turning, he walked away in silence. He had made his decision, and it cost him eternal life. Jesus and His disciples watched him go. They, especially Jesus, were sadder than the ruler. They knew that they would meet him again in the judgment day.

Thank the Lord that you can follow Jesus today! Praise Him for His invitation to walk with Him.

August   29

Etiquette

But we know that the Law is good, if one uses it lawfully, realizing the fact that law is not made for a righteous man, but for those who are lawless and rebellious, for the ungodly and sinners, for the unholy and profane. 1 Tim. 1:8, 9, NASB.

In the November 7, 1991, *Adventist Review* Dorothy Minchin-Comm wrote a beautiful devotional article titled "The Little Tablets." The article carries us back to the time of Louis XIV, who converted an ordinary country estate into one of the most magnificent palaces that Europe has ever seen.

The gardener took great pains with the flower beds that he had laid out in perfect circles, triangles, and intersected rectangles. It was a living carpet of graceful, intricately designed flower patterns. However, season after season the noblemen and great ladies trampled the flower beds without restraint. Repeatedly the gardener's skillful hands tried to repair the damage. He finally decided to do what no one else dared to do—appeal to Louis XIV himself. He asked the king if he could make some kind of law whereby a small barrier would be put up to prevent the palace's visitors from spoiling the gardens.

The king ordered "little tablets"—*etiquette* in French—to be neatly arranged along the sides of the flower beds. Then Louis XIV issued a royal decree ordering all his courtiers to walk carefully within the pathways marked out by the "etiquette"—the rows of little tablets.

The story gives us an insight to God's law. Etiquette demands that we honor our God and not trample on His commandments. Today we have signs that read "Keep Off the Grass." In essence, this is what the commandments are—notices to keep off the grass of God's will. Note carefully in our text today that the law condemns only those who violate it—the "lawless and rebellious." Those who reverence the King of the universe are happy for the divine hedge that keeps God's gardens looking beautiful. True, all of us have trampled underfoot our King's flower beds. We have broken through the hedge and wandered off the pathway, but thank God He has forgiven us and is willing to help us to respect the *etiquette of the gospel.*

As you study our text today, aren't you thankful that He has a law and that He is a God of etiquette? He has erected its barriers for our own good and for the beauty of His kingdom. How has God's law helped you keep from marring the beauty of His universe?

The Lord Will Rise Upon You

For behold, darkness will cover the earth, and deep darkness the peoples; but the Lord will rise upon you, and His glory will appear upon you. Isa. 60:2, NASB.

This prophecy met its fulfillment at the first coming of Christ. Spiritual blindness, worsening over centuries, had now reached its deepest. To a large degree tradition had replaced the Scriptures. Religious education emphasized nonessentials and elevated external forms.

Traveling from the realms of indescribable glory to the enveloping folds of darkest shadows, Jesus came to dispel the gloom of misapprehension and misunderstanding about God. Speaking of Christ, John says, "In Him was life, and the life was the light of men. And the light shines in the darkness; and the darkness did not comprehend it" (John 1:4, 5, NASB).

Jesus Himself announced, "I have come as light into the world, that everyone who believes in Me may not remain in darkness" (John 12:46, NASB). Christ was light to the human race through His words and actions.

In His famous bread-of-life message (John 6), He called upon His hearers to eat His flesh and drink His blood. Although it must have sounded strange to them, He underlined the importance of His invitation by declaring that unless they ate His flesh and drank His blood, they could have no life.

The message is clear: we receive His life by receiving His Word. "The words that I have spoken to you are spirit and are life" (John 6:63).

Although Jesus is not with us today, His Word is. When we understand the grand purpose of Scripture and realize that through its pages the human mind comes into contact with the divine and the infinite, we will covet every moment possible to spend in its study. We will consider our fellowship with the eternal One through Bible study a privilege and honor—never drudgery.

The Bible is a window through which we look into the face of God. It is a great privilege to have the Lord arise upon us and reveal His glory in us, and it will happen if we spend time with the Scriptures. Most of us live in an age when and in places where God's Word is available to everyone.

Thank God that you have the privilege of looking in the face of Jesus through His precious Word. Express your gratitude in your own words.

_____

_____

August 31

God's Love in Creation

Do we not all have one father? Has not one God created us? Mal. 2:10, NASB.

"Every manifestation of creative power is an expression of infinite love" (*Patriarchs and Prophets*, p. 33). Whether it be a newborn baby or a giant galaxy of stars, everything God made expresses infinite love. Bob has often referred to his looking through the hospital's nursery window at our first baby. He had always been mystified by the way fathers would become so excited about the arrival of their first child—the way a man would delight in pointing out his infant in the nursery and exclaim, "That's my baby!" Not until the birth of our firstborn child could he begin to understand the deep love parents have for their children—a love that no one can ever know until he or she too becomes a parent.

The whole world is a nursery. God the Father bends low in love as He sees life being reproduced through His creative power.

Have you ever considered how we might respond to our children if they were merely manufactured on some fast-moving assembly line, and all that was necessary would be to go to a store and buy a brand-new, shiny baby for

$1,000? Of course, we would be about as excited and thrilled as we are over the purchase of a new car. But there could be no deep, sacred, divine, reverential attitude toward a manufactured baby! Even the acquisition of a new pet, such as a dog, produces deeper emotions than getting a new bicycle.

Life is love. Life is sacred. Life is spiritual. Thank God for it! Praise Him for His creative powers. Why? Our Creator-God of love brought life into existence. From Him comes every intellectual and artistic talent, every emotional capacity, every gift of grace and love.

Genuine life—life breathed into all of us by a loving Creator—has an awe and grandeur beyond comprehension. God created us out of love. And through the process of human reproduction, we share in that grandeur and wonder as we have the opportunity to bring new life into existence because of love.

Praise Him for His creative power and for bringing you into existence and for the opportunity of living eternally with Him.

September 1

Singing Gladdens Our Pilgrim Life

I will sing unto the Lord, for he hath triumphed gloriously: the horse and his rider hath he thrown into the sea. The Lord is my strength and my song, and he is become my salvation: This is my God, and I will praise him. Ex. 15:1, 2, RV.

Moses led the Israelites in this beautiful triumphant anthem of thanksgiving after God delivered them from the hand of Pharaoh at the Red Sea. It is one of the most sublime songs of all ages. One could hear their voices far across the desert and sea as the mountains echoed and reechoed the words of their praise, gratitude, and renewal of faith and trust in God. As this great throng trudged through the rocky desert and united their voices in praise to God for His love and divine direction, their trials and difficulties diminished, their restless spirits grew calm, and their faith in God strengthened, bringing them closer to Him.

This great deliverance and the song commemorating it made such an impression upon Israel that it has never been forgotten. Through the ages prophets and psalmists have echoed it, testifying that God still gives strength and deliverance to those who trust in Him.

Moses' song is not only for the Israelites of old, but for those of us living during the last days of earth's history, for in it we can look forward to the final destruction of the wicked and the victory of God's people. John the revelator saw those who had overcome evil standing on the sea of glass. They held harps of God as they sang the song of Moses and the Lamb (see Rev. 15:2, 3). Let us plan today to be a part of that glorious chorus!

As singing cheered the hearts of the children of Israel on the way to the Promised Land, so "God bids His children today gladden their pilgrim life. There are few means more effective for fixing His words in the memory than repeating them in song. And such song has wonderful power. It has power to subdue rude and uncultivated natures; power to quicken thought and to awaken sympathy, to promote harmony of action, and to banish the gloom and foreboding that destroy courage and weaken effort. It is one of the most effective means of impressing the heart with spiritual truth. . . . Temptations lose their power, life takes on new meaning and new purpose, and courage and gladness are imparted to other souls!" (*Education*, pp. 167, 168).

Recall some songs that have inspired you to live a victorious life, and praise God for their influence.

_____

_____

September 2

The Best and the Worst

For we all stumble in many ways. If any one does not stumble in what he says, he is a perfect man, able to bridle the whole body as well. James 3:2, NASB.

Many people have prayed for the gift of tongues when they should have prayed for the gift of silence. One of the fables credited to the slave Aesop contains much truth. His master, Xanthus the philosopher, ordered him to purchase the best food possible from the market. He wanted to throw a party for his friends. But the only thing Aesop bought was tongue. The cook served it with different sauces. The servants brought course after course, each consisting of tongue. Xanthus became angry and said, "Did I not order you to buy the best victuals the market afforded?"

"And have I not obeyed your orders?" replied Aesop. "Is there anything better than a tongue? Is not the tongue the bond of civil society, the organ of truth and reason, and the instrument of our praise and adoration of the gods?"

Xanthus then commanded him to go again to the market and buy the worst food possible. Aesop again brought back tongues, which the cook prepared and served in various ways.

"What! Tongue again?" Xanthus exclaimed.

"Most certainly," Aesop answered. "The tongue is surely the worst thing in the world. It is the instrument of all strife and contention, the inventor of lawsuits, and the source of division and wars. It is the organ of error, of lies, calumny, and blasphemy."

This ancient fable supports James's statement, "With it [the tongue] we bless our Lord and Father; and with it we curse men, who have been made in the likeness of God; from the same mouth come both blessing and cursing. My brethren, these things ought not to be this way" (James 3:9, 10, NASB).

To speak kindly and honestly never hurt the tongue. The tongue can encourage others, especially our children, to love the Lord and serve Him. It can bring great blessing to us as we lift our minds to Him in gratitude and praise. And it is a powerful instrument in witnessing. Instruct your tongue today to be a blessing to everyone you meet.

Thank the Lord that you can use your tongue to communicate the gospel to others.

Job's Character and Wealth

There was a man in the land of Uz, whose name was Job, and that man was blameless, upright, fearing God, and turning away from evil. Job 1:1, NASB.

We think the most eloquent book in the Bible is that of Job. The language, the figures of speech, and the thoughts are truly magnificent. In Job 38 God speaks to him with words "in their majesty unequaled, unapproached, by the loftiest productions of human genius" (*Education*, p. 159).

The core theme of the book deals with one basic question: What is faith? Anyone who faces severe and overwhelming trials that raise doubts about God's love needs to study carefully this book with its powerful insight to life's problems.

Job was immensely wealthy for his time and had a family of 10 children and many servants. In our day we would classify him in the millionaire club. He had obtained his wealth honestly, or he could not have been considered blameless and upright. His devotion as a servant of God stands revealed in the fact that he feared God and turned "away from evil."

His seven sons took turns throwing feasts for the entire family. If each one did it once a year, it meant a son gave a feast about every seven weeks. After each cycle of parties, Job would get up early in the morning and slaughter 10 animals and offer a burnt offering in behalf of his seven sons and three daughters. Job expressed his concern for the salvation of his children in the words "Perhaps my sons have sinned and cursed God in their hearts" (Job 1:5, NASB).

Job's routine of sacrifices for his children did not contribute to their salvation. Neither sacrifices nor anything else can buy salvation. But their father's concern over their spirituality must have impressed them. Wayward children may not admit it, but a parent's consistent Christian spirit of kindness and love makes an impact on them. Furthermore, unceasing prayer in behalf of children increases the parents' love.

Thank God for your family, regardless of their spiritual state. All its members are precious in God's sight. List the names of your children or those for whom you would like to pray daily.

_____

_____

A Universe of Intelligent Beings

Now there was a day when the sons of God came to present themselves before the Lord, Satan also came among them. Job 1:6, NASB.

Recently we were watching a television program about scientists' attempt to discover intelligent life in our universe. The program showed extremely sensitive receivers that scan the depths of space for any radio signal that might indicate intelligent beings communicating with each other. Statements and quotations from astronomers, physicists, and other scientists indicated a widespread belief that intelligent life exists on other planets. The immensity of space, with its unnumbered galaxies and island universes, humbles even the atheist into thinking that our tiny world cannot possibly be the only place inhabited by beings who can think and act.

Our text supports such a concept. According to Ellen White, the "sons of God" who "came to present themselves before the Lord" are none other than representatives from other worlds. When the Lord asked Job some pointed questions about his knowledge and involvement in the creation of our world, He referred to the triumphal time when at the world's creation "all the sons of God shouted for joy" (Job 38:7, NASB).

Paul speaks of our Lord creating all things "both in the heavens and on earth, visible and invisible, whether thrones or dominions or rulers or authorities" (Col. 1:16, NASB). While Paul was probably thinking mainly of the forces of good and evil that struggle invisibly in this world—a belief particularly strong in his time—his statement also suggests intelligent beings or "rulers or authorities," who are presently living beyond our planet.

It is mind-expanding to imagine a universe teeming with billions of populated planets, planets inhabited by sinless beings who adoringly obey God. We, if faithful to our Lord, will spend eternity visiting such worlds and becoming acquainted with God's huge family. Our own planet, on which Jesus died, will become the command center for the universe. Satan will no longer exist, no longer be around to claim that he represents our world in the councils of heaven. We have so much to look forward to.

Let us express our thanks for this hope of a busy future making friends with other beings and sharing with them how Jesus redeemed us!

My Servant Job

And the Lord said to Satan, "Have you considered My servant Job? For there is no one like him on the earth, a blameless and upright man, fearing God and turning away from evil." Job 1:8, NASB.

Satan's bold entrance to an important heavenly council prompted the Lord to ask him about faithful Job. In addition to his wealth, Job had, through the Lord's Spirit, developed a blameless and upright character. In response to the Lord's comment about Job's trustworthy character, Satan challenged God to remove His hedge of protection around the man.

"Does Job fear You for nothing?" Satan demanded. "You have blessed his works. He has everything a heart could desire. His possessions have put him at the top of the Fortune 500 Club. The patriarch's remarkable family are known and admired for their achievements. With few or no trials and problems, he finds it easy to serve You. But if You destroy all that he has, he will surely curse You to Your face." (See Job 1:9-11.)

How would the Lord respond to Satan's shocking and arrogant challenge? God's reply reveals His immense confidence in Job. "Behold, all that he has is in your power, only do not put forth your hand on him" (verse 12, NASB).

The reality of the cosmic struggle between the Lord and Satan over the salvation of a soul is one lesson to learn from our text today. The battle over every person on earth is as real as World War II or the war in the Persian Gulf. Do not permit your busy schedules to blind you to the reality of the daily warfare being fought over you. Do you really believe that the Lord and Satan will battle over you today? You will face trials and temptations especially designed for you by Satan and permitted by the Lord. But Satan is no match for Him. Calvary was Satan's Waterloo! Cling to Jesus through prayer and Bible study.

Praise Him now for the victories He will give you over Satan this very day!

Job's Testing

Then Job arose and tore his robe and shaved his head, and he fell to the ground and worshiped. And he said, "Naked I came from my mother's womb, and naked I shall return there. The Lord gave and the Lord has taken away. Blessed be the name of the Lord." Job 1:20, 21, NASB.

Round 1 in the fight over Job ended in victory for the Lord. This amazing man held firm his faith in God in spite of horrible losses. We have tried to put ourselves in Job's place. Our wealth consists of two daughters and a home partially owned by the bank, plus our "elderly" furniture, two older cars, and some savings. To have it all wiped away virtually overnight is more than we can bear to think about. Would we—could we—still trust God if that happened?

Let's itemize Job's losses. The list begins with his 500 yoke of oxen and 500 female donkeys—all stolen by the Sabeans. The desert marauders murdered all but one of the servants tending the animals. Next on the list was the blazing destruction of his 7,000 sheep and all but one of his shepherds by a huge bolt of lightning—fire from heaven! Then came a band of Chaldeans, who raided his 3,000 camels. Job lost the entire lot, along with his camel drivers, except for the individual who escaped to tell him about it.

The worst and most heartrending misfortune was the cyclone that struck the oldest son's home, where all the children were having a feast. Again all but one of the whole family of sons, daughters, and in all probability, grandchildren, perished. Satan left one person alive in each incident to carry the shocking news to Job. The climax to this series of tragedies is Job's testimony found in verse 22: "Through all this Job did not sin nor did he blame God" (NASB).

Perhaps you have gone or are going through some tragedy in your life. If so, can you find it in your heart to still bless the Lord rather than blame Him?

September 7

"Skin for Skin!"

And Satan answered the Lord and said, "Skin for skin! Yes, all that a man has he will give for his life. However, put forth Thy hand, now, and touch his bone and his flesh; he will curse Thee to Thy face." So the Lord said to Satan, "Behold, he is in your power, only spare his life." Job 2:4-6, NASB.

After Job lost everything, including his children, he faced the supreme test of having his own body racked with excruciating physical pain. God now allowed Satan to afflict Job himself, but not to the point of death. There are many things worse than death, and Job's life and words prove this point.

A rash of "sore boils" tormented him from head to foot. He tried to scrape off the putrefying skin with a piece of broken pottery. Then just when he needed the comfort of his wife, she tried to turn him against God. "Do you still hold fast your integrity?" she taunted. "Curse God and die!" she advised (Job 2:9, NASB). What she meant was for Job to put the blame for his problems—and hers—where it appeared to belong. She too suffered over the loss of their wealth, and especially their children. In her thinking, it had to be God who had caused the calamities. Hadn't they paid their tithe, given to the poor, worshiped God every Sabbath, fed visiting saints, helped build the church, and given large sums of money for Adventist World Radio? *Now*, she thought, *look how God rewards us!* It is the same old story of people blaming God for their troubles.

But despite his mental and physical agony, Job rebuked his wife. "You speak as one of the foolish women speaks. Shall we indeed accept good from God and not accept adversity? In all this Job did not sin with his lips" (verse 10, NASB).

His reply demonstrated faith and trust in God's goodness and submission to His will. Yet Job did not have a fatalistic attitude. Rather, in his extremity he refused to turn against his Lord.

His remarkable faith can be ours if we daily cultivate our faith and confidence in the Lord's love for us. Continually praise Him for His goodness, His power, His character, and His love. Do it now, for the Lord is good no matter what happens to you!

Job Laments His Birth

Let the day perish on which I was to be born, and the night which said, "A boy is conceived." . . . Why did I not die at birth, come forth from the womb and expire? Job 3:3-11, NASB.

Has life been so difficult at times that you regret having been born? If so, know that your case is not unique. The Scriptures are wonderful in that we usually read in their pages about someone who has had an experience similar to ours and by God's grace coped with it.

Job had lost just about everything—possessions, children, health. His wife ridiculed his faithfulness. What was there to live for? In his agony he eloquently described his feelings about life itself. The third chapter of Job is a masterpiece of descriptive speech. He begins his lament by cursing not God but his birthday. "May that day be darkness; let not God above care for it, nor light shine on it. Let darkness and black gloom claim it" (Job 3:4, 5, NASB).

If Job had suffered from suicidal tendencies, he might have ended it all, but his faith rose above his indescribable troubles. Trials can always be turned into stepping-stones. Working with our members in the former Soviet Union has caused us to marvel at their faith and trust in God despite overwhelming persecution. Nearly every minister during the Stalin era suffered imprisonment or banishment to Siberia. The authorities had severely curtailed religious freedom for all religions, Christian or non-Christian. In 1916 the Russian Orthodox Church had 1,025 monasteries. Then came Communism, and by 1985 only 19 remained open. Stalin had an estimated 15 to 20 million property owners murdered or starved to death so the government could confiscate their possessions. World War II added to the immense suffering of the Soviet people when more than 20 million men, women, and children perished.

Yet our members and leaders have remained courageous in the face of such huge problems. They live for the soon return of Jesus. Their faith has been a great inspiration to us.

We should unceasingly praise the Lord for the temporal and spiritual blessings we so often take for granted. Daily we should praise the Lord for our spiritual heritage and freedom. Even though at times we face discouragement, our confidence and trust in God should provide us with a sense of peace, security, and hope.

Praise the Lord by jotting down some of your blessings.

_____

_____

Job's Concept of Death

For now I would have lain down and been quiet; I would have slept then, I would have been at rest, with kings and with counselors of the earth, who rebuilt ruins for themselves; or with princes who had gold, who were filling their houses with silver. Job 3:13-15, NASB.

Have you ever noticed the headlines and pictures on the front pages of the tabloids at the supermarket checkout counters? It appears that the subject most often headlined involves life after death. Numerous articles deal with the reports of those who thought they had died and then came back to life. The main concern of the tabloid publishers is not truth but to sell papers. They realize what attracts buyers, and the subject of death is one of the top attractions. The mystery of what happens to a person when he or she dies has led many to drink at the impure fountains of the occult in its various forms.

The first recorded lie in history concerns life and death. The serpent, Satan, assured Eve that if she ate of the forbidden fruit in Eden, she would not die. Who was right—Satan or God?

Our text today belongs to a larger section that testifies that death is a sleep. Note the words "slept" and "rest." The suffering patriarch longed for rest in the grave. He pointed out that death is the same state of unconsciousness for kings, princes, and their counselors. In the grave even "the wicked cease from raging, and there the weary are at rest. The prisoners are at ease together; they do not hear the voice of the taskmaster. The small and the great are there, and the slave is free from his master" (Job 3:17-19, NASB).

How often we have thanked the Lord for the truth of life after death, which has preserved us from the trap of spiritualism. Although death is humanity's last and greatest enemy, it soon will be swallowed up in victory at our Lord's coming. The Christian has a bright hope.

Please give a written testimony of your belief in life after death at our Saviour's return.

Is Justification Impossible?

Can mankind be just before God? Can a man be pure before his Maker? Job 4:17, NASB.

This question comes from one of Job's so-called comforters, Eliphaz. His thrust in chapters 4 and 5 is to show that innocent people do not suffer. His description of the concept is vivid as he claims that "affliction does not come from the dust, neither does trouble sprout from the ground, for man [the context implies bad men] is born for trouble, as sparks fly upward" (Job 5:6, 7, NASB).

According to Eliphaz, Job had to be guilty of something, or he simply wouldn't be suffering such terrible calamities. Eliphaz wrongly argued that the rain and sunshine come only to good people.

However, in his speech to suffering Job, he does ask a most important question: "Is it possible for a person to be just and pure before God?" He expands his question in chapter 15: "What is man, that he should be pure, or he who is born of a woman, that he should be righteous?" (verse 14, NASB).

Even Job had earlier asked, "How can a man be in the right before God?" (Job 9:2, NASB). Later he demanded, "Who can make the clean out of the unclean? No one!" (Job 14:4, NASB).

Bildad, another friend, argued: "How then can a man be just with God?" He added, "Or how can he be clean who is born of woman?" (Job 25:4, NASB).

It is a question that Satan does not want answered correctly because it focuses on how God saves a person. How we sinners, who drink "iniquity like water!" (Job 15:16, NASB), can be saved puzzled Job and his friends.

The bad news is that from a human standpoint we cannot be justified. But the good news, praise God, is that from His standpoint we can be declared innocent. We can be just before God, pure and right before our Maker! It is a marvelous, unfathomable truth that our Lord can make the clean out of the unclean. If we are in Christ, we are justified. And if we are in Christ, we are sanctified. His perfection is credited to our account. Our response to this wondrous fact, then, is to be one of loving obedience.

It is a privilege to thank Him for His marvelous salvation, which centers in His forgiveness of our sins and in His power through the Holy Spirit to create in us clean hearts. How do you feel about this magnificent truth?

Does God Trust Man?

He puts no trust even in His servants; and against His angels He charges error. How much more those who dwell in houses of clay, whose foundation is in the dust, who are crushed before the moth! Job 4:18, 19, NASB.

Eliphaz makes the comment in today's text immediately after he asks, "Can mankind be just before God?" (Job 4:17, NASB). It is a horrible indictment against God. He equates God's attitude toward the human race with his own. Evidently Eliphaz' experiences had been rather disappointing. Perhaps a fellow believer had cheated him. Too often he may have witnessed the weaknesses and failings of those who worship God. Thus he judges the human race rather severely. Is it true that God has no confidence or trust in people?

The story of Job's life proves otherwise. God had complete confidence in him, the very one to whom Eliphaz was making such discouraging statements. Scripture is filled with case histories of those whom the Lord trusted. Yes, God did bring charges against one third of His angels, who chose allegiance to Satan and made him their commander in chief, but remember, two thirds remained loyal. It is true that the broad way to death is heavily traveled by those "who are crushed before the moth." But many of "those who dwell in houses of clay" still manage to find the narrow way to life.

Our Lord Jesus "is making experiments on human hearts through the exhibition of His mercy and abundant grace. He is effecting transformations so amazing that Satan, with all his triumphant boasting, with all his confederacy of evil united against God and the laws of His government, stands viewing them as a fortress impregnable to his sophistries and delusions. They are to him an incomprehensible mystery" (*Testimonies to Ministers*, p. 18).

It is a great privilege to cause Satan to regard us as impregnable fortresses and as an incomprehensible mystery because of God's grace upon our hearts. Praise His name for what He is, and for what He can and will do for us!

Rejoicing in Pain

Would that God were willing to crush me; that He would loose His hand and cut me off! But it is still my consolation, and I rejoice in unsparing pain, that I have not denied the words of the Holy One. Job 6:9, 10, NASB.

Although Job rejoiced in his pain of body and spirit because he had "not denied the words of the Holy One," he still complained bitterly at times. After all, he was a real human being. He admitted that his words at times were those that belonged to an individual in despair and were like the wind and that at times his words had been rash (see Job 6:3, 26, NASB). Naturally it greatly puzzled him why he should suffer such losses and pain. In fact, he cried out, "Oh that my vexation were actually weighed. . . . For then it would be heavier than the sand of the seas" (verses 2, 3, NASB). Although he admitted his iniquities, he believed he was honest and sincere. At one point he asked, "Is there injustice on my tongue?" (verse 30, NASB). "Have I said, 'Give me something,' or, 'Offer a bribe for me from your wealth,' or, 'Deliver me from the hand of the adversary,' or, 'Redeem me from the hand of the tyrants'?" (verses 22, 23, NASB).

Job challenged Eliphaz' accusations of his sins being the reason for his troubles by saying, "Teach me, and I will be silent; and show me how I have erred. How painful are honest words! But what does your argument prove?" (verses 24, 25).

Rejecting Eliphaz' reasoning, Job knew that his lifestyle had not brought his problems upon himself. He was suffering, though innocent, for some reason he had yet to learn.

While it is true that we bring much calamity upon ourselves because of our own poor judgment, over and above that we are still the victims of a cosmic battle being fought between Christ and Satan—and we are caught in the middle. We pray that when adversities come our way, we will, like Job, rejoice that we have not "denied the words of the Holy One."

How do you feel about it?

God's Concern for Us

What is man that Thou dost magnify him, and that Thou art concerned about him, that Thou dost examine him every morning, and try him every moment? Job 7:17, 18, NASB.

"Does God really care for us?" is a question that plagues every one of us at one time or another. It especially disturbs us when death, terminal illness, or financial reverses strike either us or someone whom we love dearly.

Charles Lindbergh made the first solo nonstop flight across the Atlantic in a single-engine plane, his *Spirit of St. Louis.* When his infant child was kidnapped and found dead in the woods, it was headline news for weeks. As children this incident shocked us. Life had seemed glorious, but the long shadow of that crime made us wonder how the Lindberghs felt. For months while walking to school, we kept a lookout for kidnappers.

Today's world struggles not only with crime but with sickness and unexpected death. Almost daily we receive in our mail advertising cards with the picture of a missing child on one side. It is not difficult to wonder whether God really cares, especially if we are the ones who meet calamity.

Job reminds us that God really does care. The ancient patriarch believed in God's love, even though he stated, "My flesh is clothed with worms and a crust of dirt; and my skin hardens and runs" (Job 7:5, NASB).

Despite everything that had happened he still believed God to be just and fair, even though at times he asked Him, "Wilt Thou never turn Thy gaze away from me, nor let me alone until I swallow my spittle? Have I sinned? What have I done to Thee, O watcher of men? Why hast Thou set me as Thy target, so that I am a burden to myself?" (verses 19, 20, NASB).

God is interested in every individual. He concerns Himself with our welfare, especially our spiritual condition. Although He examines us every morning He does not do so as a ruthless judge but as a loving Father.

Can you testify to God's love for you despite problems? God loves you! Believe it and write about it now.

September 14

"Give Me Tomorrow!"

Now my days are swifter than a runner; they flee away, they see no good. They slip by like reed boats, like an eagle that swoops on its prey. Job 9:25, 26, NASB.

Life at best is short. Job's descriptive language of life's swiftness includes references to runners, boats, and an eagle. In Job 7:6, he declares, "My days are swifter than a weaver's shuttle" (NASB). When we finally seem prepared to really and fully live life, it departs. For most of us, in our retirement years the clock speeds up even faster.

In view of the fleetingness of time, wouldn't it be well to make the best of every moment? Savor every second of life by looking for ways to be an honor to God and a blessing to others. Time, like all lost opportunities, never returns. You have only this moment now—tomorrow may never come.

During the Korean War, when U.S. troops, facing enormous odds, had to retreat in subzero weather, Pulitzer prize-winning reporter Marguerite Higgins approached one soldier. She asked, "If I were God and could grant you anything you wished, what would you most like to have?" His famous answer "Give me tomorrow!" was widely broadcast and remembered.

It is interesting to note that at times Job's pain caused him to wish he had never been born. Then when he felt better, he complained that life was swifter than a swooping eagle. His emotions were not different from those of twentieth-century people.

Another passage in this same chapter reveals the inscrutability of God. Trying to figure out God's ways is futile, Job realized when he declared that "if one wished to dispute with Him, he could not answer Him once in a thousand times. Wise in heart and mighty in strength, who has defied Him without harm?" (Job 9:3, 4, NASB).

Job could only trust in God's goodness and believe that someday He would make things plain. We, like Job, do not understand the Lord's inscrutable ways, but we can trust His love for us. Do you? If so, why not say so in writing?

No Umpire Between Us

For He [God] is not a man as I am that I may answer Him, that we may go to court together. Job 9:32, NASB.

When applied to our Lord, the word "anthropomorphic" means to attribute to Him human characteristics and qualities, both physical and mental. In other words, we in our finite and sinful nature attempt to understand Him by bringing Him down to our level. But to do so can confuse and disappoint those trying to understand God's ways.

We are on dangerous ground if we attempt to describe God's physical qualities in detail. Daniel depicts the Ancient of Days as wearing garments white as snow and having hair on His head like pure wool. (See Dan. 7:9.) John in vision also portrays the Son of man as having hair "like white wool. . . . His eyes were like a flame of fire; and His feet were like burnished bronze" (Rev. 1:14, 15, RSV). But we must not push such descriptions too far. The prophets said that God was "like" this or that, not that He "was."

It is impossible for even a prophet in vision to describe adequately the Lord's physical appearance. Since this is true, how can we really know the depth of His mind and character? The ultimate conclusion Job came to in his experience was to accept his lot in life and to maintain his faith in God's justice and mercy, even though the Lord's ways at times were incomprehensible to him. Before Job reached that point in life, however, it is of interest to note how he reasoned with God.

He rightly recognized that God is not like a human, as our text for today reminds us. Therefore, he could not sue God at court for his problems, which Job at times believed the Lord had caused. Job exclaimed, "There is no umpire between us, who may lay his hand upon us both" (Job 9:33, NASB). He admits that God "is the strong one! And if it is a matter of justice, who can summon Him?" (verse 19, NASB).

Poor Job despairs of God's dealings with him. Finally he concludes, "I should have been as though I had not been carried from womb to tomb" (Job 10:19).

Regardless of Job's spiritual ups and downs, his testimony can be a blessing to us. We, like Job, can trust our Lord, though at times we cannot understand His ways in dealing with us. How do you feel about God?

September 16

Can We Discover God's Depths?

Can you discover the depths of God? Can you discover the limits of the Almighty? They are high as the heavens, what can you do? Deeper than Sheol, what can you know? Job 11:7, 8, NASB.

A famous Nobel prize-winning scientist in a TV interview stated that he was an atheist because of the overwhelming complexity of the universe. It was so great that no one mind or Divine Being could possibly be so intelligent and powerful as to have created it all. His comment shocked us because that is one of the main reasons we believe that a Supreme Being created, sustains, and controls the universe.

Zophar, Job's third friend to rebuke him, asked the above questions, which of themselves imply truth—truth that discloses the absolute inscrutability of the Godhead. But Zophar was dead wrong in the way he used the questions. He employed them to support the standard philosophy of his day, one still shared by most people even in our day—that is, suffering reflects punishment from God. It is the fundamental mistaken concept central to the speeches of Job's three friends—Eliphaz, Bildad, and Zophar.

Every Christian must arrive at the unalterable belief that the Lord is not responsible for the mental, physical, and social trials, tribulations, and disasters that we, to a greater or lesser degree, constantly experience. If we do not come to grips with the falsity of this idea, God's character will remain tarnished in our minds. The marvelous concept that God ever has been, now is, and ever will be pure love will be shrouded in fog!

Zophar did not understand this unalterable truth. However, he was not wrong in portraying God as one whose ways baffle the world's greatest minds. The accumulated wisdom of the human race can never touch the "depths of God." We stand before Him as poverty-stricken beggars when it comes to a knowledge of Him and His ways.

Even His magnificent love portrayed at Calvary is a mystery. We can only accept its unconditional nature, never fully understand it. Each of us can only thank Him for His love. Shall we thank Him today in writing?

_____

_____

No Excuses!

For since the creation of the world His invisible attributes, His eternal power and divine nature, have been clearly seen, being understood through what has been made, so that they are without excuse. Rom. 1:20, NASB.

If you visit any traditional society on earth, you will find that the people believe in a superior God who has created all things. They may have no concept of God's love or goodness—no understanding of His plan of salvation—but they recognize a Supreme Being who made them. Atheism and evolutionary concepts come from those taught by Western educational systems. The idea that there is no God and that life today is the product of long eons of time is a modern phenomenon.

Paul points out that what "is known about God is evident within them; for God made it evident to them" (Rom. 1:19, NASB). Then in our text for today he explains how God did so. First, through all creation we witness God's invisible attributes, such as love, beauty, kindness, patience, goodness, and liberality. Yes, because of the results of sin, we encounter one animal attacking another or a human mother leaving her newborn babe in a garbage can or armies destroying each other. But look again! Watch a mother hen protect her fuzzy yellow chicks. Observe otters teasing each other while chasing each other in a pond. Have you ever gone to Sea World? Imagine a mighty whale being trained to surface in the pool and delicately kiss a small child! Or see a lioness tenderly biting her scampering cubs. Love and caring permeates God's creation.

A pair of barn swallows built a nest on a rafter of our porch. We knew they would produce a mess, but watching them build the nest and hatch four baby swallows with clownlike mouths was worth it. What fun it was to observe their protective behavior when a mockingbird approached! Finally flying lessons began, and with delight we saw this family of six dive and climb like jet fighters around our front yard.

For every scene of violence and horror in nature, a thousand more point to a God of pure love. The things He has made clearly demonstrate His attributes.

Write down some experience you have had in nature that has brought praise to God and ecstasy to your soul.

_____

Ask the Birds, Fish, and Earth

Now ask the beasts, and let them teach you; and the birds of the heavens, and let them tell you. Or speak to the earth, and let it teach you; and let the fish of the sea declare to you. Who among all these does not know that the hand of the Lord has done this, in whose hand is the life of every living thing and the breath of all mankind? Job 12:7-10, NASB.

Yesterday we found that Paul in Romans 1:19, 20 claims that God's created works offer evidence of the eternal power and divine nature of a loving Creator-God.

Here Job, in spite of his boil-covered body, tells his accuser-comforters that even the animal kingdom and the earth itself teach us that God's hand has created every good thing. Furthermore, the existence of all things, including every breath drawn by human or beast, lies in His hands.

Charles Lyell, the British scientist regarded as the father of modern geology, ended a letter to Charles Darwin, author of *Origin of Species*, with the statement "I still see the necessity of continued intervention of creative power."

Unfortunately, Darwin stubbornly held to his evolutionary belief. He quickly replied to Lyell: "I cannot see this necessity. Its admission, I think, would make the theory of natural selection valueless. Grant a simple archetypal creature, like a mudfish or one with both gills and lungs, with five senses and some vestige of mind, and I believe natural selection will account for the production of every vertebrate animal!" (in Irving Stone, *The Origin*, p. 558).

Darwin's investigations into the birds, fish, and the earth led him far and wide, but he received a different answer than what God intended. But we who have internalized the seventh-day Sabbath hear all creation saying loudly and clearly that in the hand of God "is the life of every living thing."

Wouldn't you like to praise Him in a few words for this beautiful truth?

_____

_____

When God Laughs

Why are the nations in an uproar, and the peoples devising a vain thing? . . . He who sits in the heavens laughs, the Lord scoffs at them. Ps. 2:1-4, NASB.

Rear Admiral Robert Fitzroy commanded the ship H.M.S. *Beagle* when Charles Darwin accompanied him on his famous voyage. Darwin's journey led to the writing of his book *Origin of Species*. No publication in recent time has caused such a stir and directly or indirectly influenced the thinking of so many scientists as to the origin of life on our planet.

Fitzroy, after reading Darwin's book, became alarmed. He was now a meteorologist and working for the Meteorological Board of Trade as a statistician. Writing to Darwin, he said, "I presume that your whole time for some years has been so much engrossed by your own avocations . . . that you have scarcely used a telescope for a wide range and comprehensive view; . . . and that you have hardly read the works of later authorities except those bits of them which you could use in your own work. . . . I, at least, cannot find anything ennobling in the thought of being a descendant of even the most ancient ape" (in Irving Stone, *The Origin*, p. 559).

His friend's letter upset Darwin, since he had never specifically discussed human origins. Fitzroy simply had asked, "Why have apes not acquired the intellectual power of man?" Nevertheless, the thrust of Darwin's thesis certainly would lead one to include human beings in an evolutionary process.

As we view the immensity of space, even without a telescope, the grandeur and beauty of millions of stars and galaxies moving without any visible guidance can only awe the mind. Like a massive clock, it operates with perfect precision without any apparent winding. Christians do not know how it is done, but they know who does it.

Could our text today apply to science that attempts to devise theories about how the universe began and how it remains in operation? Do you think God responds in pity at puny people for their vain imaginations? It must break His heart to see those whom He brought into existence ignore or pervert the inspired record of how it all began.

Theories of life's origin are as changeable as fashion, but praise God, His Word stands fast. God did not lie when He said, "For in six days I made heaven and earth."

Aren't you thankful for your heritage as a person created in God's image? Express yourself about this great truth. Why are you glad for it?

Faith in the Valley of Death

Though he slay me, yet will I trust in him. Job 13:15.

When he was only 12 years old, Bob's mother died unexpectedly. His father sold their home and moved in with his parents, and Bob slept on a cot beside his father's bed. From time to time he awakened to the sound of his dad's voice in prayer. He has never forgotten his father silhouetted against the night sky and kneeling before their second-floor bedroom window. His father turned his face toward the heavens while he tearfully pleaded for strength to endure the loneliness and loss of his beloved wife, whose death he could not understand.

Trusting God in times of terrible adversity is not easy. When hope has died to little more than a spark, maintaining faith in God's love becomes the ultimate trial.

In our travels we have visited places where horrible atrocities have occurred. At Auschwitz, Poland, where several million innocent people perished in the Nazi gas chambers and the crematory ovens, we walked through empty barracks. As we viewed the conditions those not immediately murdered had to exist in and as we saw the documentary films of their emaciated bodies on Liberation Day, one question was uppermost in our minds: How could they maintain their faith in God under such horrible conditions? Repeatedly we asked each other, Could we have continued to believe that God existed and was a God of love? It is estimated that 80 percent of the Jews in Israel are atheists. Perhaps the Auschwitz atrocities at least partly account for this.

Job's declaration of trust in God even if He slew him is a marvelous hook to hang faith on. Another hook for faith in God's love is the innocent Jesus dying on the cross for guilty humans. Though His Father's presence was hidden from Him, Jesus still believed that His Father loved Him. He knew His Father's character and the reason for His being crucified. Jesus knew that He was dying as an innocent victim for guilty people. For a split second He almost doubted when, in agony, He asked His Father why He had forsaken Him. But He never gave up His trust in God.

What is your response to trusting God no matter what happens? How do you feel today about God's love for you?

_____

_____

September 21

The Resurrection Hope

Man, who was born of woman, is short-lived and full of turmoil. Like a flower he comes forth and withers. He also flees like a shadow and does not remain. Job 14:1, 2, NASB.

Job was a realist in our passage. His first point is that life is short. What is 70, 80, or even 100 years compared to 1,000 or 5,000 years or to eternity? The patriarch repeatedly refers to the brevity of life. Not only is it brief, but also there is a finality about our lives on earth.

Taking an illustration from nature, Job reveals that "there is hope for a tree, when it is cut down, that it will sprout again, and its shoots will not fail. . . . But man dies and lies prostrate. Man expires, and where is he?" (Job 14:7-10, NASB). In addition to life's shortness and finality, Job adds that it is "full of turmoil."

Learning these points about life will prevent us from being discouraged and caught off guard. They will help us cope when life seems unfair. Yes, we will have heartaches, but we know that they are inevitable in our present world. They remind us that struggles are inescapable and that death is final as far as *our present life* is concerned. The thousands of graves punctuating the landscape testify to this fact. Job gives vivid descriptions of human mortality. "As water evaporates from the sea, and a river becomes parched and dried up, so man lies down and does not rise." For how long? "Until the heavens be no more. He will not awake nor be aroused out of his sleep" (verses 11, 12, NASB).

But Job makes it unmistakably clear that death is a sleep, just as Jesus also called it a sleep. But the good news is that the sleep of death will be interrupted for the righteous. Job asked, "If a man dies, will he live again? All the days of my struggle I will wait until my change comes. Thou wilt call and I will answer Thee" (verses 14, 15, NASB).

The Christian has a marvelous hope! All pain and struggle will banish when Jesus returns and the resurrection and/or translation takes place. That moment of fantastic exhilaration will forever blot out the past with its problems.

One Christian, when asked what his favorite Bible passage was, replied, "I love all those statements that declare, 'It came to pass.'" His exegesis may have been faulty, but his conclusion was valid. The difficult and trying parts of life shall pass. We have the hope of a perfect day, a perfect life, and a perfect place in which to live forever. Do you feel like praising the Lord for this marvelous hope?

Victory Over Death

But man dies and lies prostrate. Man expires, and where is he? Job 14:10, NASB.

A 12-year-old boy timidly entered the funeral parlor, his hand clasped in his father's. Together the boy and man walked toward the casket. The boy looked at the face of his dead mother. The Grim Reaper had done his work well. A few hours before, his mother had been alive—she had had light in her eyes, speech on her lips, strength in her limbs. Then in a moment, life had passed away. Although the eyes, the lips, and the hands appeared as before—everything was so different now. Nothing visible had been taken away. The only thing gone was life.

Bob was that boy, and he has never forgotten the experience.

Death is sin's strange reward and an unnatural state. Eliphaz didn't understand this point, for he equated death with a harvest when he said to the patriarch, "You shall come to your grave in ripe old age, as a shock of grain comes up to the threshing floor in its season" (Job 5:26, RSV).

God never set an age limit on people before the entrance of sin. His original plan had no season for a harvest of death. But since sin, death is certain and unavoidable.

Philip of Macedon had a slave to whom he gave a standing order. The man was to approach the king every morning and, no matter what the monarch was doing, say to him in a loud voice, "Philip, remember that thou must die."

But the good news is that the Scriptures tell us to remember something greater than death. The time is soon coming when death's sting will forever be banished! Soon mortals will put on immortality. It will be a day of joy and gladness, a day of fantastic excitement when death will no longer summon the living. Death may be sin's messenger, but it is also just as certainly God's enemy.

We believe that the moment is fast approaching when the victory shout over death will sound. Praise God for this hope!

Sealed in a Bag

My transgression is sealed up in a bag, and Thou dost wrap up my iniquity. Job 14:17, NASB.

"Sealed up in a bag" is a unique way to describe God's forgiveness! But more than that, our God will take our bag of iniquities, tread it under His feet, and cast it "into the depths of the sea" (Micah 7:19). When God pardons, He consigns the offense to everlasting forgetfulness.

When John Wesley journeyed with General Oglethorpe to Georgia, the general threatened a servant who had offended him. "I never forgive," declared Oglethorpe.

Wesley commented, "Then I hope, sir, you never sin." The force of the rebuke mollified the general's attitude toward his servant.

God's forgiveness for our sins is our only hope. When we accept and understand God's great forgiveness, it should enable us to forgive others. The Lord's Prayer teaches us not only to ask for forgiveness of sin but also to forgive others for their sins against us. Jesus emphasized this point even more when He stated, "For if you forgive men for their transgressions, your heavenly

Father will also forgive you. But if you do not forgive men, then your Father will not forgive your transgressions" (Matt. 6:14, 15, NASB).

In Mark 11:25 our Lord taught, "And whenever you stand praying, forgive, if you have anything against anyone; so that your Father also who is in heaven may forgive you your transgressions" (NASB).

However, our attitude toward and our motivation for forgiving others always have their roots in God's forgiveness for the sins that we have committed. We praise our Lord for establishing the concept of forgiveness even before sin entered the world. It is something that Satan cannot comprehend. The ultimate greatness of our Father's forgiveness demonstrated itself in the death of His Son on Calvary. If we ever doubt His forgiveness, we should take another look at the cross of Calvary and see the amazing love of Jesus revealed.

How much do you thank Him for His forgiveness and for creating a spirit of forgiveness in your own heart? Jot down an experience in which you have forgiven others because God has forgiven you.

_____

_____

My Redeemer Lives

And as for me, I know that my Redeemer lives, and at the last He will take His stand on the earth. Even after my skin is destroyed, yet from my flesh I shall see God; whom I myself shall behold, and whom my eyes shall see and not another. Job 19:25-27, NASB.

Job's ringing testimony of his faith in the coming of the Lord and the resurrection occurred after a bitter exchange between himself and Bildad and Eliphaz. Both his professed friends did everything possible to put a guilt trip upon Job for his "sinful" life. The suffering patriarch then demanded, "How long will you torment me, and crush me with words? These ten times you have insulted me and you are not ashamed to wrong me" (Job 19:2, 3, NASB).

Both Job and his friends misunderstood God's character at this point. His friends believed that all suffering was a result of evil in one's life. While Job blamed God for his problem, He never turned against Him, but repeated consistently that God had wronged him and had "closed his net around me" (verse 6, NASB). He further stated that God "breaks me down on every side, and I am gone; and He has uprooted my hope like a tree. He has also kindled His anger against me, and considered me His enemy" (verses 10, 11, NASB).

The amazing thing is that in spite of Job's misunderstanding of God's character, he would not give up his faith in God's love for him and the hope of the resurrection and eternal life at the end of time.

Our passage today is one of the most frequently quoted texts in the book. It strongly indicates how Job has struggled in his thinking and feelings from despair to confidence and hope. "From the depths of discouragement and despondency Job rose to the heights of implicit trust in the mercy and the saving power of God" (*Prophets and Kings*, p. 163).

As far as we are concerned, the story of Job and God's dealing with him is one of the most encouraging episodes found in Scripture. Although we may puzzle over tragic events in our lives, we pray that we, like Job, will never lose our confidence in our Lord.

If this is your prayer as well, please write it out now.

_____

_____

September 25

The Fate of the Wicked

For the wicked is reserved for the day of calamity, they will be led forth at the day of fury. Job 21:30, NASB.

Chapters 20 and 21 of Job relate the discussion between Zophar and Job over the fate of the wicked. Zophar in chapter 20 gives a dramatic sermon on the short-lived triumph of the wicked. Obviously he believes that Job belongs to that category. Job's suffering proves that he is evil. In chapter 21 Job himself explains how he believes God will deal with the wicked. Clearly he envies them. "Why do the wicked still live, continue on, also become very powerful?" he asks in verse 7 (NASB). He then speaks of their descendants' prosperity. Their houses are safe from fear and God's rod does not touch them (verses 8, 9). The wicked "spend their days in prosperity" (verse 13, NASB), but they suddenly end up in the grave.

While Job agrees with Zophar that the wicked will certainly die, he emphasizes the fact that some wicked meet their end quicker than others. But regardless of how long a wicked person lives, some may die bitterly, never having tasted anything good, while others go to the grave prosperous and satisfied. The end result is the same for both. "Together they lie down in the dust, and worms cover them" (verse 26, NASB).

Job concludes his speech with the recognition that both the wicked and the righteous meet a common end in death. From the murder of Cain until the last person dies prior to Christ's coming, death will have triumphed relentlessly over the earth.

Although both chapters offer a dismal description of death being the Grim Reaper of all mankind, Job's confidence and triumph over his opponents seems secured. One can sense that he will emerge victoriously over his opponents.

Even though death awaits both the good and the evil, those who trust in God can have the confidence and assurance of a future eternal life. We praise God for this hope. Nothing on earth can compare to it.

Praise God for the fact that you know you, too, shall triumph over death through Christ.

Let's Get Acquainted

Acquaint now thyself with him, and be at peace: thereby good shall come unto thee. Job 22:21.

Today's text contains a beautiful appeal, but its speaker was actually abusing and misapplying it. Eliphaz, one of Job's so-called comforters, begged Job to be reconciled to God and establish a personal relationship with Him. But Job already had one. In fact, he knew God better than Eliphaz did! However, the text is still a beautiful one and contains much truth for all of us.

When Bob was a little boy, he began his search for the meaning of life. He still remembers the day when, as he cuddled a pet puppy, he quizzically looked at the animal and asked himself, "Why wasn't I born a dog rather than a boy?" Later he asked himself another question: "Why was I born *me*? Why wasn't I born someone else?" Eventually his Christian parents opened to him a knowledge of God and His marvelous plan of salvation. Then began his search for God—a search that hasn't ended yet.

How does a person acquaint himself with God? Before the Fall, Adam and Eve knew God face-to-face. After sin's entrance, each generation passed down to the next an indirect knowledge of Him, although much of it became perverted and confused. Yet we believe that there remains in the minds of all rational beings an intuition of God.

Who does not cry out to God at a time of terrible crisis? But this instinctive knowledge is insufficient for salvation. It cannot guarantee pardon for the past or power for the present. To believe intuitively that God exists is like a baby's first faltering step—it is only a beginning.

To progress from an intuitive to an experiential knowledge of God requires a thorough, consistent study of divine revelation as found in the Bible. Yet the Scriptures give no logical sequence of proof texts demonstrating His existence. They simply assert that God is! Surrounding those few assertions are hundreds of stories and illustrations that unmistakably testify to His actuality. "His own existence, His character, the truthfulness of His Word, are established by testimony that appeals to our reason; and this testimony is abundant" (*Education*, p. 169).

Write down an experience from your own life through which you gained a deeper acquaintance with God.

_____

_____

His Word Is More Important Than Food

My foot has held fast to His path; I have kept His way and not turned aside. I have not departed from the command of His lips; I have treasured the words of His mouth more than my necessary food. Job 23:11, 12, NASB.

If you read the part of Job 23 prior to our text today, you will find the patriarch expressing his deep longing to find God. He talks about his desire to come before God's throne and present his own case (verses 3 and 4). Then in verses 8 and 9 he speaks of his futile search for God, stating: "Behold, I go forward but He is not *there*, and backward, but I cannot perceive Him; when He acts on the left, I cannot behold Him; He turns on the right, I cannot see Him" (NASB). Then Job admits, "But He knows the way I take; when He has tried me, I shall come forth as gold" (verse 10, NASB). Job cannot understand God's ways. But the important point is that through all his questioning and through all his perplexity and confusion, he refuses to depart from God's commandments—His revelation—and proclaims, "I have treasured the words of His mouth more than my necessary food."

Most of us possess the Bible, but how many of us are possessed by it? Job is a marvelous example of an individual who accepted whatever he had of the Word of God in his era, and he believed in God and His teaching regardless of his outward circumstances. Someone has said that a Bible that is falling apart probably belongs to someone who isn't. Job was that kind of person.

If you delight to meditate on God's Word, praise Him now for what His Word means to you.

_____

_____

Job's Covenant With His Eyes

I made a covenant with mine eyes; why then should I think upon a maid? Job 31:1.

Chapter 31 of Job concludes his long speech that began with chapter 27. In this entire chapter he asserts his integrity, emphasizing in powerful language his uprightness and purity, his seriousness and sincerity, his aid to the helpless, his kindness to his enemies, his chastity, his care for his servants, his honesty, and even his victory over secret sin. If you want to study the kind of life Job really lived, these five chapters summarize his ethics.

Some feel that the book of Job is depressing, but his faithfulness in spite of undeserved calamities and trials really should give us courage. It helps us understand that despite life's reverses we can continue to trust God completely.

Our text today foreshadows the passage in Jesus' sermon on the mount in which He tells us that anyone who lusts after another person has already committed adultery. Job uses the image of making a covenant with his eyes not to gaze upon a maid or a virgin. Later he expands the concept in verses 9-11: "If my heart has been enticed by a woman, or I have lurked at my neighbor's doorway, may my wife grind for another, and let others kneel down over her. For that would be a lustful crime; moreover, it would be an iniquity punishable by judges" (NASB).

Job knew that merely avoiding immoral deeds was insufficient—he must flee from impurity even in thought. He understood clearly that what is in the heart sooner or later reveals itself in the hand.

Purity of heart is a trait of character that only God's Spirit can develop. Only the pure in heart shall see God. There is something about living a pure life through the power of God that brings great peace and satisfaction.

Have you experienced this Spirit-inspired purity in your own life? If so, what did it do for your Christian experience?

How to Preserve Your Life

The one who guards his mouth preserves his life; the one who opens wide his lips comes to ruin. Prov. 13:3, NASB.

Elihu, one of Job's professed friends, was a most eloquent debater. His speeches fill several chapters. His comment on his inability to hold his peace and not respond to what he considered to be Job's blasphemous charges against God is interesting: "I too will answer my share, I also will tell my opinion. For I am full of words; the spirit within me constrains me. Behold, my belly is like unvented wine, like new wineskins it is about to burst. Let me speak that I may get relief" (Job 32:17-20, NASB).

How many times have many of us regrettably played the part of Elihu? Talking and even arguing is for some of us a form of entertainment. It is a dangerous hobby for others.

"When a wise man has a controversy with a foolish man, the foolish man either rages or laughs, and there is no rest" (Prov. 29:9, NASB). This does not mean that a person should never offer an opinion. It is *why* it is expressed — the *way* and the *when* — that counts. True Christians will express themselves calmly and quietly, while avoiding any trace of a debating spirit. They know the truth of Proverbs 15:23: "How delightful is a timely word!" (NASB).

One of our older spiritual statesmen had a self-control that awed and baffled Bob during our mission service in Singapore. The man seldom spoke on a committee, but when he did everyone listened intently. One day Bob asked him how he could sit through committee after committee and remain so silent. He quietly replied, "Much of the discussion on any committee doesn't center on matters of real principle. It's just a matter of personal preference, and whether the vote goes one way or another really isn't too important." He continued, "Furthermore, most of everything I would have to say has already been said. If I do have something to say, I want my statement to make the greatest impact possible."

Our tongues have a relationship with us like that of a marriage — the two are one. Praise God if you have your tongue under control, and if you don't, pray for it. Put your praise or prayer into words.

God Asks Questions Humans Can't Answer

Then the Lord answered Job out of the whirlwind and said, "Who is this that darkens counsel by words without knowledge? Now gird up your loins like a man, and I will ask you, and you instruct Me!" Job 38:1-3, NASB.

The book of Job — especially chapter 38 — is the Mount Everest of the Old Testament. In many ways the book of Job is extremely complex. But as you study the book in its entirety, you find that all the deliberations and discussions between Job and his friends offer no answer to the problem of suffering other than what we understand within the framework of the great controversy between Christ and Satan.

Furthermore, God does not answer all Job's questions. Instead, He reveals Himself in wisdom and power in the final chapters of the book. Our Lord wants us to understand that our faith does not lie in philosophical explanations, but rather in trusting an all-wise God. In the end this is enough for Job.

As you study chapter 38, note the first question God asked the patriarch: "Where were you when I laid the foundations of the earth! Tell *Me*, if you have understanding" (verse 4, NASB). How was that for a starter? Then God, referring to the earth, asked, "On what were its bases sunk? Or who laid its cornerstone?" (verse 6, NASB). How can this giant hunk of rock, weighing approximately 6.5 sextillion tons, hang in space? What holds it up?

In verse 12 He silences Job by asking, "Have you ever in your life commanded the morning, and caused the dawn to know its place?" (NASB). Here is another challenge: "Where is the way to the dwelling of light? And darkness, where is its place?" (verse 19, NASB).

When he was a boy Bob would flip the light switch off and on and repeatedly wonder where the light went when the switch was off and where the darkness was banished when the switch was on. One second light flooded the room, and the next moment darkness blanketed it. All of us have had questions we cannot answer. We simply trust God.

God never answers any of His questions to Job. What He seems to be saying to Job is, Trust Me. I am omnipotent, and there is no one else like Me.

How do you feel about a God who is all-powerful and asks you to trust Him completely?

Job's Confession and Triumph

I know that Thou canst do all things, and that no purpose of Thine can be thwarted. . . . Therefore I have declared that which I did not understand, things too wonderful for me, which I did not know. Job 42:2, 3, NASB.

God answered neither Job's questions nor those of his friends. The Lord doesn't have to explain everything to us. Instead He gives us the strength to trust Him.

The climax of the book describes God's disappointment with Job's friends. He told Eliphaz, "My wrath is kindled against you and against your two friends, because you have not spoken of Me what is right, as My servant Job has" (Job 42:7, NASB). He commanded all three of them to offer burnt offerings for themselves, and added that His servant Job would pray for them. Then He said that He would accept Job's intercession for the men. The wonderful climax of the entire story is that "the Lord restored the fortunes of Job when he prayed for his friends, and the Lord increased all that Job had twofold" (verse 10, NASB).

The patriarch lived nearly a century and a half after his excruciating experience. His life, which had seemed to be totally ruined, now ended up gloriously. God restored his property, family, friends, and even his reputation. But best of all, Job had learned that when adversity strikes, it is still possible to believe in God's character of love. In many respects, Job was like the teakettle, which may be up to its neck in hot water but can whistle a merry tune.

We barely touched on the message of the book of Job, but we hope we have created in you a desire to study it more carefully.

Do you really trust God like the patriarch? Would you like to trust Him more? If so, write out your testimony in the form of an appeal for God to increase your trust and faith in Him.

Followers of the Lamb

And I looked, and behold, the Lamb was standing on Mount Zion, and with Him one hundred and forty-four thousand, having His name and the name of His Father written on their foreheads. Rev. 14:1, NASB.

The book of Revelation describes two prophetic groups. Chapter 13 portrays those who follow the beast, while chapter 14 depicts those who belong to the Lamb. The followers of the beast belong to a conspiracy that seeks to destroy the people of the Lamb. The followers of the Lamb, the ones who obey God's commandments and have their faith in Jesus, would rather die than violate the principles of the Lamb's kingdom. Their mouths are free from guile and falsehood. They will sing a new song before the throne and before the four living creatures because they deeply appreciate the sacrifice of Christ, having been "purchased from the earth" (Rev. 14:3, NASB).

Seventh-day Adventists have taught throughout their history that the second beast of Revelation 13 portrays the United States as a world superpower that will cause the rest of the world's inhabitants to worship the first beast. It is difficult to imagine America as a religious persecutor, but the Scriptures say that the beast representing America will force all to worship this first beast—apostate Christianity.

Prior to the breakup of the U.S.S.R., Communism was such a powerful force in the world that some doubted our interpretation of Revelation 13. They asked, "How can it be that the United States will become the world's superpower?" But overnight the scene totally changed. One lesson we can learn is that "the final movements will be rapid ones." Overnight, nations and empires can collapse.

Recent events have greatly strengthened our faith in our prophetic interpretation that we have developed through the decades. But the most important thing to know about prophecy is that we must remain followers of the Lamb to the very end. The three angels' messages warn us against worshiping the beast and his image and symbolically receiving a mark on our foreheads or on our hands. In order to maintain our allegiance to the Lamb, we must daily submit our wills to Him and, through prayer and study, make certain that our commitment to Him is based on love rather than fear. It is love for the Lamb that will cause us to triumph over any and all persecution. Love for the Lamb motivates us to choose death rather than to violate His commandments. Only love for the Lamb will enable us to triumph!

Some wonderful day we will see the Lamb face-to-face. Praise God for that promise and thank Him now for the privilege of being counted as one of His followers.

Is Jesus Coming Soon?

And I looked, and behold, a white cloud, and sitting on the cloud was one like a son of man, having a golden crown on His head, and a sharp sickle in His hand. Rev. 14:14, NASB.

John's description depicts the coming of Christ after God's people have carried the gospel to the world. We believe that day is coming soon. One of the reasons is the astounding collapse of Communism in eastern Europe and the former U.S.S.R. Those of us living in this period of earth's history have witnessed some of the most revolutionary political events in recorded history. In a matter of days the course of history has changed.

Our good friend Clifford Goldstein, in a guest editorial in the *Adventist Review* of January 18, 1990, wrote, "If last year someone would have told me that within a year there would be a Solidarity government in Poland, that the Berlin Wall would be null and void, that the Communists would be losing power in Czechoslovakia, Hungary, East Germany, and Bulgaria, and that the Soviets would be encouraging these reforms—I would have thought I had backslidden, left the church, and was smoking pot! Ellen White's statement that 'the final movements will be rapid ones' (*Testimonies*, vol. 9, p. 11) has taken on, for me at least, a new significance." His comments are even more true today.

Lance Morrow, in the September 9, 1991, *Time*, vividly described the breakup of the Soviet Union. "An entire empire careered through darkness with a load of nuclear weapons on board. On the winding road, it could see no farther than the beams of its headlights. And as it raced around the corners, the vehicle was disintegrating. . . . The event was unprecedented. Never before had a fully matured empire, one superpower of the world's only two, torn loose from its foundations and sped off, at such velocity, on such a journey."

We do not know what will happen next, but rest assured that our Lord is able to return triumphantly very quickly. As we have already seen in the breakup of the Soviet superpower, unbelievable and cataclysmic events can transpire overnight. Rather than be dismayed over such events, we should rejoice over the fact that Jesus is coming soon! Also thank God for the religious freedom our people in eastern Europe now have as a result of the fall of the iron curtain.

Praise the Lord that He is still in control of our planet.

October 4

A Twentieth-Century Cyrus

It is I who says of Cyrus, "He is My shepherd! And he will perform all My desire." And he declares of Jerusalem, "She will be built." And of the temple, "Your foundation will be laid." Isa. 44:28, NASB.

Isaiah's remarkable prophecy mentions a world leader by name 150 years before his time. Cyrus permitted the Jews to rebuild Jerusalem. Mikhail Gorbachev presided over the Soviet Union from March 1985 to December 1991. On December 25, 1991, Gorbachev peacefully relinquished power and transferred authority to newly independent republics. But during those years he helped set the stage for new freedom for our believers in eastern Europe.

We well remember visiting the U.S.S.R. twice before its people gained the freedoms they experience today. The difference between then and now is far greater than day and night. Prior to the dissolution of the U.S.S.R., its inhabitants could not buy Bibles, Christian books, or hear any radio or television program that dealt with Christianity. Their constitution allowed religious freedom only of the conscience. Our church members could not proclaim the good news of salvation and the soon coming of Jesus in any public auditorium. They could speak of God and religion only in our small and overcrowded church buildings.

When things totally changed in 1990, our church immediately held major public evangelistic campaigns that resulted in thousands of baptisms. In Riga,

Latvia, one of our American evangelists, Jac Colon, introduced himself to his audience as a former U.S. Air Force captain assigned to a B-52 bomber crew flying more than 100 combat missions in Vietnam prior to his becoming an Adventist Christian. During the meetings a former Soviet fighter pilot who had become an Adventist introduced himself to our evangelist and said, "We were once mortal enemies who would have shot each other out of the sky, but now we are brothers in Christ." The two hugged each other and silently wept with emotion.

Whether or not Gorbachev realized what his leadership would bring to the U.S.S.R., we believe God placed him in his strategic spot in order to help fulfill the divine command to preach the gospel to every nation, kindred, tongue, and people.

Praise God's name that hundreds of thousands of people in the former Communist countries now have the opportunity of publicly accepting Christ and joining with His people without fear of punishment. Express your thanks now.

Exaltation of Nations

Righteousness exalts a nation, but sin is a disgrace to any people. Prov. 14:34, NASB.

"In the annals of human history, the growth of nations, the rise and fall of empires, appear as if dependent on the will and prowess of man; the shaping of events seems, to a great degree, to be determined by his power, ambition, or caprice. But in the Word of God the curtain is drawn aside, and we behold, above, behind, and through all the play and counterplay of human interest and power and passions, the agencies of the All-merciful One, silently, patiently working out the counsels of His own will" (*Prophets and Kings*, pp. 499, 500).

As we have stated before, the breakup of the Communist countries in the U.S.S.R. and eastern Europe has been one of the most phenomenal historical events in the history of the world. Suddenly one of the world's two great superpowers no longer exists. Overnight the world scene has totally changed. As *Time* magazine said, "America is the world's sole remaining superpower." Charles Krauthammer, writing in the *New Republic*, stated, "There is no prospect in the immediate future of any power to rival the United States." Yassir Arafat commented on America's new status as the world's only superpower: "Washington is the 'new Rome.'"

The stage is being set for the soon coming of Jesus Christ. But the most important event taking place right now is the conversion of thousands in the various republics of the former U.S.S.R.

Can you imagine a nation of nearly 300 million people under domination for 1,000 years? First the people lived under the control of a state church. Then Communism persecuted all religions. Today they have freedom.

The reason that people throng our public meetings is that atheism has created a spiritual vacuum in their lives. The masses have a deep spiritual hunger.

During one of our meetings a woman, crying hysterically, came up to the evangelist. Tears flooded down her cheeks. Why? Because the sports palace where we were holding the meetings had been built where a cemetery and a Christian church used to be. The Communists had torn it down and, with no respect for the cemetery, had erected the sports palace. The woman was overjoyed that we were holding religious meetings over the graves of some of her ancestors.

We praise the Lord that He has broken open doors that have sealed shut millions of individuals, and now gives them an opportunity to understand the gospel. Won't you add your praise to God with ours?

A Time for Everything

There is an appointed time for everything. And there is a time for every event under heaven. Eccl. 3:1, NASB.

One guiding statement encouraged us to move ahead with public evangelism in the former U.S.S.R. "It is the very essence of all right faith to do the right thing at the right time. God is the great master worker, and by His providence He prepares the way for His work to be accomplished. He provides opportunities, opens up lines of influence and channels of working. If His people are watching the indications of His providence and stand ready to cooperate with Him, they will see a great work accomplished. Their efforts, rightly directed, will produce a hundredfold greater results than can be accomplished with the same means and facilities in another channel where God is not so manifestly working" (*Testimonies*, vol. 6, p. 24).

Note the principles involved in this passage. Ellen White defines right faith as doing the right thing at the right time, a principle that applies to the corporate body, the church, as well as the individual Christian. Noah did the right thing—building a boat—at the right time. To construct a ship to escape a world flood today would not fit either one of these two principles.

A second point to note is that God's providence prepares the way. Circumstances in our world and our lives do not happen haphazardly. God does not work by chance. Rather, He has a plan.

Third, He prepares the way for redemptive action on our part. He provides opportunities by influencing people to cooperate with us. We believe that God has surely done this in the former Communist countries of eastern Europe and the former U.S.S.R. God's blessing will be realized when we stand ready to cooperate with Him and watch for indications of His providence. We must be ready to throw our energies and resources into situations that He has miraculously opened to us.

Finally, if we follow God's plan and use the means and facilities in those channels that God has opened for us, we will see infinitely greater results than if we had gone our own way. By God's grace we believe that we have demonstrated the reality of these principles as we have evangelized these former Communist countries.

Please continue to pray that other countries, such as China, will open up quickly. Think of 1 billion—1,000 million—souls, all of whom are virtually sitting in darkness when it comes to the gospel within the framework of the three angels' messages. Will you join us in praying for God to guide us with His opening providences? List some of the events that you feel you should pray about personally.

From the East and West

And I say to you, that many shall come from east and west, and recline at the table with Abraham, and Isaac, and Jacob in the kingdom of heaven. Matt. 8:11, NASB.

Today's text is a counterpart to the great gospel commission, where Christ commanded us to go and make disciples of all the nations. The Roman centurion had asked Jesus to heal his servant. Jesus marveled at the man's request and stated that He had not found anyone with such faith in all of Israel.

Verse 12 (NASB) speaks of the sons of the kingdom (the people of Israel) being cast out into outer darkness. Why? Because His people had selfishly refused to share salvation with others. But the gospel would eventually go to everyone in every part of the world.

The Adventist Church has had phenomenal success in its mission program. But if we ever stop promoting our mission offerings and our global mission outreach, it will die. "To show a liberal, self-denying spirit for the success of foreign missions is a sure way to advance home missionary work; for the prosperity of the home work depends largely, under God, upon the reflex influence of the evangelical work done in countries afar off. It is in working to supply the necessities of others that we bring our souls into touch with the Source of all power" (*Gospel Workers*, pp. 465, 466).

In the same passage Ellen White describes an American businessman who remarked to a friend that he was involved in working for Christ 24 hours of the day. "In all my business relations I try to represent my Master. As I have opportunity, I try to win others to Him. All day I am working for Christ. And at night, while I sleep, I have a man working for Him in China" (*ibid.*, p. 466). If you belong to a church that has dropped the mission report, urge your leaders to revive it if they want to keep in touch with the "Source of all power." A nonmissionary church is a dead church. No matter how many people may attend or how large the offerings and tithe may be, a church is still dead if it does not reach out to the rest of the world.

It is a privilege and blessing to join with our Lord in sharing our faith with those people in parts of the world where angels of God are opening doors that a little while ago had been closed to us. We know from personal experience the joy and the gratitude of those who now have their first opportunity to hear the wonderful news of Christ's love.

Have you thanked the Lord recently for the knowledge you have of Him and for the religious literature you have? Millions have been deprived of the Bible and other Christian books. Millions more are virtually ignorant of the name of Jesus. The reason our Lord came to our world was to save all His people. Join us in praising God for the chance to participate in divine outreach through your prayers, offerings, and personal witness.

October 8

More Than a Prophet

Truly, I say to you, among those born of women there has not arisen anyone greater than John the Baptist; yet he who is least in the kingdom of heaven is greater than he. Matt. 11:11, NASB.

John the Baptist was languishing in prison when Jesus said this about him. John had sent some of his own disciples to find out for certain if Christ was truly the Messiah. Not too long before, the Baptist had been heralding to the multitudes that Jesus was the Lamb of God, but now as he sat in a miserable prison his faith began to waver. Jesus did not directly answer his question but continued His healing and teaching. Finally Jesus told John's followers, "Go and report to John what you hear and see" (Matt. 11:4, NASB). Jesus began to speak to the multitudes about His cousin. He asked them what they had gone out to see when they heard John preach in the wilderness—a reed shaking in the wind or a man dressed in fancy clothes fit for a king? He inquired if they thought the Baptist was "a prophet" (verses 7-9). But John was more than a prophet—he was a special messenger preparing people to meet the Messiah. Then Jesus uttered the words in our text today.

Although Jesus compared John the Baptist to men such as Moses, Isaiah, Daniel, and Jeremiah, yet as far as we know, he never wrote a book. Certainly, at least, he never authored one that was included in our present-day Scriptures. John was an "oral" prophet.

Our thoughts turn to another messenger, Ellen G. White, who too was a special messenger of the Lord whose work focused on the second coming of Christ. The thrust of her writings is to prepare a people to meet Jesus in peace and happiness. We have marveled at the broad spectrum of subjects the Lord inspired her to present as preparation for His coming. This devotional book in all probability would not be in your hands if the Lord had not led her to encourage the church to begin its publishing program. Like John, Ellen White never wrote a canonical book, but she wrote many other books for our edification in our time of the world's history.

More than 30 years ago Paul Harvey, the well-known newscaster, as he referred to her treatment of the subject of health, put things in perspective when he wrote, "Remember, this was in the days when doctors were still blood-letting and performing surgery with unwashed hands. . . . Yet Ellen White wrote with such profound understanding on the subject of nutrition."

During our own morning worship we have read through *The Ministry of Healing*, which she claimed contains the wisdom of the Great Physician. The book has touched our lives in a marked manner. We are thankful that God used messengers such as John the Baptist, Ellen White, and a host of others to bless the world and to help us prepare to meet Jesus.

If you are thankful for God's messengers, express that fact in a few words.

The King Who Was Proud of God's Ways

So the Lord established the kingdom in his control, and all Judah brought tribute to Jehoshaphat, and he had great riches and honor. And he took great pride in the ways of the Lord and again removed the high places and the Asherim [symbols of a Canaanite goddess] from Judah. 2 Chron. 17:5, 6, NASB.

We could describe Jehoshaphat, the fourth king of Judah, in one sentence: His life revealed total dependence upon God.

After coming to the throne, he immediately set about to fortify all the cities of Judah. He conducted Bible conferences that carefully taught the law to his subjects in each section of Judah. Our text states that "he took great pride in the ways of the Lord." It is an unusual event in history to find a king who is thrilled to obediently follow God. No wonder the Lord honored him. And He will honor us, too, if we serve Him with pride and gladness!

Even though Jehoshaphat had a vast army of battle-equipped warriors, when Moab and Ammon invaded Judah, he depended on the arm of the Lord instead of his armed forces! Immediately after hearing about the invasion, "Jehoshaphat was afraid and turned his attention to seek the Lord; and proclaimed a fast throughout all Judah" (2 Chron. 20:3, NASB).

A great assembly of God's people gathered in Jerusalem, and, instead of plotting how to fight the enemy, the king prayed to the Lord. His remarkable prayer teaches us some valuable lessons (see verses 6-12).

First, the king praised God for His "power and might," proclaiming that no one can stand against Him. Thus, before petitioning the Lord, Jehoshaphat praised Him. Praise before petition in our prayers is important. It reinforces our sense of God's sovereignty. Then Judah's ruler reminded the Lord how He had driven out the previous inhabitants of their land and had given it to Abraham's descendants. Furthermore, His people had built a sanctuary to the glory of God. Jehoshaphat affirmed his trust in God by pledging to come before Him at the Temple. Even in a time of national distress, he had full confidence that "Thou wilt hear and deliver us" (verse 9, NASB). This king was truly God's man. He knew the Lord, and he also knew the Lord knew him and would honor him. Jehoshaphat's relationship with God is an example for all of us today.

The God whom Jehoshaphat served stands ready today to help His church and us as its members. Follow the example of Judah's king and give your testimony of praise and adoration.

October   10

Our Eyes Are on God

O our God, wilt Thou not judge them? For we are powerless before this great multitude who are coming against us; nor do we know what to do, but our eyes are on Thee. 2 Chron. 20:12, NASB.

This text records the final words of King Jehoshaphat's prayer just prior to the enemy's attack. What makes it so marvelous is that it is a king's prayer—that of the leader of God's people. He offers our church and national leaders a marvelous example of how to handle emergencies.

In it Jehoshaphat pours out his heart in a mighty petition for God to judge the enemies of His people. Despite the fact that he has a well-trained army, he acknowledges that he is really weak. "We are powerless" are words quite foreign to most minds. Too often we assume that we can handle any emergency.

Not only does the king admit to being powerless, but he makes another extraordinary confession: "nor do we know what to do." Prayers become powerful to the degree that we admit our weakness and ignorance. If this is our true heartfelt attitude when we come to God in prayer, it reveals our utter dependence upon Him. Only then can God really help us.

Notice who heard the prayer: "And all Judah was standing before the Lord, with their infants, their wives, and their children" (verse 13, NASB). Try to imagine their feelings when they heard their king and leader offer such a prayer.

The last words of the king's prayer are memorable: "Our eyes are on Thee." It is not easy at times to keep our eyes focused on God when a child dies, a spouse runs off with someone else, we lose our job, or we come down with some terminal illness. Yet here a nation facing a terrible slaughter listened to their king say "Our eyes are on Thee."

What should they do? Trust in their own strength? Fortunately, Judah practiced what their king prayed—they kept their gaze on God.

Thank our Lord that we can still watch Him work deliverance for His people.

Success by Taking Heed

Listen to me, O Judah and inhabitants of Jerusalem, put your trust in the Lord your God, and you will be established. Put your trust in His prophets and succeed. 2 Chron. 20:20, NASB.

The last two readings focused on King Jehoshaphat's marvelous prayer for Judah's deliverance from an advancing enemy. Immediately after the king's prayer, the Spirit of the Lord came upon a man by the name of Jahaziel. As far as we know, he wrote no books and his name appears only this one time. He was definitely a prophet, but the scope of his work was extremely limited. Yet his predictions were powerful and difficult to forget. By God's authority he told the entire assembly, "Do not fear or be dismayed because of this great multitude, for the battle is not yours but God's" (2 Chron. 20:15, NASB).

The words are easy to say, but practicing them is difficult! Yet they apply to both the individual and to the many, whether church or nation.

Jahaziel proceeded to inform them about the enemy's plans and what the outcome would be. " 'You need not fight in this battle; station yourselves, stand and see the salvation of the Lord on your behalf, O Judah and

Jerusalem.' Do not fear or be dismayed; tomorrow go out to face them, for the Lord is with you" (verse 17, NASB). The prophet gave great assurance and hope to his people.

Yet, we wonder if some leaders, perhaps some of the army officers, mocked Jahaziel and thought it all ridiculous, coming as it did from a man who knew nothing about battle strategy. How can one possibly win a war by standing still and doing nothing! How could they expect God to do it all for them and they do nothing?

Actually there was something God's people needed to do. The king declared, "Have faith in God. Trust Him. Also trust, believe, and obey His prophets, and success will be ours!" To do that required the real work of faith. God was their power and strength, and He is the same today for us. "In every emergency we are to feel that the battle is His. His resources are limitless, and apparent impossibilities will make the victory all the greater" (*Prophets and Kings*, p. 202).

Belief that leads to obedience spells success for the church and for us personally. We are thankful we serve the One who battles for us. How about you? Can you testify to God's leading in your life when He gave you some victory?

October   12

Victory Through Singing and Praise

And when they began singing and praising, the Lord set ambushes against the sons of Ammon, Moab, and Mount Seir, who had come against Judah; so they were routed. 2 Chron. 20:22, NASB.

When the prophet Jahaziel encouraged Judah not to be dismayed, for the battle was the Lord's, King Jehoshaphat prostrated himself in worship. The Levites led in praising the Lord for the good news that He would give them victory. The next morning Jehoshaphat appointed certain individuals to march in front of the army and "give thanks to the Lord, for His lovingkindness is everlasting" (2 Chron. 20:21, NASB). It was a most unique way to enter battle. Judah's secret weapon was verbal and musical praise to the Lord.

Nothing can bring hope and courage to our hearts as much as praise can. The more we practice the science of praise and thanksgiving, the more we strengthen our own determination to depend upon God, and the more we put to flight Satan, who wants to depress us into defeat. As the people of Judah began their musical praise program, the Lord worked mightily in their behalf. The enemy was routed, and the spoil taken was enormous. The resulting victory caused all the surrounding kingdoms to fear the Lord, and "the kingdom of Jehoshaphat was at peace, for his God gave him rest on all sides" (verse 30, NASB).

Notice how the army of Judah returned to Jerusalem. Jehoshaphat rode at its head, and a joyous mood pervaded the entire group. "They came to Jerusalem with harps, lyres, and trumpets to the house of the Lord" (verse 28, NASB). Judah's triumph resulted from listening to and obeying the instruction given by Jahaziel the prophet.

Today the prosperity of our church has been, is now, and will ever be dependent on our heeding the voice of the Lord through His Word in both the Bible and the prophetic gift through Ellen White.

In 1907 Ellen White plainly stated, "The voice of God has come to us continually in warning and instruction, to confirm the faith of the believers in the Spirit of prophecy" (*Selected Messages*, book 1, p. 41).

God in His tender love has given us a tremendous wealth of truth and counsel to aid us in escaping Satan's snares. Have you had an experience in which God's counsel has given you courage and strength?

A Dispenser of Eye Medicine

Surely the Lord God does nothing unless He reveals His secret counsel to His servants the prophets. Amos 3:7, NASB.

Since God is love, He believes in sharing any knowledge with His followers that will guide and guard them on their journey to the heavenly Canaan. He insists on giving us this advantage. In a very specific way He has provided the Seventh-day Adventist Church detailed instruction without which we, as a rather small group, could never have achieved the success we have had in doctrinal, evangelistic, publishing, educational, and health-related areas.

The gift of prophecy through the ministry of Ellen G. White was active in our church for 70 years—from 1844 to 1915. The Lord gave her thousands of visions, and her labors shaped the church in America, Europe, and the South Pacific. Her writings have been a tremendous source of strength to every country in which we have a presence.

David Lin, who was secretary of the China Division at the time of the Communist takeover and who spent 20 years in prison for his faith, tells in an interview published in the September 12, 1991, *Adventist Review* of the influence Ellen White had on some of our members in China. Speaking of the difference between the truly converted Adventists and those who were nominal Christians, Lin credits her writings for keeping some of our members from succumbing to the pressures of Communism. All denominations suffered apostasy losses after the Communist takeover. "But," Lin stated, "our people had, in addition to the Bible, the Spirit of Prophecy, which I like to compare to an applicator or a dispenser of eye medicine. What it dispenses is the Word of God. It is Scripture, only it applies it at the right place, at the right time. So that makes us distinct."

When asked what counsel he would give to the Adventist Church in general, he replied, "The chief lesson I have learned is that the distinctive trait of the Adventist Church, aside from the Sabbath, is the gift of prophecy. When we give this due emphasis, it contributes toward a healthy situation in the church. It helps to unify the church."

He concluded, "Give the Spirit of Prophecy the place that God intended that it should occupy in the church. It has a stabilizing and a unifying influence; it makes sound, practicing Adventists."

We are happy to offer the same testimony. Can you give thanks for the marvelous gift of prophecy?

October 14

The Secret Is Out!

Now to Him who is able to establish you according to my gospel and the preaching of Jesus Christ, according to the revelation of the mystery which has been kept secret for long ages past, but now is manifested, and by the Scriptures of the prophets, according to the commandment of the eternal God, has been made known to all the nations, leading to obedience of faith. Rom. 16:25, 26, NASB.

A sincere woman once wrote to us claiming that she could not keep from committing sin even for five minutes. But she believed that she still had the assurance of salvation on the merits of Christ alone. Her statement puzzles us. Taken one way, it might cause a non-Christian to ask, "What kind of Saviour do you have? If you receive no help in overcoming evil, why become a Christian?"

However, we hope that she had in mind not overt acts of sin but the sinful state of being we all find ourselves in.

But the secret is out, the mystery revealed! Jesus stands ready to give us victory over sin. As our text today states, our Lord has made known to all nations the mystery "leading to obedience of faith." (A "mystery" in ancient religion was something that could be known only if the god revealed it to his worshipers.) It requires faith in Jesus to obey Him. Yet at the same time one of the greatest joys of living a Christian life is to grow spiritually daily and to gain victory after victory over our fallen nature. But in no way does it dispense with the fact that our nature is ever sinful, for we recognize with Paul that nothing good of ourselves dwells within us (see Rom. 7:18).

Jeremiah understood this clearly when he stated, "The heart is more deceitful than all else and is desperately sick; who can understand it?" (Jer. 17:9, NASB). Is the deceitfulness of the heart forever and totally eradicated at conversion? Did the publican's sinful nature vanish after he cried out "God be merciful to me a sinner" and went down to his house justified? No, his carnal nature still existed and was quite capable of reviving at a moment's notice! So after conversion the symptoms of sin still trouble us. But, praise be to God, we can overcome through His power.

Born-again Christians will be continually advancing in the Christian life. The ultimate purpose of our Lord's plan of salvation is to bring us into complete harmony with the principles of His law—His character. The merits of Christ given to us involve a transformation of our hearts. We believe that if what Christ has done in His gracious act of forgiveness and justification does not affect a person, he has misjudged the gospel entirely.

When we understand the full gospel, we, of all professed Christians, should be foremost in presenting Jesus before the world. We will share the divine mystery with everyone! Do you want to lift Him up in your heart and before the world today? Write down how you might tell a good friend about Him.

_____

_____

Jesus Is Wholly Desirable

My beloved is dazzling . . . , outstanding among ten thousand. . . . His hands are rods of gold. . . . His appearance is like Lebanon, choice as the cedars. His mouth is full of sweetness. And he is wholly desirable. This is my beloved and this is my friend. Song of Sol. 5:10-16, NASB.

When Bob conducted a Week of Prayer at one of our colleges in the Far East, he witnessed a heartbreaking sight. A young student, his mouth and nose streaked with blood, knelt before his angry non-Christian father. The father angrily told Bob that he was punishing his son to make him good, then began kicking the boy in the face. The youth had no tears, no signs of emotion, just a blank stare on his face as he awaited the next blow. Bob tried to reason with the father, who finally released his son and let him return to the dormitory with Bob.

The little fellow was a stranger to Christianity. Bob put his arm around him and talked to him about Jesus, who is willing to forgive us of any sin and to help us live a life of obedience to His will. The only thing that Bob could think of to stress at that moment was the love of One who is "outstanding among ten thousand." The thought of God's love brought a flood of tears to the young lad's eyes, something the beating administered by his godless, irate father could not do.

Such phrases as "the rose of Sharon" and "the lily of the valley" bring to our memory songs and choruses we have learned. But they should do more than that. Our hearts should leap with joy when we hear anything that reminds us of Jesus. In fact, our best thoughts should always center on Him.

The only permanent way our Lord can draw us as sinners to Him is through His love. He captivates us through the incomparable life He spent on earth, through His incomparable promises, and through His incomparable doctrines of the atonement and His soon coming.

Praise the Lord for His being "wholly desirable." Has something happened in your life recently that helped you to understand His love a little more? Maybe something that a child or friend said or did? Describe it and tell what you learned about God and His feelings toward you.

_____

_____

The Rose of Sharon

I am the rose of Sharon, the lily of the valleys. Song of Sol. 2:1, NASB.

John Flavel's book *The Method of Grace* contains an enormous wealth of ideas and insights on Jesus that he extracts from Scripture. Flavel, who lived in the seventeenth century, was one of the greatest Christian ministers who ever lived. We are told that his works, along with those of other Puritan writers, such as Richard Baxter and Richard Alleine, have blessed thousands of people and helped them to the kingdom (see *The Great Controversy*, pp. 252, 253).

Flavel's introduction states, "It is the one thing needful for thee to get an assured interest in Jesus Christ; which being once obtained, thou mayest with boldness say, come, troubles and distresses, losses and trials, prisons and death, I am prepared for you; do your worst, you can do me no harm; let the winds roar, the lightnings flash, the rain and hail fall ever so furiously, I have a good roof over my head, a comfortable lodging provided for me; 'my place of defense is the munition of rocks where bread shall be given, and my water shall be sure'" (*The Method of Grace*, p. 9).

How interested are we in Jesus? How real is He to us? How much time do we spend contemplating Him each day? Do we study who He is, what He did, and what He is doing now? Studying Him, meditating on Him, praying to Him, listening to the voice of His Spirit—what better way to waken our own drowsy conscience and that of our sleepy generation? If we remain strangers to the person and work of Christ, our profession of Christ will be powerless.

Flavel pointedly said, "How dangerous it is to be an old creature in the new creature's dress and habit" (*ibid.*, p. 10).

Jesus is truly the Rose of Sharon, the incomparable one. Saturate your minds and hearts with His goodness, His love, and His willingness to help you through life. The scent of His Spirit through you will pervade the lives of all those around you.

Let your paper Ebenezer today be one of praise to Jesus for His goodness.

"Fairer Than the Sons of Men"

Thou art fairer than the sons of men; grace is poured upon Thy lips; therefore God has blessed Thee forever. Ps. 45:2, NASB.

Yesterday we referred to John Flavel's book on Christ. The chapter "Christ Altogether Lovely" especially uplifts the Saviour in every sentence. In it he states that as all the rivers pour into the ocean, so Christ is the ocean in which all delights and pleasures meet. As we consider His person, offices, works, or anything else about Him, we discover Him as one "fairer than the sons of men."

Meditating on the expression "altogether lovely," Flavel makes the following points:

1. It excludes all unloveliness. Jesus even transcends everything He created in our world, for whatever beauty we find in some wonderful creature or thing, it is still imperfect. The fairest pictures have their shadows, and the most transparent stones require polished metal or gold leaf under them to set off their beauty. Life is a bittersweet experience, because no matter what we might admire, we will always find something displeasing about it mingled with the good. Jesus alone has no flaws. He alone is a sea of sweetness without one drop of gall.

2. Since we find nothing unlovely in Him, it means that everything about Him is *wholly* lovely. As every particle of gold is precious, so is every aspect of Christ. Who can weigh Jesus in a pair of balances and tell His worth? His price is above rubies, and nothing else that we might ever desire could ever compare with Him (see Prov. 8:11).

3. He is *comprehensive*, or the sum of all things lovely. As Paul states, "For it was the Father's good pleasure for all the fullness to dwell in Him" (Col. 1:19, NASB). Fix your eyes among all created beings, Flavel says, and you will observe strength in one, beauty in a second, faithfulness in a third, and wisdom in a fourth. But none excel in everything, as does Christ. Flavel describes Him as bread to the hungry, water to the thirsty, a garment to the

naked, healing to the wounded, and everything else that anyone might desire.

We will continue Flavel's insights tomorrow. But today jot down what Jesus means to you personally.

First Place in Everything

And He is before all things, and in Him all things hold together. He is also head of the body, the church; and He is the beginning, the first-born from the dead; so that He Himself might come to have first place in everything. Col. 1:17, 18, NASB.

Today we want to continue Flavel's sermon on "Christ Altogether Lovely."

4. In his fourth point he stated that nothing can be lovely in opposition to Him, or in separation from Him. That is, whatever might oppose or try to separate itself from Him can have no beauty, purity, or anything else worthwhile in it. Take away Christ, and what do you have left? For example, the best creature comfort apart from Christ is but a broken cistern. It cannot hold one drop of true comfort. Flavel compares it to the image of some lovely creature in the mirror—turn away the face, and the image vanishes. Riches, honors, and comfortable relationships are sweet when the face of Christ smiles upon us through them, but without Him they become empty trifles.

5. He transcends every excellent and beautiful thing. Compared to Christ, all other things pale into insignificance no matter how desirable they might be otherwise. As our text says, "He is before all things," not only in time, nature, and order, but also in dignity, glory, and true excellence. And in all these things He must have preeminence.

All other loveliness is derivative and secondary, but that of Christ is original and primary. Angels and men, the world and all that is desirable in it, receive whatever worth they might have only from Him. They are like streams from a fountain. Only Christ is lovely in and of Himself.

All other loveliness will ultimately prove unsatisfying and disappointing. Only Jesus will really meet our desires and needs. And only He can satisfy our dreams and aspirations.

Flavel's rich sermon on Jesus reminds us again and again that we need to turn our attention away from this world and center our thoughts and lives on Him constantly. We pray that all of us will spend every moment possible in His presence, studying and meditating on His incomprehensible wonders. Then, with hearts filled and saturated with Him, we may present Him to people in a way that they too can see His beauty and charms. No other person under heaven can save or satisfy the longings God has planted in us.

Use your creative powers to the very limit in expressing your love and appreciation for Him now.

_____

_____

Let the Earth Rejoice

The Lord reigns; let the earth rejoice; let the many islands be glad. Clouds and thick darkness surround Him; righteousness and justice are the foundation of His throne. Ps. 97:1, 2, NASB.

When you see the word "reign" or "rule," you may immediately think of people under the control of some dictator. But the Lord rules a universe of intelligent beings who love to have Him govern them. Only a few have rejected His government, and they all live on the little speck of dust known as Planet Earth.

However, the Lord reigns over more than people. He governs nature, guiding, for example, the precise movements of stars and planets. Because of God's infinite and exact control of all the objects whirling around in space and because we have discovered the precision of certain laws, such as that of gravity and the invariability of the movements of the moon in relationship to our earth, scientists can build and aim rockets in accordance with these laws. The Architect of the universe never allows the slightest error in His calculation and operation. "The Lord reigns; let the earth rejoice."

We succeed in anything only because of the invariability of God's laws of nature. Windmills capture the wind, hydroelectric plants transform the force of dammed-up water, and in our day nuclear reactions and solar energy increasingly supply us with power. God's eternal and changeless ways have enabled us to make use of natural forces.

But despite all our discoveries God is still clothed with clouds of thick darkness. There will always be a vast unknown about Him. In a sense the Christian truly bows to the unknown God. Yet at the same time he understands enough about Him through Jesus Christ to recognize that "righteousness and justice are the foundation of His throne." The Christian gladly admits that "the Lord reigns; let the earth rejoice." Aren't you thankful that God reigns and rules Planet Earth, even though at times it seems as if it is spinning out of control?

Jot down your thanks to Him now for His loving rulership.

_____

_____

A Message From Malachi, Part 1

"A son honors his father, and a servant his master. Then if I am a father, where is My honor? And if I am a master, where is My respect?" says the Lord of hosts to you, O priests who despise My name. But you say, "How have we despised Thy name?" Mal. 1:6, NASB.

The name Malachi means "my messenger." Written 2,400 years ago, his book takes less than eight minutes to read. Commentators have called Malachi "the seal of the prophets," since his work ends the Old Testament in the Protestant canon and prepares the way for the New. His message is the sunset that closes a long day of history of Israel's failings, and at the same time it is a sunrise heralding a new, glorious day.

About a century after the return of His people from the Babylonian exile God gave Malachi a special burden for their spiritual leadership. Yet the principles and admonition his book contains can apply to all of us individually. The book sadly portrays a progressive spiritual decline. The New Testament parallel to Malachi is the Laodicean message. Although Malachi attempts to correct the abuses that gradually crept in among God's people, his is certainly not a message of hopelessness.

A pivotal passage appears in Malachi 2:7: "For the lips of a priest should preserve knowledge, and men should seek instruction from his mouth; for he is the messenger of the Lord of hosts" (NASB). The principles enunciated in this text apply to everyone, whether preacher or layperson. God says this in connection with the covenant of Levi: " 'Then you will know that I have sent this commandment to you, that My covenant may continue with Levi,' says the Lord of hosts" (verse 4, NASB).

The Levi covenant traces back to the golden-calf experience. Moral restraint had evaporated, and sexual immorality threatened God's people. Moses had to stand in the gate of the camp and challenge the people to decide if they were on the Lord's side or not. All the sons of Levi gathered around Moses. It would seem that the Levites were the only ones who remained loyal at that time.

Moses ordered the Levites to strap on their swords and go through the camp, slaying the rebellious ones. Three thousand people died as a result. Although we may find the story abhorrent, the point is the Levites took a stand for God. They obeyed fully. The warfare between good and evil does not permit neutrality. We are either on God's side or on Satan's. May God help us to be faithful to our Lord Jesus Christ. We need to thank Him for the privilege of standing with Him.

A Message From Malachi, Part 2

Do not think that I came to bring peace on the earth; I did not come to bring peace, but a sword. For I came to set a man against his father, and a daughter against her mother, and a daughter-in-law against her mother-in-law. Matt. 10:34, 35, NASB.

As we stated yesterday, we can't remain neutral in the warfare between good and evil. Messengers of the Lord—and all of us are messengers of the Lord, because we believe in the priesthood of all believers—cannot come to terms with Satan and sin. Light and darkness are totally incompatible. The ultimate test then and now is whether or not we are on the Lord's side.

Will God find messengers who will stand loyal amidst today's whirlpool of apostasy? The answer is a resounding yes! He has them now, scattered like grains of salt around the world. We can be among them.

Two lessons we can immediately learn from the experience of the Levites' loyalty. Exodus 32:29 reveals lesson number one: "Today you have ordained yourselves for the service of the Lord, each one at the cost of his son and of his brother, that he may bestow a blessing upon you this day" (RSV). The Hebrew word for consecration contains the idea of being ordained to holy office. In a sense every loyal member of God's church has been ordained as a minister of God. We receive our ordination through standing for the right and upholding the character of God in kindness, forbearance, self-denial, meekness, humility, love, and firmness.

The second lesson we can learn is that God holds no grudges. Earlier Scripture records Levi's sorry participation in the massacre of the Shechemites in retaliation for what they did to his sister Dinah. It was a criminal act, which Jacob remembered when he passed by Levi and Simeon and gave Judah the firstborn blessing instead. But in spite of their marred history, God took the Levites and conferred upon them the sacred ministry of the sanctuary because of their loyalty.

These two points reveal part of God's wonderful character. First, He appreciates and honors loyalty to Him. Look upon obedience to God and His law as a great privilege and honor. In a sense it is how we "ordain" ourselves to be priests for Him today.

Second, He holds no grudges, even though our past record may be dismal. He is willing to forgive and to forget and to bless us if we remain loyal to Him.

Let the Lord know how you want to be loyal to Him now.

A Covenant of Peace

Therefore say, "Behold, I give him My covenant of peace; and it shall be for him and his descendants after him, a covenant of a perpetual priesthood, because he was jealous for his God, and made atonement for the sons of Israel." Num. 25:12, 13, NASB.

As we continue our study of the "book of Levi" we find a second time when God reaffirmed a Levi covenant. Remember that in Malachi 2:5 God said, "My covenant with him [Levi] was one of life and peace" (NASB). Let us go back to the time when Israel stayed at Shittim, the last camp before they crossed the Jordan into the Promised Land. Another rebellion took place there. God's people began to indulge in sexual immorality with the Moabite women, who led them into idolatry and Baal worship. God ordered that the rebellious leaders be killed and that their bodies be exposed to the entire camp. Plagues started through the camp, and 24,000 people died.

Zimri, leader of the Simeonite family, had brought Cozbi, a Midianite woman and the daughter of a tribal chieftain, into his tent and committed adultery at the same time Israel was pleading with God before the sanctuary doors. His brazen act caused Phinehas, grandson of Aaron, to take a spear and impale both of them. The plague halted, and the Lord renewed His covenant with Levi. That renewal appears in our text today.

It is extremely important to note that sexual immorality was present both at the golden-calf experience in Sinai and at the event at Shittim, which we have just mentioned. Sensual indulgence, whether of food or sex, has destroyed countless millions. According to Jesus, the people before the Flood were obsessed with eating, drinking, and marriage. While there is nothing wrong with either food or sex, they must remain in their proper role and under discipline and self-control.

The two experiences of Israel we have cited still have lessons for us today. God calls upon us to have clean hands and pure hearts, and to be people of integrity and purity. And of all people, ministers—Levi's modern counterparts—should take the lead in this covenant of peace with God.

Always remember that ministers and laymen alike have a powerful influence on others. " 'You have turned aside from the way; you have caused many to stumble . . . ; you have corrupted the covenant of Levi,' says the Lord of hosts" (Mal. 2:8, NASB).

We influence others, not merely through our talent or abilities, but through our holy characters. People with steadfast characters need utter no word, because their purity and goodness speak loudly enough.

Pray for purity and holiness of character, and thank God that He longs to share His goodness with you.

Our Example

For you have been called for this purpose, since Christ also suffered for you, leaving you an example for you to follow in His steps, who committed no sin, nor was any deceit found in His mouth. 1 Peter 2:21, 22, NASB.

Francis of Assisi invited a young acolyte to accompany him on a preaching expedition through the city of Florence, Italy. In silence they passed through one street after another and eventually returned to their starting point.

"But, Father," the young man said, puzzled and disappointed, "I thought we were going to preach."

"We have preached," Francis replied. "We were observed as we walked. They marked us as we went. It was thus we preached."

There is nothing more powerful for good or evil than individual example. Paul realized this when he wrote to Timothy to "let no one look down on your youthfulness, but rather in speech, conduct, love, faith and purity, show yourself an example of those who believe" (1 Tim. 4:12, NASB).

Jesus Himself proclaimed, "For I gave you an example that you should also do as I did to you" (John 13:15, NASB). As messengers of the Lord, we must not put programs and plans above character development. They must go together, but character must ever take precedence. The vast majority of all of our church problems would disappear overnight if we actually followed this principle.

The physical law of entropy states that anything left untended always goes downhill into disorder and chaos. This law applies also to human character. Character does not come naturally; it must be worked at and maintained. But we need have no fear for our church's future as long as we have men and women who seek purity, honesty, love, and kindness.

In connection with the covenant experience we have talked about the past several mornings, Malachi deals with problems that, although they involved the priesthood then, actually threaten all of us now. The book of Malachi depicts an eightfold encounter between God and His priests and people.

The eight episodes develop in three steps. Step 1: God makes an accusation. Step 2: The priests and people try to excuse themselves. Step 3: God rebuts, or refutes, their reply.

Malachi 1:2 records the first encounter. "I have loved you," the Lord told them.

Tragically His people were blind to His love. Insultingly they asked, "How hast Thou loved us?" (verse 2, NASB). It is a sad commentary that sometimes God's most favored people are often most unconscious of His love and favor. But those who keep the covenant of Levi and are messengers of the Lord will develop a spirit of constant praise, adoration, and worship. It would be well to ask ourselves what portion of our time we spend praising God and contemplating His love.

Repeatedly we have attempted to hold up in our book God's love for us. We appeal to you never to ask God, "How hast Thou loved us?" If you stop and think a moment, you will see His love exhibited in your life regardless of the tragedies and heartaches you may have experienced. As one favored by God to have His Word, why not share your heart with the Lord by writing out words of praise to Him now?

_____

_____

October 24

Abiding in His Love

Just as the Father has loved Me, I have also loved you; abide in My love. If you keep My commandments, you will abide in My love; just as I have kept My Father's commandments, and abide in His love. John 15:9, 10, NASB.

Those Christians who abide in Jesus' love cannot help radiating that same love around them. A few years ago Bob flew from Chicago to Washington, D.C., changing planes in Cleveland, Ohio. In Cleveland the airline announced that the flight to Washington would be delayed several hours. As he boarded the plane he heard the passengers complaining about missed appointments in Washington. Their mood grew increasingly hostile and angry. But a petite Black stewardess apologized for the delay, explaining that it had been caused by a storm. She cheerily announced that the crew would do everything possible to make everyone comfortable.

Bob admired her contagious smile and warm greetings as she went up and down the aisles. She showed tremendous care and concern to a girl with no arms and legs, undoubtedly the result of her mother having used thalidomide during her pregnancy. The stewardess singlehandedly transformed that planeload of passengers into such a happy group that they broke out in applause when they landed in Washington. As Bob left the plane he asked her, "You are a Christian, aren't you?"

She responded, "I am, sir, and I'm proud and happy to be one."

When we see God's love and partake of it, how can we be anything but a band of excited messengers for the Lord? Our joy and happiness should waft everywhere like a glorious perfume.

In the second of Malachi's eight confrontations with the Temple priests, he speaks for God in Malachi 1:6: "O priests who despise My name" (NASB). The mocking answer comes back, "How have we despised Thy name?" (verse 6, NASB). God's rebuttal appears in the first part of the verse: "A son honors his father, and a servant his master. Then if I am a father, where is My honor? And if I am a master, where is My respect?" (NASB).

During World War II Brigadier General Theodore Roosevelt, Jr., was waiting at an airport for a plane. A sailor stepped up to a ticket window and asked for a seat on the same plane, explaining, "I want to see my mother, and I don't have much time."

His request did not impress the young woman at the ticket window. "There's a war going on, you know," she exclaimed. At this point General Roosevelt approached the window and told her to give the sailor his seat.

A friend expressed his surprise to the officer. "Teddy, aren't you in a hurry too?"

"It's a matter of rank," came the reply. "I am only a general. He is a son!"

True sons and daughters of God have deep personal affection for their heavenly Father and reveal that love everywhere. Praise Him in your own words for that love.

"Do You Love Me?"

Jesus said to Simon Peter, "Simon, . . . do you love Me?" . . . He said to him again a second time, "Simon, . . . do you love Me?" . . . He said to him the third time, "Simon, . . . do you love Me?" John 21:15-17, NASB.

All of us are Peters needing to be asked this question on a daily basis: "Do you love Jesus?" In our study of the book of Malachi we come to the third and longest confrontation between God and His ministers. It focuses on the sacred versus the profane, the religious versus the sacrilegious, respect versus disrespect. The Lord accuses His representatives, "You are presenting defiled food upon My altar" (Mal. 1:7, NASB).

Instantly the priests protest, "How have we defiled Thee?" (verse 7, NASB).

God reminds them that they have been using blind, sick, and crippled animals for sacrifices. "You are showing contempt for My sanctuary by offering these diseased animals," He explains, adding, "Why not offer it to your governor? Would he be pleased with you? Or would he receive you kindly?" (verse 8, NASB).

The concept of defiled offerings involves every facet of our work and service. For example, God's true people should have a lifestyle that will not scorn the tremendous health principles He has presented us. Our Lord in His tremendous mercy has given us a gospel that affects the whole person, and He urges us to offer our bodies a living—not half dead—sacrifice to Him. We are to give of our best to the Master in all things.

When it came to finances, the Lord pointedly asked, "Who is there even among you that would shut the doors for nought? neither do ye kindle fire on mine altar for nought" (verse 10). True messengers of the Lord are more concerned over their service than their salary. Even those who perform services in the church should consider it a privilege to offer their talents and time without thought for remuneration if they are not full-time church employees.

"It is entirely wrong to hire every errand that is done for the Lord. The treasury of the Lord has been drained by those who have been only an injury to the cause" (*The Seventh-day Adventist Bible Commentary*, Ellen G. White Comments, vol. 4, p. 1180).

The "defiled food" principle applies also to the impact that we make before a critical world. The faults of one member can color the impression people have of the whole church. Our words, actions, or attitude affects the community's concept of the entire church structure. The world judges the church's performance and standards by the actions of the ministers and members. Every time we let the banner of purity and honesty trail in the dust, we erode confidence that can never be repaired except through the ministry of the Holy Spirit.

We come back to our beginning question: "Do we really love Jesus?" Do we love Him enough to not dishonor Him by word or deed? Do we love Him enough to never bring a stain upon Him or His body, the church? How will you answer?

October 26

Covering the Altar With Tears

And this is another thing you do: you cover the altar of the Lord with tears, with weeping and with groaning, because He no longer regards the offering or accepts it with favor from your hand. Mal. 2:13, NASB.

In the fourth confrontation between God and His ministers that Malachi records, the Lord pointedly describes how the priests and people wept and wailed because they realized that He no longer paid attention to their offerings. God then points out a problem that we still face today both in the world and in the church. "The Lord has been a witness between you and the wife of your youth, against whom you have dealt treacherously, though she is your companion and your wife by covenant" (Mal. 2:14, NASB). God unequivocally declared, "For I hate divorce" (verse 16, NASB), whether it be divorce between a husband and wife or between Him and His people.

Today we find marital divorce on the upswing among our ministers as well as the laity. Again we need to understand that a happy marriage is no accident. It takes work, but the results are infinitely worth it.

In the fifth confrontation God claims, "You have wearied the Lord with your words." When His people demand, "How have we wearied Him?" He replies, "In that you say, 'Everyone who does evil is good in the sight of the Lord, and He delights in them'" (verse 17, NASB). God has in mind here confused moral distinctions. Those determined to follow their own devices and desires eventually declare, "Evil, be thou my good." If revival, reformation, and the outpouring of the latter rain ever take place in the church in our day, there must first be a clear distinction between righteousness and evil. The dam of church discipline has all but collapsed, and unless we revive church discipline within the framework of redemptive love, the church will continue to be inundated with a flood of evil that will be difficult, if not impossible, to roll back.

However, we can be of good cheer because our Lord is preparing a people to dwell with Him in the kingdom. We want to be in that group. Why don't you put that desire into words?

Overflowing Blessings

"Bring the whole tithe into the storehouse, so that there may be food in My house, and test Me now in this," says the Lord of hosts, "if I will not open for you the windows of heaven, and pour out for you a blessing until it overflows. Then I will rebuke the devourer for you." Mal. 3:10, 11, NASB.

This is number seven of the eight confrontations that God had with His priests and people, in the book of Malachi. "Will a man rob God?" He asks them. "Yet you are robbing Me!" Then comes the usual reply, "How have we robbed Thee?" In God's rebuttal He explains, "In tithes and offerings. You are cursed with a curse, for you are robbing Me, the whole nation of you!" (Mal. 3:8, 9, NASB).

Our Lord has promised to open up the windows of heaven to those who tithe and "pour out for you a blessing until it overflows."

An old story tells about a little woman who ran a village sweets shop. The children flocked there with their pennies and came to know it as the "Bit More Store," for when she had weighed the candy, she would look into the child's eager face, and as the scales balanced, she would say, "I'll put in a bit more."

God does more than a "bit more." He gives lavishly—heaped up and running over. Not only that, but He says, "I will rebuke the devourer for you." Here the devourer was the insects that would destroy crops, but in principle the devourer can be the enemy of all souls—Satan, who destroys our faith in God. Those who are faithful with their tithe inevitably develop a sense of greater responsibility. The person who is honest with God is more likely to be honest with his fellowman.

If you have been lax in giving your tithes and offerings to God, take Him at His word. But let your motivation for giving to Him be one of overflowing love for what He has done for you. In no way can you pay the debt, but you can honor Him by giving Him the firstfruits of your increase, a concrete token of your gratitude and thankfulness.

Let your testimony ring with gratitude and praise to God for giving you so many blessings.

A Book of Remembrance

Then those who feared the Lord spoke to one another, and the Lord gave attention and heard it, and a book of remembrance was written before Him for those who fear the Lord and who esteem His name. Mal. 3:16, NASB.

In Malachi 3:13 the Lord declares, "Your words have been arrogant against Me" (NASB). The priests and people try to excuse themselves by demanding, "What have we spoken against Thee?" (verse 13, NASB). God answers them, "You have said, 'It is vain to serve God, and what profit is it that we have kept His charge, and that we have walked in mourning before the Lord of hosts? So now we call the arrogant blessed; not only are the doers of wickedness built up, but they also test God and escape'" (verses 14, 15, NASB).

But our text today describes a different type of people. They encourage each other with the thought that serving God does make a difference, and they compile written testimonies and praises for God to sustain their faith.

God urged those who rejected Him to "return to Me, and I will return to you" (verse 7, NASB). The New Testament counterpart appears in the message to the Laodicean church, where Jesus says, "I stand at the door and knock." God is merciful, long-suffering, patient, and unbelievably forbearing. There is none like Him.

We have a beautiful and brilliant future ahead of us if we will be like the people described in Malachi 3:16 and fill our books of remembrance with praises to God. How will God bless those who have adopted the principle of paper Ebenezers? " 'And they will be Mine,' says the Lord of hosts, 'on the day that I prepare My own possession, and I will spare them as a man spares his own son who serves him.' So you will again distinguish between the righteous and the wicked, between one who serves God and one who does not serve Him" (verse 17, NASB).

A Native American, when asked what the Lord had done for him, gathered some dry leaves into a circle and, placing a worm in the center, set the leaves on fire. As the flames drew nearer on every side and were about to consume the worm, he lifted it out and, placing it safely on a rock, looked up and said, "This is what Jesus did for me."

Although the wicked and arrogant may seem to be blessed, the time is coming when they will lose everything. But Jesus has rescued us, and soon He will lift us out of this world of sin altogether at His return.

Praise His name for the privilege of filling up our book of remembrance with testimonies of love and praise to Him. Add to that book today by writing a few words of gratitude to our Lord.

The Futility of Fun Without God

I said to myself, "Come now, I will test you with pleasure. So enjoy yourself." And behold, it too was futility. I said of laughter, "It is madness," and of pleasure, "What does it accomplish?" Eccl. 2:1, 2, NASB.

The book of Ecclesiastes is Solomon's mournful autobiography written in his old age. His life started on an upbeat note but ended sadly on a low one. He found out by experience that a life of sin and foolishness is like "striving after wind and there was no profit under the sun" (Eccl. 2:11, NASB).

Fortunately, in spite of his profligate life, he repented in his later years. But the damage had been done both to himself and his kingdom. Although God forgave him, the scars of sin remained.

The only true joy, and even fun, in life is always found within the framework of loving and obeying God. Life without God is just plain empty!

One evening in 1808, a gaunt, sad-faced man entered the office of Dr. James Hamilton in Manchester, England. His visitor's melancholy appearance instantly caught the doctor's attention.

"Are you sick?" Hamilton asked.

"Yes, Doctor, sick of a mortal malady."

"What malady?" the doctor inquired.

"I am frightened of the terror of the world around me. I am depressed by life. I can find no happiness anywhere, nothing amuses me, and I have nothing to live for. If you can't help me, I shall kill myself."

"The malady is not mortal," Hamilton replied. "You need only to get out of yourself. You need to laugh, to get some pleasure from life."

"What shall I do?" the patient demanded.

"Go to the circus tonight to see Grimaldi, the clown," the doctor answered. "Grimaldi is the funniest man alive. He'll cure you."

A spasm of pain contorted the poor man's face as he said, "Doctor, don't jest with me. I am Grimaldi, the clown!"

As you visit some of the former Communist-controlled countries, you can see what happens when you teach people for decades that there is no God. Where there is no God, the people live a profitless, boring, empty existence. "For who can eat and who can have enjoyment without Him?" (verse 25, NASB).

Praise the Lord for the fact that you know that life is meaningful and pleasure is fantastic when you serve the Lord. Even though we may have only a limited knowledge of God, we still find our happiness and our joy in our submission to Him. And the greater the submission, the greater the happiness.

Jot down the ways He has made life interesting for you.

External Portrays Internal

And let not your adornment be merely external—braiding the hair, and wearing gold jewelry, or putting on dresses; but let it be the hidden person of the heart, with the imperishable quality of a gentle and quiet spirit, which is precious in the sight of God. 1 Peter 3:3, 4, NASB.

At Halloween many children use face masks to create a magical illusion of being something they are not. Throughout history nearly every culture on earth has used masks as an element of ceremony, tradition, custom, and ritual. According to experts who study and collect masks, there are several principles behind their use, whether as theatrical devices, art forms, or religious symbols. For some a mask reflects what is going on inside them. Others use masks to identify not only occupations and political persuasions but religious status. Again, what we are or want to be finds expression in a mask.

Now let's transfer this concept to our entire being. The heart, meaning the mind, will find expression in our everyday regular mask, or looks. How we dress, whether we wish to admit it or not, is in most cases an outward testimony of what's going on inside us. Corporations such as IBM have strict dress codes. Why? They want the world to know they are solid, high-performing, trustworthy institutions, and therefore those who work for them must reflect these qualities. The employees must become what their company is like. Even their technicians who repair equipment in our offices dress conservatively. They know the way they look either builds or destroys confidence in the company they represent.

What about Christians who are waiting for our Lord to return? What kind of masks are we wearing? What are we telling the world about ourselves? More important, what are we telling God with our looks? It is our privilege to match our looks with our Lord's desire for us. It truly is an honor to make God look good by the way we look! If we resemble Him in principle, such as with a "gentle and quiet spirit," it becomes most "precious" in His sight.

Do you want everything in your life to be a symbol that praises His goodness and reflects the transformation that He is making in your life? We do! But more important, the mask we wear for God through the Holy Spirit becomes what we really are. He makes us into His image through and through. Can you praise Him for this wonderful reality?

Fight One More Round

I press on toward the goal for the prize of the upward call of God in Christ Jesus. Phil. 3:14, NASB.

James J. Corbett was a professional pugilist who won the world's heavyweight boxing championship in 1892.

"What," someone asked him, "is most important for a man to do to become champion?"

Corbett replied, "Fight one more round."

The most important thing to do to become a spiritual champion is also to "fight one more round." Paul did. He never gave up.

Thomas Edison, known as the greatest inventor in history, patented more than 1,000 inventions in 60 years. In his attempts to develop a storage battery he conducted more than 10,000 experiments before he succeeded. Edison knew better than anyone else in the scientific world what it meant to "fight one more round" to become a champion—the lesson the apostle Paul had learned.

Penniless Carrie Jacobs Bond, a semi-invalid, tried hand painting china and singing in vaudeville. Her lot was bitter failure. She tried songwriting, but the publishers would not buy. Then she fought "one more round" by composing "A Perfect Day," "I Love You Truly," and other songs that finally made her famous.

George Washington Carver started out in life as the son of slave parents. When he was a baby, a band of night raiders kidnapped him and his mother. It is said his master bought him back in exchange for a race horse. Carver's determination to fight "one more round" resulted in the development of more than 300 products from the lowly peanut.

The first time George Gershwin played the piano in public, his audience laughed him off the stage. As a composer he met with terrible disappointment, writing almost 100 tunes before he sold his first—for $5. But his motto was to fight "one more round," and a year later he wrote "Swanee," which sold millions of copies. He also won a Pulitzer Prize.

Jesus fought "one more round" and became a champion in Gethsemane.

When you are weary of fighting the fight of faith, remember the many others who have pressed toward the mark in a spiritual sense and fought "one more round" to became champions.

State your determination to fight "one more round" today.

"Heaven Is All Health"

The thief comes only to steal, and kill, and destroy; I came that they might have life, and might have it abundantly. John 10:10, NASB.

What you have just read is the finest and shortest description of the great spiritual struggle waging between Christ and Satan. On one side is Satan, the thief, whose only—we repeat, only—objective is to kill and destroy. And on the other side is Jesus, whose only goal is to give us unlimited life.

When Satan attacks the individual he goes after the entire person. His aim is to destroy us, not just spiritually, but physically as well. One way he has done so is by convincing most of Christianity that our physical nature is unimportant or even evil. As Greek dualism—the concept that spirit and body are separate and the latter inferior or even evil—crept into the early Christian church, it led to the doctrine of a separate, distinct, immortal soul. This dividing of the body from the soul grew out of Greek philosophy, which viewed the soul as a superior form or essence held captive in a gross body.

A. T. Robinson colorfully states this false concept as "an angel [soul] in a slot machine [body]." According to this theory, man's soul was a pearl trapped in a cesspool of a body. Thus many looked upon the body as evil, while considering the soul as divine.

But the Scriptures teach that the individual is an indivisible unit. A person is one being! We may use such terms as *body, mind,* and *soul* to discuss a human being's individual aspects, but in reality there is no mind apart from the body and no soul apart from either body or mind. Jesus, replying to a scribe who asked Him which commandment was most important, quoted from Deuteronomy 6:4, 5: "Love the Lord your God with all your heart, and with all your soul, and with all your mind, and with all your strength" (Mark 12:30, NASB). Both the Old and New Testaments teach that we must totally commit every part of our being—every cell in our body—to Him in order that we may experience His promise of abundant life.

Furthermore, a person will have a healthier spiritual life if the body is in good physical health. A sick body will block or even destroy a strong spiritual experience.

The abundant life our Lord promised comes both now and in the future. The gospel, when properly understood, reveals a treatment for both the physically and spiritually sick person. Daily we thank the Lord for the instruction in both the Scriptures and in the writings of Ellen White that teach us how to live Christ's wonderful new life.

Praise Him for the health-giving, life-giving joy that is ours through the Holy Spirit!

November 2

Life at Its Best

And Jesus kept increasing in wisdom and stature, and in favor with God and men. Luke 2:52, NASB.

This is one of the few verses recorded in Scripture that mention the childhood and youth of Jesus. It reveals the beautiful balance in our Lord's growth. Note the words "kept increasing," which indicate a constant development of His entire person. One writer compares it to Jesus "cutting his way forward as through a forest or jungle, as pioneers did." Our Lord was a pioneer in a perfect development of all His powers. Note the totality of His growth. Jesus advanced "in wisdom [mind] and stature [body], and in favor with God [spiritual nature] and men [social nature]."

Again we find ourselves confronted with the incontrovertible point that we are an indivisible unit. Whatever impacts on our mind affects our body. And whatever touches our body influences the rest of our being. Have you ever hit the wrong nail with a hammer when hanging a picture? To smash your thumbnail disturbs the entire person from head to toe. You cannot isolate the pain to the thumb. It even affects a person spiritually—some people begin to curse God, and no one feels like singing at that moment "Praise God From Whom All Blessings Flow."

It is easy to write and speak about the total interrelatedness of the individual, but it takes time to internalize the concept and apply it to ourselves. If through the Holy Spirit we do grasp this vital fact, we then can begin to appreciate how our entire system of doctrinal beliefs impinges upon our total being. For the next few readings we plan to share our thoughts on the holistic approach to life at its best.

Our pattern is Jesus. Having created us, He knows better than anyone else, including ourselves, how we function and what it takes to keep the living machinery in the best possible operating condition. Jesus knew how to live, and He lived every moment in the best possible manner. He never used His mental, physical, or moral powers in a reckless way. The way He lived is the way He desires us to live. As He traveled from village to village His vibrant, energetic life brought hope and help to the multitudes suffering either from ignorance or from willful violation of the laws of nature that our Lord Himself had created.

This same Jesus lives today. He is dispensing His Spirit to all who are willing to receive Him. He longs to give each one of us a better life now and an eternal one when He returns. Please praise His blessed name for His balanced example and desire to help us now and forever.

The Sanctuary of God

You are ... God's building. ... Do you not know that you are a temple of God, and that the Spirit of God dwells in you? If any man destroys the temple of God, God will destroy him, for the temple of God is holy, and that is what you are. 1 Cor. 3:9-17, NASB.

Today's passage applies to the body of Christ, the church, as well as to the individual Christian. The Greek word for *temple* does not refer to the courtyard, but to the inner chambers of the sanctuary itself. The illustration of our being God's building, His temple, is a powerful one. We are sacred temples, made in a fantastic, intricate way by the Lord's own hands. He desires more than anything else to dwell in us. Many in Paul's time thought the body was evil, but the apostle emphasizes that it is really sacred.

Paul appeals to us to carefully treat these temples—our entire beings—in a way that will honor Him and bless both others and ourselves. God made every part to work together. Like an automobile engine, every part must function harmoniously for it to run properly. You cannot compartmentalize an engine—separate each part by itself; it is a unified whole. So it is with us, God's temples.

We could illustrate in a thousand ways how every piece of our living machinery interacts with the other. A lie detector, or polygraph, records changes in a person's blood pressure, pulse rate, breathing, and muscular movements. If you connect a criminal to one of these sensitive instruments

314

and question him about an illegal activity, his whole being usually reacts immediately, indicating whether he is lying or telling the truth.

Even the animal kingdom shows similar tendencies. For example, we can test the impact a kind word or an affectionate pat or stroke can have on an animal's blood pressure. When a stranger walks into a dog's home, the dog's blood pressure rises as the hair on its back stands on end. (If the dog appears vicious, the stranger's blood pressure goes up too!) But after getting acquainted with the visitor, the dog calms down, and when petted and stroked, according to veterinarians, the animal's blood pressure drops below normal.

You ask What has this to do with human beings? If an animal's blood pressure soars when meeting a stranger, what about people gripped with fear, anxiety, remorse, guilt, consuming ambition, and greed? God designed our body temples in a much more sophisticated way than that of any dog or cat. Animals cannot think and reason as do humans. And we have still another advantage over them. We have Jesus, the great restorer and healer, and His marvelous Word to meditate on and to study. Listen to His promise: "Because I live, you shall live also" (John 14:19, NASB).

Praise Him today for His willingness to dwell in our body temples.

Paul's Six Arguments Against Impurity

Do you not know that your body is a temple of the Holy Spirit who is in you, whom you have from God, and that you are not your own? For you have been bought with a price: therefore glorify God in your body. 1 Cor. 6:19, 20, NASB.

Again Paul employs the analogy of our bodies being sanctuaries of the Holy Spirit. However, his temple illustration climaxes his six arguments against immorality. Sexual impurity was a common problem in the Corinthian church. In verse 13 Paul answers a ridiculous argument used by some in Corinth to justify immorality. Evidently they reasoned that since "food is for the stomach, and the stomach for food," wouldn't it follow that one could use the body to gratify the sensual appetite? After all, isn't that what the body is for? But Paul reminded them that the Lord made the body not for prostitution, but as a vessel of honor for Himself. Therefore, His people should never consider it a vehicle for immorality.

Paul's second objection to impurity appears in verse 14. Since God raised Jesus from the tomb, likewise He "will raise us up through His power" from base sensuality.

Verses 15-17 contain the apostle's third reason to reject immorality. He argues that not only are our bodies made for the Lord, but they are members

315

of Christ. Then he adds that it is unthinkable to take these members of Christ and join them to harlots. This idea must have staggered Paul's mind, and it should do the same for us!

The fourth argument, in verse 18, indicates that while lying, stealing, and covetousness are sins outside the body, fornication, adultery, and sexual impurity involve the body in a very direct manner. If our bodies are a part of Christ's body, how can we indulge in immorality? It destroys the true marriage union, which represents the oneness between Christ and His church. Our passage today presents Paul's fifth argument. Since our bodies are shrines for the Holy Spirit to dwell in, we dare not pollute them with impurity of any kind.

Finally, Paul's sixth reason to avoid immorality is that we don't belong to ourselves. We are not at liberty to do what we feel like doing at the expense of defiling ourselves. To cap off all his arguments, he beautifully reminds us that Christ has bought us with a price—an extremely high one. Nothing could be more costly than what heaven paid to redeem us.

Please praise the Lord for this lofty passage that elevates our beings to the level of a sanctuary inhabited by Christ Himself through the Holy Spirit. How will you protect yourself as His honored dwelling place?

November 5

Peace of Mind

And let the peace of Christ rule in your hearts, to which indeed you were called in one body, and be thankful. Col. 3:15, NASB.

We have known for some years that the relationship between the mind and body is far greater than many of us realize. Each has an enormous effect on the other either for good or for ill. Modern medicine has in recent years coined the word *psychoneuroimmunology*. This relatively new science has refined the focus of the mind-body relationship. Scientists are now finding that our thoughts have a powerful influence on our nervous system, which in turn affects our immune system. Thus *psycho* (mind) *neuro* (nervous system) *immunology* (immune system).

Recently we have heard much about AIDS (acquired immune deficiency syndrome). It is a medical term for a depressed immune system. The immune system of a person with AIDS has little or no capacity to battle bacteria and viruses that invade the body. From the Adventist viewpoint, a basic reason for having a strong healthy mind, body, and spirit is to maintain a strong defense force—our immune system—against disease. The new emphasis on the role the mind plays in affecting our physical health—which in turn either depresses or strengthens the immune system—has implications far beyond what we have traditionally understood and believed in the past.

The amazing point is that the Scriptures foreshadow these recent scientific discoveries. For instance, our text today, when seen in the light of psychoneuroimmunology, shows us that a mind or heart ruled by Christ generates a life-giving peace that permeates our entire being. The peace Christ gives lifts the spirits, calms the nerves, and brings health to both mind and body.

Nearly 100 years ago Ellen White told us that "many of the diseases from which men suffer are the result of mental depression. Grief, anxiety, discontent, remorse, guilt, distrust, all tend to break down the life forces and to invite decay and death" (*The Ministry of Healing*, p. 241). Her statement gives an excellent description of the psychoneuroimmunological concept.

Paul in our passage admonishes the Colossians to be thankful. A spirit of thankfulness and praise has much to do with the health of our body, mind, and spirit. Enhance your health by writing a sentence or two of praise to the One who has made us and redeemed us.

Gaining New Strength

He gives strength to the weary, and to him who lacks might He increases power. Though youths grow weary and tired, and vigorous young men stumble badly, yet those who wait for the Lord will gain new strength; they will mount up with wings like eagles, they will run and not get tired, they will walk and not become weary. Isa. 40:29-31, NASB.

This passage is a beautiful example of the total integration of the mind and body. When he preached on these verses years ago, Bob limited the effects of waiting on the Lord to the spiritual nature. Today we know that the person who makes friends with the Lord gains not only spiritual strength, but physical as well. Those who know Jesus and serve Him receive abundant life. It has been shown scientifically that a courageous, hopeful, loving attitude can promote health and prolong life.

Yesterday we touched briefly on psychoneuroimmunology, the influence of our mind on our nervous system, which in turn affects our immune system. As we have seen, the term *psychoneuroimmunology* may be relatively new, but the concept is as old as life itself, and our text today supports it.

What about our attitudes? "There is little hard evidence that attitude alone can cure serious disease. There is, however, new evidence that people can voluntarily improve their own immune function and thus prevent disease" (*Psychology Today*, March 1987, p. 51).

Isn't this what Solomon knew when he wrote "A joyful heart is good medicine but a broken spirit dries up the bones" (Prov. 17:22, NASB)? Studies have shown that mentally depressed heart patients show less improvement than happier heart patients. Some have claimed that depression can be a better predictor of medical problems than even physical tests. An individual may have excellent vital statistics—blood pressure, low cholesterol readings, normal blood chemistry, and proper weight—yet have severe physical problems. Could it be that the sufferer's attitude is one of the culprits? All too often this is true.

One of the reasons we have provided space at the end of each reading for you to write down a sentence or two of daily praise and thanksgiving is to give not just a spiritual uplift, but a physical one as well. We firmly believe in the interaction of the body, mind, and nervous system, and its effect on the immune system. It is an inescapable fact that our attitudes have a profound influence on our body's resistance to disease.

In view of this, why not begin to thank Jesus constantly for His love? Thank Him for His promise that new strength is ours if we wait on the Lord. Make happiness in the Lord your first order of the day.

November 7

The Mountains of Blessings and Curses

And all Israel with their elders and officers and their judges were standing on both sides of the ark before the Levitical priests who carried the ark of the covenant of the Lord, the stranger as well as the native. Half of them stood in front of Mount Gerizim and half of them in front of Mount Ebal, just as Moses the servant of the Lord had given command at first to bless the people of Israel. Joshua 8:33, NASB.

Two of the highest elevations in central Palestine are Mount Gerizim and Mount Ebal, each around 3,000 feet (915 meters) in elevation. At the eastern exit of the valley, between the two mountains, lies the city of Shechem, near where Jacob's well still exists. There Jesus had His unforgettable encounter with the unnamed Samaritan woman.

Before Moses died and the children of Israel under Joshua's leadership invaded Canaan, God instructed them to erect on Mount Ebal an altar and large plastered stones on which they were to write all the sacred laws He had given them. (Unlike most of the people around them, Israel did not carve its memorials on stone, but inscribed them in ink on plastered surfaces. That is why archaeologists, to their disappointment, find few Hebrew inscriptions.) Then the congregation was divided approximately in half by tribes to form two antiphonal choirs. The group standing on the slopes of Ebal was to pronounce the curses, while those on Gerizim recited the blessings. Each section would respond with a strong "amen" to each item read aloud. It was a most solemn occasion in a geographical area that held sacred memories from the history of Jacob, Abraham, and others.

It would be wonderful if we had a videotape of the event. Perhaps our church should have a similar plan for a General Conference session somewhere in the mountains where we would divide the audience in half and prepare a twentieth-century list of blessings and curses based upon the principles God gave Israel of old.

As we study the blessings and curses in Deuteronomy 27 and 28, we should understand that we do not serve a God who arbitrarily curses or blesses people. He does not operate on whims and notions. The laws of His government rest on logical and practical principles. Each law contains within itself the specific blessing or curse if obeyed or disobeyed. True, we live in a world of sin where the rain and sunshine fall on both sinners and saints, but generally speaking, many of the mental, physical, and spiritual problems we face are those we bring upon ourselves through either plain old-fashioned disobedience, carelessness, or ignorance. We cannot blame God for any of our difficulties. He loves us as He loved Israel, and He desires nothing more than to shower us with blessings—but there are conditions, as we shall see.

Praise our Lord for every heartbeat. Praise Him for answering your prayer, even if He says no. List some of the blessings that you have enjoyed recently.

Head or Tail?

And the Lord shall make you the head and not the tail, and you only shall be above, and you shall not be underneath, if you will listen to the commandments of the Lord your God, which I charge you today, to observe them carefully, and do not turn aside from any of the words which I command you today to the right or to the left, to go after other gods to serve them. Deut. 28:13, NASB.

Yesterday's reading gave the background of the two mountains—Mount Ebal and Mount Gerizim—where Joshua had the people of Israel antiphonally read the blessings and curses. Our passage today reveals the criteria for being blessed.

The condition of obedience to our Lord's commandments determines whether God will make His people the head or the tail. This principle of obedience and blessing is easier to recognize in some situations than in others. For example, death awaits anyone who jumps out of an airplane without a parachute. Obviously, the person who does so drastically disregards the law of gravity. But it is not so obvious if a person suffers kidney problems simply because he or she violates a health rule by not drinking enough water each day. That is why we should study carefully the laws of physiology in order to live life at its best.

Deuteronomy 27 and 28 contain a series of blessings and cursings, all of them related either to obedience or disobedience. The first curse involves the violation of the first and second commandments of the Decalogue. "Cursed is the man who makes an idol or molten image, an abomination to the Lord, the work of the hands of the craftsman, and sets it up in secret" (Deut. 27:15, NASB). Let us study this verse in the light of the mind's effect on the body. The person who clandestinely makes an idol or worships it certainly knows better or he would not do it secretly. To knowingly break any of God's commandments produces guilt, and guilt depresses the immune system.

Doing what is right gives one a sense of well-being. Thus, to do right promotes health. While the way of obedience is the road to life and happiness, disobedience leads to depression, sorrow, and unhappiness, which tend to break down our mental and physical constitution.

Our Lord created us for happiness. He knows that obedience to His will brings mental and physical blessing. Aren't you thankful for His laws and for a desire to obey them? Express your thankfulness now!

November 9

How to Be Blessed

Now it shall be, if you will diligently obey the Lord your God, being careful to do all His commandments which I command you today, the Lord your God will set you high above all the nations of the earth. And all these blessings shall come upon you and overtake you, if you will obey the Lord your God. Deut. 28:1, 2, NASB.

We are still thinking about Mount Ebal and Mount Gerizim, the mountains of cursing and blessing. Deuteronomy 27 and 28 teach that for every effect there is a cause. Why do so many individuals fail to recognize this unchangeable fact? It is a law of heaven and earth. God told His people that life has only two options—obey and be blessed, or disobey and be cursed.

As you study these blessings and cursings, keep in mind that both result from choices that we personally make. Israel's prosperity or defeat did not come by chance. So it is with us today, either as individuals or as a corporate church. Does that mean that we will escape all problems if we render perfect obedience? No! The struggle between good and evil, between Christ and Satan, still continues. We are in a raging war, and its fallout often affects even the innocent. In the physical realm many, through no fault of their own, have congenital weaknesses, a legacy from birth or childhood. Accidents and aging contribute to life's problems. All are part of sin's effect on humanity.

But what we are saying is that those who by God's grace obey His laws to the very best of their knowledge and ability will be blessed far above those who disobey. The second commandment supports this concept when it concludes: "But showing lovingkindness to thousands, to those who love Me and keep My commandments" (Ex. 20:6, NASB). The theme of obey and live, disobey and die, runs like an unbroken cord from Genesis to Revelation.

In the spiritual realm we can always be assured of blessing if we obey all of God's laws. And in the physical world we may have better health and greater happiness in spite of those illnesses that we did not bring upon ourselves through disobeying God's mental, physical, and moral laws.

Praise and thanksgiving will always bring great blessing. The more you lift your mind to Him in thanksgiving and praise Him, the healthier and happier you will be. Write down several sentences of praise to Him who alone gives us the strength to obey His marvelous life-giving laws.

_____

_____

Serve the Lord With Joy and Gladness

So all these curses shall come on you and pursue you and overtake you until you are destroyed, because you would not obey the Lord your God by keeping His commandments and His statutes which He commanded you. . . . Because you did not serve the Lord your God with joy and a glad heart, for the abundance of all things. Deut. 28:45-47, NASB.

Our passage today expresses a key to mental, physical, and spiritual health. The blessings and cursings at Mount Gerizim and Mount Ebal are linked to obedience or disobedience to God's laws. But in the case of blessings for obedience, God seeks joyful service. Why? Those who study the concept of psychoneuroimmunology stress the importance of attitudes in relationship to sickness or health. The Lord, having created us as we are, is well aware of this. To fully experience the blessings that result from obedience we need a happy, joyful attitude. In fact, it is vital in maintaining health.

As you study the blessings and curses in Deuteronomy 27 and 28, note the effects of the blessings and curses on the physical, mental, and spiritual faculties. A curse awaits those who dishonor parents; who illegally move a boundary marker; who mislead a blind person; who pervert the justice due an alien, orphan, or widow; who commit incest; who accept bribes.

Do such curses affect only our spiritual nature? Listen to the results of disobedience. The offenders will find themselves afflicted with mental confusion, insanity, fever, inflammation, tumors, incurable itching, blindness, boils on the knees and legs, and other chronic sicknesses. Read these chapters carefully and thoughtfully. We believe that you will be surprised how God used the holistic approach behind both the blessings and curses. More than 3,000 years before modern medical science proved the intimate relationship between the mind and the immune system, God through Moses shared this concept with His people.

We always need to keep in mind that the mental and physical problems Israel endured were not arbitrarily caused by the Lord; rather, they were the natural results of disobedience and disloyalty to the principles that God has ordained life to operate on.

On the other hand, the marvelous blessings of obedience affect every aspect of life. If Israel had obeyed, it would lead to blessings upon them in both city and country, in their marriage relationships, in their rearing of children, in their increase of possessions, in their breadmaking.

God desires that we serve Him with joy and glad hearts. Write down a few words of your happiness in the Lord now!

_____

_____

November 11

Healing of Mind and Body

And behold, they were bringing to Him a paralytic, lying on a bed; and Jesus seeing their faith said to the paralytic, "Take courage, My son, your sins are forgiven." Matt. 9:2, NASB.

Christ's healing of the paralytic demonstrates how God made us. We are a unit in body, mind, and spirit. Here was a person racked with both physical and mental pain. The fact that Jesus forgave his sins indicates the major problem in the paralytic's life. Because of his life of sin, his conscience was destroying his peace of mind, which in turn affected him physically, as well. Nothing destroys health of mind and body more than guilt. And any kind of sinful behavior warps one's mental outlook, which in turn adversely affects every cell of the body. Good health depends on a person's attitude much more than we realize.

We hesitate to use the word *health* without showing its all-inclusiveness. The biblical sense of health is wholeness or complete soundness. Salvation seeks to make a person healthy and whole mentally, spiritually, and physically. From a secular viewpoint, individuals may have physically sound bodies, but if they are not healthy mentally or spiritually, they are not healthy or whole in the biblical sense.

When Jesus healed people and made them whole, He also touched them spiritually. Why did Jesus say to one individual "Go and sin no more"? Our

Lord knew it was useless to heal a person who would continue in the same path of sin that may have triggered his or her physical illness in the first place. In the incident recorded in today's text, the man Jesus healed had been sick for 38 years. After telling him to sin no more, He added, "so that nothing worse may befall you" (John 5:14, NASB). The story clearly illustrates the tie-in between body, mind, and spirit.

Much of our suffering today results from our own disregard of God's laws, whether of nature or the Ten Commandments. All God's laws are sacred and cannot be violated without paying a penalty. Yet in spite of our rebellion, our Lord forgives us and stands ready to give us another opportunity. Often we can alleviate our physical suffering by bringing our lifestyle back into harmony with God's laws. Sometimes, though, nothing we can do will correct the physical problem. Yet even then we can be assured of His forgiveness, which then results in peace of mind.

Thank Him for His efforts to save us from evil and lead us to the good, and praise Him for His forgiving power, which gives us new life.

The Golden Eight

But to you who fear My name the Sun of Righteousness shall arise with healing in His wings; and you shall go out and grow fat like stall-fed calves. Mal. 4:2, NKJV.

As we study the causes of physical disease and illness, we discover that many of them involve the violation, either intentionally or otherwise, of certain basic laws of health. Adventists often label the laws as natural remedies. What are they? "Pure air, sunlight, abstemiousness, rest, exercise, proper diet, the use of water, trust in divine power—these are the true remedies" (*The Ministry of Healing*, p. 127). These eight golden elixirs of life, when carefully practiced, will do a world of good to either restore or maintain health.

One of our leading lay-owned and -operated Adventist health centers, Weimar Institute, has worked them into an acronym: New Start (nutrition, exercise, water, sunshine, temperance, air, rest and relaxation, trust in divine power). This acronym is an excellent way to remember the eight rules for health. When we attempted to practice the eight principles daily, we found from our own experience that the Sun (Son) of righteousness did, indeed, bless us with the healing in His wings! To understand them better, we suggest that you read as a part of your daily devotion the marvelous book *The Ministry of Healing*. In the words of its author, Ellen G. White: "This book contains the wisdom of the Great Physician" (*Testimonies*, vol. 9, p.

71). We have read it through together and plan to do so again. The grand principles it reveals are balanced and all center on the One who has healing in His wings.

In the ancient world, where people struggled to exist from harvest to harvest, the idea of growing fat like the stall-fed calves in our text today was appealing. Fatness was a sign of wealth. In the modern world, with its more abundant food supply, we know that too much weight can be unhealthy. But we can grow fat in the area of spiritual, mental, and social qualities, as well as physical soundness.

It is wonderful to enjoy life at its best. In fact, we get so excited over practicing these principles that sometimes we find it hard to contain ourselves. We feel like the ant that found some crumbs we left on the sidewalk for our beloved barn swallows, who have a nest with four baby birds in our porch ceiling. When we checked to see if the mother swallow had gotten the food, we discovered that one ant had spread the good news of the unexpected food supply to all the citizens of his ant city. Streams of ants were excitedly carrying away the crumbs. In the same way as the little ant, we want to share the wonderful news of health with everyone who will listen.

God wants to heal us and to help us to enjoy life thoroughly. Won't you thank Him for the gift of health?

Renewing of the Mind

In reference to your former manner of life, you lay aside the old self, which is being corrupted in accordance with the lusts of deceit, and that you be renewed in the spirit of your mind, and put on the new self, which in the likeness of God has been created in righteousness and holiness of the truth. Eph. 4:22-24, NASB.

The thrust of our passage today is Scripture's call for the believer to lay aside the old life of sinful pursuits and let the Holy Spirit renew, or transform, our minds into a brand-new person in the likeness of God. Such renewal is the healing process of a born-again mind. It is not just a superficial change, but rather a renovation that affects the whole person, and it is a supernatural process, not one the believer himself does.

The mind and its operation are more intricate than that of any computer. We need to treat it with the greatest respect. The mind is the actual functioning of that marvelous organ of the body known as the brain.

Scientists have attempted to compare the brains of outstanding individuals with those of ordinary people. When Lenin died, the Soviets established a special institute to study his brain. They sliced its tissue into more than

30,000 sections and over a period of years counted the cells in the various layers like the stars in a photograph of the heavens. When they examined the brain of a common Russian in a similar manner, they did find that Lenin's cerebral cortex had about 25 percent more cells. But whether Lenin's brain or that of an ordinary person, our Lord created them to function as the capital of the body.

The influence of the mind on the body is remarkable. Charles Mayo, cofounder of the Mayo Clinic, claimed that 80 percent of all the illness seen at their clinic originated in the mind. Long before Mayo made his observation, Ellen G. White observed: "Satan is the originator of disease. . . . Sickness of the mind prevails everywhere. Nine tenths of the diseases from which men suffer have their foundation here. Perhaps some living home trouble is, like a canker, eating to the very soul and weakening the life forces" (*Testimonies*, vol. 5, pp. 443, 444).

Neither Mayo or Ellen White are talking about a neurosis, in which people think they are sick but aren't. Rather, they are saying that the actual sickness a person suffers from originates or has its foundation in the mind itself. Again this shows the powerful influence the mind has over the body.

On the other side of the coin, you have the body affecting the mind through the nourishment and other substances it feeds the brain. This is why we should be careful with our diet and anything else that affects all the organs of the body, whether positively or negatively.

God loves His creatures with a strong and tender love. Every "Thou shalt not" contains a promise. Praise Him for the ability to obey and live. Thank Him for His laws that have as their purpose to bring us into a closer fellowship with Him. And thank Him for His help in putting on the "new self."

Deliver Us From Evil

Then David said to Abigail, "Blessed be the Lord God of Israel, who sent you this day to meet me, and blessed be your discernment, and blessed be you, who have kept me this day from bloodshed, and from avenging myself by my own hand." 1 Sam. 25:32, 33, NASB.

Nabal, a wealthy farmer whose name means "foolish" or "reckless," was Abigail's husband. During David's flight from Saul, he and his men camped in the wilderness where Nabal's servants were located. David's men treated the servants with kindness and courtesy and stole nothing from them. They acted as Nabal's protectors from bandits and desert marauders. Then David sent 10 young men to Nabal at a festive time to ask for life-sustaining supplies.

Rather than helping David, Nabal stupidly demanded, "Who is David?" Then he proceeded to compare him to a slave who had deserted his master.

David and his men had performed a greatly needed service in such troublous times. Nabal and everyone else in Israel knew about David and his problems. But the wealthy man's harsh, selfish nature took control. When David received the report, his anger boiled over. *No one will treat the future king of Israel this way!* is probably what he thought. He armed his men and started toward Nabal's home.

But a servant told Abigail the whole story, and immediately her good judgment took over. She loaded up plenty of food on donkeys, without telling her husband, and started toward the mountain where David had his camp. On the way she met him and his men on their way to slaughter every male in Nabal's household.

Her diplomatic approach brought David to his senses. Read again his response found in our text today. It is a beautiful confession. Blessed be the peacemakers. Thank God for individuals who kindly and tenderly say or do things that keep us from falling into evil. Perhaps a husband or a wife, a friend, a relative, or a loving church member has said or done something that kept you from making a foolish move. Thank the Lord for such people. Do it in writing today, and even name the person who may have helped you.

The Man Who Became as Stone

But it came about in the morning, when the wine had gone out of Nabal, that his wife told him these things, and his heart died within him so that he became as a stone. And about ten days later, it happened that the Lord struck Nabal, and he died. 1 Sam. 25:37, 38, NASB.

Today's passage comes from the climax of yesterday's story. Abigail's gift of food diverted David from his murderous mission. When she returned to Nabal she found him drunk at the sheep-shearing feast. After he sobered up the next morning, she told him about his close brush with death. His response was physical, not verbal. "His heart died within him so that he became as a stone."

Most of us do not fully grasp the complexity and interrelatedness of our bodies. When we say "bodies," we refer to the total person—what we call mind, body, and spirit. Nabal's experience illustrates how a person's mind—or heart, as the Bible expresses it—affects the body.

When Abigail's account of David's intent to kill him at last registered in Nabal's brain, fear left him paralyzed like "a stone." In just 10 days his horror-filled mind so ravaged him—mentally, physically, and spiritually—that he died.

Our text states: "The Lord struck Nabal, and he died." What it means is that Nabal's selfish, greedy, uncontrollable lifestyle violated the laws of his very being. That violation and misuse of his God-given powers resulted in death. It is in this sense, and this sense only, that the Lord "struck Nabal."

Rejoice today that you have life and another opportunity to live, think, and act properly for the Lord. Put your praise in writing, and it will have a positive impact on your whole being.

Under Whose Control?

Now the man's name was Nabal, and his wife's name was Abigail. And the woman was intelligent and beautiful in appearance, but the man was harsh and evil in his dealings, and he was a Calebite. 1 Sam. 25:3, NASB.

The name Abigail in Hebrew means "father is rejoicing," and in the Greek, "source," or "cause of delight." It was a most fitting name for the woman portrayed in 1 Samuel 25. What a contrast we see in her name and her life to that of her husband. David had planned to destroy Nabal (whose name means "fool") and his clan for the rude treatment the future king of Israel had received from them. When interceding with David, Abigail described her husband as being a "worthless man, . . . for as his name is, so is he" (1 Sam. 25:25, NASB).

Abigail's Spirit-filled life radiated through her personality. Although married to a cantankerous man, she did not allow his behavior to tarnish her character. His despotic ways could not stop her from being a tactful, peace-loving, kind, charming, courteous woman. Nor did Nabal's harsh dealings intimidate her.

Abigail knew the secret of happiness, even though outward circumstances were anything but desirable. She and the Holy Spirit were close friends, and the result was a close daily walk with God. Her intimate relationship with God exerted a powerful influence for good in her home and community throughout her life.

This incident in David's life teaches two important lessons—lessons needed in our lives today. The first appears in the marked contrast between the characters of Abigail and Nabal, a vivid illustration of what a person can become when under either the Lord's control or Satan's. Those who serve God and those who don't have character traits and personalities that are as different as lemonade is from lemon juice. Men and women filled with God's

327

Spirit inevitably develop such qualities as kindness, patience, and long-suffering. The longer and closer we walk with God, the more Godlike characteristics we develop. On the other hand, if under the influence of the evil one, the longer we live, the more we develop Satan's attributes.

The second lesson to learn is that we are all under the control of one of the two powers—Christ or Satan. Once we really understand that there is no neutral ground in life, it should drive us to our knees and the Word. We can choose to let God's Spirit guide and transform us. If we make the right choice, Abigail's experience of developing a beautiful character can be ours.

Praise God in a few words below for those individuals who, because they feared the Lord, were an influence for good in your life.

_____

_____

November 17

Things of God or Things of Men

But when Jesus turned and looked at his disciples, he rebuked Peter. "Out of my sight, Satan!" he said. "You do not have in mind the things of God, but the things of men." Mark 8:33, NIV.

Our text clearly portrays the great conflict between Christ and Satan. First of all, what Jesus said to Peter was a rebuke—a strong one for an ordained church leader. If Jesus called you Satan, how would you feel? Of course, how Jesus said it—the tone of His voice and the look on His face—is one of the keys in understanding this passage. Undoubtedly He was one of the inner circle of three—Peter, James, and John—the leading officers of the newly established church. Anything Jesus said to Peter He did not utter to hurt him. Never! Jesus' entire life, including His death and resurrection, had only one purpose—to save men and women from eternal death.

But here Jesus knew that it would require strong language spoken in the right way to awaken Peter to the real purpose of Christ's mission. To compliment the disciple or to use sweet talk at this point could be fatal.

Another point we should keep in mind is that only a prophet should and could make a true statement like this to another person. Some publicly attempt to destroy the influence of certain church leaders through verbal or written attacks. When we encounter such attacks we should always ask ourselves, "Are they prophets? Do they know by revelation the inmost soul of the people they've targeted?" Even the way that we use strong biblical or Spirit of Prophecy passages can do more harm than good if we do not keep this fact in mind.

Inspired authors had a right to say what they did, and they also said and wrote things to individuals under certain circumstances. We who are uninspired can use the principles behind such prophetic statements, but how careful, loving, and kind we should be in whatever we say or write.

Finally, why did Jesus say what He said to Peter? Jesus was attempting to prepare His disciples for the awesome events of Calvary. It was terribly painful for our Lord to talk about His coming death as a human being. He did not want to suffer and die. Peter took Jesus aside and began to rebuke Him, exclaiming, "God forbid it, Lord! This shall never happen to You" (Matt. 16:22, NASB). On the surface Peter seemed to want to protect our Lord. In reality, however, by rejecting Jesus' death he selfishly desired Him to establish a world kingdom in which he would be at least one of the vice presidents! In order to help the disciple understand His true motivation, Jesus gave him a strong rebuke. Not only did He refer to him as Satan, but He added, "You are a stumbling-block to Me; for you are not setting your mind on God's interests, but man's" (verse 23, NASB).

What about our own Christian experience? Are we able to praise our Lord for helping us to realize the purpose behind His mission?

Can we thank Him for the establishment of the kingdom of grace?

Answering God's Call

But you shall receive power when the Holy Spirit has come upon you; and you shall be My witnesses both in Jerusalem, and in all Judea and Samaria, and even to the remotest part of the earth. Acts 1:8, NASB.

Ellen Lane sat beside her husband's bed in a small rented room in Tennessee, watching him shake with the chills and fever of malaria. She kept thinking to herself, *The hall is rented, the handbills distributed, and everything has been arranged for the evangelistic effort.* Falling to her knees, she prayed, "Oh, God! What shall we do? Everything is ready, but now my husband is sick and cannot preach tonight. Please send help!"

As if hearing a voice, the message came to her mind, "Ellen, you must preach in your husband's place." Had God spoken to her? she wondered. Would she—could she—stand before the crowd and preach? Although hesitant, she knew that if God wanted her to do it, He would send the Holy Spirit to help her. And preach she did! Night after night the crowd grew larger. Through her messages the Holy Spirit touched the hearts of many, and a Seventh-day Adventist church began in that town.

Blessings never cease to flow when we are willing to answer God's call. We may feel inadequate, thinking someone else can do the job better, but when God summons He will supply our need. "As the will of man cooperates with the will of God, it becomes omnipotent. Whatever is to be done at His command may be accomplished in His strength. All His biddings are enablings" (*Christ's Object Lessons*, p. 333).

Accepting these words of assurance will give us courage for any task God may ask us to perform. God, in His love, does not expect us to employ abilities we do not possess! He has given to all of us certain talents, and if we use them effectively and faithfully, He is content. His main concern is for us to be in a state of readiness so He can bless our efforts when He assigns us a task.

Tentmakers Priscilla and Aquila accepted the Lord's call when Paul asked them to accompany him to Ephesus. They had a deep knowledge of the gospel. In Ephesus they met Apollos, who was an "eloquent" preacher and "mighty in the Scriptures." The couple could have reasoned that being humble tentmakers, they were not in a position to instruct such a powerful preacher. But when God called, "they took him aside and explained to him the way of God more accurately" (Acts 18:26, NASB).

Thank the Lord that He often uses people unrecognized by human wisdom to glorify His name. Most of us are in that category. Praise Him for using you even in a small way to advance His cause. Thank Him by recording one of your experiences in which you know the Lord worked through you.

The Attitude of Christ

Have this attitude in yourselves which was also in Christ Jesus. Phil. 2:5, NASB.

If we read this verse in its context, then we understand what type of mind or outlook on life we should have. Furthermore, it is the same attitude that Jesus had.

Paul introduces this passage by urging believers to be "of the same mind, maintaining the same love, united in spirit, intent on one purpose" (Phil. 2:2, NASB). Then he defines it by explaining, "Do nothing from selfishness or empty conceit, but with humility of mind let each of you regard one another as more important than himself" (verse 3, NASB). Jesus was so unselfish that He gave even His life to save us, considering the human race as more important than His very own human existence.

The apostle expands on this concept by saying: "Do not merely look out for your own personal interests, but also for the interests of others" (verse 4, NASB). After this he tells us to have this kind of mind or attitude because it is the way that Jesus thought and acted.

Two words summarize the mind of Christ: *unselfishness* and *humility*. Jesus is the most unselfish person who ever walked the earth. His love led Him down the ladder step by step, from being God the Son, to God the unique

God-man, to the depths of death in our place. Nothing like the Incarnation event had ever occurred before in the history of the universe. When Jesus deliberated over our salvation—whether He should come down to save us—He did not consider what was best for Himself, but rather what was best for us.

When it comes to humility, no one in heaven or earth ever humbled himself as Jesus did. Yet this humility testifies to His greatness as a human being and overwhelms us with awe. It is an attitude that every one of us desperately needs. His powerful example of unselfishness and humility makes us long to be like Him. Why not praise Him for His attitude that not only led Him to save us but can be ours for the asking?

It's Your Choice

Jesus said to him, "If you want to be perfect, go, sell what you have and give to the poor, and you will have treasure in heaven; and come, follow Me." Matt. 19:21, NKJV.

We feel it important to consider two other aspects of the story of the rich young ruler. The first is that he operated on a righteousness-by-works plan. He knew he was a lawkeeper, even if only from an outward motivation. When he asked Jesus what good thing he needed to do in order to secure eternal life, the answer Christ gave pleased him. After Jesus listed six of the seven rules dealing with our relationships with others, the young leader eagerly responded, "Well, Teacher, I have done all this and more, too, ever since I was a boy" (Matt. 19:20). We wonder if he added, "If what You say are conditions for salvation, then I am extremely proud to announce to You and Your disciples that You won't find a better candidate than me. My record of works is impeccable. There is nothing between me and perfection!"

What minister or congregation would even think of refusing church membership to him? From all appearances he was an extremely wealthy, honorable, upright, and morally pure individual. As he waited for Jesus to compliment him, he received the jolt of his life when he heard the words "One thing thou lackest." But that one thing embodied the very heart of his problem. He was a legalist! His obedience did not have as its motivation love for God or man. Unless he experienced a true conversion with the Holy Spirit controlling him, he was a lost man. Proud of his near faultless performance, he could not understand how the Lord would dare to point out any weakness in his life—after all, he had none!

A second point we must learn is that this ruler had freedom of choice. Back in 1979 at New York's Kennedy Airport ballerina Ludmila Vlasova, wife of Alexander Godunov, a former Bolshoi Ballet star who'd defected, chose to return to the U.S.S.R. rather than join her husband in the United States. Soviet officials had held her prisoner for several days. After that they escorted her to the Aeroflot terminal, but the U.S. government would not permit the plane to leave unless she made a clear decision as to whether she wanted to live in the U.S.A. or go back to her place of birth. After a lengthy interrogation she chose to return. In view of her choice, no U.S. diplomat or even the president of the United States could have or would have held her against her will. To deny her that choice would be to deny the very democratic freedoms for which our country stands.

So Jesus, Creator and Ruler of the universe, who stood in human form in front of the young man, asked him if he wanted freedom—eternal life. The young man was free to accept or reject it. Unfortunately, he turned down the offer and remained in the bondage of selfish greed and self-righteousness. Jesus "longed to see in him a humble and contrite heart, conscious of the supreme love to be given to God, and hiding its lack in the perfection of Christ" (*The Desire of Ages*, p. 519).

Praise the Lord for the choice you have made to hide yourself in His perfection. Thank Him for the freedom you enjoy in Him.

Cast Into Outer Darkness

Then the king said to the servants, "Bind him hand and foot, and cast him into the outer darkness; in that place there shall be weeping and gnashing of teeth." For many are called, but few are chosen. Matt. 22:13, 14, NASB.

Nothing is of greater importance than our eternal salvation, and since this parable has a direct bearing on our salvation, we believe it will help us spiritually to study it.

The real problem with the king's friend who came without the wedding garment is explained in another parable: the parable of the sower and the seed with the four types of soil, three of them being the wrong kind. About every problem that can inflict the human race appears in it. The wayside represents the inattentive hearer, where the soul becomes "hardened by the deceitfulness of sin" (Heb. 3:13, NASB). The friend without the wedding garment could have been in this class if he concluded that the king's clothes weren't that important. Or he could have had the experience of a stony-ground hearer, who has little depth to his Christian experience. He really had no great respect for the king and the king's word. Had he a great love for the king, he surely would have put on the wedding garment. Or he could have

332

been a thorny-ground banquet guest. His refusal to wear the king's wedding garment was because his heart soil was filled with "fleshly lusts, which wage war against the soul" (1 Peter 2:11, NASB).

All three types of bad soil have a common characteristic. They minimize sin and maximize self-desires. We concentrate on what we want, not on what God desires for us. Righteousness-by-works garments are really garments of selfishness that we have personally designed. We often today refuse Christ's wedding garment, but we do it in a very sophisticated, polite way. But the end result is that we still don't allow Christ to cover us with His righteousness. It is one thing to *say* that we are Christians, but quite another to *be* Christians.

There is no reason in heaven or earth for a person not to covet the privilege of wearing Christ's wedding garment, the righteousness of Christ, or the putting on of Christ. If we put on Christ we have every reason to believe that we can and will be among the saved. Although Jesus makes the garments at great cost, He gives them to us free of charge. What more can He do? Can you possibly grasp our Lord's love in offering to impart His character to us? Can you comprehend His not only being willing to clothe us but also to dwell in us, as Paul declares: "Christ in you, the hope of glory" (Col. 1:27, NASB).

Jesus longs to forgive and transform us. His only desire is to keep us supremely happy by saving us from Satan! Praise Him for His love and goodness.

God's Art Gallery

The heavens are telling of the glory of God; and the firmament is declaring the work of His hands. Day to day pours forth speech, and night to night reveals knowledge. There is no speech, nor are there words; their voice is not heard. Their line has gone out through all the earth, and their utterances to the end of the world. Ps. 19:1-4, NASB.

God's universe is the book of nature, the "second Bible" for lost man. Our personal experience as we have traveled around the world has given us an overwhelming appreciation for God's revelation of Himself through nature. We thrill to see the love God displays through His handiwork.

As we look upon the mountains we consider them God's communication to man in Braille and the heavens as His voice. No display of fireworks can ever compare with the Milky Way, especially as seen in the Southern Hemisphere. From Australia to Alaska no man-made glory can compare to a night when teasing clouds play hide-and-seek with the full-faced golden moon.

Numerous night flights have given us a fantastic collection of pictures of setting suns, fields of clouds, reflecting moonlight beams, and stars scattered like diamonds across a velvet sky. Each of these paintings we have carefully stored away in the art museum of memory. If we have any doubts of God's love or existence, they vanish instantly when we take a memory-walk through the hallways of our art gallery.

If ever you become discouraged and don't know which way to turn, take a look at the sky when the moon is out and the stars are twinkling, and lift up your heart to Him in praise and gratitude. When you look at a tree, a flower, a bird, a star, a lake, let your soul spill over with gratitude and praise. You will be instantly and forever convinced that our God is great. That He lives, He rules, He guides, He sustains, and above all, that He wants to bless you.

For what scenes from nature do you praise God the most? How have they helped when you have struggled with doubt and discouragement?

_____

_____

November   23

Godliness With Contentment

But godliness actually is a means of great gain, when accompanied by contentment. 1 Tim. 6:6, NASB.

Paul in his letter to Timothy is not referring to a Laodicean apathy, but rather a restfulness and tranquillity in Jesus Christ. How many people do you meet who are really content with their position and wages? That is not to say that people should not strive to use their talents to the very best of their ability. But are they content with their lives, or are they hopelessly restless, always frustrated and seeking something else?

One day some soldiers came to John the Baptist and asked what he suggested they should do with their lives. John replied, "Do not take money from anyone by force, or accuse anyone falsely, and be content with your wages" (Luke 3:14, NASB). Long ago we observed that if you doubled the wages of some people, in a short time they would again find themselves in financial difficulty.

To have the kind of contentment we are talking about, we must separate the essential from the nonessential, a never-ending task. Our Lord was simplicity personified. Jesus wasn't driven to want what He really didn't need. He knew what was important in life and what was useless or irrelevant. One of the most thrilling things Christ could ever say about us would be what He said about Mary: "The part that Mary has chosen is best" (Luke 10:42, NEB). She knew what was most important in her life and concentrated on that.

One of the best ways to achieve godly contentment is to begin to praise God for what you have and the work that He has given you. Rather than watching others, coveting what they may have, look to Jesus Christ and thank Him for clothes to wear, a house to live in, a car to drive, food to eat. Thank God even for the weather!

A man once asked a shepherd what the weather would be like. The shepherd replied, "It will be whatever weather pleases me."

Asked for an explanation, he replied, "Sir, it shall be what weather pleases God, and what weather pleases God pleases me."

Contentment does not result by accident. It comes by design. Practice thanking the Lord for every blessing that you can think of. Do it daily. Begin now to record some of God's gifts that bring you contentment.

Jesus, Our Defender

Simon, Simon, behold, Satan has demanded permission to sift you like wheat; but I have prayed for you, that your faith may not fail; and you, when once you have turned again, strengthen your brothers. Luke 22:31, 32, NASB.

Try to imagine in your mind Jesus personally praying for Peter so that Satan could not claim him. The battle between Christ and Satan over every soul is as real as rain. Every one of us is the object of his attacks. It is a solemn thought that Satan demands permission to sift us like wheat. His whole objective, along with that of his cohorts, is to destroy us and separate us from our Saviour.

During our travels through India and other countries, we have watched individuals in the grainfields using the ancient method of winnowing grain. A man or a woman holds a round, flat tray covered with wheat. He or she tosses the grain high in the air and catches it while the wind carries the chaff away. Unfortunately, almost always a few grains of wheat will miss the tray and plunge to the ground, where birds and mice will eat it. So our enemy tosses us to and fro, hoping we will fall by the wayside to be devoured.

But we have the assurance that Christ will pray for us. What the Saviour did for Peter, He is doing for all of us. The problem was that Peter, totally oblivious to his danger, emphatically declared: "Lord, with You I am ready to go both to prison and to death!" (Luke 23:33, NASB). Jesus sadly had to inform the disciple that he would deny Him three times within a short time. During Christ's trial Peter was unprepared even to admit he knew Christ, much less to die for Him. When he came to his senses he repented, and finally the Spirit transformed his life into a powerful witness for the Lord.

What did the Lord pray for? That the disciples' faith would not fail. The Greek word translated "fail" is the root word for our English word *eclipse*. The worst possible condition a person can slip into is to have his faith eclipsed by doubt and fear.

Praise the Lord that today He is praying for you as an individual, that you will not fail. Let your mind dwell on our High Priest, who is in the heavenly sanctuary interceding by praying for us. Before you start this day, jot down your deep appreciation for Christ's concern over you.

November 25

Thanksgiving

Praise the Lord! Praise the Lord from the heavens; praise Him in the heights! Praise Him, all His angels; praise Him, all His hosts! Praise Him, sun and moon; praise Him, all stars of light! Praise Him, highest heavens, and the waters that are above the heavens! Let them praise the name of the Lord. Ps. 148:1-5, NASB.

Contrary to popular opinion, the *Mayflower* colonists had a Thanksgiving dinner fit for dieters. Archaeologists at the Massachusetts Plimoth Plantation believe the food consisted of vegetables and fruit, such as pumpkins, squash, wild onions, Jerusalem artichokes, corn, plums, cranberries, parsnips, carrots, turnips, cabbage, radishes, and beets. They may have served some wild turkey, fish, and venison, but certainly had no cranberry sauce or pumpkin pie.

The main objective of Thanksgiving is not food, although most make it that. Nor is it to be a day of fasting. According to Benjamin Franklin, the first settlers of New England were actually in a despondent mood over the struggles they had gone through during their first winter in the new land. Someone proposed that they proclaim a fast in recognition of the hardships they had endured. But then, according to the story, an old farmer spoke of their provoking heaven with their complaints. Showing that they really had much to be thankful for, he urged that instead of appointing a day of fasting, they should have a time of thanksgiving.

There is always something to be thankful for, regardless of our circumstances. The key to being thankful is to look for things to be grateful for.

We have a relative who is crippled by an extremely severe case of arthritis. It started more than 40 years ago when she was a small child. Today she can barely walk. Her hands are so damaged by it that she finds it difficult to hold a knife or fork, yet her pleasant smile and positive attitude seem to be telling the Lord and others that she is thankful for life itself. Her life has especially blessed the young people in the church where she has led youth activities for years.

Above everything, we can be thankful for Jesus Christ. Every day we should sing His praises and talk courage!

As you study the last few psalms in the Bible, you will find them filled with praise to God for His sanctuary, His mighty deeds, His greatness, and His creative power. On this Thanksgiving Day may it be a special time of praise and prayer.

Why not jot down a few things for which you are especially thankful?

There Is Health in Happiness

A joyful heart is good medicine, but a broken spirit dries up the bones. Prov. 17:22, NASB.

While in a concentration camp, Victor Frankl found himself stripped of everything he owned, including the very hair on his body. He said he learned from the experience that society can take everything from a person but one thing—the attitude one chooses to have in any given set of circumstances. We can be disgruntled, critical, or feel sorry for ourselves. On the other hand, we can avoid much distress, ill will, weariness, and even ill health if we decide to be optimistic and full of courage.

Again and again experience, and now even science, has proved that people can improve their health by altering their attitude. "Between the mind and the body there is a mysterious and wonderful relation. They react upon each other" (*Counsels on Health*, p. 122).

Norman Cousins, former editor of *Saturday Review of Literature*, came down with a serious and potentially fatal disease. When the doctors couldn't help him, he began taking the "merry heart" medicine described in our text. He secured all the humorous books that he could find and concentrated on making himself laugh. After recovering, he claimed that he had laughed himself to health!

If laughter had a positive effect on Norman Cousins' health, how about the Christian, who has additional resources, such as the quiet spirit of gratitude and praise that center on Jesus? Shouldn't he or she have even better health? If focusing on funny things was effective, wouldn't dwelling on everything that is noble, good, and pure be even more beneficial? Undoubtedly, a positive, happy attitude is a powerful coping mechanism for harmful stress.

Paul knew the power in having a good attitude when he wrote in Philippians 4:8: "And now, my friends, all that is true, all that is noble, all that is just and pure, all that is lovable and gracious, whatever is excellent and admirable—fill all your thoughts with these things" (NEB).

We all love to be in the presence of people whose happy, contented spirits give us a lift. It is sheer joy to associate with those who have outgoing and positive attitudes. Such people are a real tonic to all those they meet.

Our daughter gave us a tiny plaque with the picture of a rabbit doubled up in laughter because he sees a ladybug sitting on a leaf. The caption reads "A giggle a day keeps the glums away."

As you look in people's faces in every walk of life, many seem to reflect "a broken spirit." It is estimated that more than 40 percent of all male Americans suffer from hypertension. How much does a "broken spirit" contribute to the fact that every hour nearly 200 people in the United States have a heart attack—for many their first and last. The true Christian does not allow his heart to fail from fear, but he is happy in the Lord. He or she has many reasons to have a merry heart.

Why not choose to be happy and thankful? We have the assurance that unseen agencies walk with us, both on the mountaintops of joy and in the valleys of tribulation. Practice being happy in the Lord. Think of at least two reasons why you should be happy today, and then thank the Lord for them.

November 27

Jesus and a Joyful Attitude

These things I have spoken to you, that My joy may be in you, and that your joy may be made full. John 15:11, NASB.

Although the word "attitude" does not appear in the King James Version, the concept is certainly there. We are attracted to people with a joyful, positive attitude and repelled by those who have gloomy spirits. Christ's attitude must have been a joyful one, or people, including little children, would never have been drawn to Him.

Three important things will help cultivate a joyful attitude: (1) promoting self-development, (2) having a purpose in life, and (3) looking unto Jesus. "Our first duty toward God and our fellow beings is that of self-development" (*Counsels on Diet and Foods*, p. 15). Ellen White does not mean that we should consider ourselves number one in life. No, she means instead that we should improve our talents and abilities so that we can use them to bless others.

For you to bless the world with your life, it is important that you take time each day for spiritual, physical, mental, and social growth. Others hear the gospel best when it comes through a healthy, whole person. Christian self-development is not something we do when we have finished everything else, but is something we must schedule in each day's activities.

Gail Sheehy, author of several books, surveyed 60,000 people between the ages of 18 and 80 and personally interviewed several hundred individuals. She found that the one constant in the lives of people who enjoy a strong sense of self-worth and well-being was a dedication and devotion to some cause or purpose beyond themselves. A sense of purpose is to the mind what good health is to the body. We can choose how we will live our lives, deciding what is the most important course to pursue, only when we have a goal in life.

Feelings are not a safe criterion when measuring our religious life. Looking unto Jesus is the secret of a joyful attitude. Any potter molding a lump of clay will tell you that the key to making successful pottery is centering. Once you center the clay on the wheel, you can have control over what you will do with it. When each of us centers our life on Christ, He gives us direction.

A joyful attitude and having a definite direction to our lives require careful planning. Paul sensed this clearly when he wrote to his young friend Timothy: "Pay close attention to yourself and to your teaching" (1 Tim. 4:16, NASB). That is self-development. Then he added, "Persevere in these things" (verse 16, NASB). The idea of persevering is to have direction in life. The things the apostle urged him to persevere in had to do with centering his life on Christ.

Praise God that Jesus is the center of our lives, enabling us to develop self and have a purpose in life. He is the hub of our wheel of existence. Express your thanks to Him for His being the hub.

The Assurance of Salvation

See how great a love the Father has bestowed upon us, that we should be called children of God; and such we are. For this reason the world does not know us, because it did not know Him. 1 John 3:1, NASB.

Does John call us children of God because we have earned the title by our own good works? Do we start the Christian life *by becoming* the sons of God through the merits of Jesus Christ and then switch to remaining His sons through our own meritorious efforts? No, salvation begins and ends with Christ. Salvation is through grace by faith alone in Jesus Christ at the beginning, the middle, and the end of our Christian experience.

Only recently has our church begun to discuss our assurance of salvation. Thus the vast majority of our books and magazines have ignored the topic. As a result many in the church are confused about the certainty of their salvation.

The man had worked for the church for many years. Now retired, and seriously ill, he had requested prayer and anointing. As Bob stood beside the hospital bed, the patient told him the inner longing of his heart. While he naturally wanted to be healed, he was even more concerned about his salvation. He expressed his agony over the possibility of dying without being ready to face God. As he looked over his past life with its shortcomings and numerous failures, he wondered whether the Lord had accepted him. His voice cracked and tears began to flow as his hidden fears at last came to the surface.

Only God had a correct and intimate knowledge of his heart. But those of us who knew him could only speak words of highest praise. His lifestyle, personality, and service record recommended him as one of God's true saints. The fruits of his life were untainted with rebellion, and his loyalty to Christ and His church was unquestioned. Somehow, though, he had failed to understand a most important facet of God's great plan of salvation. But he was not alone—countless others struggle with the same question.

In our own lives we have discussed this subject numerous times. The Holy Spirit has impressed us that the assurance of salvation is a truth that needs to be handled properly and with care. We can and must have such assurance, and we praise God for it in our own experience.

Has the Holy Spirit brought confidence in your salvation to your heart? Why not ask for Him to strengthen your confidence in His desire and ability to redeem you?

November 29

Children of God

The Spirit Himself bears witness with our spirit that we are children of God, and if children, heirs also, heirs of God and fellow heirs with Christ, if indeed we suffer with Him in order that we may also be glorified with Him. Rom. 8:16, 17, NASB.

Once more we ask the question "Are we the children of God because of our own meritorious works?"

"Never!" you instantly reply.

But does that mean that we do not attempt to obey His commandments? Again, never! If we understand the assurance of salvation correctly, we will find ourselves irresistibly compelled to greater surrender and obedience to Him.

We sing the song "Just as I Am." But do we really believe that when we come to Christ, we then have the assurance of salvation? Or does a nagging fear linger that we must reach a certain standard of obedience before we have that assurance? If the latter, then how can we ever have any real assurance, for we can never know just how far we must climb the ladder of obedience and perfection.

We have mentioned John Wesley's experience before, but it might be helpful to expand on it more. Ellen White summarizes it beautifully in *The Great Controversy*, pages 255 and 256. Wesley's encounter with German Moravians aboard a ship during a violent storm left a great impression on his mind. They faced the storm with serenity, while Wesley and others feared for their lives. Mystified, Wesley later asked a Moravian if he had been afraid. The simple reply was, "I thank God, no." Wesley then asked about the women and children. The answer: "Our women and children are not afraid to die."

Only after his return to England did he clearly understand that he must renounce "all dependence upon his own good works for salvation and must trust wholly to 'the Lamb of God, which taketh away the sin of the world.' " During this time he attended a Moravian meeting and found his heart strangely warmed. He finally reached the point where he felt that he really did trust Christ and Christ alone for salvation. The Holy Spirit gave him assurance that the Lord had taken away his sins and had saved him from the law of sin and death.

"Through long years of wearisome and comfortless striving, years of rigorous self-denial, of reproach and humiliation, Wesley had steadfastly adhered to his one purpose of seeking God." Although he had scrupulously obeyed every ray of light that came to him, they were still "long years of wearisome and comfortless striving." But Wesley's profound conversion experience brought a great change. "Now he had found Him [God]; and he found that the grace which he had toiled to win by prayers and fasts, by almsdeeds and self-abnegation, was a gift, 'without money and without price.' "

Please understand that all your obedience and all your humbling of yourself every minute of every day will not merit salvation. You are the child of God through the merits of His Son alone, the Lord Jesus Christ.

Express your thanks to God for His priceless Gift, who alone brings the assurance of salvation.

Lord, Save Me

And He said, "Come!" And Peter got out of the boat and walked on the water and came toward Jesus. But seeing the wind, he became afraid, and beginning to sink, he cried out, saying, "Lord, save me!" Matt. 14:29, 30, NASB.

Peter was confident that Jesus could make it possible for him to walk on water. He stepped out of that boat and started walking toward Jesus. But then he let his own strength, his own willpower, and trust in himself get in the way. And he became afraid when he suddenly realized that his own accomplishments were insufficient to keep him on top of the water.

The story teaches us that we must keep our eyes on Jesus and trust Him for salvation. If in any way we depend on our spiritual performance to recommend us to God, the stormy winds of uncertainty will sweep away our assurance of salvation in Christ and Him alone.

Wesley's experience reveals two important points. He realized that the merits of Christ alone constituted the grounds and root of his assurance. Nothing he said or did could ever provide him salvation. For us to think otherwise steals from Christ the glory that is His for saving us.

But there is a second aspect to consider, and here professed Christians can easily get tripped up. After Wesley's conversion he continued his strict and self-denying life, but now it was the "*fruit* of holiness. The grace of God in Christ is the foundation of the Christian's hope, and that grace will be manifested in obedience" (*The Great Controversy*, p. 256). Even Wesley's strict lifestyle was a gift from God.

"You will know them by their fruits" (Matt. 7:20, NASB). What is the fruit of depending on Christ's righteousness for our assurance of salvation? If it is more devotion, greater spirituality, more faithful obedience, and more sacrificial giving, we may be sure that we have correctly understood and appropriated the righteousness that comes solely by faith. But if it is carelessness in spiritual things, self-confidence, and laxness in obeying God's will, then we may be equally sure that we have failed to understand the righteousness that is by faith. By presumption we have slipped into unrighteousness. Properly understanding this subject of righteousness by faith, we believe, will produce a latter-rain revival and reformation in our midst greater than our church has ever experienced. With our assurance of salvation established solely on the merits of Christ we will be motivated to live like Jesus, and our souls—like Wesley's soul—will burn with the desire to carry the glorious gospel of God's free grace to everyone.

The central core of our message is to "behold the Lamb of God, which taketh away the sin of the world" (John 1:29). Let our crucified, risen, and ministering Saviour in the sanctuary be the center of our attention, our hopes, and our desires.

Praise God for His complete salvation and the assurance we can have in Him.

"Son of God, Where Are You?"

And it will be said in that day, "Behold, this is our God for whom we have waited that He might save us. This is the Lord for whom we have waited; let us rejoice and be glad in His salvation." Isa. 25:9, NASB.

Only the Christian faith, as far as we know, has the unique belief of a Saviour-God who will return to earth to take His people home with Himself. The Creation story portrays God's first visit to our planet, when He formed it, and our first parents. Sin created an invisible barrier between God and man, and ever since that day those who serve the Lord have looked wistfully heavenward for His return.

Genealogies are usually boring, but there is one that is absolutely thrilling in its climax. It reads: "the son of Enosh, the son of Seth, the son of Adam, the son of God" (Luke 3:38). "Son of God"—it is hard to believe that we are the literal actual offspring of God by creation. From that moment when Adam sprang to his feet and stood erect before his Maker, an intense, intimate relationship between them began. God had intended that the union between Him and the first couple would never cease. But tragically "Son of God" degenerated to the three sad words "Where are you?" (Gen. 3:9). To our minds, the terrible day when God cried out "Where are you?" was overshadowed only by the Friday of Jesus' crucifixion. It was the beginning of a long separation between the Lord and His people that was both spiritual and physical as the personal, face-to-face relationship shattered. We thank God that Jesus' blood healed the broken spiritual relationship. But people still wait for the physical reunion.

It should stir our souls to their very foundations at the thought of a soon-coming day when the physical separation between Jesus and us will end and we will be in His presence face-to-face. Our emotions almost overwhelm us when we sing "Face to face with Christ my Saviour, face to face, what will it be, when with rapture I behold Him, Jesus Christ, who died for me?" (*The SDA Hymnal*, No. 206).

We praise the Lord with ever-growing excitement as we anticipate that moment when we shall join the mighty chorus of voices around the earth who will cry out, "This is the Lord for whom we have waited; let us rejoice and be glad in His salvation." We know this is what you are longing for too. Please describe how you feel as you await His return.

343

"And He Died"

So all the days that Adam lived were nine hundred and thirty years, and he died. Gen. 5:5, NASB.

In yesterday's reading we noted two sets of three words each, "Son of God" and "Where are you?" The first set climaxed Luke's genealogy of Christ, revealing that Adam was the son of God. The second set dealt with God's searching for Adam and Eve as they hid from Him in the Garden of Eden. We now come to the conclusion of Adam's life. Adam had brilliantly started out as "son of God" with Eve, then a short time later after sinning heard God's cry, "Where are you?" and now nearly 1,000 years later we read in the Genesis 5 obituary list, "and he died." This is the true meaning of evolution in the Scriptures. Since the entrance of sin, life evolves downward, not upward.

We believe that Adam and Eve had the saddest experience of any couple on earth. They lived through numerous generations of people and witnessed sin expand like a torrent of water to cover the earth. Many of us as parents have observed wrong traits develop in our children that are carbon copies of our own. It tears our hearts out. Sin exploded through the human race. It started with Cain, the child over whom Eve exclaimed at his birth, "I have gotten a man, the Lord" (see Gen. 4:1, margin, NASB).

Remembering the Genesis 3:15 promise that a Deliverer would come, Adam and Eve "joyfully welcomed their firstborn son, hoping that he might be the Deliverer" (*The Desire of Ages*, p. 31). They little realized what sorrow lay ahead for them when the one whom they thought might become their Saviour-son would become a slayer-son instead. From the day of that murder on, every night that Adam and Eve went to their rest they undoubtedly talked about the terrible results of their disobedience as they witnessed it in their children, grandchildren, great-grandchildren, and each succeeding generation.

For nearly a millennium they anxiously looked forward to a coming Redeemer when at last they would be reunited with their Creator. But before any reunion could take place, their Creator would humble Himself and come as the Second Adam, an incarnation the first Adam never saw. Someday, however, not too far off, the first Adam will witness the Second Adam approaching in heaven's cloud-filled skies. Adam and Eve sincerely repented of their sin, and "they believed the precious promise of God, and were saved from utter ruin" (*The Seventh-day Adventist Bible Commentary*, Ellen G. White Comments, vol. 1, p. 1084).

We rejoice over the thought that someday not far distant we shall see the first Adam meet the Second Adam. Live for that day that Adam and Eve longed for—the coming of Jesus. Get cemented to Christ through praise, prayer, and Bible study. Every night when you go to bed, let your last thoughts be *Come, Lord Jesus; please come quickly. We want to go home with You.* Write out how you feel about wanting Him to return.

Seeing Jesus

Take now your son, your only son, whom you love, Isaac, and go to the land of Moriah; and offer him there as a burnt offering. Gen. 22:2, NASB. "Your father Abraham rejoiced to see My day; and he saw it, and was glad." John 8:56, NASB.

It was early in the morning when Abraham saddled his donkey and took two young men, some split wood for the burnt offering, and his most precious son of promise, Isaac, and started off on a three-day journey to a place where God had ordered him to go. What Abraham experienced in those three days was far worse than what Jonah went through during his three days in the stomach of a great fish.

God's command repeatedly ran through Abraham's mind: "Take your son, your son of promise, and offer him as a burnt offering." Abraham went through a Gethsemane experience. His sleepless nights he spent in prayer pleading with God to take the bitter cup from him. Isaac and the two young friends were mystified over his father's behavior. The son did not know until they reached the place of sacrifice that he was to be the offering.

If you are a parent, try to put yourself in Abraham's shoes, and if a child, imagine you are in Isaac's place. Abraham had told the servants to stay behind, but his faith never faltered even at this point. He said, "I and the lad will go yonder, and we will worship and return to you" (verse 5, NASB). Note the words "we will worship and return to you."

The record of the conversation between Abraham and Isaac stands as a monument of tenderness and overwhelming emotion. Isaac speaks: "My father!"

The father replies, "Here I am, my son."

The younger man continues, "Behold, the fire and the wood, but where is the lamb for the burnt offering?"

Brokenhearted, Abraham struggles to come up with an answer. Finally, by faith alone, he replies, "God will provide for Himself the lamb for the burnt offering, my son." So the two of them walk on together (Gen. 22:7, 8, NASB).

They build the altar, Abraham arranges the wood with the help of Isaac, and then comes the terrible moment of truth when the father tells his son of promise—the son he had waited for a century—what God has ordered him to do.

Can you imagine Isaac's feelings? "Me, I am to be sacrificed by my own father—no—how can it be? How could God give such a cruel command!" We

345

know for certain that Isaac surrendered his will and obeyed, since he could have easily overpowered his elderly father.

The sacrifice of the ram caught in a thicket instead of Isaac climaxes this story of stories. Abraham and Isaac had a greater understanding than any other human being of the agony that God the Father and Jesus went through to save the human race. As he stood on Mount Moriah, "Abraham learned of God the greatest lesson ever given to mortal. His prayer that he might see Christ before he should die was answered. He saw Christ; he saw all that mortal can see, and live" (*The Desire of Ages*, p. 469).

We rejoice over people of faith like Abraham and Isaac. Their experiences make us love Jesus more and more for being the lamb Himself. Join us in praising His wonderful name.

December 4

Not a Dull Dogma!

And I saw heaven opened; and behold, a white horse, and He who sat upon it is called Faithful and True; and in righteousness He judges and wages war. And His eyes are a flame of fire, and upon His head are many diadems. . . . And on His robe and on His thigh He has a name written, "KING OF KINGS AND LORD OF LORDS." Rev. 19:11-16, NASB.

We concur with the English author Dorothy L. Sayers, who once stated, "We are constantly assured that the churches are empty because preachers insist too much upon doctrine—'dull dogma,' as people call it. The fact is the precise opposite. It is the neglect of dogma that makes for dullness. The Christian faith is the most exciting drama that has ever staggered the imagination of man—and the dogma is the drama."

The greatest event in all history will soon take place, and it involves the doctrine—the dogma—of the second coming of Jesus. Our text is a fabulous description of Jesus with fiery eyes sitting on a white horse, His robe inscribed with the omnipotent name KING OF KINGS AND LORD OF LORDS. Here we have no dull dogma—rather, that scene is the most electrifying picture human eyes will ever behold. When we see Jesus come, the sight and sound of it will brand itself on our minds for eternity!

Jesus said, "Abraham rejoiced to see My day; and he saw it, and was glad" (John 8:56, NASB). When the Lord promised Abraham that through his descendants all the nations on earth would be blessed, He was specifically referring to His first advent as the Messiah and His return as King of kings. Christ was *the seed* of Abraham above all others.

But when Abraham saw the crucified Christ through the offering of Isaac, he also saw the return of Christ. The cross guarantees the second advent of

Jesus. Christ's death would be utterly pointless if He doesn't come again. As Paul stated so clearly: "If we have hoped in Christ in this life only, we are of all men most to be pitied" (1 Cor. 15:19, NASB). Should you ever wonder whether Christ will return, think back to His first advent and ask yourself, "Why would He come the first time if He isn't going to complete His mission?" The answer will obviously strengthen your faith.

Moses, like Abraham, predicted the coming of a Messiah. "The Lord your God will raise up for you a prophet like me from among you, from your countrymen, you shall listen to him" (Deut. 18:15, NASB). Jesus testified to the fulfillment of Moses' prophecy when He said, "For if you believed Moses, you would believe Me; for he wrote of Me" (John 5:46, NASB).

"Mommy," a little one confided at bedtime while talking about Jesus, "I'm so lonely for my Friend Jesus. When is He going to come?" It was the heart cry of Abraham and Moses, and still is of all the rest of us who love Him. Our lives would be bleak without the blessed hope.

Thank You, Jesus, for the hope of Your soon return. I look for Your return because

_____

_____

December 5

King David and the Coming of King Jesus

When your days are complete and you lie down with your fathers, I will raise up your descendant after you, who will come forth from you, and I will establish his kingdom. . . . And your house and your kingdom shall endure before Me forever; your throne shall be established forever. 2 Sam. 7:12-16, NASB.

At the Lord's direction the prophet Nathan spoke these words to King David. The prophet had in mind David's son Solomon. But the concept of David's throne enduring forever ultimately refers to the eternal kingdom of glory God will establish when King Jesus returns. This illustration of a historical event in which the actual kingdom of David and Solomon became a model or pattern of God's future kingdom of grace and glory is a beautiful example of biblical typology. The theme of the marvelous consummation of the ages is not a new belief but is as old as Adam. Abraham, Moses, Noah, David, and a host of others were Adventists in a very definite sense of the word.

Many of the psalms powerfully refer to the coming of the Lord in spectacular glory. Just one example: "The Lord is at thy right hand; He will shatter kings in the day of His wrath. He will judge among the nations" (Ps. 110:5, NASB).

Isaiah, speaking of the Messiah's first coming, proclaims, "Therefore the Lord Himself will give you a sign: Behold, a virgin will be with child and bear a son, and she will call His name Immanuel" (Isa. 7:14, NASB). Then, after referring to Jesus as the Wonderful Counselor and Mighty God, he states, "There will be no end to the increase of His government or of peace, on the throne of David and over his kingdom, to establish it and to uphold it with justice and righteousness from then on and forevermore" (Isa. 9:7, NASB). This mixing of the first and second advents of Jesus is similar to Christ's intermingling of the destruction of Jerusalem and the end of the world in Matthew 24.

When King Jesus arrives, can you possibly imagine how thrilled David and Isaiah will be? We rejoice in the hope of the second coming of Christ that is so prominent in both the Old and New Testaments.

December 6

Destruction and Restoration

Shout for joy, O daughter of Zion! Shout in triumph, O Israel! Rejoice and exult with all your heart, O daughter of Jerusalem! . . . The King of Israel, the Lord, is in your midst; you will fear disaster no more. Zeph. 3:14, 15, NASB.

"I live from one deliverance experience to another," someone has said, "and the space between them can be measured in minutes! I seem to live either in the frying pan or the fire. When will it all end?" Unfortunately, we cannot permanently escape life's difficulties until either death or translation, when Jesus returns. We could compare the Christian life to a classical music station broadcasting in a never-ending storm of lightning and thunder. We hear only snatches of music between the static. But we can rejoice and exult with our whole heart that eternity is almost here!

Zephaniah, a relative of King Hezekiah, wrote our text today. His tiny three-chapter book forecasts the terrible events to befall Judah and Jerusalem during the repeated invasions of the Babylonian Empire. He calls his prophecies of doom "the great day of the Lord." They have an application to our time just before Jesus returns. But Zephaniah presents not only destruction but also restoration.

It is the element of restoration that gives us the courage and stamina to hope, believe, and live for the Soon Coming. "The Lord your God is in your midst, a victorious warrior. He will exult over you with joy" (Zeph. 3:17, NASB). God is with us and ecstatic over us!

He weeps when you weep, and He rejoices when you rejoice. And this same wonderful God is coming to our world. Nothing can equal the sustaining power in our lives of the hope of His soon return. Phoebe Cary said it beautifully: "One sweetly solemn thought comes to me over and over; I am nearer home today than I ever have been before."

The Old Testament writers only dimly understood the concept of the consummation of the ages, but multitudes of God's children lived and died hoping to see the Messiah. As the centuries passed, humanity scarred old Mother Earth with the graves of billions, but those faithful who died breathed their last knowing that someday Jesus would settle the conflict between good and evil. That day is not far distant.

Strengthen your faith by writing out a testimony of your confidence and assurance of His soon coming.

Be on the Alert

Therefore be on the alert, for you do not know which day your Lord is coming. Matt. 24:42, NASB.

The attack on Pearl Harbor 52 years ago today still teaches us important lessons. Articles and books continue to point out the seemingly unimportant details that joined together to produce disaster for our forces in Hawaii. Neither government or military leaders in Hawaii were prepared for this sudden event. Even though radar and other warnings indicated an attack was imminent, they were ignored. The evening before the attack many of the military top brass had gone to a party, little realizing the danger.

As we ponder the return of our Lord Jesus Christ, we see significant parallels between the events of Pearl Harbor and the Second Coming. The element of unpreparedness looms especially large on the prophetic horizon. New Testament writers give as one of the signs of the end certain widespread character traits—dissipation, drunkenness, anxiety, greed, lack of self-control, treachery, brutality, boastfulness, lawlessness, and abusiveness. They are the inevitable result of turning one's back on God. Those who continue to ignore Him will have the shock of their lives when Christ returns. Even those who have been preparing for this great event will be surprised when it takes place.

Jesus makes it clear that no one—not even the angels—knows the day or the hour of His return, only the Father. To emphasize the element of surprise, He compares the time of the Second Coming to the days before the Flood, when people went about their lives as usual, eating, drinking, marrying, and all the other daily routines. Even when Noah entered the ark, the record states, "They did not understand until the flood came and took them all away; so shall the coming of the Son of Man be" (Matt. 24:39, NASB).

349

All those in Noah's day knew that when the lightning and thunder burst across the sky and rain started that the flood he had warned them about had at last arrived. But what they had not known was when it would begin. So with our Lord's return.

Jesus reemphasizes this point with another illustration in verses 43 and 44. Robbers were constantly breaking into homes. What the home owner could not know was when the thief might strike his house. "For this reason you be ready too; for the Son of Man is coming at an hour when you do not think He will" (NASB).

One other important factor to remember is that we also do not know the moment of our death. The Lord, in a very definite sense, comes for those who die before He actually returns. No, He is not taking their souls back to heaven, but rather they will sleep in the grave, totally unconscious of time, until He returns. Thus our last heartbeat will instantly, in terms of experience, place us at the point of our Lord's second coming, and we must be always ready for that possibility.

We have a precious privilege and tremendous responsibility to share the good news of the gospel in such a way that men and women will willingly and eagerly prepare to meet Jesus in peace when He returns. Are you prepared for His return?

December 8

Right on Time

But when the fulness of the time came, God sent forth His Son, born of a woman, born under the Law. Gal. 4:4, NASB.

As days turned into months, and months into years, and years into millenniums after Adam and Eve had their last face-to-face conversation with Jesus, many of God's people exclaimed as they struggled to await the Messiah's arrival, "The days are long and every vision fails" (Eze. 12:22, NASB). So today some ask in frustration, "When will Jesus return?" Those of us reared in the church probably never expected to live this long without seeing the Lord's return. When we entered the ministry, we believed Jesus would return quickly. Our only objective was to prepare people to meet Him in peace.

Our text today is one of reassurance. When the time had been reached for the appearance of Jesus as Messiah (as foretold by the 70 weeks of years prophecy in Daniel 9), our Lord came. While we have no specific prophecy in Scripture that reveals the time of His second appearance, we can know when it is near, "right at the door" (Matt. 24:33, NASB). We can easily hear the sound of His approaching footsteps.

Expectations of the first coming of Jesus gradually increased during Old Testament times. When the moment arrived for Jesus' birth in Bethlehem, a few faithful people were intensely anticipating the Messiah's arrival. Among them was an aged and pious man named Simeon. Although not a priest, he had studied the Old Testament prophecies carefully, enabling the Holy Spirit to perform a special work in his and our behalf. We say "our" because it strengthens our confidence in the soon coming of Jesus. Dr. Luke describes the incident beautifully. "And behold, there was a man in Jerusalem whose name was Simeon; and this man was righteous and devout, looking for the consolation of Israel; and the Holy Spirit was upon him" (Luke 2:25, NASB).

We need to ask ourselves, "Am I also a devout, Spirit-filled person looking for Jesus to come soon?"

When Simeon saw Jesus' family, clothed in poverty, presenting their firstborn son to the priest, the Spirit came upon him. He took the infant Jesus in his arms, lifted his eyes toward heaven, pronounced a blessing, and said, "Now Lord, Thou dost let Thy bondservant depart in peace, according to Thy word" (Luke 2:29, NASB).

Let heaven rejoice over our joy in Jesus' first and second comings. He will return soon! Praise His name today for that blessed hope.

Sanctuary or Snare?

And Simeon blessed them, and said to Mary His mother, "Behold, this Child is appointed for the fall and rise of many in Israel, and for a sign to be opposed." Luke 2:34, NASB.

As mentioned yesterday, the Holy Spirit led Simeon, an ordinary person "looking for the consolation of Israel" (the advent of the Messiah) into the Temple, where he would take Jesus in his arms and make a Spirit-inspired pronouncement. Although the attending priest did not recognize Jesus as God's Son, Simeon did.

When the priest went home that day and his wife asked him how things had gone in the Temple, he probably yawned and replied, "Nothing unusual, dear. I officiated over six babies and their presentation in the Temple. However, there was one odd happening. Some old fellow came up to us during the dedication of the child of one poor couple. The man took this little fellow and cradled him in his arms and began to say some very strange things. First, he said he could now die in peace, for his eyes had seen God's salvation. I thought that a bit unusual. The baby he was holding didn't look any different than any of the others I've dedicated."

"Did this old man say anything else?" the priest's wife asked.

351

"Oh yes, a lot more. He called the infant 'a light, a revelation to the Gentiles, and the glory of God's people, Israel' (see verses 29-32, NASB). Can you imagine talking about a baby's being a blessing to both Jews and Gentiles? That's ridiculous, for God does not care for the Gentiles any more than we Jews do."

"Is that all he said?" the wife continued. "How did the parents respond?"

"Well, his father and mother were amazed at what the old man was saying about the child" (see verse 33).

"Is that all?"

"No. This fellow began to say some real weird things I don't understand at all. He told the mother that her child had been appointed for the fall and rise of many in Israel and for a sign to be opposed. I just don't understand what he meant—it's a mystery to me."

It would not have been a mystery had the priest been a diligent student of the Word. He would have known that, according to Isaiah, the people would see the coming of the Messiah either as a blessing or a curse. To some, Jesus would "become a sanctuary" and to others, "a stone to strike and a rock to stumble over, and a snare and a trap for the inhabitants of Jerusalem. And many will stumble over them. Then they will fall and be broken; they will even be snared and caught" (Isa. 8:14, 15, NASB). Jesus is either a sanctuary or a snare.

Let Christ be your sanctuary! Thank Him for His first advent and for the promise of His return.

December 10

The Piercing Sword

And a sword will pierce even your own soul—to the end that thoughts from many hearts may be revealed. Luke 2:35, NASB.

After Simeon spoke these words to Mary, try to imagine the conversation at her and Joseph's table that evening.

"Joseph, did you understand what Simeon meant about a sword piercing me? Was he talking about a coming war in Palestine where I will be killed?" Mary might have asked.

"My dear, it puzzled me, too. First, Simeon seemed so thrilled over holding our Son, Jesus. He spoke of our Boy being a light to both Jews and Gentiles. The old man even said that Jesus would be the glory of God's people Israel. Finally he mentioned this sword business. The word he used for sword means a long javelin or saber. That really mystifies me."

Poor Mary never understood until she stood at the foot of the cross. When the Roman soldier thrust the javelin into the side of Jesus, it went through her heart as well. Here was her Son, an obedient boy who had never done anything wrong and whose life had blessed multitudes, now dying as a criminal. She could have turned bitter against both Rome and her people, but she didn't. Her dying Son set her an example by asking His Father's forgiveness for His persecutors.

Mary had been blessed above all other women, for she had had the privilege of bearing to the world the incarnate God the Son. She was the human mother of "the Son of the Highest." In humility she had accepted the honor. From that moment until the cross, Mary knew that her Son was special.

The last biblical record of Mary appears in Acts 1:14, which records her presence in the upper room with the disciples prior to Pentecost. Undoubtedly she had been with the group who stood gazing into the skies when a cloud hid Jesus from their sight as He ascended to heaven. We wonder if Jesus didn't have something to say to her then. Perhaps He said, "Be faithful, Mother; I will return. Someday you will be with Me forever." The wound in her soul was now healed. She died a good Adventist, knowing for certain that her Son would return and she would come forth in the resurrection.

This hope is ours today. Let your heart ring with thoughts of praise over His second coming. Write a few words down to make His coming real.

_____

_____

She Never Left the Temple

And at that very moment she came up and began giving thanks to God, and continued to speak of Him to all those who were looking for the redemption of Jerusalem. Luke 2:38, NASB.

We have shared with you the story of Simeon blessing Jesus and His parents in the Temple. While he was prophesying, under the Spirit's direction, of the sword that would pierce Mary's heart, someone else entered the scene. A prophetess and well advanced in years, her name was Anna. If you study Luke 2:36 and 37 carefully, you will probably conclude that she was more than 100 years of age. The record states, "She never left the temple, serving night and day with fasting and prayers" (verse 37, NASB). The priests probably assigned her a room in which to stay.

"At that very moment" while Simeon was uttering his prophetic words, Anna joined them and "began giving thanks to God." She was praising the Lord, along with Simeon, for the privilege of seeing the infant Jesus, the long-looked-for and hoped-for Messiah! Had we the same dedication she had, we too would be joyfully praising God. Try to experience what it must have been like for both Simeon and Anna to know and believe, as they looked into the peaceful, beautiful face of the infant child, that He was the Messiah, the

Redeemer that humanity had waited thousands of years for! How long Anna lived afterward we do not know, but probably not too long. But if this was the only time she gazed on the face of Jesus, she died knowing that she would see it again, not as a baby, but as a coming King.

Every one of us can have that same hope. We, along with Simeon, Anna, and a multitude of others, will see Jesus returning in the clouds of heaven as the King of the universe. He came the first time to prepare the world through the preaching of the gospel so that He could later return and take us home to Himself. We, like Anna, can continue "to speak of Him to all those" who will listen and who long for the redemption not only of Jerusalem but of the entire world.

Praise Him for His love, redemption, and promise to return.

December 12

Jesus' Testimony on His Own Return

And the high priest said to Him, "I adjure You by the living God, that You tell us whether You are the Christ, the Son of God." Jesus said to him, "You have said it yourself; nevertheless I tell you, hereafter you shall see the Son of Man sitting at the right hand of power, and coming on the clouds of heaven." Matt. 26:63, 64, NASB.

In our text today Jesus spoke under oath to Caiaphas, the high priest in Jerusalem. Both Caiaphas and his father-in-law, Annas, the former high priest, were determined to have Jesus killed, and unfortunately they were successful. To be in the shoes of either one of them when Jesus comes would be a terrible experience. Contrary to Jewish law, Caiaphas put Jesus under oath in an attempt to get Him to incriminate Himself. But regardless of the oath's illegality, Jesus knew He had to answer. Although given under most unpleasant circumstances, His response is a ringing affirmation of His promise in John 14:1-3 that if He went back to heaven to prepare a place for us, He would come again! Now He tells His accusers and murderers that in the future they would see Him, the Son of man, sitting at the right hand of God in heaven's clouds.

When Jesus assured the two priests that they would see Him when He returned, it made His promise to come even stronger. Christ arrives as King and Saviour to those who truly love Him, but as a Judge to those who have disobeyed and rebelled against Him. We want to live as though Jesus died for us yesterday, rose this morning, and will return tomorrow. To do otherwise will lead only to spiritual complacency or indifference.

Jesus left no doubt about His return at the Last Supper. "But I say to you, I will not drink of this fruit of the vine from now on until that day when I drink it new with you in my Father's kingdom" (Matt. 26:29, NASB). He clearly taught His second advent in many parables, such as the one about the tares, or weeds, growing among the wheat. It is at the end of the world during the harvest when God's harvesters burn the tares and save the wheat. Elsewhere the wicked husbandman will be dealt with when the owner of the vineyard, Jesus, returns. The ten virgins and the sheep and goats parables all refer to the coming of Jesus. The Second Advent saturates all of His teachings.

Again we praise Him for His promises of His return. Our confidence is stronger than ever in the truth that soon we shall see Him face-to-face. Do you feel the same way?

December   13

God's Kindness Shown to Elijah

But he himself went a day's journey into the wilderness, and came and sat down under a juniper tree; and he requested for himself that he might die, and said, "It is enough; now, O Lord, take my life, for I am not better than my fathers." 1 Kings 19:4, NASB.

Have you ever felt that you wanted to die? Have you ever prayed for death? Elijah, the greatest prophet to the northern kingdom, begged for exactly that. Once he had fearlessly stood before wicked King Ahab and predicted a drought for the entire country at a time when everything was green and beautiful.

Then, after three and a half painful years—when the searing heat of the sun had baked man, beast, and crops—Elijah returned to summon the godless people to meet him on Mount Carmel. There he had stood alone against not only the prophets of Baal but also the entire nation. He had surveyed the emaciated bodies of men, women, and children who had suffered needlessly. Through the power of God he had brought fire from heaven. A cloudburst had flooded the countryside, vindicating him. Then when he had been emotionally drained, Queen Jezebel sent Elijah a death threat. It was more than he could take. The prophet was not superhuman, but a man "subject to like passions as we are" (James 5:17). Depression seized him, he fled, and finally he collapsed in sheer exhaustion.

He made a mistake by not trusting God, but how did the Lord handle the situation? Did He castigate Elijah? Did He start preaching at him for his lack of faith? Absolutely not! Rather, God sent an angel with a specially prepared meal. The angel gently touched him and with a lovely voice said, "Arise, eat." Elijah did, and fell back into his exhausted sleep again. A second time the angel awakened him and invited him to another delicious meal. That kindness and food strengthened Elijah so he could hike the 40 days and nights to Mount Horeb, where he found refuge in a cave.

We serve a wonderful, thoughtful God. Praise Him for His concern about not only our spiritual needs but our physical ones as well. Join us in expressing adoration to Him. _____

Happiness in the Lord

Happy are you, O Israel! Who is like you, a people saved by the Lord, the shield of your help and the sword of your majesty! Your enemies shall submit to you, and you shall tread down their high places. Deut. 33:29, NKJV.

These are the last words of Moses' final blessing on Israel before he climbed Mount Nebo to die. The words "happy" and "blessed" are interchangeable. What constitutes happiness? It is no secret that everyone on earth searches for it. Dr. Albert Schweitzer, the famed clergyman, philosopher, physician, missionary, and music scholar, made a brief but true statement about being happy. "Happiness," he said, "is nothing more than good health and a poor memory." When we first heard this, we thought we ought to be about the happiest couple on earth, since we both have good health and not-so-good memories—especially for names!

Life is not easy, and the older you get the less easy life seems to be—at least for some. One prominent preacher was so convinced that people have greater problems after 50 years of age that he claimed that if he were president of the United States he would give every person older than 50 and still out of jail a Purple Heart. Of course, this is an extreme position and even ridiculous, for the fabulous 50s and the soaring 60s can be the greatest years of our lives!

When the Battle of Waterloo ended on that historic June day in 1815, British officers wanted to find out just what happened. They interviewed a number of soldiers who had participated in the decisive struggle against Napoleon. One soldier in the infantry said, "Don't ask me, for I know nothing about the matter, since I was all day trodden in the mud and ridden over by every scoundrel who had a horse."

So it is with most of us. Life is a real earthly battle in the mud! Great things may be happening around us, even though we may not realize it. We may receive little glory in the present struggle, but that does not matter. We are blessed and happy, for the Lord loves and has saved us, and we are contributing to His final and ultimate victory. He is our shield of help and the sword of our majesty.

The way to really feel happy is to share it. Tell how you feel happy in the Lord. To your surprise, you will feel even more joyous than you did before.

The Day Is Coming!

"For behold, the day is coming, burning like a furnace; and all the arrogant and every evildoer will be chaff; and the day that is coming will set them ablaze," says the Lord of hosts, "so that it will leave them neither root nor branch." Mal. 4:1, NASB.

Our text comes from the last chapter of the Old Testament. The coming of Jesus with a renewed earth ends the Old Testament. Please remember that you do not have to be in this group of arrogant evildoers. The Lord, through Malachi, is using what you might call negative encouragement. God wants to motivate us toward life, not death. But more than that, this passage assures us that heaven is a place free from harassment or anything else that can possibly cause one second of stress.

At the moment it is impossible for us to grasp what it will be like to live forever in an environment where we have nothing to fear, whether disease, death, accident, or assault. There will be nothing that degrades, nothing that destroys, nothing that corrupts. In fact, the Lord through Malachi promises that the saved will walk on the ashes of all that was evil. No longer will the innocent suffer. No longer will God's children be the object of Satan's wrath. We shall flourish in a place called the new earth that is utterly purified and restored to the condition it was prior to the great struggle between sin and righteousness.

Just after World War II Marie's brother-in-law who worked at the Newport News Ship Building Company took us to see the restoration of one of the largest passenger ships that our country had ever built up to that time, the S.S. *America*. During the war the government had borrowed the vessel and stripped it of all of its luxurious furnishings, carefully putting them in storage. Then it was converted into a troop ship carrying thousands of soldiers back and forth between Europe and the United States. Now every detail, including rugs, mirrors, chairs, drapes, lamps, was all carefully being put back exactly as it had been originally.

So with our world. Every tree, flower, lake, hill—all will be restored. Even the tree of life, carefully preserved in heaven for thousands of years, God will place back on our world. In addition He will add some extra things, such as the beautiful New Jerusalem, our eternal capital city.

But best of all, Jesus will once more be personally with us! Malachi 4:2 describes that those who fear His name "will go forth . . . like calves from the stall" (NASB). Have you ever watched young calves leap about in the fresh air and pasture after being penned up in a dark, smelly place for weeks? They are acrobatic clowns, twisting, turning, and dancing in their excitement. We do not know about you, but we know that when we get to the new earth, we will leap and shout for joy because we are home at last with Jesus forever!

As we stand on the verge of these overwhelming events, how can we help but praise and glorify His name?

December 16

Apollos, Paul, or Christ

It is better to take refuge in the Lord than to trust in man. It is better to take refuge in the Lord than to trust in princes. Ps. 118:8, 9, NASB.

While there is nothing wrong with receiving encouragement and help from fellow believers, we must be careful not to become dependent upon another person. We know of some individuals who cling to counselors and others for emotional, intellectual, or even spiritual support on a continuing basis. It can become almost a form of mental slavery as dangerous as that demonstrated by the people who followed Jim Jones of Jonestown fame to their suicidal death some years ago.

A friend once wrote to us, "I consider _____ the consummate theologian in the Adventist Church today." The fact is that we have no single "consummate theologian" in the church! We have many qualified dedicated Bible scholars and theologians who have expertise in many areas. But even our most brilliant minds have barely tapped the enormous amount of knowledge available. To put one person at the top of the list is simply another way of saying, as Paul pointed out (see 1 Cor. 1:12), "I belong to Paul," or "I belong to Apollos," or "I belong to Peter." Paul ends his statement with "I belong to Christ."

For a true knowledge of God, we need to depend directly on Christ alone and not on any other person. We may study with individuals, hear excellent sermons, but the most important things we can learn only as we directly study the Word.

We will always have deep appreciation for our Bible scholars and depend upon their abilities constantly. But in the final analysis God holds us responsible for our own beliefs and decisions. Our only safety lies in placing our confidence in the Lord and His revealed will as found in the Scriptures. Let the Spirit speak through the Word and direct our minds as we read it. Allow Him to enable us to be individuals and, under His guidance, help us to do our own thinking.

It is a wonderful privilege to come humbly to the Scriptures, asking for the Spirit's enlightenment, and to study its great truths. No one else can do it for us. It is our privilege and our duty alone. In this way we can testify to our experience by saying "Christ is my life; Christ is my joy; Christ is my Saviour; Christ is my pattern."

Praise God in your own words for the direct access we have with Christ through His Word.

The Brain Strain

But seek first His kingdom and His righteousness; and all these things shall be added to you. Matt. 6:33, NASB.

When we purchased our first microwave oven, it sat unused for several weeks simply because neither of us had time to master the voluminous book of instructions! At times we wondered if an ordinary person could possibly learn to operate such a sophisticated piece of kitchen machinery. The point is that knowledge is increasing at a fantastic rate. Years ago someone pointed out that the brain processes, on an average, handle an astonishing 41,000 words a day. What are we handling today?

Brain overstimulation inevitably leads to bewilderment and confusion. Although the brain is a fabulous instrument, more marvelous than any computer, it still has its limitations. Those who fail to recognize this point and subject themselves to an information overload may end up with various forms of mental illness, including depression.

The only answer to this problem is to be very selective of what information we feed our brain computers. All of us face seemingly endless demands today. We have so much to listen to, to look at, and to read. Even the news of world problems strains the mind.

We have often wondered what kind of life Jesus would live if He were in our world today. How much would He know about automobiles? Would He try to keep up with all the world events? What would His library look like? Would He be conversant on every new religious concept? How many conventions would He attend? How many seminars would He include in His schedule? What amount of time would He spend watching television? What news journals would He take? How many book clubs would He belong to? If He had a home, how many gadgets, relics, and souvenirs would He have sitting around waiting to be dusted?

Or would Jesus practice the "seek ye first" principle? We believe that our Example and Guide—the Master Example—would have probably avoided most activities that did not help salvage a soul from ruin and death. We do know that He refused to permit Himself to become entangled in the politics of Rome and declined to counsel a man on how he should settle the family estate.

Jesus valued every moment spent improving His own personal relationship with His Father. Life can be much more uncomplicated if we walk in the steps of Jesus. Praise Him for His example now.

December 18

From Humiliation to Triumph

Behold, My servant will prosper, He will be high and lifted up, and greatly exalted. Just as many were astonished at you, My people, so His appearance was marred more than any man, and His form more than the sons of men. Isa. 52:13, 14, NASB.

The chapters and verses in our Bibles are a purely human invention, and sometimes they separate things that should go together. Our text today should really form part of Isaiah 53, the great prophetic revelation of Christ's humiliation and exaltation.

Isaiah 53 is an Old Testament passage that clearly applies to the Messiah. The Lord sent Philip to help the Ethiopian eunuch understand this passage. The record states that the eunuch asked Philip, "Please tell me, of whom does the prophet say this? Of himself, or of someone else?" (Acts 8:34, NASB). (Philip knew what the eunuch was reading because people in the ancient world always read out loud.) In reply Philip began his Bible study with Isaiah 53 and preached about Jesus.

The opening words of our text today begin with Christ's triumph. The marring and disfiguring refer not only to Jesus' crucifixion but also to His wilderness temptation. His struggle against evil in both living and dying affected His appearance to the extent that even His friends had difficulty recognizing Him.

To the angels, Jesus' humiliation began at Bethlehem when He was born as a baby. Even then, when compared to His former glory the face of the infant Jesus was "marred more than any man."

Despite the fact that we will study it throughout eternity, we will never really understand a love that drove the Creator to become one with His creation. We will only be able to marvel at it. No wonder the prophet says that the masses will be astonished at Him, and "kings will shut their mouths on account of Him; for what had not been told them they will see, and what they have not heard they will understand" (Isa. 52:15, NASB).

Don't you think you should kneel in awe before your Saviour? Praise His name for accepting humiliation in order to pay your penalty on the cross.

Spectator or Participator?

Now therefore arise, O Lord God, to Thy resting place, Thou and the ark of Thy might; let Thy priests, O Lord God, be clothed with salvation, and let Thy godly ones rejoice in what is good. 2 Chron. 6:41, NASB.

Our passage comes at the climax of Solomon's magnificent prayer at the dedication of the Jerusalem sanctuary. "When Solomon had finished praying, fire came down from heaven and consumed the burnt offering and the sacrifices; and the glory of the Lord filled the house" (2 Chron. 7:1, NASB). God's glory prevented the priests from entering the house of the Lord, and all the people bowed down, "their faces to the ground, and they worshiped and gave praise to the Lord, saying, 'Truly He is good, truly His lovingkindness is everlasting' " (verse 3, NASB).

As we read of this fantastic worship experience, we feel that there ought to be more praise and thanksgiving in our church services.

Several years ago we visited South Africa and worshiped with our Black members several times. Limited finances prevented them from owning a piano or organ, but that in no way stopped them from worshiping in song. They sang hymns not only at the usual points in the service, but also at every other opportunity. For instance, during the intermission they lifted their voices to God in song. As the ministers entered, the congregation's voices became the organ and piano, softly singing an appropriate hymn. While deacons collected the offering, they again sang a hymn, expressing in melody their praise and gratitude for God's material and spiritual blessings. Following the benediction, the congregation broke out anew in a joyous rendition of "Blessed Be the Tie That Binds" as the ministers went to the rear to greet the parishioners. All this was in addition to the traditional hymns and the special music presented by a choir.

These worship services were not only memorable but deeply moving. We left with a warm glow in our hearts because we had actively participated in worshiping our God in a very special way through singing.

Too often in more affluent countries members are becoming spectators rather than participators. The church is rapidly becoming a theater in which the performers do their part. Even when the members sing a congregational hymn, it often consists of only one or two verses. Most of the other music comes from performers and not from the congregation.

It is an honor to join in worshiping God in singing and in uplifting our hearts in prayer. Even during the offering, let our minds dwell on the magnificent sacrifice Jesus made for us.

Let the worship service be one of participation on your part, and thank the Lord for the honor and opportunity of doing so. List some things you want to bring to God in prayer and praise this coming Sabbath.

The Power of the Cross

For Christ did not send me to baptize, but to preach the gospel, not in cleverness of speech, that the cross of Christ should not be made void. For the word of the cross is to those who are perishing foolishness, but to us who are being saved it is the power of God. 1 Cor. 1:17, 18, NASB.

To the Jews the cross was "a stumbling block, and to the Gentiles foolishness" (1 Cor. 1:23, NASB). The concept of the stumbling block really means a scandal. The Jews believed that anyone who died on a cross was under a curse from God, so how could anyone claim that Jesus was the Messiah? God's anointed one would never fall under a curse. The manner of His death was shameful in their eyes. Thus the cross is a destroyer of prestige, honor, reputation, pride, self-sufficiency, and independence.

To the Gentiles the cross was foolishness and absurdity, ridiculousness, and unphilosophical nonsense. A divine being would never perish that way. The Christians believed He was God, and gods cannot die. If He died on a cross—a most shameful form of execution—then the Gentiles concluded He obviously could not be God. Thus at the heart of the gospel stands an ignominious symbol, the cross of Christ. But to the surrendered Christian the cross stands for real life.

Some years ago Bob visited Florence, Italy, where the fifteenth-century Dominican Reformer Savonarola lived. He visited his cell and saw the Bible and books that he used. But it was a framed faded and tattered flag hanging on the wall that attracted his attention. It was the flag that Savonarola used in leading marches through the streets of Florence, and on it were the words "We preach Christ crucified." For upholding the cross of Christ, Savonarola was tortured, hanged, and burned in 1498.

The carnal heart resists God and His government, and this is where the cross comes into effect. When we see Christ becoming sin for us on the cross, when we hear Him cry out, "It is finished," we find ourselves viewing sin differently. To really look upon Jesus, who suffered the wrath of God against sin, will truly humble and crucify self. If you find yourself caught up in a conflict between self and God, there is only one solution. Focus everything on Jesus, especially His sacrifice on Calvary. What is your response?

Was Jesus God?

"Your father Abraham rejoiced to see My day; and he saw it, and was glad." The Jews therefore said to Him, "You are not yet fifty years old, and you have seen Abraham?" Jesus said to them, "Truly, truly, I say to you, before Abraham was born, I AM." John 8:56-58, NASB.

This passage powerfully supports the claim that Jesus was truly God. When He used the phrase "Before Abraham was born, I AM," He knew that His opponents would employ "I AM" against Him as a claim to be God. "I AM" traces back to Exodus 3:13, 14. When God called Moses to deliver the children of Israel from Egypt, Moses asked, "What shall I say to them?" In other words, "How do I answer 'Who sent you?' " Then the Lord told him to use the term "I AM WHO I AM," and that "I AM has sent me to you."

In Hebrew, as in English, this name is a form of a verb "to be," implying that the One who carries this name has always existed, with no beginning and no ending. The Jewish leaders instantly understood Jesus' allusion, and "therefore they picked up stones to throw at Him; but Jesus hid Himself, and went out of the temple" (John 8:59, NASB). To them, Jesus was committing blasphemy because He claimed to be God. They would not have tried to stone Him otherwise, because stoning was the scriptural punishment for blasphemy.

To believe that Jesus is God is important in our Christian life. C. S. Lewis, writing to those willing to accept Jesus as a great moral teacher but not as God, said, "A man who is merely a man and said the sort of things Jesus said would not be a great moral teacher. He would either be a lunatic—on a level with the man who says he is a poached egg—or else he would be the devil of hell. You must make your choice. Either this man was, and is, the Son of God, or else a madman or something worse. You can shut him up for a fool, you can spit at him and kill him as a demon; or you can fall at his feet and call him Lord and God. But let us not come with any patronizing nonsense about his being a great human teacher. He has not left that open to us. He did not intend to" (*Mere Christianity*, pp. 52, 53).

Admittedly it was difficult for the Jews and would be just as difficult for us to believe that Jesus was God if He lived among us today. If we saw Him associating with notoriously dishonest people like Zacchaeus, or the tax collector Matthew, or the woman taken in adultery, we would naturally wonder, "How can this be God?" But the fact that He associated with such people—seeking to redeem them—is supreme evidence that He is indeed God. He wants to save sinners, and He has saved untold numbers of them through the centuries.

Praise our heavenly Father for sending God the Son to redeem us. He was fully God and fully man. What is your response to the God who became one with us?

An Unwitting Testimony

Now Zedekiah . . . reigned as king in place of Coniah. . . . But neither he nor his servants nor the people of the land listened to the words of the Lord which He spoke to Jeremiah the prophet. Jer. 37:1, 2, NASB.

Over and over the Old Testament tells of God's people turning against His messengers. When they listened to His prophets, they prospered. But when they rejected or ignored them, they suffered terribly.

In his book *Why I Believe in Mrs. E. G. White* (pp. 126, 127) F. D. Nichol tells about a conversation he had years before with an aged leader of the Advent Christian Church, probably the largest of the groups—outside of the Seventh-day Adventist Church—that survived from William Miller's movement. Both the Advent Christian Church and the Seventh-day Adventist Church organized approximately at the same time. Membership in the Advent Christian Church, however, peaked about the end of the nineteenth century at 30,000. Today the Seventh-day Adventist Church has 7 million members.

Nichol was doing research at the Advent Christian College, in Aurora, Illinois, which has a large collection of Miller's original writings. The elderly church leader assisting Nichol proved to be quite knowledgeable about the growth of the Seventh-day Adventist Church and its activities throughout the world. One evening near sunset, as they rode in the car together, he said to Nichol, "Your church leaders through the years have been wiser men than ours. They saw the need of a publishing work and started it, the need of medical work, of educational work, and of a great mission program. And they also saw the need of a close-knit organization. And so today you are strong and growing rapidly, while we are not."

Instantly Nichol replied, "My dear brother, I don't think that is quite an accurate statement. Our leaders were not wiser than yours, nor more far-visioned. The record will show that they were ordinary flesh and blood, like your men, with great limitations of vision and faith. But the difference was that we had in our midst a most singular woman. She marked out what we ought to do in the different branches of our work. She was specific, emphatic, and insistent. We accepted her counsel and direction, for we believed she had visions from God. That is the reason we have this marvelous organization and have grown."

Recalling the incident, Nichol said that the man immediately became silent, for the Advent Christian people had long ago rejected our belief that Mrs. White possessed the prophetic gift. Eloquently though unwittingly, the Advent Christian leader had given a most impressive testimonial to God's leading of this movement through a messenger. Will you praise God for His special gift to our church?

Unconditional Love

Love knows no limit to its endurance, no end to its trust, no fading of its hope; it can outlast anything. Love never fails. 1 Cor. 12:7, 8, Phillips.

Some years ago Bob traveled in South America with Pastor Hector J. Peverini, one of our division administrative leaders. There from others he learned an amazing story of this man's unconditional love for his wife. When he was a young minister, only four years married and with three small children, Peverini's wife suffered a serious postpartum illness that practically incapacitated her for the rest of her life.

During the next four decades Pastor Peverini cared for, supported, and loved his wife, even though she did not recognize him and treated him as a stranger. Several friends, and even administrators of the church, counseled him to divorce her, but his love to her was unshakable. He had promised to love her always, "in sickness and in health, in prosperity or in adversity." How could he abandon her?

The years passed slowly while she was institutionalized. Numberless prayers ascended to God for the restoration of his wife and for strength to raise his children. Thirty-five years later the discovery of new medicines partially restored her to health. Although the long years of illness took their toll, the point is that love triumphed! Surely, this wonderful love story magnifies the power of God's grace in the midst of adversity. God's grace enabled Peverini to continue to love his wife, raise his family, and remain loyal to his commitment to preach the gospel.

God's love is unconditional. He doesn't love us because of any inherent goodness that we have or for any good thing that we may have done. Instead, He loves us no matter what our performance is. The greatest demonstration of God's love for us was in the giving of His Son to die on the cross that we might in turn be able to love. It is this kind of love that should bind husbands and wives and families together. The secret of happy relationships is unselfish love, a love that "seeketh not her own." Such love is the glue to bind us together in a caring, accepting attitude.

Thank God for His unconditional love that has brought us not only life eternal but the ability to love one another unconditionally. Express your desire that God will give you the power to love in such a way.

Giving All We've Got

He also saw a poor widow put in two very small copper coins. "I tell you the truth," He said, "this poor widow has put in more than all the others. . . . She out of her poverty put in all she had to live on." Luke 21:2-4, NIV.

If you ever feel tempted to think that you are unimportant and that whatever you can contribute in the way of time, talent, or treasure is insignificant, please remember the story of the widow. We don't know her name, but her influence is still around after 2,000 years!

Telemachus, a monk who lived more than 1,500 years ago, spent most of his life secluded in a monastery, praying, studying, and raising vegetables for the institution. One day he felt deeply impressed by the Lord to go to Rome, the political center of the world. Once there, he couldn't figure out why God had led him to the busiest, wealthiest, and largest city on earth, because his life and background did not fit into the culture of Rome.

As he traversed the streets of Rome, the people's preoccupation with vice and violence stunned him. One day he found himself swept along by the crowd into a place that he had never known existed—the Colosseum, where animalistic gladiators fought and killed each other. He stared in disbelief at the sight of one man slaughtering another.

Finally he couldn't stand it any longer, so he ran and jumped on top of the perimeter wall and shouted, "In the name of Christ, forbear." He could not endure the horrible killing. "Stop this now!"

But no one listened. The applause drowned out his pleas. Unable to contain himself, he leaped down to the sandy floor of the arena. The frail little man, dressed in a monk's habit, began dashing back and forth between the muscular, brutal fighters, still pleading to them, "In the name of Christ, forbear." The crowd looked and sneered at him. Finally someone shouted, "Run him through! Kill him!" One of the fighters pierced his stomach with one flash of the sword, and as he slumped to his knees, the little monk gasped once more, "In the name of Christ . . . forbear."

According to Charles Colson's book *Loving God*, the spectators, after seeing what happened, grew deathly silent, and one by one people left until the huge stadium had emptied. It was the last gladiatorial contest in the Roman Colosseum. Men never again entertained the crowds by killing each other there.

This monk, like the widow, gave all he had—his very life. You may not be called upon to offer up your life in such a manner, but God can use you in your small way to make an impact for good on the life of someone today. Pray for that opportunity, and praise Him for the privilege of lending your influence in favor of the gospel.

Wonderful! Wonderful!

For a child will be born to us, a son will be given to us; and the government will rest on His shoulders; and His name will be called Wonderful Counselor, Mighty God, Eternal Father, Prince of Peace. Isa. 9:6, NASB.

Try to think of the most wonderful event that has ever happened to you. As we look back on our own lives, our wedding day and the birth of our two daughters stand out in unforgettable glory. And from a spiritual viewpoint we will never forget our baptismal day.

But above and beyond any personal experience is that of the Christ event. God's Spirit certainly inspired Isaiah to describe the person and life of our Saviour. The secret of the prophet's ability to express such divine concepts so beautifully is the fact that he had a vision in the Temple that compelled him to exclaim, "I saw the Lord" (Isa. 6:1, NASB). Isaiah powerfully describes Christ, His salvation, and His ultimate rulership of heaven and earth. It all begins with the birth of a Child. A baby's birth always produces intense feelings, but the Infant described in our verse as the Eternal Father and Prince of Peace had a far more wonderful entrance into the world.

Search a thesaurus for descriptive words, and you will find yourself left bewildered at the lack of language to describe such a magnificent event. Think of the mighty God coming in a manger. Impossible! you say. But it happened!

Who is this Child? What is His position? He is the leader, the president, the king of the universe. This supernatural Being who became a baby proves to the universe that God is love! No one, not even Satan and his mob of disloyal angels, can ever challenge His position as ruler of the entire limitless universe. After that night in Bethlehem, no one in heaven or earth can ever rightfully doubt God's claim to love us.

Imagine it—God coming as a little baby, born in a stable in a tiny Palestinian village. No concept of any other religion on earth can ever match this event of indescribable love.

Many versions of the Bible employ the words "Wonderful" and "Counselor." The fact is that His name embodies every good quality we can think of. Can you imagine how at His birth heaven must have rung with music from angel choirs? All the orchestras on earth put together could not match the magnificent music they produced when Jesus, the Son of God, was born of a sinful woman!

Praise and honor are His forever and ever. Every event in history is important only as it relates to the supreme event of Christ's coming as a babe to our planet to save us. How can we help thanking Him, praising Him, honoring Him, and adoring Him for His sacrificial love! Do your best to find words of praise to Him for His first coming to earth.

Redemption Rock

Be strong and courageous, do not be afraid or tremble at them, for the Lord your God is the one who goes with you. He will not fail you or forsake you. . . . And the Lord is the one who goes ahead of you; He will be with you. He will not fail you or forsake you. Do not fear, or be dismayed. Deut. 31:6-8, NASB.

While we were visiting our friends Otho and Kathryn Eusey a few years ago, they took us to a spot known as Redemption Rock, near South Lancaster, Massachusetts, where they live. They also loaned us a book describing the experience of Mrs. Mary Rowlandson. The story began in February 1675, when a large force of Indians descended at sunrise upon the little village of Lancaster, Massachusetts. They burned the log houses and killed more than 50 colonists. Among the 20 persons they took prisoner was Mrs. Mary Rowlandson, the wife of a minister. During her 82-day captivity, the Indians moved camp 20 times.

She wrote a small book of her torturous experience titled *The Narrative of the Captivity and Restoration of Mrs. Mary Rowlandson.* Although wounded, she survived the famine conditions and forced marches during freezing weather, but her 6-year-old daughter, mortally wounded, died after a few days. Fortunately, her husband was in Boston when the attack came.

Her story is filled with the divine promises she read from a Bible one of the Indians had given to her. Many of the promises she clung to were similar to our text today. The thrilling climax of her story concerns the agreement made between the Indians and the English to ransom her for the sum of 20 pounds. The spot where the exchange took place was at an isolated granite ledge now located in Princeton, Massachusetts. This spot acquired the name of Redemption Rock. A bronze plaque on the rock reads in part, "Upon this rock, May 2, 1676, was made the agreement for the ransom of Mrs. Mary Rowlandson of Lancaster."

We have visited it several times, and each time our minds always turn to our Lord, who ransomed us. Our planet, like a giant redemption rock, is where Jesus made Heaven's exchange for the human race. He bought us back from the enemy, not with silver or gold, but by His own even more precious blood. Satan has dragged us through the harsh winter of evil, buffeting and wounding us, and he has sought to destroy us. But the ransom was paid, and Christ, our substitute and surety, gives us the security of eternal life. Although the guilt of every human being weighed heavily upon His heart, He refused to come down from the cross, in order that we rebellious sinners might have the opportunity of accepting Him as our eternal Saviour.

How Would Jesus Treat His Yard Boy?

Is this not the fast which I choose, to loosen the bonds of wickedness, to undo the bands of the yoke, and to let the oppressed go free, and break every yoke? Is it not to divide your bread with the hungry, and bring the homeless poor into the house; when you see the naked, to cover him; and not to hide yourself from your own flesh? Isa. 58:6, 7, NASB.

Some years ago while attending the New York World's Fair, we visited the National Council of Churches pavilion. It continuously screened a film depicting Christ as a circus clown. Religious reviewers of the film condemned it severely. We too were shocked at the idea of portraying Christ as a clown, complete with paint and costume, and still consider the concept tasteless. But as the years have passed, certain impressions the film made on our minds have not faded.

This Christ-clown was not the usual joker, but rather a meek, quiet, and extremely helpful person. He treated all types of people with love and respect, and helped other circus personnel lug the heavy buckets of water to the elephants. Constantly he alleviated suffering, not only for the circus personnel but for the circus animals, as well. His life finally ended in a painful death, with the crowds mocking him. Although he had done nothing wrong, people could not endure such a marvelous character.

One application or lesson we learned from this portrayal is that whatever station in life we find ourselves, we certainly, by God's grace, can act like Jesus in our relationship with others.

To our way of thinking we must dress up Christ not in clown clothes, but in late-twentieth-century garb. When you view Crucifixion scenes painted by Renaissance Dutch artists, for example, you see that they used contemporary Dutch citizens on the hillside. In other words, Christ is ever contemporary, ever present—everlasting. His actions in life are as relevant and valid today as they were 2,000 years ago. If He were a person on earth today, would He thank the lad at the supermarket for transferring His groceries to the trunk of His car? Would He speak a word of encouragement and appreciation to the yard boy who cut His grass? Would He tell the janitor in any building that he is doing a good job? How would He answer a telephone? crudely, abruptly, or courteously? If someone mistakenly dialed His number, would He become angry? How would He respond to someone telling Him a juicy rumor, the content of which placed a cloud over an individual's reputation? How would He respond to those making racial slurs?

Jesus was a perfect gentleman, beautifully courteous and extremely helpful. His presence powerfully encouraged the weary and heavy laden.

Praise Him today for His marvelous example to you.

Don't Worry Yourself Out of God's Hand

I was at ease, but He shattered me, and He has grasped me by the neck and shaken me to pieces; He has also set me up as His target. Job 16:12, NASB.

Job's words reflect the unending pain of an emaciated body covered with painful boils. His life had been one of ease and prosperity until a string of mental and physical disasters devastated him. His vivid language portrays what all of us have seen at one time or another—a dog or a cat grabbing a rabbit or a rat by the neck and shaking it to death. In Job's case, he wrongly credits God for seizing and tormenting him.

When Bob had quadruple-bypass open-heart surgery some time ago, he said that it was the closest he had ever come to experiencing the sufferings of Job. Bob felt as if the operation had mutilated his chest and leg beyond recovery. Afterward he could identify with Job's description of being shattered and grabbed by the neck. He could not understand why he was the target for such an experience. Had he not lived a good life—vegetarian, nonsmoker, and nondrinker? The question "Why me?" repeatedly tormented his mind.

Yet, through it all, Bob trusted the Lord instead of blaming Him. The physicians had warned him of the possibility of depression occurring after this type of surgery, but we praise the Lord that he never once experienced the problem.

"When brought into trial, we are not to fret and complain. We should not rebel, or worry ourselves out of the hand of Christ. . . . The ways of the Lord are obscure to him who desires to see things in a light pleasing to himself. They appear dark and joyless to our human nature. But God's ways are ways of mercy and the end is salvation" (*The Desire of Ages*, p. 301).

We want to magnify the Lord that He has put His peace in our hearts. Also, we pray that we will never want to worry ourselves out of His hands. Is this your desire? If so, express your gratitude to Him now.

Jesus Is Our Hero

And when I saw Him, I fell at His feet as a dead man. And He laid His right hand upon me, saying, "Do not be afraid; I am the first and the last, and the living One; and I was dead, and behold, I am alive forevermore." Rev. 1:17, 18, NASB.

It is a sad commentary on our culture that, according to the *World Almanac* in its twelfth annual poll of the heroes of young Americans, the winners all came from either the sports, entertainment, military, or political world. The major reason such people get selected as heroes is, according to Andy Worhal, author of the book *The Frenzy of Renown*, promotion by the mass media. Throughout history people have looked for hero symbols. The psalmist David as a young army commander had his admirers who sang about his killing of 10,000 to King Saul's 1,000.

But no one can compare to Jesus as the greatest hero of all time. He embodied a whole constellation of marvelous traits. His claim to fame especially includes His humility, which eventually led Him to the cross. Although He never endorsed breakfast cereals, fast-food restaurants, tennis rackets, or clothes, He did endorse the character of His Father, both by word and example. Jesus unceasingly promoted God the Father. Jesus' sole aim while living on earth was and even now in heaven is to forgive people their sins and recreate in them a desire to live a lifestyle that fits them for heavenly citizenship.

Jesus is the greatest statesman who ever lived. His aim is to save a nation of people from destruction if they will but follow Him.

He is the greatest teacher who ever lived, because He has redirected the minds of millions into channels of saving knowledge.

He is the Physician of physicians. His knowledge of the mind and body makes Him a specialist in every area of health practice. And He has graciously shared His knowledge with us in both the Scriptures and the Spirit of Prophecy. We could make the list much longer of the traits that make Him the greatest hero of multiplied millions throughout the ages.

How we wish that all baseball, tennis, football, and basketball fans would worship Jesus as their hero. If only every executive, every entrepreneur, every professional person trying to climb the success ladder, would make Jesus his or her beloved hero. And if every blue-collar and white-collar worker would set Jesus up as his or her number one hero, what a different world it would be.

At least we who read these words can make Jesus our hero. What qualities do you especially admire about Him?

_____

_____

The Birds and Fish Reveal God's Majesty

O Lord, our Lord, how majestic is Thy name in all the earth, who hast displayed Thy splendor above the heavens! . . . Thou hast put all things under [man's] feet, . . . the birds of the heavens, and the fish of the sea, whatever passes through the paths of the seas. O Lord, our Lord, how majestic is Thy name in all the earth! Ps. 8:1-9, NASB.

An article titled "Secrets of Animal Navigation," in the June 1991 *National Geographic*, describes certain astounding feats in the animal kingdom that have baffled scientists for centuries. Now, however, they think they have a better understanding of what lies behind them. One example is that of the Pacific salmon, which wander around the Pacific Ocean several thousand miles from their birthplace until, when the migrating mood strikes them, they head for home. We humans have trouble finding places even with detailed road maps. But fish, as well as birds, butterflies, turtles, insects, and other animals, can travel incredible distances to preordained destinations.

The legendary swallows of San Juan Capistrano, California, spend the summer there, then leave the mission each year on October 23 and fly 6,000 miles to their winter home in Goya, Argentina. This remarkable annual pilgrimage poses a number of puzzling questions: How do they know when to depart? How do they find the place they have come from? Some believe that birds use the sun as a compass, together with an internal clock that compensates for the sun's changing position. Others believe star patterns guide night migrants. Whatever the reason, we know for sure that a loving Creator majestically displays His power in the birds of the heavens and the fish of the sea.

Imagine what a thrill it will be to sit at the feet of the supreme naturalist of the universe, Jesus, and listen to Him reveal these and a million other secrets of life that we can only guess at now!

As we close out this year, think of God's love exhibited in the splendor of His Creation. "The perfection of God's work is as clearly seen in the tiniest insect as in the king of birds" (*Testimonies*, vol. 4, p. 591).

When you see nature as an evidence of God's love and power, you cannot help lifting your heart to Him in appreciation and adoration. Pay our Creator a written tribute of praise now!

December 31

Our High Priest

He is able to save forever those who draw near to God through Him, since He always lives to make intercession for them. For it was fitting that we should have such a high priest, holy, innocent, undefiled, separated from sinners and exalted above the heavens. Heb. 7:25, 26, NASB.

George Whitefield, the powerful eighteenth-century English evangelist, endured constant insults from many so-called theologians of his day. When urged by friends to reply to certain false accusations, lest they stigmatize him for life, he replied, "I am content to wait till the judgment day for the clearing up of my character. When I am dead I desire no epitaph but this: 'Here lies George Whitefield. What kind of man he was the great day will discover.' "

Adventists have a doctrine known as the investigative judgment, based on the Old Testament sanctuary system. When correctly understood, this doctrine proves both the marvelous mercy and the blameless justice of God. The accountability factor in the plan of salvation not only is an absolute necessity but constitutes a wonderful motivation in our lives to look to our Great High Priest for help. Referring to this concept, Carrol Johnson Shewmake beautifully describes in her book *Practical Pointers to Personal Prayer* her own experience. "It was exciting news to find that the work of investigation that Jesus was doing now was not an impersonal study of the records of heaven but a searching of *my* heart and life" (pp. 54, 55).

The concept of our High Priest examining our life's records causes two major things to happen. First, it makes us think seriously about the direction we are headed in life. It emphasizes the need to carefully consider our thoughts, words, and actions. Also it convicts us of the terribleness of sin. Second, it drives us to our knees before our High Priest as He ministers on our behalf in the heavenly sanctuary, heaven's salvation command center. Not only do we need forgiveness but we need power to overcome sin itself.

Our High Priest defends us against Satan's constant accusations. He can and will save us. We, like George Whitefield, can be content that our High Priest will clear our record if we trust and obey Him.

As you look back over the year 1993, ask yourself, "Have I formed a deeper bond with Jesus? Is my life more like His today than it was 12 months ago?" We surely hope so! Finally, on this last day of the year, spend a few moments expressing your love for Him as your personal High Priest, Defender, and Helper.

INDEX

8:3, 4	JAN. 29
8:11	FEB. 25
8:16, 17	NOV. 29
8:31, 32	APR. 24
12:3-6	JAN. 6
16:25, 26	OCT. 14

1 CORINTHIANS

1:17, 18	DEC. 20
3:9-17	NOV. 3
6:18	MAY 20
6:19, 20	NOV. 4
9:24, 25	MAY 3
10:13	APR. 21
10:14	MAY 20
11:24, 25	JAN. 26
13:7, 8	DEC. 23
15:21-23	FEB. 26

2 CORINTHIANS

5:1, 2	JUNE 8
5:17	JULY 4
8:9	JAN. 10
8:12	APR. 10
10:3-5	JUNE 15
12:7	MAR. 7
12:9	MAR. 8

GALATIANS

4:4	DEC. 8
5:6	JAN. 19

EPHESIANS

2:8	AUG. 5
3:8	AUG. 22
4:1, 2	JULY 12
4:13, 14	JULY 8
4:22-24	NOV. 13
5:20	MAR. 26
5:25-27	MAY 15

PHILIPPIANS

2:3	JULY 31

2:5	NOV. 19
3:4	APR. 8
3:8-10	AUG. 10
3:13	AUG. 23
3:14	OCT. 31
4:2, 3	JUNE 7
4:8	MAR. 5

COLOSSIANS

1:17, 18	OCT. 18
2:9, 10	APR. 11
3:1-3	MAR. 24
3:15	NOV. 5

1 THESSALONIANS

4:16, 17	FEB. 22
5:3, 4	MAR. 3

1 TIMOTHY

1:8, 9	AUG. 29
1:15	JULY 3
4:7, 8	MAR. 30
4:16	MAY 22
6:6	NOV. 23
6:7, 8	APR. 27
6:11	MAY 20

2 TIMOTHY

1:11, 12	JAN. 16
2:13	FEB. 7
2:15	JULY 6
2:22	MAY 20

TITUS

2:13, 14	FEB. 24

HEBREWS

2:17, 18	JULY 14
4:13	FEB. 4
4:15, 16	APR. 1
7:25, 26	DEC. 31
9:13, 14	JAN. 24

9:28	MAY 27
10:25	APR. 4
11:6	AUG. 9
11:8	MAY 30
12:2	JAN. 11
13:5	FEB. 7

JAMES

3:2	SEPT. 2
4:1, 2	MAY 18
4:11, 12	JUNE 12
5:15	MAY 1

1 PETER

2:2	JULY 5
2:21, 22	OCT. 23
3:3, 4	OCT. 30
3:10, 11	JUNE 18
4:1	APR. 23

1 JOHN

1:7	JAN. 22
3:1	NOV. 28
5:4, 5	JULY 11

REVELATION

1:17, 18	DEC. 29
3:18	APR. 25
5:9	APR. 9
12:10	FEB. 6
12:11	JAN. 25
13:8	MAR. 13
14:1	OCT. 2
14:14	OCT. 3
19:11-16	DEC. 4
20:4	MAY 11
22:20	FEB. 28

For Your Spiritual Growth

Wising Up

The *Adventist Review* editor tells about the experiences through which God's grace opened his eyes and wised him up. His topics are as diverse as tomatoes and fatherhood, but he always presents sparkling insights on the Christian life. This is the wit, wisdom, and spiritual vibrancy of William Johnsson at his best. Paper, 124 pages. US$7.95, Cdn$9.95.

Heaven

David Smith turns our focus from this troubled world to a place where pain, sorrow, and death shatter into obsolescence, and gives us a foretaste of what it will be like to live in the presence of Jesus forever! Paper, 96 pages. US$7.95, Cdn$9.95.

Every Time I Say Grace, We Fight

Sandra Finley Doran offers practical help to marriage partners who don't share the same religion or see eye-to-eye on their Christian lifestyles. Readers learn how to establish open communication, nurture individuality, and protect their family from well-meaning relatives. Paper, 94 pages. US$7.95, Cdn$9.95.

Forgiveness

Discover how God's forgiveness was shown in the lives of such Bible characters as Adam, Rahab, Peter, and Mary Magdalene. Walton Brown provides us with strong assurance that we will always find a forgiving friend in God. Paper, 121 pages. US$8.95, Cdn$11.20.

The Great Visions of Ellen G. White

Roger W. Coon takes an intriguing look at the historical context of 10 of Ellen White's key visions. Filled with human interest stories and enlightening commentary, this book will help you to understand better the culture and setting in which these visions were given. You'll see how they have charted the course for the SDA Church and discover their urgent message for today. Hardcover, 158 pages. US$12.95, Cdn$16.20.

Inspiration

Did every fact and idea in the Bible come straight from God? If we read Scripture too closely, could we find something that will destroy our faith? Dr. Alden Thompson shows us how to read the Bible so that God's will shines through puzzling commands and apparent contradictions. Hardcover, 332 pages. US$15.95, Cdn$19.95.

How to Be Filled With the Holy Spirit and Know It

This book by Garrie Williams will help you experience the joy of fellowship with the Spirit and the power of the latter rain now! It answers such questions as How do I receive the Spirit? What will the evidence be? How can I know the difference between imagination and impressions of the Spirit? Paper, 188 pages. US$7.95, Cdn$9.95.

The Power of the Spirit

By examining closely the apostolic church's experience with the Holy Spirit, Elders Neal Wilson and George Rice show us what God wants to accomplish through His remnant people. Paper, 138 pages. US$8.95, Cdn$11.20.

To order, call **1-800-765-6955** or write to ABC Mailing Service, P.O. Box 1119, Hagerstown, MD 21741. Send check or money order. Enclose applicable sales tax and 15 percent (minimum US$2.50) for postage and handling. Prices and availability subject to change without notice. Add GST in Canada.

WHAT HAS GOD DONE FOR US LATELY?

Remember the way the Lord has led us in our past history. And if you want something more current, subscribe to the *Adventist Review*, and see what God did for us last week.

You'll read wonderful stories about doors opening in countries where we once faced a brick wall. You'll hear about big baptisms. And you'll share in the inspiring experiences of other Adventists.

Subscribe to the weekly *Adventist Review*, and see what God has done for us lately.

Blessings reported as they happen. In the weekly

ADVENTIST REVIEW

To order, call your local Adventist Book Center:

1-800-765-6955

Inspirational Stories

Because of Patty

Paula Montgomery. When a phantom illness struck Sam and Mella's infant daughter, it should have been a tragedy. But their night of despair turned to joy because of Patty. A heartwarming story about a little girl who always gave more than she took, written by Patty's sister. Paper, 126 pages. US$7.95, Cdn$9.95.

Flesh and Blood

Vatha Pheng and Melvin Adams. Vatha shares the incredible story of how her family survived the Killing Fields of Cambodia and the intriguing circumstances that led to their becoming Seventh-day Adventists. Paper, 144 pages. US$8.95, Cdn$11.20.

The Man From Lancer Avenue

Trudy Morgan. Experience what it would be like to live down the street from Christ. Get to know the very ordinary people whose lives He changed. This intriguing story brings Jesus into our time and blows the dust of antiquity off the Gospel characters. Paper, 191 pages. US$9.95, Cdn$12.45.

To order, call **1-800-765-6955** or write to ABC Mailing Service, P.O. Box 1119, Hagerstown, MD 21741. Send check or money order. Enclose applicable sales tax and 15 percent (minimum US$2.50) for postage and handling. Prices and availability subject to change without notice. Add GST in Canada.

The *Paint the World With Love* Books

Inspiring stories about what ordinary Adventists are doing to share God's love

---

Paint the World With Love

In her first *Paint the World With Love* book Jeannette Johnson introduces you to some unsung heroes—Adventists who are humbly brightening their corner of the world by touching people's lives and making a difference. They aren't powerful or rich. All they have to give God is themselves. But you'll be amazed and your heart warmed as you read about what God has accomplished through them. Hardcover, 158 pages. US$9.95, Cdn$12.45.

Paint the World With Love, Second Coat

Each chapter in this "second coat" by Jeannette Johnson will leave you with a warm and joyous feeling. Read the thrilling stories of how God brought martial arts champion Steve Mackey into the church and how Olia Dixon triumphed over her handicaps. Meet Mutley, the wonder dog who has her own TV show and a ministry for others. You'll come away with the unshakable belief that God can do extraordinary things with our ordinary lives. Paper, 158 pages. US$8.95, Cdn$11.20.

To order, call **1-800-765-6955** or write to ABC Mailing Service, P.O. Box 1119, Hagerstown, MD 21741. Send check or money order. Enclose applicable sales tax and 15 percent (minimum US$2.50) for postage and handling. Prices and availability subject to change without notice. Add GST in Canada.

Cabin Boy to Advent Crusader

The life story of Joseph Bates, by Virgil Robinson

On his first voyage at sea Joseph Bates fell overboard and was providentially rescued from a shark. So begins this fascinating story of one of the most colorful pioneers of the Adventist Church. From the seafaring town of New Bedford, Massachusetts, to the broad expanse of the world's great oceans, follow the events of his incredible life.

Read the intriguing story of how he was impressed into the British Navy and made a prisoner of war. Watch him rise to the position of captain and learn about the curious events that led him to forsake his successful career and join ranks with the Advent movement.

Listen with Captain Bates to the stirring messages of William Miller and Ellen White. Wait with him those last hours before the expected return of Christ. Share in his life-changing discoveries about the seventh-day Sabbath, and journey with him as he brings this precious truth to hundreds of searching Christians.

This special edition of *Cabin Boy to Advent Crusader* marks the 200th anniversary of Joseph Bates' birth.

Paper, 190 pages. US$7.95, Cdn$9.95.